OBJECT-ORIENTED COBOL

T0155677

Advances in Object Technology Series

Dr. Richard S. Wiener
Series Editor

Editor
Journal of Object-Oriented Programming
Report on Object Analysis and Design
SIGS Publications, Inc.
New York, New York

and

Department of Computer Science
University of Colorado
Colorado Springs, Colorado

Additional Volumes in Preparation

OBJECT-ORIENTED COBOL

Edmund C. Arranga
Frank P. Coyle

SIGS
BOOKS & MULTIMEDIA

New York • London • Paris • Munich • Cologne

CAMBRIDGE UNIVERSITY PRESS
Cambridge, New York, Melbourne, Madrid, Cape Town, Singapore, São Paulo, Delhi

Cambridge University Press
The Edinburgh Building, Cambridge CB2 8RU, UK

Published in the United States of America by Cambridge University Press, New York

www.cambridge.org
Information on this title: www.cambridge.org/9780132611404

First published by SIGS Books, Inc. 1996
Digitally reprinted by Cambridge University Press 2008

A catalogue record for this publication is available from the British Library

Library of Congress Cataloguing in Publication data

Arranga, Edmund C., 1952–
   Object-oriented COBOL / Edmund C. Arranga, Frank P. Coyle.
     p.   cm — (Advances in object technology series; 12)
   Includes bibliographical references and index.
   ISBN 1-884842-34-8 (pbk.)
     1. COBOL (Computer program language)   2. Object-oriented
programming (Computer science).   I. Coyle, Frank P., 1945–
II. Title.   III. Series: Advances in object technology; 12.
QA76.73.C25A77   1996
005.13′3—dc20   96-19201
                                                      CIP

ISBN-13 978-0-132-61140-4 paperback

ABOUT THE AUTHORS

Edmund C. Arranga is a cofounder and vice-president of Object-Z, Inc., a company specializing in Object-Oriented COBOL training and consulting. He is also on the editorial board of *The COBOL Report,* a newsletter for COBOL programmers. Arranga has had numerous articles published in technical journals and magazines and conducts object-oriented training classes around the country for business and academia. He teaches Object-Oriented COBOL at UCLA and UCI Extensions.

He has held positions as a project manager and software engineer at McDonnell Douglas and TRW and has over 20 years of experience in COBOL and software development. He received a bachelor's degree from Texas A&M University, College Station, Texas, and is completing his master's degree in software engineering as time permits. He can be reached at 74651.2630@compuserve.com.

Frank Coyle was raised in The Bronx, where he graduated from Fordham College while working part-time collecting tolls on the Triborough Bridge and driving a New York City taxi. Lured by warmer weather, he migrated south to Atlanta, to attend graduate school at Georgia Tech, where he lost most of his New York accent. After receiving his M.S. degree in computer science in 1974, he taught computer science at Morehouse College and consulted on COBOL-based information systems projects. From this experience, he discovered what software development was really all about.

In 1987, he returned to academia to work on his PhD in computer science at Southern Methodist University (SMU) in Dallas, Texas. After attending the OOPSLA87 conference on object-oriented programming systems and languages, he was drawn into the world of Smalltalk, thus beginning his journey into object technology. In 1992 he received his PhD from SMU, where he is currently on the faculty and is Director of the Software Engineering Program. He teaches courses on object-oriented analysis, design, and programming and is engaged in research on design patterns and on the reengineering of legacy systems. He has presented talks and tutorials on Object-Oriented COBOL at national and international conferences and finds it fascinating that people always react, in some way, to the words "Object-Oriented COBOL."

He resides in Dallas with his wife, Judy, and two sons, Alex and Nick, with whom he has to compete for the family computer. In his spare time, he enjoys shooting hoops and cranking up his Fender Stratocaster to play along with ZZ-Top and Neil Young.

FOREWORD

For my entire working life, I and The COBOL Foundation have been involved with implementing the world's diverse programming languages. Between 1961 and 1988, my association with Digitek Corporation and Ryan-McFarland (RM) Corporation resulted in the implementation of over 200 unique compilers. In the early period, companies such as Digital, IBM, NCR, et al. purchased our compilers and resold them under their own names. Later on in this 28-year period, we marketed our compilers under the RM name for the most part. The languages included BASIC, C, COBOL, FORTRAN, Jovial, Pascal, PL/I, Simscript, and many others.

One of the biggest disappointments of my career has been the lack of progress in application development tools. Certainly the languages of FORTRAN and COBOL were major inventions in the late 50s. Simply the fact that they are still heavily used after 35 years is testimony to that. During the 70s and 80s, minor evolutionary progression continued, but in the last five years, the COBOL implementers have begun to evolve the COBOL application development tools more rapidly.

We all know that the hardware side of the equation has moved along at a blistering pace. The software side, however, has not kept up.

Sometimes we have to step back and take a long look at the big picture of what we are doing in the computer world. We are about 40 years into a 200-year information revolution, which is progressing in a way not unlike the industrial revolution and other transformatory events. In actuality, we are only about 20 percent of the way through the task of automating the world. We need the best tools we can possibly get.

Object-Oriented COBOL is certainly a major evolutionary step ahead. Going beyond the significantly enhanced COBOL that I have alluded to, this book will help developers work with COBOL in an even more productive way than previously. I like to think of Object-Oriented COBOL as a higher-level language than the COBOL we all know—a language that will soon be viewed as an extremely powerful tool.

This book includes an excellent example to lead COBOL-literate developers through the process of developing a real application using Object-Oriented COBOL.

The COBOL users of the world should definitely use Object-Oriented COBOL to develop a small application at first. After acquiring some experience, I'm confident they will begin to implement larger and larger applications. A major retraining of development personnel is not required for a COBOL programmer to become fluent with Object-Oriented COBOL.

Object-Oriented COBOL may very well be the largest step forward in commercial application development tools since the development of COBOL itself in 1960.

David E. McFarland
The COBOL Foundation
http:/ /www.Cobol.org

PREFACE

Programming languages, in attempting to move forward, often move more crab-like than ahead. Since its inception software engineering has been looking to establish a beachhead that could turn the tide of handcrafting applications to designing applications for reuse so as to return the type of benefits that have been the hallmark of hardware in all its transistorized glory.

Software has found its transistors—they are called objects. Objects allow programmers to build with components rather than piecemeal, particle by particle. With objects, software "comes of age." Already objects have been responsible for a metamorphosis across all phases of the software life cycle, spawning new subdisciplines that include object-oriented analysis and design, object-oriented databases, object-oriented operating systems, and object request brokers.

Objects are not limited to a single platform; they are equally at home on a personal computer (PC) as on a mainframe, client–server network, or the global Internet. Objects are not a fad but the extension of abstraction and encapsulation techniques that have been evolving since the earliest versions of COBOL (COmmon Business Oriented Language) and FORTRAN. Objects are the future; by the year 2000, 80% of all distributed software will be object oriented.

Object-Oriented COBOL (OOCOBOL) is the latest evolutionary step in COBOL's long history. COBOL is a survivor with a long, rich, colorful, and at times turbulent history of adaptation to change. Although COBOL's robustness and scalability have served it well, the limitations of the structured paradigm have taken their toll.

In many ways, the history of COBOL is the history of data processing. Today, Object-Oriented COBOL stands at the crossroads of two paradigms: structured methods and object technology. Although structured methods and procedural COBOL have created many successful systems, structured methods have outgrown their own rules of self-regulation and anecdotal techniques.

The emergence of OOCOBOL provides a unique opportunity for COBOL programmers, who, with their experience and broad systems knowledge, are uniquely qualified to harness the power of objects to extend legacy systems and develop new applications. It is time to move to the future, it is time to move to Object-Oriented COBOL.

GOALS

This book has three major goals.

1. To provide a firm understanding of object-oriented concepts
2. To furnish an introduction to the syntax and semantics of Object-Oriented COBOL
3. To provide enough background in object-oriented analysis and design so that readers may begin to implement their own small- to medium-sized applications.

STRUCTURE

This book is divided into four major sections.

- *Section I—Concepts.* The first section introduces object technology and Object-Oriented COBOL. Chapter 1 takes a historical perspective of COBOL and object technology. Chapter 2 introduces Object-Oriented COBOL language fundamentals in order to lay a foundation for the syntactic details of Section II.

- *Section II—Constructs.* The second section addresses the syntax of the language, focusing primarily on object-oriented features. Although there is still some debate on the most important features of an object-oriented language, there is agreement that it must support classes, objects, and inheritance. These are the topics of Chapters 3–5.

- *Section III—Objects in Action.* The third section focuses on the dynamic aspects of Object-Oriented COBOL. Chapter 6 discusses messages, Chapter 7 talks about creating and destroying objects, Chapter 8 covers working with objects, and Chapter 9 examines collection classes.

- *Section IV—Putting Objects to Work.* The fourth section deals with putting

Object-Oriented COBOL to work. Chapter 10 shows how a small system is developed using responsibility-driven object-oriented analysis and design techniques. Chapter 11 discusses issues surrounding migrating legacy code. The appendixes include a fully implemented version of the application begun in Chapter 10.

AUDIENCE

This book is intended for those with a background in procedural COBOL. The examples used in the book avoid, for the most part, COBOL 85 constructs. Where COBOL 85 constructs are used, however, they are noted. Although COBOL 85 introduced significant new capabilities to the language, we realize that many organizations have not adopted them. Because COBOL 97 is compatible with COBOL 85, Appendix F includes an explanation of some of the more useful COBOL 85 features.

This book focuses on the COBOL 97 language standard as defined by ANSI (American National Standards Institute) and the ISO (International Standards Organization). COBOL 97's object-oriented features are a subset of the COBOL 97 language definition, and are of such critical importance that several major vendors, including Hitachi, IBM, and Micro Focus, have released compilers implementing the new object-oriented features. Thus, Object-Oriented COBOL, similar to C++, has compilers available even as the language moves toward standardization.

Not all the features discussed in the book are supported by all the compilers, however. Hitachi, IBM, and Micro Focus are continually releasing updates, working toward the language standard (see Appendix A for vendor-specific details).

A NOTE ON TYPEFACE AND FONTS

We follow the convention of putting COBOL reserved words and methods in a square font; for example, Identification Division, Perform, Method-1. The names of classes and objects are italicized, as in *Class-1, anObject*. In addition to italicizing object names, camelback is sometimes used to distinguish an instance object from a class as *aBook* (instance name) and *Book* (class or factory name). Camelback, widely used with other object-oriented languages, concatenates multiple words, capitalizing all but the first letter of each new word. Thus, rather than specify *A-Customer-Object* we use *aCustomerObject*.

WORDS OF CAUTION

Questions express a certain point of view. Procedural programmers, when learning a new language, commonly ask questions that focus on data and input/output operations. With procedural languages this makes sense, because once input and output operations are understood, data-manipulation operations fall into place.

However, focusing on data reflects a certain point of view—a preoccupation based on a prior structure of our programming languages and patterns of imagination. COBOL has been, and continues to be, a strong data-manipulation language. Certainly data is important. Yet data is important only within a context. Often a COBOL programmer will encounter five, six, seven, or more file definitions in a legacy system, lost in a sea of data and endless **Redefines** even before getting to the **Procedure Division**. A design by data philosophy has not worked. Data-driven design produces programs that are hard to understand, harder to modify, and just plain hard.

Determining the context—what the data means and how it is used—is one of the keys to understanding application. Object-oriented languages allow us to seal off the data, relegating it to its rightful position in support of an object's responsibilities. With objects, we move from an open universe, where every variable is visible to every operation, to a closed universe where data has context and supports responsibilities.

With responsibility, though, comes delegation—another concept that may be new to COBOL programmers. COBOL programs often begin with **A100-Main**, or a similar paragraph name, which outlines the basic structure of a program. Again, a word of caution. Do not look for one program or paragraph called **Main** to control an object-oriented application. In object-oriented systems, application logic is not centralized but distributed among collaborating classes and objects. Ironically, this is both a source of power for object-oriented systems and a source of confusion for those beginning their journey with objects. Our advice: stay the course. The journey is well worth the effort.

ACKNOWLEDGMENTS

C OBOL programmers are, above all else, practical. It is the COBOL programmer who must deliver working systems day in and day out. We know firsthand the problems encountered, the demands made, and the unrealistic goals often imposed.

With this thought in mind, we would like to acknowledge COBOL programmers the world over, who with great skill, dedication, and imagination have collectively changed the face of business. You have produced many of the finest applications in the world for over three decades, at times by force of will more than anything else.

Our thanks to the students at UCLA Extension, who with their enthusiasm and real-world experience, have proved that COBOL programmers can become good Object-Oriented COBOL programmers in as little as 12 weeks; to Kasum Bajaj, Tu-uyen A. Can, Brenda Sharpless, and Danny Miller for reviewing and making wonderful suggestions; to Jack Alanen for teaching; to Ray Obin and Donald Schricker at Micro Focus, Shinobu Satoh at Hitachi, and Ann Wallace and Ron Langer at IBM for taking the time to answer questions; to Kurt Kaltschmidt and Ernie Escuton for their enthusiasm and support; to Charles Finley and his machines; to Laura Long and her artistry; to Barbara Crawford, our compositor; to F. Peter Arnold, our managing editor, and Don Jackson, our director, at SIGS Books & Multimedia; and of course to our family members Lisa, Jarad, Judy, Alex, and Nick for their patience, love, and support and to whom we dedicate the book.

E.C.A.   Long Beach, California
F.P.C.   Dallas, Texas

CONTENTS

APPENDIXES

CONCEPTS

LOOKING

Object-oriented languages, in general, and Object-Oriented COBOL, in particular, represent an evolutionary step in the progression from procedural code to objects. The focus of procedural programs is on data and algorithms; the focus of object-oriented programs is on classes, objects, responsibilities, and collaborations. The fundamental elements are the same; it's the focus that's different.

This change in focus means a new way to think about software. Making the transition to a different mindset can often be difficult, however. Psychologists use the word epiphany to describe the phenomenon in which the essence of something is revealed in a sudden flash of recognition. The classic example is the picture that is at once a young woman and an old lady (Figure I.1). From one perspective it shows a young woman. Stare and stare and it suddenly becomes an old lady. Sometimes we continue to stare but there is only one picture. Then a tilt of the head or a sidelong glance and suddenly the other image jumps into view. Yet the picture hasn't changed. The lines and shading are the same. What's different? Only our perception; a change in perspective.

FIGURE I.1.   The variability of perception: young woman or old lady? [With permission of John Wiley & Sons, Inc. from Weinberg, *An Introduction to General Systems Thinking*.]

Understanding objects also involves an epiphany. We stare and stare at the lines of code and data through procedural eyes, seeing only a familiar picture. To see the difference, however, our perception must change. As with the young lady and the old lady, we sometimes need someone to stand behind us and say "the young lady's chin is the old lady's nose."

These chapters will provide similar cues on where and how to look. It will take time, but a perception of objects will emerge from the lines of code and data. It is a picture worth the effort.

CHAPTER 1

COBOL AND OBJECTS?

Software developers may wonder whether the combination of COBOL and object technology makes sense. At first glance, COBOL, with its associated green screens, core dumps, and traditional mainframe connections, seems strangely at odds with the push button GUIs (Graphical User Interfaces) and interactive development environments of the personal computer (PC) and workstation worlds. This perceived incongruity, however, is actually more a reflection of the mainframe's inability to keep pace with the innovations of the PC world than a flaw in COBOL. Since its beginnings in 1959, when leaders from business and government gathered to outline their ideas for a new language, COBOL has continued to meet its objectives as the programming language of business.

In the late 1950s, only proprietary assembly languages and FORTRAN, the new scientific programming language, were available to grapple with the complexity of first-generation computers. Help was needed in other areas—specifically business. CODASYL (Committee on Data Systems Language), the committee that defined COBOL, reached a number of important decisions that have influenced the language to this day. First, the language needed to handle large quantities of data. Second, the

language needed to be machine independent. And third, the language needed to be "readable" so that it could be more easily maintained. After 18 months of discussion, beginning in 1959, a COBOL standard was defined and the COBOL language was born.

Four decades and four ANSI revisions later, COBOL has lived up to its promise as a business-oriented language, except that now businesses require enterprisewide, client–server solutions. Amazingly, COBOL has kept pace, 180 billion lines of code strong, and ready to tackle the increasing needs of greater productivity demanded in today's business climate.

Focus of This Chapter

Object technology did not arrive on the software scene devoid of parentage or struggle. Object technology grew out of past successes and failures and the realization that we can do better. It is a struggle every discipline cycles through—from theory to science to engineering to standard practice, with a cycle typically taking anywhere from twenty to thirty years.

Object technology has served its incubation period. Today object technology stands on the verge of entering the standards practice phase. To understand how and why object technology came to be we must examine its roots in the procedural and structured methods of the past. The focus of this chapter is uncovering those roots. The following topics are covered:

- COBOL's Evolution
- The Programming Revolution
- Object-Oriented Languages
- Methodologies

COBOL's Evolution

Much of COBOL's success may be attributed to its very specific design objective—the support of general business data processing. COBOL's first-class treatment of data made file and record reuse easy. Because data manipulation was the key to success for many organizations moving to automation, COBOL's data-centric, hardware independent features brought wide-scale adoption and success.

Over the years, COBOL has not been a stranger to change. The addition of object-oriented features is only the most recent evolution. Since its introduction, COBOL has been enhanced in 1968, 1974, and again in 1985/89 by the American National Standards Institute (ANSI). The latest ANSI/ISO (International Standards Organization) standard, COBOL 97, includes both conventional improvements as well as object-oriented features. Object-Oriented COBOL (OOCOBOL) is a subset of COBOL 97.

Influenced by other object-oriented languages, such as C++ and Smalltalk, COBOL 97 supports strong typing and dynamic object creation, while respecting the legacy base of COBOL code. One new verb, **invoke**, coupled with the preservation of COBOL's basic program structure, makes the language a viable alternative for organizations looking to make the move to object technology.

But before assessing Object-Oriented COBOL's future, we first need to understand why object technology offers a solution to many of software's toughest problems.

WHY OBJECTS?

If we have learned one lesson over the past several decades of software development, it's that software is hard to get right. Software's innate flexibility allows for arbitrarily complex programs in which changing a single byte can have drastic effects far removed from the original point of modification. Software, unlike any other engineering enterprise, is unconstrained by the laws that govern how bridges, dams, and skyscrapers are constructed. Anyone who has ever tried to maintain software knows that attempting to fix a bug often introduces additional bugs more difficult to find and eradicate than the original.

One of the strengths of object technology is its ability to model business processes with constructs that can be directly translated into code. The continuity of concepts from analysis, to design, to code, directly supports traceability throughout the entire software development life cycle. Rapid application development (RAD) can be used by quickly verifying and testing user requirements in the early stages of development, when changes are less costly and easier to implement.

Object technology manages software's inherent complexity by partitioning programs into manageable components known as objects. When done correctly, distributing a program's functionality across objects reduces the impact of change to limited areas within the total program space. Objects with well-defined interfaces make programs easier to understand and reuse, thereby allowing objects to live more productive lives within the business enterprise.

WHAT IS AN OBJECT?

Quite simply, an object is a packaging of code and data, which are fundamental components of all software. COBOL programmers have long understood how code and data combine to create an executable program unit. Object-orientation doesn't change that fact, it only changes the focus to packages of code and data. These mini-programs, or objects, function as service providers in an application that includes other objects and program components.

Code and Data

Code and data are at the heart of all programs. Experienced programmers, looking at objects for the first time, are often surprised to discover that they do not have to relearn everything they know about software. The code and data are still there; it's the packaging that is different. Rather than one large program, objects cooperate and communicate with one another to get programming tasks done.

Interfaces

An object's interface is a boundary or external layer that handles requests for services (see Figure 1.1). A service request may take different forms. It may request data from

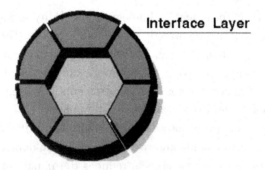

FIGURE 1.1. An object with its interface layer.

an object or ask for computational services, such as an interest calculation or a file update. All service requests must go through the object interface. Therefore, clients must know what messages are available and whether any parameters are required.

In OOCOBOL, individual paragraphs or *methods* are specified as part of the object's interface, visible to clients. Collectively, all the externally visible methods of an object define the object's interface. Clients may include other objects, modules, or programs either locally or dispersed in a network. Methods serve as the entry points for object services.

Information Hiding

Because the object interface regulates access to an object's code and data, a program's implementation details can be hidden from other program components. This aspect of object technology supports long-term maintenance because now a programmer can make the distinction between public and private parts of a program.

This capability to keep certain code and data inaccessible is not something new. Conventional programs support information hiding by suggesting applications be constructed as modules. Object-oriented languages, however, take the concept one step further by protecting both data and code through the object interface.

COBOL Objects

In COBOL 97 the view of objects as packages of code and data is made explicit in the syntax of an object definition. Objects in COBOL resemble conventional COBOL programs, complete with their own Identification, Environment, Data, and Procedure Divisions (see Figure 1.2).

Messages

Object-oriented programs are collections of collaborating objects. Messages are the means of communication between objects. Basically, a message is a request for service (Figure 1.3). Sending a message causes the execution of a block of code within the receiving object. In object-oriented systems, methods are the executable blocks of code that receive messages. Thus, messages invoke methods, similar to how a call transfers control to a subprogram. Again, like subprograms, data may be passed back and forth in the process of invoking a method (sending a message).

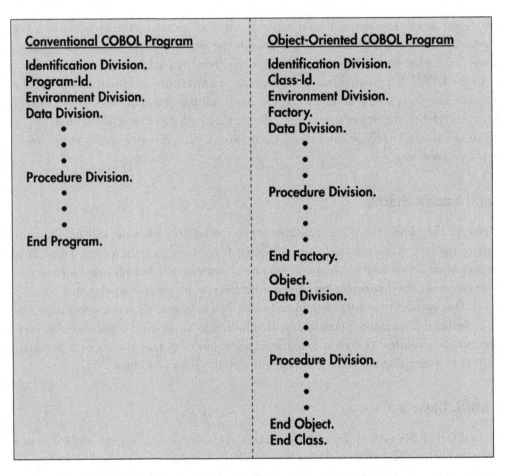

FIGURE 1.2. Conventional and Object-Oriented COBOL programs.

Invoke is used to request services from an object. For example, if customer1 were an object that contained a method called getDate, a COBOL program requesting date information from the object would be written as follows:

Invoke customer1 'getDate' returning WS-Date.
where WS-Date might be defined in Working-Storage Section as:

01   WS-Date.
05   Month   PIC 99.

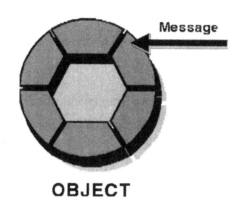

FIGURE 1.3. Messages as requests to objects.

```
05      Day       PIC 99.
05      Year      PIC 99.
```

Using a method properly means understanding the object interface: using the proper method name, the sequencing of parameters, and the structure of any returned value. The job of the client (the user of an object's services) is to understand what an object is capable of doing. The task of the server (the object itself) is to get the job done.

WHY OBJECT-ORIENTED COBOL?

Before Object-Oriented COBOL, organizations had few options in moving to object technology. Neither C++ nor Smalltalk provided attractive choices. Object-Oriented COBOL, on the other hand, by extending the basic COBOL language, provides a graceful path for organizations looking to make the move to object technology. As a result, organizations can use Object-Oriented COBOL in a variety of ways.

- **Support for legacy code.** The sheer quantity of COBOL legacy code is staggering. Industry estimates place the quantity of legacy code at over 180 billion lines—enough for every man, woman, and child on earth to have his or her own COBOL program. Object-Oriented COBOL is a world standard, supported and backed with the full weight of both the ANSI and the ISO organizations.

Because Object-Oriented COBOL is supported on PCs, midrange computers, and mainframes, its multiplatform availability opens up possibilities for developing distributed systems, adding GUI front-ends, as well as extending the functionality of legacy code.

- **Code Reuse.** By developing code within an object-oriented framework, organizations can leverage programming efforts through code reuse. Because the focus in object-oriented development is on functionality rather than lines of code, organizations using Object-Oriented COBOL will be better able to leverage their investment in program development and minimize their investment in program maintenance.

- **Development Options.** Object-Oriented COBOL's multiplatform availability allows organizations to offload costly development cycles to less-expensive platforms. With Object-Oriented COBOL now available for UNIX, MVS, Windows 95, OS/2, and Windows NT, the opportunities for cross-platform development are significant.

- **Client–Server Computing.** Networks, not platforms, are fast becoming the defining element for computing in the 21st century. The rise of client–server distributed computing, coupled with the explosion in the Internet, is forcing companies to rethink their computing strategies. Networking technologies allow existing programs to connect with other programs and to act as servers for new categories of clients without having to rework existing code. Object-Oriented COBOL is uniquely positioned to bridge the gap between mainframe applications and networks, opening the door to flexible computing strategies for transaction-based and data warehousing applications.

- **People Reuse.** Reuse is a term most often applied to software. Reuse, however, can be equally applied to people and with greater results. Object-Oriented COBOL builds naturally on the language understood and used by more programmers than any other language in the history of computing. Programmers with business knowledge bring a wealth of experience and problem-solving skills to organizations.

Although OOCOBOL's most notable features are object oriented, there have been many other important improvements to the language. Table 1.1 shows a partial list of both the conventional, as well as some of the object-oriented features of COBOL 97.

TABLE 1.1. Conventional and Object-Oriented Features of COBOL

Conventional features	Object-oriented features
Common exception processing	Class and object definitions
Bit and Boolean data types	Data encapsulation for class and instance objects
Free format source code	Methods for class objects and instance objects
In-line comments	Multiple inheritance and subclassing
Table sort	Polymorphism
Recursion	Data items maintaining object references
Call . . . Return parameter for subroutines	Garbage collection

A Brief History of Objects

Object technology is not a fad or a radically new technology. The fundamental ideas behind objects have been around since 1966 when a programming language known as Simula was developed in Oslo, Norway by two computer scientists. The maturation of object-oriented languages, object-oriented analysis, and object-oriented design have positioned object technology as the successor to the conventional structured languages and methods of the past.

Recent collaborative work by the Object Management Group (OMG), a consortium of over 300 major hardware and software vendors, has resulted in the specification of CORBA (Common Object Request Broker Architecture), a framework for transparent access to remote objects across distributed networks. Developments such as these underscore the importance of object technology as an enabling factor in enterprisewide computing efforts.

To appreciate where we are it is often helpful to look back and examine the path we've taken. The following sections describe the evolution of object technology illustrating how it is a natural extension of what has come before and a basis for what is to come next.

Early Days

Many look to the 1950s as the beginning of the modern computer era. Yet, in the early 1900s IBM and others were selling specialized, punched-card, electromechanical devices to count, sort, and categorize data. Like the computers of today, these early machines were programmed, but in specific patterns of fixed hardwired connections. They performed their tasks relentlessly, but lacked a key ingredient—software.

In the 1940s, a simple idea by John von Neumann changed the face of computing. Von Neumann proposed a model of computing known as the *stored program concept* in which both a program and its data resided in memory. Until that time, computing machines were fed data, but what they *did* with the data was predetermined by hardwired connections. Von Neumann's brilliant insight was to feed the instructions in just like data. Rather than machines running on hardwired connections, instructions became responsible for determining what operations were executed and in what order.

This simple change meant that computers were not constrained to performing one task. Machines could assume any number of roles by simply changing their programs. Once the concept of programs as data was understood, the computer industry took off. Vacuum tube behemoths such as ENIAC, EDVAC, and UNIVAC became the legendary giant brains of the late 1940s and early 1950s, leading the charge into a new era of computing.

It soon became apparent, however, that computers were limited by the very source of their power—their programs. Each machine contained its own set of built-in primitive operations on which programs were constructed. Writing a program was extremely complicated, error-prone, and time-consuming.

Some relief was provided by assemblers that allowed programmers the luxury of using mnemonics (semi-readable instructions such as LOAD or MOV) instead of cryptic binary codes. But even with the alphabet soup of assembly language, programmers still had to understand the underlying architecture of the machine.

Even after the introduction of UNIVAC, the first commercial computer, few took the computer industry seriously. Computing machines were seen as of interest to only a limited audience of scientists and technicians. It took programming languages to get the ball rolling.

The Programming Revolution

The emergence of high-level programming languages is a milestone in the history of computing. Rivaling the importance of the stored-program concept, languages such as FORTRAN and COBOL unlocked the power of von Neumann's ideas, launching the computer industry on its present-day path.

Although we now take computer languages for granted, many early pundits believed that it was impossible to get a computer to write a program—to generate the complex stream of machine instructions that tells a CPU (central processing unit) what to do. The assumption was that writing a program was beyond the capability of a machine. The success of FORTRAN, the first high-level language, proved the early pundits wrong.

FORTRAN was designed to ease the burden of mathematical programming by translating complex formulas into intricate machine-level instructions. FORTRAN made programmers out of scientists and engineers, opening the door to a new world of applications.

The computational prowess of FORTRAN was of only marginal use to businesses seeking to automate their data-intensive operations. Finding FORTRAN unsuited to business applications, in 1959 a committee of government and business leaders decided on a framework for a new programming language, better suited to processing large quantities of data. COBOL, or the COmmon Business Oriented Language, emerged as a machine-independent, human-readable language, tailored to the data-processing requirements of business and government.

The Language Landscape

For over two decades, FORTRAN and COBOL dominated the language landscape. FORTRAN met the needs of science and engineering and COBOL served the needs of business.

Figure 1.4 illustrates the parallel threads of code-centric versus data-centric languages. For example, ALGOL, Pascal, and C followed FORTRAN in the code-centric camp, generally ignoring issues of data and file manipulation. In fact, Pascal, C, and C++ studiously avoid any connections to file and data from within the language.

COBOL is on the data side, with its important variants: COBOL 68, COBOL 74, COBOL 85, and the latest, COBOL 97. Other important languages developed in the data-centric tradition, not shown in Figure 1.4, were PL/I, SNOBOL, and ICON. Part of COBOL's uniqueness is its support for files at the language level. Over the years COBOL has continued to extend its data manipulation capabilities, keeping pace with the changes in secondary-storage technology.

Object-Oriented Languages

Whereas C++ and OOCOBOL represent object-oriented languages that have evolved from code- and data-centric languages, there has been another quiet thread based on

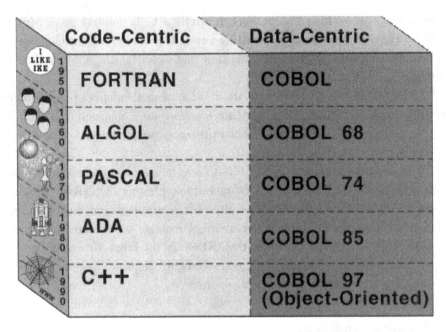

FIGURE 1.4. Code and data trends in computing.

the notion of pure object orientation that has flourished on the fringes of mainstream computing. Simula, the first object-oriented language, was developed in the mid-1960s to help solve problems that did not fit into either a data-centric or computation-intensive framework. Many problems in transportation and scheduling simply could not be computed with formulas and equations, but instead required modeling and simulation.

Simula achieved considerable success in the simulation world. Its real impact, however, was on the researchers at Xerox PARC (Palo Alto Research Center) in the 1970s, who were building simple, easy-to-use, graphical computing languages and environments. Smalltalk, an object-oriented language based on Simula's notion of objects and classes, was the result.* In many ways Smalltalk established a standard against which other object-oriented languages were measured. Smalltalk is considered a pure object-oriented language in which everything is an object, including numbers.

---

* During Smalltalk's incubation at Xerox, an upstart garage-programmer named Steve Jobs was inspired by what he saw while visiting PARC, and several years later the Apple Macintosh was born.

C++, on the other hand, is a hybrid object-oriented language, designed by Bjarne Stroustrup at AT&T's Bell Labs. C++ very much retains the flavor of C while bringing object-oriented constructs to what is basically a lower-level programming language.

Object-Oriented COBOL's style reflects the influence of Smalltalk and C++ in that objects may be created dynamically at run time or statically at compile time. Object-Oriented COBOL, while traveling a different path than either Smalltalk or C++, arrives into the object arena, in many ways, a more powerful and capable language than either of its contemporaries.

Like Smalltalk, Object-Oriented COBOL allows a programmer to define everything, numbers included, as objects, while respecting the need to be upwardly compatible with earlier COBOL applications. Unlike Smalltalk, Object-Oriented COBOL gives developers the freedom to incorporate both object and procedural constructs according to the needs of their applications.

Object-Oriented COBOL is similar to C++ in that both are hybrid languages. Unlike C++, Object-Oriented COBOL is a subset of COBOL. C++ and C are different languages, each defined by their own ANSI committees. C is not a proper subset of C++, which means that the two languages will evolve differently with only informal agreements to keep the commonality between the languages standard. Object-Oriented COBOL, on the other hand, is a proper subset of COBOL, meaning earlier versions of COBOL code are guaranteed to be compatible with the newer versions of the language.

As shown in Figure 1.5 there are two paths to object orientation. For code-centric languages, data is combined with functions to produce member functions. For

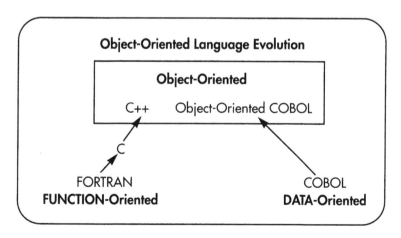

FIGURE 1.5. Two paths to object-orientation.

data-centric languages, data is combined with procedures to produce methods. Both member functions and methods are encapsulated by an interface. Different paths, same result—objects.

Methodologies

Without an idea of what we are trying to build and a vision of how to get there, our software, whether conventional or object oriented, will more than likely fail to fully meet the needs of the user. That is why we have software methodologies.

Methodologies tell us how best to use our language tools. Tracing the history of languages and methods, we can see that there is a connection. Over time, the best ideas from various methodologies are solidified into syntax, resulting in new languages and extensions to existing languages.

As shown in Figure 1.6 advances in computing may be seen as the interaction among three separate but interrelated technologies: hardware, programming languages, and software methodologies, each with its own separate thread of development, each influenced by the other.

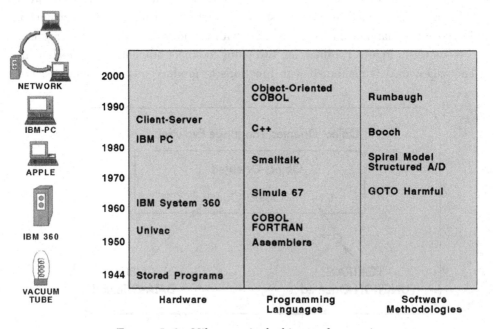

FIGURE 1.6. Milestones in the history of computing.

Object technology continues this interdependency. Object-oriented languages, object-oriented design, and object-oriented analysis emerged out of a need for better abstraction, encapsulation, and reuse. Object technology does not solve all our software development problems. It does, however, provide a better tool for modeling, capturing, and implementing business systems than are provided by the methods and languages of the past.

SIMULA

The Simula programming language was created and developed from 1962 to 1967 by Ole-Johan Dahl and Kristen Nygaard at the Norwegian Computing Centre (NCC) in Oslo, Norway. Simula shared the same fate as many other excellent programming languages, such as Modula-2 and ALGOL, that were much more widely used and appreciated in Europe than in the United States.

Simula was originally developed as an extension to ALGOL 60 (*ALGO*rithmic *L*anguage), the leading programming language of the day in Europe. The motivation to link Simula with ALGOL was to reach as broad an audience as possible (the same reason C++ was added to the C language). Simula grew out of a need to program simulations using the Monte Carlo method. Univac provided equipment and other resources in an attempt to counter the success of IBM and their FORTRAN compiler. It was thought that ALGOL combined with Simula would effectively neutralize the IBM offering, which did not provide a simulation capability. In 1964 the first commercial offering of Simula was made available as an extension to the UNIVAC ALGOL 60 compiler.

This first implementation of Simula lacked classes, subclasses, and objects. Dahl and Nygaard always envisioned Simula as a general-purpose programming language and began work in that direction in 1965. In an attempt to find general unifying concepts that would support more than Monte Carlo simulation, Dahl and Nygaard conceived the concept of class hierarchies, class types, and objects (at that time called processes). These ideas were refined and incorporated in the definition of what was to become Simula 67. At that time the tie between ALGOL and Simula was severed and Simula 67 became a programming language in its own right. The commercial debut of Simula 67 was in 1971 on a UNIVAC 1100 series. An IBM version that ran on the 360/370 series followed in 1972, and a version was installed on a DEC PDP-10 in 1975.

In 1986 the name of the language was shortened to Simula. Simula is in use today and enjoys modest success in Europe. Simula compilers are available for mainframes and PCs. Its greatest success and continuing legacy remain, not the language itself, but the seminal ideas of Dahl and Nygaard.

Key Points

- COBOL has a long-standing history of supporting business applications.

- Objects are packages of code and data.

- An object's interface hides the implementation details and encapsulates code and data.

- By incorporating object-oriented features, Object-Oriented COBOL does not abandon its data-centric framework.

- Object-Oriented COBOL is a subset of the ANSI/ISO COBOL 97 standard.

- Object-Oriented COBOL builds on the strength of its data-manipulation capabilities, adding support for objects directly into the language.

Suggested Readings

Berard, E. (1993). *Essays in Object-Oriented Software Engineering.* Englewood Cliffs, NJ: Prentice Hall.

Goldberg, A., & Robson, D. (1989). *Smalltalk-80: The Language.* Reading, MA: Addison-Wesley.

Love, T. (1993). *Object Lessons.* New York: SIGS Books.

Stroustrup, B. (1991). *The C++ Programming Language* (2nd ed.). Reading, MA: Addison-Wesley.

Taylor, D. (1990). *Object-Oriented Technology. A Manager's Guide.* Alameda, CA: Servio Corporation.

Wegner, P. (1992). Dimensions of Object-Oriented Modeling. *IEEE Computer, 25,* 12–20.

Welburn, T., & Price, W. (1995). *Structured COBOL* (4th ed.). San Francisco: McGraw-Hill.

Review Questions

1.0   What is meant by the term *object-oriented programming?*

1.1   What is the role of an object interface?

1.2   How does Object-Oriented COBOL compare with other object-oriented languages, such as Smalltalk and C++?

1.3   Describe some of the different ways that organizations can make use of Object-Oriented COBOL.

1.4   Describe how object-orientation is an extension of programming ideas begun in the 1950s.

CHAPTER 2

An Object-Oriented COBOL Model

S cience and engineering routinely use models to manage complexity and explain the world around us. Science constructs models using abstractions and hierarchies to explore everything from the age of the universe to the components of matter. Applying the concept of abstraction to the subject of matter reveals a hierarchy of compounds, elements, molecules, atoms, protons, neutrons, electrons, and quarks. A model of the atom, or a model of the solar system, captures both the spirit and specification of the subject.

Object technology brings the same fundamental modeling capability to software, taking abstractions and hierarchies directly from the cloth of the problem domain to capture the spirit and specification of a system. It is a watershed time in the history of software development—a time when the tools and techniques of software development have moved beyond the realm of crafting an application to the arena of engineering a solution.

FOCUS OF THIS CHAPTER

This chapter illustrates the key concepts of the object model. Its goal is to introduce fundamental object-oriented concepts in order to provide a foundation to begin a discussion of object technology in general, and Object-Oriented COBOL in particular.

Do not be alarmed if certain constructs are given only brief treatment in this chapter. Each construct is fully developed in later chapters. This early introduction is focused on simplicity rather than completeness. The following topics will be covered in this chapter:

- Classes
- Inheritance
- Messages
- Objects
- Polymorphism
- Responsibility-Driven Design

The Waterfall Model

Traditional software development typically relies on the waterfall model for managing the phases in a project's life cycle. A picture of the waterfall model is shown in Figure 2.1.

The Spiral Model

Responsibility-driven design operates within a spiral model of development, with rings of effort as opposed to the cascading tasks used in the waterfall model. A linear approach is replaced by one of discovery, design, and coding, over and over again. Both design and the act of coding uncover other objects that are required in an application. Stages of development are not stand-alone labors divorced from other phases. Instead, feedback occurs as knowledge is gained in a continuing cycle of refinement. There is no arbitrary, fixed number of cycles around the spiral. Instead there is incremental development that emphasizes "growing" a system as opposed to building a system. Figure 2.2 shows a picture of a spiral model of software development.

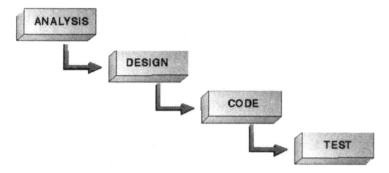

FIGURE 2.1. The waterfall model.

RESPONSIBILITY-DRIVEN DESIGN

Responsibility-driven design is an approach to object-oriented software development, based on the work of Rebecca Wirfs-Brock, which begins by asking the question: what classes, objects, and messages are required to meet the goals of an intended application? The process begins more by discovery, and less by invention, than with methods of the past. Objects are discovered or "unearthed" during the initial phases of design, just as a chemist might search for compounds, or a geologist for minerals.

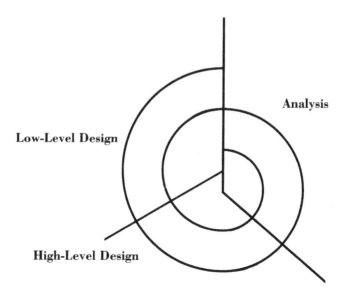

FIGURE 2.2. The spiral model.

In responsibility-driven design, objects serve as both a start and an end point of the design process. The process begins by finding and ends by implementing the same unit ideas—objects. From analysis to design to implementation there is a symmetry of thought, that is at once pleasing and correct, because the units of expression remain consistent across the different phases of software development.

A central idea in responsibility-driven design is one of delegating responsibility to objects. For example, in the real world, one might expect to delegate responsibility for flying an airplane to a pilot, or performing surgery to a doctor. In this delegation, however, there is a mutual understanding between the person delegating the responsibility and the person being given the responsibility to correctly carry out the task.

The same principle of delegating responsibility to pilots or surgeons can be applied to objects. In object-oriented software, objects know how to perform their tasks and contain certain knowledge about themselves. For example, it would be fair to say, a *customer* object would know the last purchase it made. On the other hand, it would *not* be fair to assume a *customer* object would know where the product was manufactured. That information may instead be part of the *product's* knowledge. There is a limit to what an object knows, just as there is a limit to what a pilot or a surgeon knows. Objects only know as much as they need to carry out their assigned tasks and nothing more.

In this world of responsible objects, it is the collaboration between objects that moves the process forward and accomplishes work. The collaboration between objects is called a *contract*. A set of contracts is the "understanding" built into an object-oriented system that objects will respond to requests (messages) from other objects and supply the necessary information or perform the necessary task.

With this basic backdrop of assigning responsibility to objects, we can define the goal of object-oriented programming as *an attempt to simulate reality by developing models of the real world in software.* And define object-oriented programming as *a modeling technique applied to software whose units of expression are objects that communicate by sending and receiving messages.*

THE COMPONENTS OF CONSTRUCTION

Objects

The basic building blocks of object-oriented software are objects. Objects *encapsulate* or protect their inner workings from outside interference. Objects may be thought of as self-contained units or modules protected by an interface.

There are different objects in object-oriented software, just as there are different objects in the real world. In the real world, people, places, and things are all examples of objects. In object-oriented software, people, places, and things are also examples of objects.

Objects contain *methods* and *data*. In Object-Oriented COBOL, methods are similar to conventional COBOL programs, complete with their own **Identification**, **Environment**, **Data**, and **Procedure** Divisions. Interfaces are implemented in the methods. An interface specifies the acceptable format of a message and optionally includes a returned argument (reply). Figure 2.3 illustrates the structure of an object with its methods and data.

An object contains all the information it needs to carry out its responsibilities and interactions with other objects. Objects are responsible for managing themselves. For example, a library book is a real-world entity that can be modeled as an object. Applying the technique of responsibility-driven design, the following is a list of possible responsibilities (methods) that could be expected of a library-book object:

- Information—report the title of a book.
- Status—report if a book is in the library.
- Check-Out—check a book out of the library.
- Check-In—return a book to the library.

The following is a list of items (data) that one might expect a library-book object to maintain:

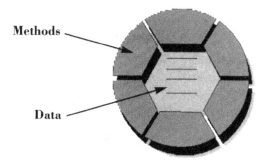

FIGURE 2.3. An object with methods and data.

- Title, author, ISBN, publication date, and other related information
- The book's current status—checked out? overdue?
- A history of borrowers

A book's methods (code) in combination with a book's data items, define the capabilities of a book object.

A *Book* object, in carrying out its assigned tasks, may need help from other objects. For example, a *Book* object may be responsible for reordering additional copies and may require the help of another object, *Reorder,* that is part of the system. Working together, the *Book* object is said to *collaborate* with the *Reorder* object to get the job done. Figure 2.4 illustrates a library-book object with its methods and associated data items.

Only an object's methods may reference and change its data items. In this way, objects are protected from the possible side effects of other operations in an application. Should an object need to be changed, the changes are localized to the changed object.

Objects are highly cohesive, loosely coupled components. Cohesion is the degree of connectivity among the elements of an object, and coupling is the degree of connectivity between objects. An object exhibits cohesion if there is a unity of purpose in its design. A library-book object, for example, should not include a method that converts meters to yards. Coupling, *unlike* cohesion, should be low. The connections between objects should be simple and straightforward, keeping objects relatively independent.

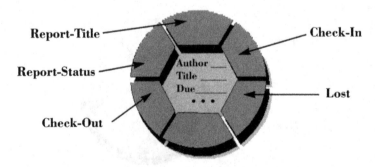

FIGURE 2.4. A library-book object.

Defining Objects

The part of an Object-Oriented COBOL program that defines the object begins with the reserved word **Object** and is delimited by the reserved words **End Object**. A period directly follows the **End Object** with no other words allowed. The **Object** paragraph is nested within an object-oriented program. Nested within the **Object** paragraph are the methods. Here is an **Object** declaration within the program *Book*.

Format: an Object paragraph within the class program Book.

```
Identification Division.
Class-Id. Book.
  <methods and data>
Object.
  <methods and data>
End Object.
End Class Book.
```

Declaring an object does not create one. Object declarations are similar to record declarations. Declaring a record does not create the record, it provides a description. Declaring an object does the same thing, it provides a description. Objects are first declared and then created after the program begins execution.

Just as a record description may describe an infinite number of records, one object declaration may describe an infinite number of objects. During the running of a program, each object created is unique, just as each record is unique. In a library application, for example, each book in the library could be modeled as an individual object, created after program start-up based on the definition in class *Book*.

An object's responsibilities are taken care of by an object's methods. Methods are specified in COBOL by the reserved word **Method-Id** followed by a user-defined method name. Methods are delimited by the reserved word **End Method** followed by the method name.

Data within an object may be global to all methods of an object or specific to an individual method. Because of this, COBOL supports a **Data Division** for the object as well as for the method(s). Data declared in an object's **Object Data Division** is available to all object methods. Data declared in a method **Data Division** is available only to the method.

In the following example, the method "Report-Status" references both global object data (Book-Status) and data local to the method (LS-Book-Status). Note that method names are placed in quotation marks.

Format: an Object and its method, within the class program Book.

```
Identification Division.
Class-Id. Book.
  <class methods and data>
Object
Data Division.
Working-Storage Section.
01 Book-Status              Pic X(03).
Method-Id. "Report-Status".
Data Division.
Linkage Section.
01 LS-Book-Status           Pic X(03).
Procedure Division Returning LS-Book-Status.
  Move Book-Status to LS-Book-Status.
End Method "Report-Status".
  <other methods>
End Object.
End Class Book.
```

Messages

Objects communicate by sending and receiving messages. In close conjunction with client–server terminology, the object initiating the message is called the *client*, whereas the target object is referred to as the *server*. When an object receives a message it responds by executing one of its methods.

A message consists of three parts: (1) the identity of the target object, (2) the name of the method, and (3) any arguments required by the method. Figure 2.5 illustrates a message requesting a library book object to report its status.

Within an Object-Oriented COBOL program, every object has a unique identifier. In Figure 2.5, *Hamlet* is the unique object identifier and *Status* is the method. The object, depending on the availability of the book, may respond with "In" or "Out."

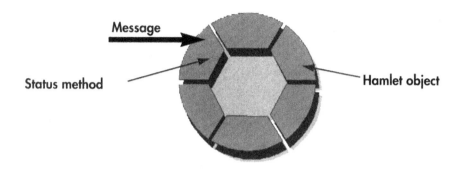

FIGURE 2.5. Message sending.

Simple messages involve only the recipient and the message name. More complex messages may have additional arguments or parameters and may return a value.

Message Syntax

In Object-Oriented COBOL the verb, **Invoke,** is used to send messages (request services) from another object. For example, in the following message, *Hamlet* is asked to report its status:

Invoke Hamlet "Report-Status" Returning Status.

Polymorphism

With objects, it is the responsibility of the object receiving the message to execute code in response to the message. The client, the object sending the message, is simply interested in getting a job done. Thus with objects it is possible to use the same message name with different objects. This flexibility is called *polymorphism* (from the Greek meaning "many forms"). For example, a library may lend both videos and books, each with its own **Report-Fines** method. Because objects are self-contained units, the same method name may be used conceptually for the same effect (to calculate fines) but have different underlying code (based on different fine schedules).

Polymorphism corresponds to the way we use words. In English, we understand the meaning of a word by its context. For example, the word "object" in a courtroom has a different meaning than the word "object" used at a software engineering convention (Figure 2.6).

FIGURE 2.6. Polymorphism in action.

In traditional COBOL, **If** statements along with unique identifier names are necessary to select and process the correct segment of code. For example, the following series of nested **If** statements would be needed to implement the **Report-Fines** capability previously described.

```
If Video-Request
   Perform A100-Video-Fines
Else
   If Book-Request
      Perform A100-Book-fines
   End-If
End-If.
```

Polymorphism reduces the need for many of the branching statements found in traditional programs. Polymorphism also simplifies the act of writing and maintaining software. The struggle of naming similar operations is eliminated. Instead, context determines which method is correct at any given moment. As every professional programmer knows, complex **If** statements, commonly found in applications, are often difficult to decipher and dangerous to change. Polymorphism greatly reduces the incidental errors by reducing the dependency on switching logic.

Of even greater importance, however, is the ease of enhancement that polymorphism brings to software. For example, should the library decide to begin lending other materials, such as audiotapes, these new objects would simply implement their own method of **Report-Fines**. Introduction of new objects has minimal impact on the operation of a system. Polymorphism and objects help solve the problem of constantly retooling existing code by allowing systems to be extended in a more natural, unobtrusive manner.

For example, when both *Book* objects and *Video* objects implement their own versions of **Report-Fines**, the programmer does not have to keep track of different method names for different fine calculations. Responsibility for maintaining the different rates falls to the objects themselves. Thus, if *Hamlet* is an object handle that can refer to either *Book* or *Video* objects, the following code will correctly calculate the fine, irrespective of whether Hamlet is actually a *Book* or *Video* reference.

> Invoke Hamlet "Report-Fines" Returning Fine.

Classes

Classes provide the same function as blueprints, templates, or molds. All objects must be an *instance* of some class. The terms *object, instance,* and *object instance* are synonymous.

In an object-oriented application there may be dozens of classes that interact to get various tasks accomplished. Each class is responsible for creating its own type of object. For example, in a library application, there may be *Customer, Book,* and *Video* classes, just to name a few. The library book, *Hamlet,* may be an instance of the class *Book*. There may be thousands of books in a library and thousands of *Book* objects in a system, each object instance created by its class.

Another way of thinking about the class-object relationship is to view the class as a cookie cutter or template. A cookie cutter, like a class, creates form where none existed before (from the cookie dough). Cutting usable classes from the problem domain is accomplished by defining classes that are relevant to the application being developed. For example, an automobile manufacturing application would need *Car, Truck,* and *Minivan* classes (Figure 2.7). The *Car* class (cookie cutter) would be used to create *Car* objects. Figure 2-8 illustrates a *Car* class (factory object) creating *Car* objects.

All the objects created by a class share the same interface, the same methods, and the same data items based on the class definition. It is important to realize, however, that each object instance will maintain its own data *values*. The book object,

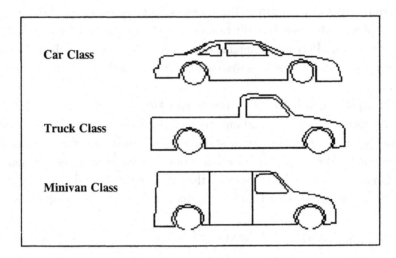

FIGURE 2.7. Three different classes.

FIGURE 2.8. A car class creates three car objects.

Hamlet, for example, will differ from *Macbeth* in title and date of publication. The values, of course, may be the same, but only if by intent. Each object is unique, just as each copy from the same printing of *Macbeth* is unique. During the running of an Object-Oriented COBOL program, when objects are created, they are assigned a unique system identifier, distinguishing them from all other objects.

The Class and Factory Objects

Class definitions serve as templates for the creation of objects during the running of a program. Object creation is not automatic, however. Typically, the message NEW is sent to a class and an object instance is returned, just as pressing a cookie cutter into dough yields a new cookie. However, because NEW is a message, there must be an object recipient—something more than just a class definition in a COBOL program.

To make this all work there is a special object associated with each class. This object is called the FACTORY OBJECT, which actually carries out the creation of object instances. Thus, the requirement that all messages be sent to some object can be satisfied.

Class Methods and Class Data

Programmers can specify factory methods and factory data. The more common term for factory methods and data is *class methods* and *class data* (not to be confused with the methods and data that the object instances will have, which are referred to as *instance methods* and *instance data*). The two most common class methods are *constructor* and *destructor* methods, used for creating and destroying objects.

Just like object definitions, a class may contain a Class Data Division as well as a Data Division for each method. Data from the Class Data Division is shared by the methods of the class. Data from the method Data Division is accessible only to the declaring method.

Class Definitions

A class definition begins with the reserved word Class-Id, followed by a user-defined class name. The end of the class is marked by the reserved words End Class, followed by the class name. Notice that there is no period directly following the words End Class. Instead, the period comes after the class name. The following is an example of a class program named *Book*, with a class method called Report-Object-Count.

Format: a class program called Book.

```
Class-Id. Book.
Factory.
Data Division.
```

```
        Working-Storage Section.
        01 Object-Count              Pic s9(05).
```

```
        Method-Id. "Report-Object-Count".
        Data Division.
        Linkage Section.
        01 LS-Object-Count           Pic s9(05).
        Procedure Division Returning LS-Object-Count.
           Move Object-Count to LS-Object-Count.
```

```
        End Method "Report-Object-Count".
        <other methods>
        End Factory.
        Object.
        <object methods and data>
        End Object
```

```
        End Class Book.
```

The **Identification Division** is optional. The class program shown above could be rewritten to include the optional **Identification Division**, which we will often omit for readability purposes. The following is an outline of a class program with the **Identification Division**.

Format: a class program called Book.

```
        Identification Division.
```

```
        Class-Id. Book.
           <class methods and data>
        Object.
           <object methods and data>
        End Object.
```

```
        End Class Book.
```

Every class program must include the **Class-Id**. Each class program only has one **Class-Id**. The **Class-Id** notifies the compiler that this is a class program.

Inheritance

Inheritance structures classes in hereditary relationships for the purpose of providing methods and data items to descendant classes. In object-oriented programming, descendant classes, often called *subclasses,* can inherit the methods (behavior) of ascendant classes, often called *superclasses.*

The term inheritance as it applies to object-oriented software is equivalent to its more general biological usage. In other words, subclasses inherit from superclasses in the same manner that the characteristics of children are inherited from their ancestors. Inheritance is one of object-oriented software's most powerful features, providing for code reuse, the evolution of systems, and most important, an ability to classify and construct software in layers of functionality.

Returning to our example, a library may lend books, videos, and audiotapes to the public. Rather than duplicate code that is common to all three items, a class hierarchy may be established so that common methods are inherited by the subclasses. For instance, the act of borrowing and returning a book, video, or audiotape may be the same for all three items. In this case a more general superclass called *Item* is defined, with the more specific subclasses, *Book, Video,* and *Audio,* inheriting the Check-Out and Check-In methods. The inheritance arrow starts at the subclass and points toward the superclass to emphasize that subclasses are derived from superclasses. Figure 2.9 offers a visual representation of class hierarchy.

The methods defined in a superclass are also methods of all subclasses. The role of the superclass is to provide a set of behaviors (methods) for its subclasses.

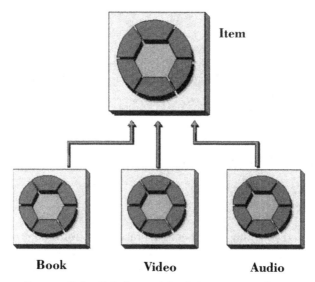

FIGURE 2.9. Subclasses inherit from a superclass.

This hierarchical arrangement means that any modification to methods in a super-class are automatically part of the subclasses through inheritance.

Inheritance applies to both class and object methods. Class methods, defined as part of the factory object, are inherited by descendant factory objects. Object methods, defined in a class Object paragraph, are inherited by descendant objects. Because of inheritance, there is localization of effort in modifying or extending systems because the effort can be localized at the superclass level.

For example, a library may decide to offer a new level of service in which books, videos, or audiotapes may be borrowed over the phone and mailed to a home or business. In an object-oriented system, where *Book, Video,* and *Audio* are subclasses of class *Item*, implementation is possible by making one change in the Check-Out method of the superclass *Item*. Because of inheritance, the subclasses *Book, Video,* and *Audio* have the changes available and can immediately support telephone borrowing.

Inheritance helps alleviate the problems data items cause when format changes are necessary. Data items (variables), common to many subclasses, can be defined in the superclass to avoid duplication of effort when changes need to be made. For example, in a library system, by defining an internal tracking number in the super-class rather than the subclasses, a change in format from eight digits to ten digits can be accomplished with a single change at the superclass level rather than making three individual changes to *Book, Video,* and *Audio*.

Inheritance Implemented

Object-Oriented COBOL introduces a new reserved word, Inherits, to structure class-es in hereditary arrangements. The following declaration allows the subclass *Book* to inherit from the superclass *Item*.

Format: a class program called Book inherits from the class Item.

Class-Id. Book Inherits Item.

Object References

In an object-oriented program, objects collaborate to get work done, often containing references to other objects. Objects that maintain references to other objects are known as *composite* or *aggregate* objects.

In a library system, for example, customers borrow books. The customer and the book may both be represented as objects, with the customer object maintaining references to the books that have been checked out. In previous examples, object data was restricted to simple values. Composite objects represent a more realistic view of objects, however, as object collaboration is an important aspect of object-oriented programming. Figure 2.10 illustrates a *Customer* object that maintains data items (variables) that reference two *Book* objects.

As can be seen in Figure 2.10, the *Customer* object does not actually contain the *Book* object. Rather, the *Customer* object contains a *reference* or *object-handle* to the *Book* object. The advantage references have over direct containment is that referenced objects are free to be part of any number of composite objects. For example, a library may have many different applications, such as lending, billing, and fund raising, all of which are interested in referencing the object *Customer*. By allowing different variables in different applications to reference a *Customer* object, the same *Customer* object may participate in as many application objects as needed. The *Customer* object may also change without affecting the objects that reference it. For example, customers may change their addresses, or the library may decide to supplement customer information. With object reference, changes to *Customer* can be made with minimal impact on the subsystems and objects that reference it.

Composition is a fundamental building block of complex systems. Allowing software to accurately mimic nature's strategy provides the ability to construct systems with crisply defined boundaries composed of subsystems.

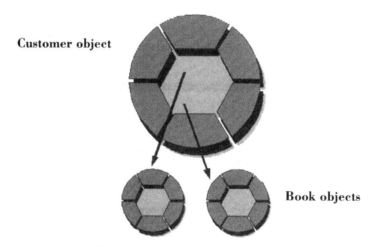

Customer object

Book objects

FIGURE 2.10. A composite object.

CLASS LIBRARIES

Object-oriented environments provide libraries of reusable classes called *class libraries*. There are a number of sources for class libraries. Vendors of object-oriented compilers often provide class libraries, as do third-party software houses. In addition, Object-Oriented COBOL provides a class library as part of the standard language.

Commercially developed class libraries drastically reduce the effort associated with system development. Library classes are designed, tested, optimized, and documented, allowing developers to concentrate their efforts on problems unique to their application. Commercial class libraries offer packaged solutions to many of the most common problems associated with software development. Commercial library classes may be extended via inheritance to add application-specific functionality. Figure 2.11 illustrates a commercial class library inherited by user-developed classes.

Class libraries may also be developed within organizations to foster reuse. Internally developed class libraries can reduce development costs because business and commercial class libraries give companies tremendous advantage in developing

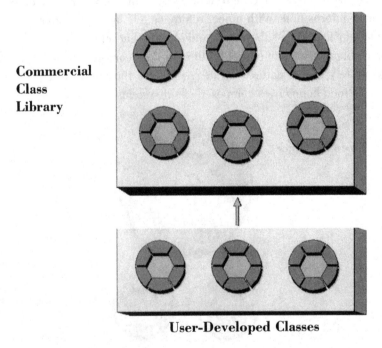

Commercial Class Library

User-Developed Classes

FIGURE 2.11. Inheritance and class libraries.

applications quickly and economically. Companies with effective class libraries often experience a 50% to 80% reduction of effort in developing systems by reusing previously developed code.

Object-Oriented COBOL provides the class **Base** to support essential object-oriented programming functionality. Every user-defined class may inherit the class **Base** by specifying the **inherits** phrase along with the class name. The following is an example of the class *Book* inheriting the Object-Oriented COBOL Library Class **Base**.

Format: the class Book inherits Base from the class library.

Class-Id. Book Inherits Base.

Object Technology—A Consistent Approach

Object technology offers a consistent, unifying theme to software development. Object technology deals in units of expression that are consistent across analysis, design, and programming. This commonality of concepts, classes, and objects establishes a common foundation that replaces the chaotic attempts to impose an artificial structure on software development. Figure 2.12 illustrates this continuity of development across an object-based software development process.

This continuity provided by objects contrasts sharply with structured methods that deal in different units of expression during the different phases of software development. Structured analysis builds on data-flow diagrams, whereas structured design specifies modules and structured programming uses single-entry/single-exit paragraphs. These differences create an *impedance mismatch* or a resistance to the development flow of software construction. Mapping the outputs of one phase to the inputs of the next resists and, in many cases, defies translation. Figure 2.13 illustrates the mismatch.

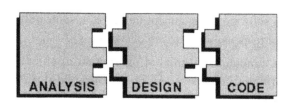

Figure 2.12. The continuity of objects.

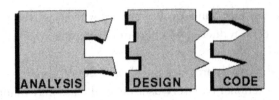

FIGURE 2.13. An impedance mismatch.

Out of the Great Divide

Object technology raises the level of abstraction for software development in a manner similar to the way virtual machines extend the capabilities of hardware. Programming languages exist as vehicles of thought that capture ideas and express solutions. The early programming languages required very small slices of logic, restricting program logic to the machine's circuits and gates—an intimate connection that incorrectly bound programs to the computing hardware. The early programming languages were languages of calculation. Unfortunately, computers as calculators do not contribute much toward solving complex business problems or in supporting reusable code.

Object-Oriented COBOL enables programmers to build systems of greater complexity with less difficulty. Object-Oriented COBOL does this in ways we will explore over the next several chapters. As we shall see, there is *not* one specific reason for the increased capability of Object-Oriented COBOL. Rather, it is a combination of features that include classes, objects, polymorphism, and inheritance. Taken together, they permit object-oriented languages to reach beyond the accepted limitations of conventional procedural languages.

Key Points

- Object-oriented software development delegates responsibility to objects with a technique called responsibility-driven design.
- Objects are the fundamental units of expression in object-oriented programming, object-oriented analysis, and object-oriented design. Objects are the products of classes.
- Messages are the means of communication among objects.

- Classes are an organization scheme used to identify and classify logical groupings of like things.

- Inheritance structures classes in hereditary relationships for the purpose of providing methods and data items to descendant classes.

- Object-Oriented COBOL uses a factory object to create object instances.

- The terms object, instance, and object instance are synonymous.

- Class libraries provide for code reuse with commercially, as well as independently, developed classes.

Suggested Readings

Boehm, B. (1988). A Spiral Model of Software Development and Enhancement. *IEEE Computer, 21*(5).

Cox, B., & Novobilski, A. (1991). *Object-Oriented Programming: An Evolutionary Approach* (2nd ed.). Reading, MA: Addison-Wesley.

Royce, W. (1970). Managing the Development of Large Software Systems. *IEEE WESCON*, 1–9.

Wegner, P. (1995). Interactive Foundations of Object-Based Programming. *IEEE Computer, 28*(10), 70–72.

Whorf, B.L. (1956). *Language, Thought & Reality.* Cambridge, MA: MIT Press.

Review Questions

2.0   Find three hierarchies that we deal with in our everyday lives.
2.1   List some of the responsibilities one might routinely delegate.
2.2   What is the *goal* of object-oriented programming?
2.3   Name the phases in the waterfall model of software development.
2.4   Compare and contrast the waterfall model to the spiral model for developing software.
2.5   How do objects communicate?
2.6   Give a brief description of polymorphism.
2.7   List the Object-Oriented COBOL model's components of construction.
2.8   Name a difference between a factory object and an object instance.

CONSTRUCTS

CHAPTER 3

CLASSES—A MATTER OF STRUCTURE

In object-oriented programming the class is a key foundational concept. Although objects are the stuff of object-oriented programming, it all begins with the class.

Classes partition a domain into logical groupings, describing entire categories of objects. Just as a blueprint describes a house, a class contains the description of an object. Although a class includes the object definition, however, it is more than just a blueprint. A class also includes the machinery to construct its objects, machinery known as class methods and data. Thus, classes provide the essential functionality as well as the framework for constructing object-oriented applications.

FOCUS AND FORMAT OF THIS CHAPTER

The primary focus of this chapter is to introduce the syntax of classes. In addition, we introduce the Unified method as a notation to model object-oriented software systems, and discuss some of the basic concepts of responsibility-driven design to begin to better understand the role of classes in applications. The following is a list of topics covered in Chapter 3:

- Definitions
    Class Definition
    Factory Definition
    Method Definition
- Paragraphs
    Class-Id
    Factory
    Method-Id
    Repository
- Concepts
    Class Data Interface
    Class Methods
    CRC Cards
    Factory Object

A QUICK LOOK AT THE SYNTAX

Before getting involved in the specifics of classes and their implementation, the basic structure of an Object-Oriented COBOL program is presented below to provide a quick glimpse at the structure and syntax. Object-Oriented COBOL remains a combination of **Identification, Environment, Procedure,** and **Data** Divisions. Several new paragraphs and reserved words have been added to the language. Also, extensions to some existing language usage have been introduced whereas restrictions have been placed on others, which we will cover.

A class program in Object-Oriented COBOL (OOCOBOL) begins with the **Identification Division** containing the **Class-Id** paragraph and ends with the **End Class** delimiter. Listing 3.1 below outlines the major constructs for defining a class, a factory object, methods, and objects. A standard COBOL program is shown as a comparison. For a complete look at the format of an Object-Oriented COBOL program, see the list at the end of this chapter.*

---

* See Appendix H for conventions on interpreting program formats.

OOCOBOL

[Identification Division.]
Class-Id. class-name-1 Is [attributes].
[Environment Division.]
[Identification Division.
Factory.
[Environment Division.]
[Data Division.]
[Procedure Division.
[{Methods}...]]
End Factory.]
[Identification Division.]
Object.
[Environment Division.]
[Data Division.]
[Procedure Division.
[{Methods}...]]
End Object.]
End Class.

COBOL

[Identification Division.]
Program-Id. program-name Is
[attributes].
[Environment Division.]
[Data Division.]
[[Procedure Division.]
  {procedure division entries}]
End Program.

LISTING 3.1. A class and procedural program outlines.

THE CLASS PROGRAM

The easiest way to understand the construction of Object-Oriented COBOL class programs is to understand a few basic rules. An Object-Oriented COBOL class program is assembled using all or some of the four definitions given below.

1. Class Definition—a source unit that contains the Class-Id paragraph.
2. Factory Definition—a source unit that contains the Factory paragraph.
3. Method Definition—a source unit that contains the Method-Id paragraph.
4. Object Definition—a source unit that contains the Object paragraph.

A source unit is a sequence of syntactically correct COBOL statements optionally beginning with an **Identification Division** and terminating with an end header (delimiter). A source unit may contain zero, one, or many other COBOL source units. Figure 3.1 illustrates how the definitions fit together.

The term *source unit* has replaced the term *source program*. Below are the parts, some of which are optional, that are required of each definition.

Class Definition
  Identification Division
  Class-Id Paragraph
  Environment Division
  Factory Definition
  Object Definition

Factory Definition
  Identification Division
  Factory Paragraph
  Environment Division
  Data Division
  Procedure Division
  Method Definitions

Method Definition
  Identification Division
  Method-Id Paragraph
  Environment Division
  Data Division
  Procedure Division

Object Definition
  Identification Division
  Object Paragraph
  Environment Division
  Data Division
  Procedure Division
  Method Definitions

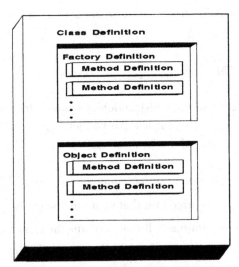

FIGURE 3.1. The pieces of an OOCOBOL program.

Syntax diagrams can be used to specify the form of class programs. Following the diagrams, assembling syntactically correct class programs becomes a matter of substitution. Here are the four syntax diagrams.

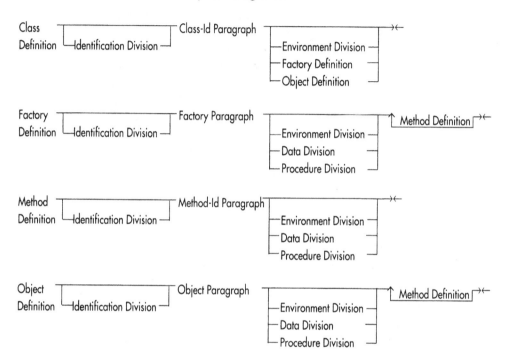

THE CLASS DEFINITION

The Class Definition begins with an **Identification Division** containing the **Class-Id** paragraph. A Class Definition is a source unit (a syntactically correct set of COBOL statements). Optionally included in a Class Definition are an **Environment Division**, a Factory Definition, and an Object Definition. A Class Definition is delimited by the reserved words **End Class**. We will use the convention of highlighting lines that are discussed in the examples given.

To assist in navigating the examples, Quick Reference Maps will be used to pinpoint where we are in the program with an arrow (←). A list of entries to be discussed is included alongside the map. In addition, the four major definitions of a class program—the Class, Factory, Method, and Object Definitions—are underlined.

Quick Reference Map:
Class-Id paragraph

Identification Division.	Identification Division.
Class-Id. ←	Object.
Environment Division.	Environment Division.
Identification Division.	Data Division.
Factory.	Procedure Division.
Environment Division.	{Methods.}
Data Division.	End Object.
Procedure Division.	End Class.
{Methods.}	
End Factory.	

Format: permitted and required entries for defining a class.

[Identification Division.]
Class-Id. class-name-1 [class-attributes].
[Environment Division.]
[Factory Definition.]
[Object Definition.]
End Class class-name-1.

The Identification Division header (the words Identification Division) is optional in the Class Definition. The Identification Division header is assumed to be present if not explicitly coded when the reserved words Class-Id are encountered. The Identification Division header is optional in each of the four Object-Oriented COBOL definitions (Class, Factory, Method, Object).

Format: a basic outline of a class program shown in comparison to a standard COBOL program.

OOCOBOL	COBOL
[Identification Division.]	[Identification Division.]
Class-Id. class-name-1.	Program-Id. program-name-1.
all other declarations	all other declarations
End Class class-name-1.	End Program program-name-1.

Example: a class program with the class name of "Class-1" shown alongside a standard COBOL program with the name of "Program-1".

OOCOBOL	COBOL
Identification Division.	Identification Division.
Class-Id. Class-1.	Program-Id. Program-1.
all other declarations	all other declarations
End Class Class-1.	End Program Program-1.

Example: Here again is a class named Book.

[Identification Division.]
Class-Id. Book.
   all other declarations
End Class Book.

The **Class-Id** paragraph includes a required user-defined name to uniquely identify the class program. The user-defined **class-name** follows standard COBOL naming conventions. There are two types of words in COBOL.

1. Reserved words
2. User-defined words

The rules for forming user-defined words

1. User-defined words are 1–31 characters in length (this has been increased from the previous limit of 30).
2. User-defined words contain a combination of alphabetic or numeric or the hyphen (A–Z, a–z, 0–9 "–").
3. The word must not begin or end with a hyphen (-).
4. Embedded blanks are not permitted.
5. The word must not be a COBOL reserved word (e.g., **Identification, Division**).

The rules for user-defined words apply to the name selected for the class. Class names must be unique within the same run-unit.

The Class Environment Division

The Class Environment Division may optionally include a Configuration Section. The Configuration Section may contain a Source-Computer paragraph, an Object-Computer paragraph, a Special-Names paragraph, and a Repository paragraph. A Class Environment Division may not contain an Input-Output Section.

Quick Reference Map:
Environment Division.
  Configuration Section.
  Source-Computer.
  Object-Computer.
  Special-Names.
  Repository.
	Identification Division.
	Class-Id.
	Environment Division. ←
	Identification Division.
	Factory.
	Environment Division.
	Data Division.
	Procedure Division.
	  {Methods.}
	End Factory.
		Identification Division.
		Object.
		Environment Division.
		Data Division.
		Procedure Division.
		  {Methods.}
		End Object.
		End Class.

Format: permitted and required entries for the class Environment Division.

```
[Identification Division.]
Class-Id. class-name-1 [class-attributes].
Environment Division.
[Configuration Section.]
[Source-Computer.]
[Object-Computer.]
[Special-Names.]
[Repository.]
End Class class-name-1.
```

The Source-Computer paragraph provides a description of the computer on which the program will be compiled. The Object-Computer paragraph describes the computer on which the program will be run. Both paragraphs are optional and are treated as comments.

Example: a Class Environment Division.

```
Identification Division.
Class-Id. Class-1.
Environment Division.
Configuration Section.
Source-Computer.          IBM-PC.
Object-Computer.          IBM-3090.
Special-Names.            Class A-Color Is "Red" "Blue".
Repository.
End Class Class-1.
```

The **Special-Names** paragraph in the above example uses an enhancement introduced to the COBOL 85 standard. "**Class**" in this context is a clause that allows enumerated data types to be declared. The use of **Class** in the **Special-Names** paragraph is in no way related to the concept of Class as applied to object-oriented programming. COBOL 85 features the reader may want to investigate further are provided in Appendix F.

The Class Environment Division Repository Paragraph

The **Repository** paragraph allows specification of class names used within the scope of the declaring **Environment Division**. A class-specifier begins with the reserved word **Class** followed by a user-defined class name and optionally includes the reserved word **Is** followed by a system-name.

Quick Reference Map:	Identification Division.	Identification Division.
Environment Division.	Class-Id.	Object.
Configuration Section.	Environment Division. ←	Environment Division.
Repository.	Identification Division.	Data Division.
	Factory.	Procedure Division.
	Environment Division.	{Methods.}
	Data Division.	End Object.
	Procedure Division.	End Class.
	{Methods.}	
	End Factory.	

Format: a class Environment Division Repository paragraph.

> [Identification Division.]
> Class-Id. class-name-1.
> <u>Environment</u> <u>Division</u>.
> [Configuration Section.]
> <u>Repository</u>.
>> {<u>Class</u> class-name-1 [Is system-name}...]
>> End Class class-name-1.

The **Repository** paragraph operates in much the same manner as the **Select** statement. The **Select** statement establishes a connection between the internal name of a file used by the program with an external file-name known to the system.

Format: the class-specifier shown in comparison to the Select statement.

<u>OOCOBOL</u>	<u>COBOL</u>
Identification Division.	Identification Division.
Class-Id. class-name-1.	Program-Id. program-name-1.
Environment Division.	Environment Division.
Configuration Section.	<u>Input-Output</u> <u>Section</u>.
<u>Repository</u>.	<u>File-Control</u>.
<u>Class</u> class-name-1 Is system-name.	<u>Select</u> file-name Assign To system-name.
other entries	other entries.
End Class class-name-1.	End Program program-name-1.

The **Repository** paragraph establishes a connection between the internal class name used by the program with the external file-name known to the system.

Example: a class-name known to a program as "Class-1" and known to the system as "CLASS1". A file-name known to a program as "100-INFILE" and known to the system as "INFILE1".

<u>OOCOBOL</u>	<u>COBOL</u>
Identification Division.	Identification Division.
Class-Id. Class-1.	Program-Id. Program-1.
Environment Division.	Environment Division.
Repository.	File-Control.
Class Class-1 Is "CLASS1".	Select 100-INFILE Assign "INFILE1".

The class name of the **Repository** paragraph should match the class name specified in the **Class-Id** paragraph. The system-name follows the naming rules of the particular system. On OS/2 and Unix machines the system-name may be identified by its name including all directories and subdirectories up to 160 characters in length.

Example: a class-name known internally as "Class-1" and externally as "C:\COBOL\PROGRAM\CLASS1".

>   Identification Division.
>   Class-Id. Class-1.
>   Environment Division.
>   Repository.
>   Class Class-1 Is "C:\COBOL\PROGRAM\CLASS1".

Every class that is accessed in the program must be identified in the **Repository** paragraph.

Example: Class-1 identifies two additional class programs.

>   Identification Division.
>   Class-Id. Class-1.
>   Environment Division.
>   Configuration Section.
>   Repository.
>   Class Class-1 Is "CLASS1"
>   Class Class-2 Is "CLASS2"
>   Class Class-3 Is "CLASS3".
>   End Class Class-1.

Example: Returning to the library example, here is the Customer class, declared in the class Book.

>   Identification Division.
>   Class-Id. Book.
>   Environment Division.
>   Configuration Section.
>   Repository.
>   Class Book   Is "BOOK"
>   Class Customer   Is "CUSTOMER".
>   End Class Book.

THE FACTORY OBJECT

Object-oriented applications operate by sending and receiving messages. This also applies to creating objects. In Object-Oriented COBOL, every class has its own factory object, which handles messages related to object creation and destruction.

In Object-Oriented COBOL, a class definition is both a template that specifies what object instances will look like and forms the basis for creating the factory object. Details of the factory object appear in the Factory Definition. There is only one factory object per class (Figure 3.2). The factory object, with its own methods and data, operates behind the scenes to create object instances.

The data in a factory object is defined within the Factory Definition. Factory object data is available only to the methods of the factory object. This data, although technically defined in the factory object, is also referred to as *class data.*

The factory object is different from object instances in that it is automatically generated by the Object-Oriented COBOL run time environment at program startup. Memory is allocated for the factory object at compile time, whereas memory is allocated for object instances dynamically, at run time.

THE FACTORY DEFINITION

A Factory Definition is a COBOL source unit that includes the **Factory** paragraph. A Factory Definition may contain an **Environment Division**, a **Data Division**, a **Procedure**

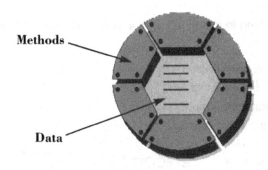

FIGURE 3.2. A factory object.

Division, and Method Definitions. The Factory Definition is delimited by the reserved words **End Factory**.

Quick Reference Map:	Identification Division.	Identification Division.
Factory.	<u>Class-Id.</u>	<u>Object</u>.
Environment Division.	Environment Division.	Environment Division.
Data Division.	Identification Division.	Data Division.
Procedure Division.	<u>Factory</u>.←	Procedure Division.
Method Definitions.	Environment Division.	{<u>Methods</u>.}
	Data Division.	<u>End</u> <u>Object</u>.
	Procedure Division.	<u>End</u> <u>Class</u>.
	{<u>Methods</u>.}	
	<u>End Factory</u>.	

Format: a basic outline for declaring a factory object.

[Identification Division.]
<u>Factory</u>.
[Environment Division.]
[Data Division.]
[Procedure Division.]
<u>End</u> <u>Factory</u>.

The Factory Environment Division

The **Environment Division** of the Factory Definition applies to every method defined within the scope of the Factory Definition. The Factory **Environment Division** may include an **Input-Output Section**. The **Input-Output Section** may contain a **File-Control** paragraph and a **I-O-Control** paragraph. The **Environment Division** of a Factory Definition is not permitted to contain a **Configuration Section**.

Quick Reference Map:
Environment Division.
  Input-Output Section.
  File-Control.
  I-O-Control.

Identification Division.
Class-Id.
Environment Division.
Identification Division.
Factory.
Environment Division. ←
Data Division.
Procedure Division.
  {Methods.}
End Factory.

Identification Division.
Object.
Environment Division.
Data Division.
Procedure Division.
  {Methods.}
End Object.
End Class.

Format: a basic outline for declaring a factory object with Environment Division entries.

> [Identification Division.]
> Factory.
> [Environment Division.]
> [Input-Output Section.]
> [File-Control.] {file-control-entries}...
> End Factory.

A file-control-entry in the Input-Output Section of the Factory paragraph makes the file available to every method of the factory. The file-control-entry also establishes the file's organization (indexed, relative, sequential), access mode (dynamic, random, sequential), file status, and other information about the files.

Example: a factory object declared with an Input-Output Section.

> Identification Division.
> Factory.
> Environment Division.
> Input-Output Section.
>
> File-Control.   Select 100-Infile Assign to "INFILE1"
>   Access Mode   Is Sequential
>   File Status   Is Status-of-File.
> End Factory.

The Factory Data Division

A Factory Data Division may contain a File Section, a Working-Storage Section, and a Report Section. The Data Division of a Factory is not allowed to contain a Linkage Section or Communication Section.

Quick Reference Map:	Identification Division.	Identification Division.
Data Division.	Class-Id.	Object.
File Section.	Environment Division.	Environment Division.
Working-Storage-section.	Identification Division.	Data Division.
	Factory.	Procedure Division.
	Environment Division.	{Methods.}
	Data Division. ←	End Object.
	Procedure Division.	End Class.
	{Methods.}	
	End Factory.	

Format: a factory object's Data Division.

    [Identification Division.]
    Factory.
    [Environment Division.]
    Data Division.
    File Section.
    Working-Storage Section.
    End Factory.

The Data Division File Section defines and reserves storage for files and their related records. The Working-Storage Section defines and reserves space for additional data used in the program. Data Division entries in the Factory paragraph are available to every method of the factory object.

Example: a factory object's Data Division entries.

    Identification Division.
    Factory.
    Environment Division.
    Data Division.

```
File Section.
FD 100-Infile
   Record Contains 80 Characters.
01 100-Record                 Pic x(80).
Working-Storage Section.
01 Switches.
   05 EOF-Switch   Pic x(01)     Value 'N'.
      88 EOF-On                  Value 'Y'.
      88 EOF-Off                 Value 'N'.
End Factory.
```

Note that the **Data Records** clause, **Label Records** clause, and **Value Of** clause of the file description entry (**FD**) are now obsolete. Obsolete items may or may not be supported depending on the implementor's compiler. They should be avoided if possible to avoid future potential conflicts.

Consider again the example of a library book and a variable called **Count** that tracked the total number of books checked out of a library. An implementation of the library application could declare **Count** in the **Data Division, Working-Storage Section** of the **Factory** paragraph.

A Factory's Procedure Division

A Factory **Procedure Division** may only contain declaratives and Method Definitions. No other statements, section headers, or paragraph headers are permitted. When used, declaratives immediately follow the **Procedure Division** entry and are executed automatically when an I/O error occurs.

Quick Reference Map: Procedure Division. Method Definitions	Identification Division. Class-Id. Environment Division. Identification Division. Factory. Environment Division. Data Division. Procedure Division. ← {Methods.} End Factory.	Identification Division. Object. Environment Division. Data Division. Procedure Division. {Methods.} End Object. End Class.

Format: a factory object's Procedure Division.

[Identification Division.]
Factory.
[Environment Division.]
[Data Division.]
Procedure Division.
   Method Definitions
End Factory.

METHODS

The procedural code in an object is placed in methods. Each method has its own method name and its own **Identification, Environment, Data**, and **Procedure** Divisions. When a method is invoked (called) the procedural code it contains is executed.

In object-oriented systems, methods may contain their own local data. Method data is only accessible to the procedure code of that method. Method data is assigned an initial value when a method is invoked (called) and discarded when the method completes. This is similar to the **Initial** attribute of the **Program-Id**, which restores data to its initial value (state) each time the program is called.

For example, a method called *Convert* that converts yards to meters may define a constant method data variable of 39.37 inches (inches in a meter) in addition to other variables that hold values needed for the conversion calculation. Each time the *Convert* method is called, the constant value is initialized to its constant value and any other method variables are initialized to zeros unless otherwise specified.

In addition to data local to individual methods, data defined in the **Data Division** of the Factory paragraph or in the **Data Division** of the Object paragraph are global to all methods defined in the corresponding **Procedure Division**.

Methods are executed, or in the vocabulary of object-oriented programming, services are requested, by using the reserved word **Invoke**, followed by the object name, the method name and optionally, any parameters. The following is an example of a request to the class *Book* (actually the Factory object for the class) for execution of the method **Report-Overdue-Books**.

Invoke Book "Report-Overdue-Books" Returning Overdue-Count.

Methods may be declared in the **Procedure Division** of a factory object or in the **Procedure Division** of objects. Methods declared in a factory object are known as *class methods* or *methods of the class*. Methods declared in object instances are known as *object methods, instance methods,* or simply *methods.* Class methods are responsible for object creation and destruction as well as tasks that span the entire class. Object methods do much of the detailed application programming work.

THE METHOD DEFINITION

A Method Definition is a COBOL source unit that begins with an **Identification Division** and contains the **Method-Id** paragraph. A Method Definition may contain an **Environment Division**, a **Data Division**, and a **Procedure Division**. A Method Definition is terminated by the delimiter **End Method**.

Quick Reference Map:	Identification Division.	Identification Division.
Method-Id.	Class-Id.	Object.
Environment Division.	Environment Division.	Environment Division.
Data Division.	Identification Division.	Data Division.
Procedure Division.	Factory.	Procedure Division.
	Environment Division.	{Methods.}
	Data Division.	End Object.
	Procedure Division.	End Class.
	Identification Division.	
	Method-Id. ←	
	Environment Division.	
	Data Division.	
	Procedure Division.	
	End Method.	
	End Factory.	

Format: a basic outline for declaring a method.

[Identification Division.]
Method-Id. method-name-1 [method attributes].
[Environment Division.]
[Data Division.]
[Procedure Division.]
End Method method-name-1.

Method-name-1 of the Method-Id paragraph, like the class name, is a required user-defined name that follows standard COBOL naming conventions. Method-name-1 of the Method-Id paragraph must match method-name-1 of the End Method delimiter. Method names must be unique within a Class Definition. Although not required, method names are generally placed within quotation marks. Placing method names in quotation marks allows a method to have the same name as a reserved word without causing problems. For example, a method could be called Identification, as long as it was surrounded by quotation marks.

Example: a method with the name of "Method-1".

Identification Division.
Method-Id. "Method-1".
Environment Division.
Data Division.
Procedure Division.
Exit Method.
End Method "Method-1".

The Method Environment Division

A method Environment Division may contain a Configuration Section and an Input-Output Section. The Configuration Section may contain a Source-Computer paragraph, an Object-Computer paragraph, and a Special-Names paragraph. The Input-Output Section may contain a File-Control paragraph and an I-O-Control paragraph.

Quick Reference Map:
Method-Id.
Environment Division.

Identification Division.	Identification Division.
<u>Class-Id</u>.	<u>Object</u>.
Environment Division.	Environment Division.
Identification Division.	Data Division.
<u>Factory</u>.	Procedure Division.
Environment Division.	{<u>Methods</u>.}
Data Division.	End <u>Object</u>.
Procedure Division.	End <u>Class</u>.
Identification Division.	
Method-Id.	
Environment Division. ←	
Data Division.	
Procedure Division.	
End Method.	
End <u>Factory</u>.	

Format: a basic outline for declaring a method with its Environment Division entries.

[Identification Division.]
<u>Method-Id</u>. method-name-1.
<u>Environment Division</u>.
[Configuration Section.]
[Source-Computer.]
[Object-Computer.]
[Special-Names.]
[Input-Output Section].
[File-Control.] [{file-control-entries}...]
[I-O-Control.] [{i-o-control entries}...]
<u>End</u> <u>Method</u> method-name-1.

Example: a method declared with Configuration and Input-Output Section entries.

Identification Division.
Method-Id. "Method-1".
Environment Division.
Configuration Section.
Source-Computer.   IBM-PC.

```
Object-Computer.        IBM-3090.
Special-Names.
Input-Output Section.
File-Control.   Select 100-Infile Assign to "INFILE1"
                Organization Is Sequential
                Access Mode Is Sequential
                File Status Is Status-of-File.
End Method "Method-1".
```

A file-control-entry is required for each file to be used by the method. Files declared in method Input-Output Sections are only accessible to the declaring method.

The Method Data Division

The Data Division of the Method Definition may include a File Section, a Working-Storage Section, a Linkage Section, and a Report Section. The Data Division may not contain a Communication Section.

Quick Reference Map:	Identification Division.	Identification Division.
Method-Id.	Class-Id.	Object.
Data Division.	Environment Division.	Environment Division.
	Identification Division.	Data Division.
	Factory.	Procedure Division.
	Environment Division.	{Methods.}
	Data Division.	End Object.
	Procedure Division.	End Class.
	Identification Division.	
	Method-Id.	
	Environment Division.	
	Data Division. ←	
	Procedure Division.	
	End Method.	
	End Factory.	

Format: a method Data Division.

    [Identification Division.]
    Method-Id. method-name-1.
    [Environment Division.]
    Data Division.
    File Section.
    Working-Storage Section.
    Linkage Section.
    Report Section.
    End Method method-name-1.

The Linkage Section describes parameters (data items) received and possibly returned by the method. The Linkage Section in concert with the Procedure Division header defines the interface to the object. Note Linkage Section data items are not allowed to include initial values.

Example: a method's Data Division entries.

    Identification Division.
    Method-Id. "Method-1".
    Environment Division.
    Data Division.
    File Section.
    FD 100-Infile
        Record Contains 80 Characters.
    01 100-Record   Pic x(80).
    Working-Storage Section.
    01 Switches.
        05 EOF-Switch   Pic x(01)   Value 'N'.
            88 EOF-On   Value 'Y'.
            88 EOF-Off   Value 'N'.
    Linkage Section.
        01 Invoked-Count   Pic s9(04).
    End Method "Method-1".

The Method Procedure Division

A method's **Procedure Division** may contain any **Procedure Division** entry. In addition, a method **Procedure Division** contains an **Exit Method** statement, which marks the logical end of the method.

| Quick Reference Map:
Method-Id.
Procedure Division. | Identification Division.
Class-Id.
Environment Division.
Identification Division.
Factory.
Environment Division.
Data Division.
Procedure Division.
Identification Division.
Method-Id.
Environment Division.
Data Division.
Procedure Division. ←
End Method.
End Factory. | Identification Division.
Object.
Environment Division.
Data Division.
Procedure Division.
  {Methods.}
End Object.
End Class. |

Format: a method Procedure Division.

> [Identification Division.]
> **Method-Id. method-name-1.**
> [Environment Division.]
> [Data Division.]
> **Procedure Division.**
>   procedure division entries
> Exit Method.
> End Method method-name-1.

The **Exit Method** statement provides a common end point for a series of procedures and is only allowed in the **Procedure Division** of a method. The **Exit Method** delimiter returns control to the invoking statement.

Example: a method Procedure Division.

    Identification Division.
    Method-Id. "Method-1".
    Environment Division.
    Data Division.
    Procedure Division.
      Display "Hello World".
    Exit Method.
    End Method "Method-1".

THE CLASS INTERFACE

To communicate with an object one must understand its interface—the set of messages understood by the object. An object interface serves as a point of connection between two software components, just as with real-world components one only needs to understand the interface to use the device.

The interface to an object is the key to that object. An interface is defined by

- the object name (the class name in the case of the factory object)
- the method name
- any parameters required by the method

The simplest interface is an object name, followed by a method name. Consider again the class *Book* with a class method called **Perform-Inventory**. An interface to the class *Book* would be:

Book "Perform-Inventory"

If the class *Book* had two methods, there would be two interfaces. An interface may also use parameters. For example, the following method uses a **Returning** parameter.

Book "Report-Overdue-Books" Returning Overdue-Count

Parameters to a method are defined in the method's **Procedure Division** header and corresponding **Linkage Section**. For example, here is the method **Report-Status** with its **Status** parameter.

Class-Id. Book.
...
Factory.
Method-Id. "Report-Overdue-Books".
Data Division.
Linkage Section.
01 Overdue-Count   Pic s9(05).
Procedure Division Returning Overdue-Count.
...

Objects (and this includes factory objects) encapsulate the details of their implementation. Using an object only requires knowledge of the interface. As a user, how the method works is not a requirement for using the class effectively.

PUTTING THE PIECES TOGETHER

Class programs might at times seem to require a bewildering number of Identification, Environment, Data, and Procedure Divisions. The illustration below shows the relationship of the Class, Factory, Method, and Object Definitions.

Format: the Class, Factory, Method, and Object Definition relationships.

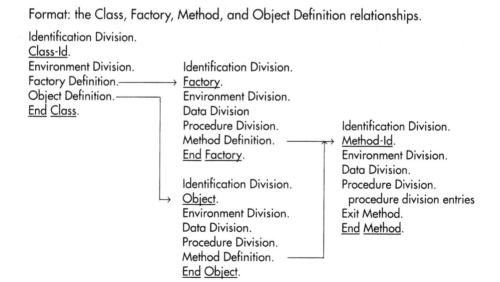

```
Identification Division.
Class-Id.
Environment Division.        Identification Division.
Factory Definition.————→     Factory.
Object Definition.———        Environment Division.
End Class.                    Data Division
                             Procedure Division.
                             Method Definition. ————→   Identification Division.
                             End Factory.               Method-Id.
                                                        Environment Division.
                                                        Data Division.
                             Identification Division.   Procedure Division.
                             Object.                      procedure division entries
                             Environment Division.      Exit Method.
                             Data Division.             End Method.
                             Procedure Division.
                             Method Definition. ————
                             End Object.
```

The following illustrates the structure and visibility of class data.

Format: the structure of a class.

```
begin class
    <class-data>                data global to the factory object
    begin method-1
        <method-data>           local data
        <method-code>
    end method-1
    begin method-2
        <method-data>           local data
        <method-code>
    end method-2
end class
```

The <class-data> is visible to both method-1 and to method-2. The <class-data> is global to the factory object. The <method-data> is only visible to its respective method. The <method-data> is local.

Procedural applications may be viewed as one huge factory object in which class data (data visible to the entire program) is the only option available. In contrast, the architecture of object-oriented applications encapsulates the data to well-defined areas. Structured programming *encourages* and object-oriented programming *enforces* modular programming.

The minds of maintenance programmers may rest a little easier when encountering applications designed by the principle of encapsulation enforcement rather than the principle of structured encouragement. There is a saying in object-oriented programming that "objects are correct by construction." While not literally true, the idea is valid. Small, well-defined modules are much more likely to be correct than are giant monolithic programs.

Example: the encapsulation of data within the class and class methods.

```
Class-Id. Class-1.
...
Factory.                                          Class Data
Data Division.
Working-Storage Section.                                        scope Class-1
01 Value-1      Pic 9(02) value 1.                              Value-1
Procedure Division.

    Method-Id. "Method-1".
    Data Division.                              Method data
    Working-Storage Section                      scope Method-1
    01 Value-2          Pic 9(02) value 2.       Value-2
    Procedure Division.
        procedure division statements.
    Exit Method.
    End Method "Method-1".

    Method-Id. "Method-2".
    Data Division.
    Working-Storage Section.                    Method data
    01 Value-3          Pic 9(02) value 3.       scope Method-2
    Procedure Division.                          Value-3
        procedure division statements.
    Exit Method.
    End Method "Method-2".

End Factory.
End Class Class-1.
```

As we will see in the next chapter, the structure of objects is identical to the structure of the factory object. Each contains its own global data (by global, we mean visible to the entire object) and local method data.

Scope

One of the significant changes in the COBOL 85 standard was the ability to enhance modularity and localization. Modularity and localization are served by limiting the area of influence of data and operations to well-defined areas. Scope is the range over which data is visible or operations have influence. Global data is visible to every operation in a program, whereas local data is only visible to operations within a well-defined area.

Although scope most often refers to data, the concept of scope equally applies to operations. COBOL 85 introduced scope delimiters for almost every operation. READ is delimited by END-READ, COMPUTE by END-COMPUTE, and IF by END-IF. Noise words, like END-IF, are our friends; they catch the eye and delimit the operation. But scope rules do more than engage the senses. Through delimiters, control over operations, particularly nested overlapping operations, is enhanced and maintenance is simplified.

Prior to COBOL 85, there were no controls limiting the scope of data. Scope did not figure prominently in the COBOL vocabulary. Every variable declared in the Data Division was global. There was no way to specify that certain data items in the Data Division could only be accessed by some subset of operations in the Procedure Division.

It is not unusual to find page after page of Data Division entries in large COBOL applications. Twenty to 30 pages of data variables are not uncommon, including a few dozen redefines thrown in for good measure, and good luck. Sifting through this maze to modify one variable can be a chilling experience. COBOL 85 is less thrilling.

One of the important features of COBOL 85 was CALL by CONTENT. Previously COBOL only supported CALL by REFERENCE, which passes the address of the calling parameters to a subprogram. Passing the address permits the subprogram to modify the parameter values (which may or may not be the intention). CALL by CONTENT passes a temporary copy of the parameters to the subprogram, thus ensuring there can be no change (accidental or otherwise) to the original data.

Data Name Conflicts

Both Factory (Class) definitions and Object definitions have two Data Divisions—one global to all methods and one local to methods. COBOL allows the same name to be used in both the global and local Data Divisions. When this occurs, however, the method Data Division gets priority and makes the global declaration invisible.

For example, if a data item called Count is declared as class data and the same data name Count is declared in a method called Method-1, the class data item called Count will not be accessible to the Procedure Division of Method-1.

Example: a data name conflict.

        Class-Id. Class-1.
        ...
        Factory.
        Data Division.
        Working-Storage Section.
        01 Count   Pic 99.   Count definition #1
        Method-Id. "Method-1".
        Data Division.
        Working-Storage Section.
        01 Count   Pic 99.   Count definition #2
        Procedure Division.
        < this procedure division will not have access to Count definition #1>
        Exit Method.
        End Method "Method-1".
        End Factory.
        End Class Class-1.

The American National Standards Institute (ANSI) committee may rectify this limitation in the future, allowing duplicate names to be uniquely distinguished by some kind of qualifier, such as data-name-1 of method-name-1.

A Detailed Object-Oriented COBOL Outline

Format: a detailed outline for defining classes programs.

        Identification Division.
        [Class identification division header is optional.]
        Class-Id. class-name.
        [Class-id and class-name are required.]
        Environment Division.
        [Class environment division is optional.]
        Configuration Section.
        [Class configuration section is optional.]
        Source-Computer.
        [Specifies the computer on which the program is written. Treated as a

comment by many compilers.]

Object-Computer.

[Specifies the computer on which the program is run. Treated as a comment by many compilers.]

Special-Names.

[Allows enumerated data types, alternate character sets, and specific mnemonic names.]

Repository.

[Repository paragraph is required. Identifies class-names and system-names.]

class-name Is system-name.

[Entry is required.]

Identification Division.

[Factory identification division header is optional.]

Factory.

[Factory paragraph is required.]

Environment Division.

[Factory environment division is optional.]

Input-Output Section.

[Factory input-output section is optional.]

File-Control.

[Factory file-control is optional. Files specified here are only accessible to the individual method.]

  Select File-name ... assign to ....

I-O-Control.

[Factory i-o-control is optional. Specifies special i/o processing.]

Data Division.

[Entire factory data division is optional.]

File Section.

[Factory file section is optional. Specify files and records.]

FD description entries.

[Block size, record contains clause, along with other possible file description entries.]

01 file record description entries.

Working-Storage Section.

[Factory working-storage section data variables are visible to all class

methods.]
Report Section.
[Factory report section is optional. Describes reports to be written onto report files.]
Procedure Division.
[Factory procedure division is optional.]
Declaratives.
[Declaratives is optional. Section is executed automatically when i/o errors occur.]

Identification Division.
[Method identification division header is optional.]
Method-Id. method-name-1.
[Method-id paragraph is required along with the method-name-1. There may be as many methods declared as needed. In this example there is only one.]
Environment Division.
[Method environment division is optional.]
Configuration Section.
[Method configuration section is optional.]
Source-Computer.
[Specifies the computer on which the program is written. Treated as a comment by many compilers.]
Object-Computer.
[Specifies the computer on which the program is run. Treated as a comment by many compilers.]
Special-Names.
[Allows enumerated data types, alternate character sets, and specific mnemonic names.]
Input-Output Section.
[Method input-output section is optional.]
File-Control.
[Method file-control is optional. Files specified here are only accessible to the class methods.]
  Select File-name ... assign to ....
I-O-Control.

[Method i-o-control is optional. Specifies special i/o processing.]

Data Division.

[Entire method data division is optional.]

File Section.

[Method file section is optional. Specify files and records.]

FD description entries.

[Block size, record contains clause, along with other possible file description entries.]

01 file record description entries.

Working-Storage Section.

[Method working-storage section data variables are visible only to the declaring method.]

Linkage Section.

[Method linkage section is optional. Establishes an area for passing parameters—the signature.]

Report Section.

[Method report section is optional. Describes reports to be written onto report files.]

Procedure Division.

[Method procedure division is optional. Any data described in the method would be unreachable without the method procedure division.]

Declaratives.

[Declaratives is optional. Section is executed automatically when i/o errors occur.]

all other procedure division entries.

Exit Method.

[Exit method is optional. Marks the logical end of the method.]

End Method method-name-1.

[End method ends the current method with the unique tag of the method-name-1. Required.]

End Factory.

[End factory delimiter is required.]

Identification Division.

[Object identification division header is optional.]

Object.

[Object paragraph is required to declare objects.]

Environment Division.
[Object environment division is optional.]
Data Division.
[Entire object data division is optional.]
Method Definitions
[Object method definitions are optional.]
End Object.
[End object is required.]
End Class class-name-1.
[End class ends the class program with the unique tag of the class name.
Required.]

CLASSES IN APPLICATIONS

In object-oriented software development, doing analysis and design means coming up with class definitions. To place the COBOL class syntax in perspective, we introduce some analysis and design issues by posing and answering commonly asked questions about classes and objects.

How Many Classes Should An Application Contain?

The actual number will be dependent on the application domain. Different solutions will most likely implement a different number of classes. Classes are a means of classification, a taxonomy for grouping like things. The classification, and consequently the number of classes implemented, is an analysis and design decision. Generally the number of classes in small- to medium-sized business applications will range from 20 to 100 or more.

Often, the majority of classes in a system will come from commercial class libraries or internally developed class libraries, as a business begins to define and implement its own specific libraries. Generally, it takes three or four internally developed applications before dividends are paid in the form of business class libraries suitable for reuse.

Classes may be divided into categories called *stereotypes*. A *stereotype* tells what "kind" of class it is. There are a number of different stereotype classifications. The following is one classification scheme:

- *Presentation/Interface classes and objects*—are responsible for presenting and retrieving information for users. These classes/objects are typically responsible for displaying graphical user interfaces or retrieving information, for example, from a point-of-sale system.

- *Data Management classes and objects*—are responsible for managing data structures. They hide the details of data structures, allowing the structure to potentially change without affecting the other classes and objects in the system.

- *Application Domain classes and objects*—perform tasks or contain information specific to an application.

- *Control classes and objects*—are responsible for coordinating the services provided by different classes and objects. This category manages many of the operations in an application acting as a go-between or as middleman in carrying out requests for service.

How Does One Begin Identifying Classes?

CRC (Class, Responsibility, Collaborator) sessions have proven highly effective in discovering candidate classes in the problem domain. During a CRC session, CRC cards, standard 3 x 5 index cards, are used to simulate system behavior and assign responsibilities to candidate classes.

A CRC card is an index card with a line drawn down the middle. The class name is written at the top of the card. The left column contains the class responsibilities and the right column contains the class collaborators. For example, a *Book* class may be responsible for reporting its status as well as basic information such as title, publication date, and so on. The *Book's* collaborators are the objects the book sends messages to, in order to carry out its tasks. Figure 3.3 illustrates the class *Book* CRC card with the class noted at the top and a few responsibilities listed on the left.

For each class in the application there will be a CRC card. Some classes are immediately obvious. For example, in a system that models arena ticket sales for a business like Ticketmaster, obvious classes are the customers, the arenas, and the events (baseball games, music concerts, track and field competitions). Other, not so obvious, classes may include sponsors, promotions, and possibly city ordinances.

When doing CRC analysis it is best to work in a team and include experts from the problem domain who will invariably suggest classes that otherwise would be over-

Class: Book	
(Responsibilities)	(Collaborators)
report status	
report title	
...	

FIGURE 3.3. A Book class CRC card.

looked. Other members of the team should include someone from design, mainte-nance, and at least one or two end-users.

Is There a Standard Way to Represent Classes?

The Unified Method, a third-generation object-oriented analysis and design method developed by Grady Booch and Jim Rumbaugh, is on its way to becoming a standard way to represent classes. The Unified Method combines the Booch and the OMT (Object Modeling Technique) methods, combining several modeling constructs and graphical notations.

The Unified Method uses a rectangle with three compartments to represent classes. The top compartment lists the class name, the middle compartment lists attributes, and the bottom compartment provides a list of the methods as shown.

Book
attributes are listed here
methods are listed here

How Can One Distinguish Between Class and Object Methods and Attributes?

The '$' symbol is used to distinguish between class and object methods and attributes. Below, the variable Total-Fines is shown as a class attribute, and the variable Book-Fine is shown as an object attribute.

Book
$Total-Fines Book-Fine

In addition, attributes may specify a data type and an initial value in the following format:

attributeName:type=initialValue

Book
$Total-Fines:numeric=0 Book-Fine:numeric=0

Below the class *Book* lists a class method, **Report-Total-Fines**, and an object method, **Check-In**.

Book
$Total-Fines:numeric=0 Book-Fine:numeric=0
$Report-Total-Fines Check-In

Methods may also provide additional details. Here is the format that may be used.

methodName(parameters:type=defaultValue,...)=resultType

Class stereotypes (what "kind" of class it is) may be shown in parentheses above the class name. Here is the class *Book* with its class stereotype.

(domain) Book
$Total-Fines:numeric=0 Book-Fine:numeric=0
$Report-Total-Fines Check-In

The class figure may be enlarged to accommodate any number of attributes, methods, and additional methodName and attributeName information. It is not a requirement to provide every detail when diagramming class figures. Compartments may be omitted to reduce the detail and amplify the important aspects of the figure. In practice, one displays only the more relevant attributes and methods.

Why So Many Duplicate Divisions?

The Class, Factory, Method, and Object Definitions may all contain Identification, Environment, Data, and Procedure Divisions, making for a host of duplicate divisions. The reason is not to make things confusing for the programmer, but to give the programmer flexibility in moving paragraphs around between objects and between objects and conventional programs.

Each Division within a Definition has scope (is in effect) until the next nested Division is encountered. Each definition may be considered a module that can be combined (nested) with other modules so that programmers can reuse definitions to suit their purposes.

Is There a Typical Class Definition?

Class definitions are typically fairly straightforward, with a factory object that contains a constructor method (for creating objects) and possibly a destructor method (for destroying objects). The following is a typical class definition.

Example: The format of a common class definition.

```
Class-Id. Book Inherits Base.
Environment Division.
Repository.
 Class Book Is "Book".
Factory.
<a constructor method>
<possibly a destructor method>
End Factory.
Object.
<object data and methods>
End Object.
End Class Book.
```

Are Object-Oriented Programs Less Efficient Than Conventional Programs?

Some of the early object-oriented languages, including Smalltalk, were interpreted rather than compiled, resulting in slower performance than in the comparable compiled languages. Object-Oriented COBOL, however, is compiled and therefore does not pay a performance penalty.

Common Concepts: Different Words

Programming languages generate their own dialects and often use different words to talk about concepts that are essentially the same. Different terms for similar ideas tends to confuse rather than clarify the concepts. COBOL is no exception to this and although this list is by no means exhaustive, several terms of the COBOL culture are related here to the more general terms used in software engineering and other programming languages.

COBOL	*Other Languages*
computational-1	binary*
computational-3	packed-decimal*
condition name	enumerated data type
data conversion	data casting
data item (data-name)	variable
data name or identifier	unsubscripted variable
data representation or data category	data type
figurative constant	constant string (but somewhat different)
identifier	subscripted variable
intrinsic function	function
not discussed before COBOL 97	abstract data type
non-numeric literal	literal string or character string
numeric literal	literal string
record	structure
reserved word	keyword

subprogram	subroutine or procedure
table	array
a kind of imperative statement	assignment
supported in COBOL 97	boolean
supported in some COBOL implementations	pointers
Pic 9	real data
Pic 9	integer data
Pic 9v9	fixed point data
Pic 9 Usage Display	zoned decimal
methods (Object-Oriented COBOL)	member functions, operations

* supported in COBOL 85

Levels of Abstraction

Abstraction deals with separating the necessary from the unnecessary to gain conceptual clarity. By focusing on essential properties, an abstraction reduces problem complexity. The more powerful abstractions are those that are useful across a variety of problems. Most programming language improvements since the late 1970s have been aimed at increasing the ability to express and use abstractions.

One useful abstraction mechanism is that of hierarchy. A hierarchy divides a domain into levels, each of which is understandable as a unit, while hiding details of the level below. In software, at the lowest level, everything is either a 1 or a 0. Moving up a level raises the abstraction level by interpreting strings of 1s and 0s as numbers and words. The numbers and words are built from the same primitive material, 1s and 0s.

Classes and objects are conveniences constructed to give descriptive power beyond the boundaries found in procedural programs. Classes and objects are groupings that allow us to deal in broader concepts more easily. In programs we prefer to talk about logically related abstractions as one unit.

(continued on next page)

Computers today are considered multilevel machines of abstractions.

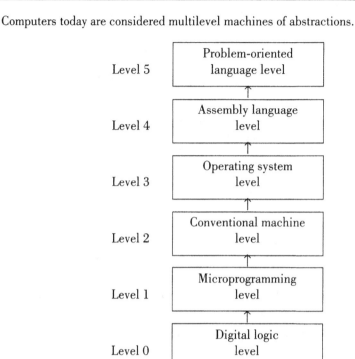

Levels of abstraction

In terms of physical reality, only the current running through the machine exists. Every level above that is an abstraction. A data record doesn't exist at Level 0. Only the interpretation we apply to ranges of voltage makes it a data record. At Level 0 we are concerned with circuits and gates; at Level 5 we are concerned with modeling a business. [From Tanenbaum, Andrew S. (1990). *Structured Computer Organization*, 3rd ed. p. 5. Reprinted by permission of Prentice Hall, Upper Saddle River, New Jersey.]

Key Points

- A class program is constructed using class, factory, method, and object definitions.
- The factory definition declares the factory object.
- The factory object may be considered, in many ways, the class.
- Methods and data are defined in the factory object.

- Methods contain their own data.

- Data defined in a factory paragraph is called class data.

- Data defined in a factory object method is called method data.

- Class data is visible to all of the methods of the factory object.

- Method data is only visible to its method.

- Classes and objects are generally categorized in one of four groups, according to what type of services they provide.

- There are different aspects and different views of a class/object depending on the user's perspective.

Suggested Readings

Beck, K., & Cunningham, W. (1989, October). A Laboratory for Teaching Object-Oriented Thinking. *OOPSLA 89 Proceedings, SIGPLAN Notices 24*(10), 1–6.

Booch, G., & Rumbaugh, J. (1995). *Unified Method for Object-Oriented Development: Documentation Set,* version 0.8. Santa Clara, CA: Rational Software Co.

Dijkstra, E. (1968). The Structure of "THE" Multiprogramming System. *Communications of the ACM, 11*(5), 341–346.

Information Technology—Programming Languages, their Environments and System Software Interfaces—Programming Language COBOL. Working Draft 1.1, October 1995. An *ISO/IEC JTC1 SC22/WG4* Document.

Obin, R. (1995). *Object Orientation: An Introduction for COBOL Programmers,* 2nd ed. Palo Alto, CA: Micro Focus Publishing.

Tanenbaum, A. (1990). *Structured Computer Organization,* 3rd ed. Englewood Cliffs, NJ: Prentice-Hall.

The 1985 COBOL Standard X3.23—1985/X3.23a—1989.

Review Questions

3.0   Name the four major definitions of a class program.

3.1   What is the purpose of the Repository paragraph?

3.2   Where are class methods declared?

3.3   What is the difference between class data and class method data?

3.4   Is the Linkage Section allowed in a class Data Division?

3.5   True or false: The Identification Division header is optional.

3.6   What is a stereotype? Give an example.

3.7   Diagram (using the Unified Method) a class called *Pilot* and populate the class with several methods and attributes one might expect to find in such a class. Show diagrammatically which are the class methods and attributes, and which are the object methods and attributes.

3.8   The different words for common concepts, found across programming languages, give rise to tribal knowledge. Discuss ways in which software engineering as a discipline might begin to address this problem.

3.9   Find three levels of abstraction commonly found in software applications.

CHAPTER 4

OBJECTS

Complex systems assume characteristics that go beyond their constituent elements. The collective synergy that occurs between system elements reflects the fact that the whole is greater than the sum of its parts. In chaos theory this phenomenon is called emergent behavior; in software it is called confluence.

With synergy a team can accomplish much more than individuals working alone. The interaction between team members gives rise to higher orders of ability. In object-oriented systems we build simple components that are understandable and combine them in ways that capture complex system behavior. The interaction between objects weaves a fabric that imitates reality. Objects break down mammoth systems into manageable cells; small constellations of machines—versatile, combinable, and less likely to fail.

FOCUS AND FORMAT OF THIS CHAPTER

In this chapter we explore the Object-Oriented COBOL syntax associated with object definitions. In addition, we continue to explore the object-oriented software development process from a responsibility-driven design perspective.

Chapter topics include the following:

- Definitions
    Object Definition
    Method Definition
    Object Reference
- Paragraphs

    Object
    Method-Id
- Concepts
    Object identifier

THE CONTEXT OF AN OBJECT DEFINITION

The following outline defines the structure of an Object-Oriented COBOL program.

OOCOBOL

[Identification Division.]
Class-Id. class-name-1 Is [attributes].
[Environment Division.]
[Identification Division.
Factory.
[Environment Division.]
[Data Division.]
[Procedure Division.
[{Methods}...]]
End Factory.]
[Identification Division.]
Object.
[Environment Division.]
[Data Division.]
[Procedure Division.
[{Methods}...]]
End Object.]
End Class.

COBOL

[Identification Division.]
Program-Id. program-name Is
[attributes].
[Environment Division.]
[Data Division.]
[[Procedure Division.]
{procedure division entries}]
End Program.

The four major components of a class program are as follows:

1. Class Definition—the source unit that contains the **Class-Id** paragraph.
2. Factory Definition—the source unit that contains the **Factory** paragraph.
3. Method Definition—the source unit that contains the **Method-Id** paragraph.
4. Object Definition—the source unit that contains the **Object** paragraph.

The components of an Object Definition and a Method Definition are given below:

Object Definition	Method Definition
Identification Division	Identification Division
Object Paragraph	Method-Id Paragraph
Environment Division	Environment Division
Data Division	Data Division
Procedure Division	Procedure Division
Method Definition(s)	

To construct objects and methods the following syntax charts may be followed.

Object Definition ⌐ Identification Division ⌐ Object Paragraph ⌐ Environment Division — Data Division — Procedure Division ⌐ Method Definition ⤲

Method Definition ⌐ Identification Division ⌐ Method-Id Paragraph ⌐ Environment Division — Data Division — Procedure Division ⤲

Format: the Class, Factory, Method, and Object Definition relationships.

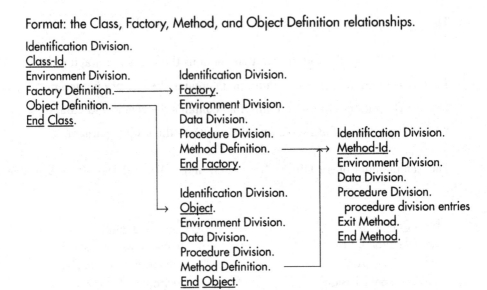

THE OBJECT DEFINITION

The Object Definition is a source unit introduced by an **Identification Division** containing the **Object** paragraph. Optionally included in an Object Definition are an **Environment Division**, a **Data Division**, and a **Procedure Division**. The Object Definition is delimited by **End Object**.

	Identification Division.	Identification Division.
Quick Reference Map:	Class-Id.	Object. ←
Object paragraph	Environment Division.	Environment Division.
Environment Division	Identification Division.	Data Division.
Data Division.	Factory.	Procedure Division.
Procedure Division.	Environment Division.	{Methods.}
	Data Division.	End Object.
	Procedure Division.	End Class.
	{Methods.}	
	End Factory.	

Format: permitted and required entries for defining an object.

> [Identification Division.]
> <u>Object.</u>
> [Environment Division.]
> [Data Division.]
> [Procedure Division.]
> End <u>Object</u>.

Example: an object with required and permitted entries.

> Identification Division.
> Object.
> Environment Division.
> Data Division.
> Procedure Division.
> End Object.

The Object Environment Division

The Object **Environment Division** may include an **Input-Output Section**. The **Input-Output Section** may contain a **File-Control** paragraph and an **I-O-Control** paragraph. An Object **Environment Division** may not contain a **Configuration Section**. The definitions in the **Environment Division** apply to the Object Definition and to every method declared in the Object Definition.

Quick Reference Map:	Identification Division.	Identification Division.
Environment Division.	<u>Class-Id.</u>	<u>Object</u>.
Input-Output Section.	Environment Division.	Environment Division. ←
File-Control.	Identification Division.	Data Division.
I-O-Control.	<u>Factory</u>.	Procedure Division.
	Environment Division.	{<u>Methods</u>.}
	Data Division.	End <u>Object</u>.
	Procedure Division.	End <u>Class</u>.
	{<u>Methods</u>.}	
	End <u>Factory</u>.	

Format: permitted and required entries for an object Environment Division.

> [Identification Division.]
> <u>Object.</u>
> **[Environment Division.]**
> [Input-Output Section.]
> [File-Control.]
> [I-O-Control.]
> End <u>Object</u>.

Example: an object declared with input and File-Control.

> Identification Division.
> Object.
> **Environment Division.**
> Input-Output Section.
> **File-Control.**   Select 100-Infile Assign to "INFILE1"
>   Organization Is Sequential
>   Access Mode Is Sequential
>   File Status Is Status-of-File.
> End Object.

The file-control-entry establishes the file's name, organization, access mode, file status, and other information about the file.

The Object Data Division

The Object Data Division may contain a File Section, Working-Storage Section, and a Report-Writer Section. The Object Data Division may not contain a Linkage Section or Communication Section.

Quick Reference Map:	Identification Division.	Identification Division.
File Section.	<u>Class-Id.</u>	<u>Object</u>
Working-Storage	Environment Division.	Environment Division.
Section.	Identification Division.	Data Division. ←
Report-Writer Section.	<u>Factory</u>.	Procedure Division.
	Environment Division.	{<u>Methods</u>.}
	Data Division.	End <u>Object</u>.
	Procedure Division.	End <u>Class</u>.
	{<u>Methods</u>.}	
	End <u>Factory</u>.	

Format: permitted and required entries for an object's Data Division.

> [Identification Division.]
> Object.
> **[Data Division.]**
> [File Section.]
> [Working-Storage Section.]
> [Report-Writer Section.]
> End Object.

Example: an object declared with Data Division entries.

> Identification Division.
> Object.
> **Data Division.**
> File Section.
> FD 100-Infile.
>   Record Contains 80 characters.
> 01 100-Infile-Record   Pic x(80).
> Working-Storage Section.
> 01 Switches.
>   05 Eof-Switch   Pic x(01)   Value 'N'.
>   88 Eof-On   Value 'Y'.
>   88 Eof-Off   Value 'N'.
> 01 Record-Count   Pic s9(04) Value +0.
> End Object.

An Object's Procedure Division

An Object's **Procedure Division** may only contain declaratives and method definitions. No other statements, section headers, or paragraph headers are permitted. When used, declaratives immediately follow the Procedure Division entry and are executed automatically when an I/O error occurs.

Quick Reference Map:
Procedure Division.
  Method Definitions

Identification Division.	Identification Division.
<u>Class-Id.</u>	<u>Object</u>.
Environment Division.	Environment Division.
Identification Division.	Data Division.
<u>Factory</u>.	Procedure Division. ←
Environment Division.	{<u>Methods</u>.}
Data Division.	<u>End</u> <u>Object</u>.
Procedure Division.	<u>End</u> <u>Class</u>.
{<u>Methods</u>.}	
<u>End Factory</u>.	

Format: an object's Procedure Division.

    [Identification Division.]
    <u>Object.</u>
    [Environment Division.]
    [Data Division.]
    <u>Procedure Division</u>.
      Method Definitions
    <u>End</u> <u>Object</u>.

METHODS

Methods hold the procedural code of an object. In an Object-Oriented COBOL program there are two kinds of methods. These are depicted in Figure 4.1.

1. Class methods—methods declared in **Procedure** Divisions of the **Factory** paragraph.
2. Object methods—methods declared in **Procedure** Divisions of the **Object** paragraph.

In Figure 4.1, both the factory object and the object instance have six methods. Objects may have an arbitrary number of methods, although for program comprehension it is a good idea to keep the number of methods fewer than 10. Because the data

Factory Object   Object Instance

Both have
Methods

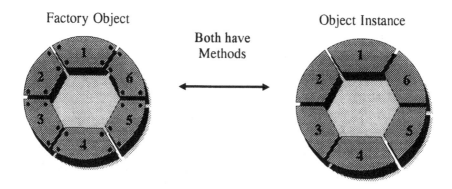

FIGURE 4.1. Object methods.

stored within an object is accessible only via methods, an object instance without methods is useless.

Methods are very much like individual programs, each method with its own name and its own Identification, Environment, Data, and Procedure Division. The methods of an object are called *object methods* or *instance methods*. The methods declared in a factory are called *class methods*.

Data

Data, like methods, may also be defined as part of a class or an object instance. There are four possibilities.

1. Class data—the data in the Data Division of the Factory paragraph.
2. Class method data—the data in the Data Division of a Method-Id paragraph in a factory object.
3. Object data—the data in the Data Division of the Object paragraph.
4. Object method data—the data in the Data Division of a Method-Id paragraph in an object.

The following code shows the structure of a class program with class and object instance data.

```
Identification Division.
Class-Id.   class-name-1.
Environment Division.
Identification Division.
Factory.
Environment Division.
Data Division.            class data—declared here
Procedure Division.
[{Methods}...]]          factory object method data—declared here
End Factory.
Identification Division.
Object.
Environment Division.
Data Division.            object data—declared here
Procedure Division.
[{Methods}...]]          object instance method data—declared here
End Object.
End Class.
```

Figure 4.2 depicts the class and object data.

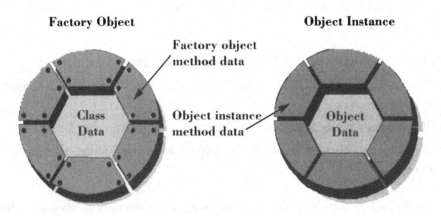

FIGURE 4.2. Methods and data of a Factory Object and Object Instance.

Method data is only available to the **Procedure Division** of the declaring method. Class data is available to all class methods; object data is available to all object methods.

THE METHOD DEFINITION

A Method Definition for an Object is similar to that of a Class Factory, introduced by an **Identification Division** and containing the **Method-Id** paragraph. A Method Definition may contain an **Environment Division**, a **Data Division**, and a **Procedure Division**. A Method Definition is terminated by the delimiter **End Method**.

Quick Reference Map:	Identification Division.	Identification Division.
Method-Id.	Class-Id.	Object.
Environment Division	Environment Division.	Environment Division.
Data Division.	Identification Division.	Data Division.
Procedure Division.	Factory.	Procedure Division.
	Environment Division.	Identification Division.
	Data Division.	Method-Id. ←
	Procedure Division.	Environment Division.
	Identification Division.	Data Division.
	Method-Id.	Procedure Division.
	Environment Division.	End Method.
	Data Division.	End Object.
	Procedure Division.	End Class.
	End Method.	
	End Factory.	

Format: a basic outline for declaring a method.

[Identification Division.]
Method-Id. method-name-1.
[Environment Division.]
[Data Division.]
[Procedure Division.]
End Method method-name-1.

The **method-name-1** of the **Method-Id** paragraph, like the **class-name**, is a required user-defined name that follows standard COBOL naming conventions.

A user-defined method name of the **Method-Id** paragraph must match the name given at the **End Method** marker. Method-names, with the exception of override methods (discussed in Chapter 6), must be unique within a Class Definition.

OBJECT HANDLES

Object handles are variables that hold the references to objects. Handles permit references to objects to be passed around within a program without having to move the actual object itself. Similar to their real-world use, handles protect and make a variety of things easier to use (Figure 4.3). COBOL handles also make objects easier to use.

Using Object Handles

Object-Oriented COBOL does not provide for the direct declaration of objects. Objects cannot be declared directly, as can predefined data types. To specify objects, the **Usage** clause has been extended with **Object Reference** syntax to declare object handles. A data item declared with **Object Reference** holds a handle or reference to an object; it does not hold the object itself. Just like handles we use all the time, we hold the handle of an item, not the item itself (Figure 4.4).

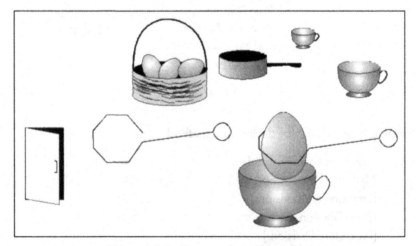

FIGURE 4.3. Some real-world handles.

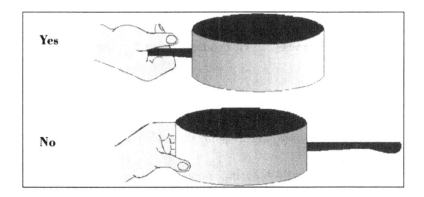

FIGURE 4.4. Using a handle.

The following is the format for declaring an object handle.

Format: a Usage Object Reference clause.

[Usage Is] <u>Object Reference</u> [Class-Name]

The following is the format of a **Usage Object Reference** for a data name.

Format: Usage Object Reference declared with a data name.

0x data-name   [Usage Is] Object Reference [Class-Name]

where:
0x is the level number
data-name is the user-defined data name object identifier (object handle)
Class-Name is the user-defined class name (the type of object the data
    name contains)

The Extended Usage Clause

In COBOL numeric (**Pic 9**) data types may be further defined with the **Usage** clause.
The **Usage** clause specifies the storage format of numeric data types. When omitted
the default is **Display**.

Format: the Usage clause.

> 0x   data-name   Pic character string   Usage Is clause.

where:

> 0x is the level-number
> data-name is a user-defined name to identify a data item
> Pic character string declares the allowable data types, size and editing
>   characters
> Usage Is clause declares the optional numeric data types

Here are some familiar data-type declarations with the Usage clause.

Example: specifying data types with the Usage clause.

> 01 data-1   Pic 9(06) Usage is Comp-3.
> 01 data-2   Pic 9(06) Usage is Display.

The key word Usage is optional and may be omitted. Here is an example.

Example: specifying data types without the optional key word Usage.

> 01 data-1   Pic 9(06) Comp-3.
> 01 data-2   Pic 9(06) Display.

The following example illustrates the declaration of an object handle capable of holding a reference to an instance object of type *Book*, based on the definition of a class called *Book*.

Example: a data-name of Object-Handle capable of holding objects of type Book.

> Class-Id. Book.
>
> ...
>
> 01 Object-Handle   Usage Is Object Reference Book.

The keyword Usage is optional and may be omitted as in:

> Class-Id. Book.
>
> ...
>
> 01 Object-Handle   Object Reference Book.

Object References provide the ability to declare object identifiers (handles to objects). Some object-oriented programming languages use pointers to objects. When pointers are used the data within an object is vulnerable to unauthorized access and change. Encapsulation cannot effectively be enforced. Object-Oriented COBOL requires object handles to access object data, guaranteeing that the data in an object will only be changed by the methods of the object.

Tables of Objects

When multiple objects need to be referenced, tables of object handles may be declared using the Occurs clause. In this respect, object handles are similar to other COBOL data types. To declare a table capable of holding 100 entries of alphanumeric data, the following table might be defined.

Example: a one-dimensional table for holding alphanumeric data, defined as Pic X(06).
```
01 Table-Name.
   05 Table-of-Names  Occurs 100 Times
                      Pic X(06).
```

Declaring a table for holding object handles uses the same syntax, except for the data type.

Example: a one-dimensional table that will hold 100 object handles of data type Book.
```
01 Object-Table.
   05 Objects-Table   Occurs 100 Times
                      Object Reference Book.
```

Tables of object handles follow standard COBOL table syntax. Multidimensional tables may be declared and tables may be declared with indexes. As in standard COBOL, tables are declared in the Data Division and processed in the Procedure Division. In Chapter 6 we will discuss loading tables of object handles. Although tables provide one format for holding object handles, Object-Oriented COBOL and object-oriented programming in general uses a much more powerful data structure for holding and manipulating objects, called collections. Collections will be discussed in Chapter 9.

OBJECT NOTATION

Object instances are represented in the Unified Method by drawing a hexagon with vertical sides and a slightly peaked top and bottom.

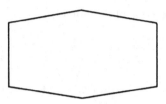

The name and type of object are written inside the figure as *objectName: className*. For example, a book object called *Hamlet*, of type *Book* would be drawn as follows:

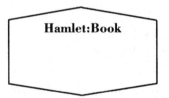

Object attributes, including name, type, and value(s), may optionally be listed in a second compartment below the object name and type as *attributeName:type=value*. For example, the data item **Status** would be represented thus:

A third compartment may be drawn to specify particular object methods as opposed to class methods. The $ notation, used in the class diagram to distinguish class methods from object methods, will suffice. The same format used to specify class methods is used to specify object methods. The following example shows the method **Report-Status**.

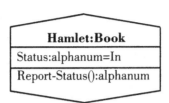

The object diagram may be enlarged (if necessary when using a word processor or diagramming tool) to include any number of attributes and methods. In addition, notes may be attached to the figure to provide additional information as needed. The following diagram shows a note attached to the method **Report-Status** to indicate that the only permissible returned values are "In" or "Out."

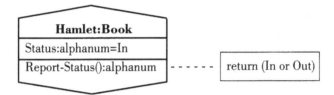

THE EVOLUTION OF PROGRAMMING LANGUAGES

The evolution of programming languages is typified by the progression from the fairly limited vocabulary of Assembler Man to the more meaningful vocabulary of Procedural Man to the extended vocabulary of Object-Oriented Man (Figure 4.5).

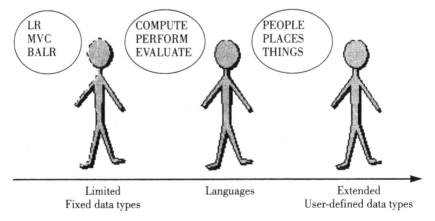

FIGURE 4.5. The evolution of programming languages.

To fully appreciate the power of Object-Oriented COBOL, it is useful to examine how the concept of objects evolved from basic concepts beginning in the 1950s.

In the 1950s, primitive and simple aggregate data types were the only ones supported by programming languages. The intended use and instruction set of the host machine dictated which data types were supported by a language. There was a very intimate connection between the programming language and the underlying hardware.

Throughout the 1950s, until the early 1960s, the world of computing was sharply divided into two realms: business data processing and scientific computing. Programming languages were targeted toward architectures that reflected their intended use. FORTRAN was developed for scientific computing on the IBM 704 with an instruction set geared to efficiently process numbers. COBOL was developed for the IBM 702 with an instruction set equipped to process character data. However, this separation between science and business computing began to blur in the 1960s, with the development of general purpose computers and operating systems.

As programming languages broke free of hardware constraints, language developers introduced more sophisticated data types. During this time *abstract data types* were suggested by Strachey and Standish, who recognized that data could be viewed from the perspective of the operations that could be carried out on the data. Abstract data types were a huge leap forward and are one of the keys to understanding objects.

Abstract data types have four characteristics.

1. A collection of one or more data items.

2. A relationship (physical or logical) among the data items.

3. A set of operations that may only be performed on the data items through an interface.

4. The concept that the data type is separate from specific examples of that structure.

Abstract data types are new to COBOL. Except for primitive types such as Pic X and Pic 9, type has not been a separate idea in COBOL. With the introduction of objects, however, the concept of types, long an integral feature of other languages, is now part of COBOL.

State Persistence in Procedural COBOL

In procedural COBOL the programmer has the ability to control the persistence of a sub-program's state. State persistence is the default in subprograms. Every time a main program calls a subprogram, the subprogram remains in the state it was exited. The data variables maintain their values as they were last updated. This may or may not be what is wanted, depending on the application. However, a subprogram responsible for maintaining running counts may want persistent state. On the other hand, a subprogram responsible for performing a new calculation every time it is called may not want data persistence. COBOL gives the programmer the option. The programmer may use the default persistent state or may instead return the subprogram to its initial state every time it is called.

Persistence may be implemented in one of two ways. The subprogram may control its own state or the state of the subprogram may be controlled by the calling program. For example, assume a subprogram called "TOTAL" is responsible for reading a file and counting the number of records in the file. After reading each record, the subprogram increments its counter by one and returns control to the calling program. When the calling program needs the next record it calls the subprogram to read another record. At the end of the application the subprogram prints the total number of records in the file. For this application, the subprogram "TOTAL" needs to remain in the last condition it was called to accurately compute the sum. It needs state persistence. Because persistence is the default for subroutines, the programmer may decide only to comment or document the fact that the subprogram needs to have state persistence.

On the other hand, a calling program might read a file and pass a date to a subprogram to determine the number of days until an employee's anniversary date. After each calculation, control is returned by the subprogram to the calling program. In this case, the subprogram needs to be returned to its initial state each time it is called. The programmer has two options: control the state of the subprogram via the calling program or control the state of the subprogram within the subprogram itself.

To control the state of the subprogram via the calling program, the programmer may use the CANCEL statement immediately before issuing a call to the subprogram:

```
CANCEL "TOTAL"
CALL "TOTAL" USING EMPLOYEE-DATE.
```

where EMPLOYEE-DATE is a parameter passed to the subprogram.

To control the state of the subprogram within the subprogram itself, returning it to its initial state each time it is called, the INITIAL statement is used in the Program-ID paragraph as in:

```
PROGRAM-ID. TOTAL INITIAL.        // Subprogram Program-Id paragraph
```

RESPONSIBILITY-DRIVEN DESIGN AND OBJECTS

During the early stages of object-oriented software development, responsibility-driven design and CRC (class, responsibility, collaborators) sessions do not differentiate between the class and the objects of the class. The objective of CRC sessions is to define classes, which by implication define the objects that will be used in an application. Specifics about the objects, such as when and how long an object lives, are determined during later design phases.

In the library application we have outlined several classes: *Customer, Book, Video,* and *Audio.* Assigning the class *Book* the responsibility to report its status means that a *Book* object must respond with "In" or "Out" when sent the **Report-Status** message. The following is an implementation of the **Report-Status** method in the class *Book.*

> Example: the class Book with an object method called Report-Status.

```
        Class-Id. Book.
        ...

        Object.
        Data Division.
        Working-Storage Section.
        01 Status          Pic X(03).
        Method-Id. "Report-Status".
        Data Division.
        Linkage Section.
        01 LS-Status       Pic X(03).
        Procedure Division Returning LS-Status.
           Move Status to LS-Status.
        Exit Method.
        End Method "Report-Status."
        End Object.
        End Class Book.
```

Key Points

- An object is declared in the Object paragraph.

- The textual declaration of an object does not create an object, it only provides a potential.

- An object instance, like a factory object, has data and methods.
- **Object Reference** is a new data type used to declare data items to hold object handles.
- Classes and objects are abstract data types.
- Responsibility-driven design assigns responsibilities to classes/objects during the early stages of software development without defining when and how the object is created.
- The Unified Method uses a hexagon-type shape to represent objects.

Suggested Readings

Beck, K., & Cunningham, W. (1989). A Laboratory for Teaching Object-Oriented Thinking. Proceedings of the 1989 OOPSLA Conference on Object-Oriented Systems, Languages and Applications: reprinted in *Sigplan Notices, 24*(10), 1–6.

Booch, G. (1983). *Software Engineering with Ada.* Menlo Park, CA: Benjamin/ Cummings.

Brooks, F. (1987). No Silver Bullet: Essence and Accidents of Software Engineering. *IEEE Computer, 20*(4), 10–19.

Budd, T. (199). *An Introduction to Object-Oriented Programming.* Reading, MA: Addison-Wesley.

Sammet, J. (1969). *Programming Languages: History and Fundamentals.* Englewood Cliffs, NJ: Prentice Hall.

Standish, T. (1984). An Essay on Software Reuse. *IEE Transactions on Software Engineering, 10*(5), 494–497.

Review Questions

4.0   What are the components of an Object Definition?
4.1   What Divisions are allowed in an **Object** paragraph?
4.2   Give a brief description of a method.
4.3   What **Usage** clause is used to declare object handles?
4.4   Define a table capable of holding 10 object handles.
4.5   List three primitive data types found in COBOL.
4.6   What are the three characteristics of an object?
4.7   Is a subprogram an abstract data type? Why or why not?
4.8   Using the Unified Method, diagram an object of the class *Automobile*.

CHAPTER 5

INHERITANCE

Aristotle once described man as "the animal possessed of the capacity for articulate speech." His classical definition is an example of the effectiveness of hierarchy in describing categories in the real world. The ability to arrange classes in hierarchies gives object-oriented programming its tremendous expressive power.

Hierarchies are a kind of definition. They specify what something is like and at the same time, describe how it is different. This is the classical approach to understanding—an approach based on class hierarchies.

Hierarchies are canonical forms of description for many disciplines, serving as a principle for organization and an aid to understanding. All scientific and technical knowledge is based on hierarchies, the classic example being the phylum–order–class–genus–species biological ordering of life.

Hierarchies may be thought of as factored solutions, which, as Dijkstra points out, are a key to problem solving. Hierarchies are an important aspect of an object-oriented system, forming the basis for inheritance. Classes inherit code from each other, forming hierarchies that model the real world in software.

FOCUS AND FORMAT OF THIS CHAPTER

The primary focus of this chapter is on inheritance, describing how it may be used in Object-Oriented COBOL and how variables may be used within the inheritance hierarchy. We also examine how class methods (defined in the **Factory** paragraph) are inherited by descendant factory objects and how object methods (defined in the **Object** paragraph) are inherited by descendant object instances.

- Reserved Words
  - Invoke
  - Property
  - Override

- Concepts
  - Abstract class
    - Is-A
    - Mixin
  - Association
    - Has-A
    - Multiple Inheritance
  - Class Library
    - Method resolution
    - Single Inheritance

INHERITANCE

Inheritance is the mechanism by which classes can share methods. The class that inherits is called the *subclass*. The class from which it inherits is called the *superclass*. A class can inherit from a superclass by specifying the **Inherits** phrase in the **Class-Id** paragraph. The inherited class (superclass) must also be specified in the **Repository** paragraph of the descendant class.

Quick Reference Map:
Class-Id paragraph.
Repository paragraph.

Identification Division.	Identification Division.
<u>Class-Id.</u> ←	<u>Object</u>.
Environment Division.	Environment Division.
Identification Division.	Data Division.
<u>Factory</u>.	Procedure Division.
Environment Division.	{<u>Methods</u>.}
Data Division.	<u>End</u> <u>Object</u>.
Procedure Division.	<u>End</u> <u>Class</u>.
{<u>Methods</u>.}	
<u>End Factory</u>.	

Format: permitted and required entries for inheriting a class.

<u>Class-Id.</u> class-name-2 Inherits class-name-1.
[Environment Division.]
Configuration Section.
<u>Repository.</u>
    class-name-1 Is Class "system-name"
    class-name-2 Is Class "system-name".
[Factory Definition.]
[Object Definition.]
<u>End</u> <u>Class</u> class-name-2.

The following is the definition for **Class-2**, which inherits from **Class-1** (where **Class-1** has been defined elsewhere).

Example: Class-2 Inherits from Class-1.

Class-Id. Class-2 Inherits Class-1.
Environment Division.
Configuration Section.
Repository.
    Class-1 Is Class "Class1"
    Class-2 Is Class "Class2".
Factory Definition.
Object Definition.
End Class Class-2.

ABSTRACT CLASSES

In the library example introduced in Chapter 2, a class hierarchy was established based on a superclass called *Item* and several subclasses: *Book, Video,* and *Audio.* The real-world difference between items and books, videos, and audiotapes is that only books, videos, and audiotapes may be physically checked out. Item is an abstraction of all three.

Item is an example of an *abstract* class. Abstract classes are not meant to have object instances but to act as templates for other classes. In the class *Item,* object methods exist for the purpose of providing common behavior to inheriting subclasses. Abstract classes are also called *deferred* classes, in that their operations may be specified, but the implementation is deferred until their subclasses are defined.

The opposite of an abstract class is a *concrete* class. In the library example, the class *Book* is a concrete class, whereas *Item* is an abstract class, specifying the general properties of its concrete subclasses. Here again, is the structure of the library system (Figure 5.1).

In Chapter 2, the class *Item* included the methods **Check-In** and **Check-Out**. Thinking of class *Item* as an abstract class, two other methods, **Report-Title** and **Report-Status**, can also be included in the class *Item* for inheritance by the subclasses *Book, Video,* and *Audio.* By specifying methods in an abstract class, we define a set a behaviors common to all subclasses, such as the following:

1. **Report-Title**—report the title of an *Item* (*Book, Video,* and *Audio* objects).
2. **Report-Status**—report if an *Item* is in or out of the library.
3. **Check-In**—return an *Item* to the library.
4. **Check-Out**—check an *Item* out of the library.

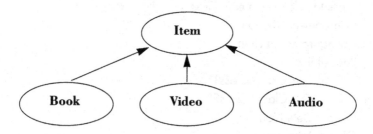

FIGURE 5.1. Structure in the library system.

Each of the above object methods, intended for *Book*, *Video*, and *Audio* objects, are defined in the **Object** paragraph of the class *Item*. A common confusion is to mix the roles of object methods (intended for object instances) with class or factory methods (intended for more general classwide functionality).

Class Methods

Class methods, also called Factory methods, are most commonly used for object creation and destruction. However, they may also be used to support functionality across all objects or a subset of objects within a class. For example, calculating a total or averaging over all instances of a class may be implemented as a class method. Class methods for the library example include: determining the total number of items checked out, tracking the number of items overdue, and calculating the total amount of fines imposed on overdue items. The following is a list of possible class methods.

1. Total-Out—calculate and report the total number of *Items* checked out of the library.
2. Total-Overdue—calculate and report the total number of *Items* currently overdue.
3. Total-Fines—calculate and report the total amount of fines imposed on overdue *Items*.

The following program, in outline form, shows how class and object methods may be defined in the superclass *Item*.

Example: The class Item defines class and object methods.

```
Class-Id. Item.
Environment Division.
Configuration Section.
Repository.
   Item Is Class "Item".
Factory.
Method-Id. "Total-Out".
Method-Id. "Total-Overdue".
Method-Id. "Total-Fines".
Object.
```

```
Method-Id. "Report-Title".
Method-Id. "Report-Status".
Method-Id. "Check-In".
Method-Id. "Check-Out".
End Class Item.
```

Given the above class definition for *Item*, the following is the class definition for *Book*, which inherits both the class and object methods from *Item*.

Example: The class Book inherits class and object methods from the class Item.

```
Class-Id. Book Inherits Item.
Environment Division.
Configuration Section.
Repository.
    Book Is Class "Book"
    Item Is Class "Item".
<Factory Definition.>
<Object Definition.>
End Class Book.
```

The other two library classes, *Video* and *Audio*, may *also* inherit class and object methods from *Item* by specifying the **Inherits** phrase in their **Class-Id** paragraphs and by declaring the class *Item* in their **Repository** paragraphs.

THE INHERITANCE HIERARCHY

A subclass inherits all the methods of its ancestors. A subclass inherits not only from its most immediate superclass but from all classes higher in the inheritance chain. For instance, consider a new class, *Rare-Book*, a more specialized version of the class *Book*. It exists below *Book* in the inheritance hierarchy. Figure 5.2 depicts the extended inheritance tree. Inheritance flows only in one direction, from the top down. Methods defined in *Rare-Book* are not available to the *Book* class and methods defined in the class *Book* are not available to the class *Item*.

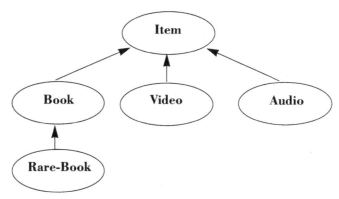

FIGURE 5.2. The extended inheritance tree.

How Inheritance Works

Inheritance is often viewed as a descending chain, with methods declared in ancestor classes inherited by classes lower in the hierarchy. Each descendant object on the chain can invoke methods inherited from superclasses. Subclasses may override inherited methods; they cannot, however, limit or restrict inheriting methods. In this respect, inheritance is an all-or-nothing proposition. One way of thinking about inheritance is shown in Figure 5.3.

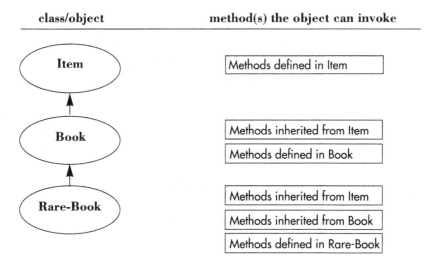

FIGURE 5.3. The descending method chain of inheritance.

In actuality each method is not duplicated for each object. Here is another portrayal, indicating with arrows which methods may be invoked by which objects (Figure 5.4).

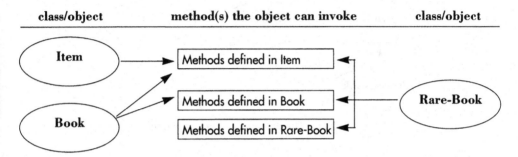

class/object	method(s) the object can invoke	class/object

FIGURE 5.4. Methods and their availability to objects.

Inheritance and Data

As illustrated in Figure 5.4, the actual code that constitutes a method is not duplicated within each inheriting object. Data items, however, *are* duplicated for each object created. Note, however, that it is the data items, *not* the data values that are duplicated for each object in the inheritance chain. This is an important distinction. When an object is created, memory is allocated for all data items declared in the Object section of the class and all data items declared in the Object sections of all superclasses.

Inheritance works similarly for each factory object associated with each class definition. Memory is allocated for any data items declared in the Factory paragraph of a class definition as well as any factory data specified in superclasses.

As an illustrative example, assume that the class *Item* defines a class method called **Running-Count**. The method [1] displays the value of a variable called Counter, [2] adds 1 to the value, and [3] redisplays the value. The following is the **Running-Count** method defined in the Factory paragraph of class *Item*.

Example: The class Item defines a class method to be inherited by descendant classes.

Class-Id. Item.

...

Factory.

```
Data Division.
Working-Storage Section.
01 Counter          Pic 9(02) Value 0.
Method-Id. "Running-Count".
Procedure Division.
    Display "Counter: " Counter.
    Add 1 to Counter.
    Display "Counter: " Counter.
    Exit Method.
End Method "Running-Count".
    ...
End Class Item.
```

The classes *Book* and *Rare-Book* may inherit the **Running-Count** method either directly from *Item* or indirectly from a subclass of *Item (Book)*, as in:

```
Class-Id. Book Inherits Item.
```

```
Class-Id. Rare-Book Inherits Book.
```

Both the class *Book* and the class *Rare-Book* may now **invoke** the **Running-Count** method using the following statements:

```
#1.   Invoke Book "Running-Count" End-Invoke.
```

```
#2.   Invoke Rare-Book "Running-Count" End-Invoke.
```

Because memory is allocated for all data in every factory object, the values associated with the variable **Counter** will be unique for the invoking *Book* and for the invoking *Rare-Book* statements. Executing statement #1 produces the following output:

```
Counter:   0
Counter:   1
```

Executing statement #2 10 times produces the following, after the tenth iteration:

```
Counter:   9
Counter:   10
```

Executing statement #1 one more time yields the following:

Counter: 1
Counter: 2

Figure 5.5 depicts the classes *Item, Book,* and *Rare-Book* executing the method Running-Count and showing that the variable Counter, associated with each class, holds different values.

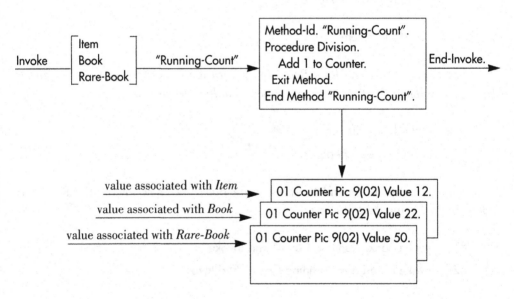

FIGURE 5.5. Item, Book, or Rare-Book may Invoke the Running-Count method.

It is important to note that data items, defined at the superclass level, are not directly accessible to methods of the inheriting subclasses. The procedural code in a subclass may reference data defined in its own class, but superclass-defined data is accessible only through access methods inherited from the superclass.

For example, consider a superclass named *Parent* and a subclass named *Child,* where *Parent* defines a single class data item and one class method called Parent-Method-1 that adds 1 to Counter.

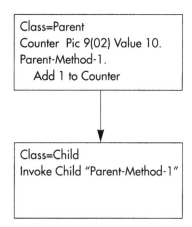

FIGURE 5.6. A subclass inherits a method of a superclass.

Because Counter is defined in *Parent,* no code in subclass *Child* may directly reference the variable **Counter**. If *Child* defined its own variable called **Counter**, the **Counter** variable in *Parent* would be invisible to methods of *Child*. **Counter** in *Child* would be a completely different variable because of local scope, and only methods declared in *Child* would be able to access the variable.

Earlier, we outlined three class methods and four object methods in the class *Item.* Through inheritance, these methods become available to the *Book, Video,* and *Audio* classes. For example, the following **Invoke** statements may be executed by the subclasses based on the class methods inherited from the class *Item.*

Invoke Book "Total-Out" ... End-Invoke.

Invoke Book "Total-Fines" ... End-Invoke.

Invoke Video "Total-Overdue" ... End-Invoke.

Invoke Rare-Book "Total-Fines" ... End-Invoke.

Any methods defined in *Rare-Book,* however, can *not* be invoked by the *Book* object. The rules of inheritance prohibit ascendant objects from invoking methods defined in descendant classes. For example, the **Invoke** statement in the method below causes an error.

```
Class-Id. Book Inherits Base.
...
Method-Id. Error-Method.
Procedure Division.
    Invoke Book "A-method-defined-in-Rare-Book" End-Invoke.
Exit Method.
End Method Error-Method.
```

Method Resolution

When an object attempts to invoke a method, the system performs a search to identify whether the object may invoke the requested method. The search and identification process is called *method resolution*. The system determines or resolves the request (the **invoke** statement) by searching for the method and the objects that are allowed to invoke them.

For example, consider the method **Total-Fines** defined in the class *Item*. When *Rare-Book* invokes this method the system searches first for the method-name in the *Rare-Book* class. If the *Rare-Book* class has implemented its own version of **Total-Fines,** the search stops and the method is executed. Because the method was not implemented in the class *Rare-Book,* the search continues for the method-name in the methods defined by the class *Book*. Failing to find the method, the system continues to search for the method-name in the methods defined by the class *Item*. At this point the method is found and the method executes.

If the class *Item* inherited the class **Base,** the system would continue the search for the method in **Base.** If a method is not found an error occurs. The following is an **Invoke** statement and a trace of the subsequent method search.

```
Class-Id. Rare-Book Inherits Book.
...
Method-Id. Find-Method.
Procedure Division.
    Invoke Rare-Book "Total-Fines" ...End-Invoke.
    Exit Method.
End Method Find-Method.
```

In Figure 5.7, the search concludes successfully when the method, **Total-Fines,** is found in the methods defined in the class *Item*.

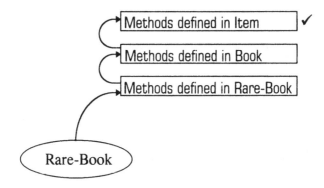

FIGURE 5.7. Successful completion of the search.

Overriding Inheritance

Object-Oriented COBOL provides a mechanism to override inherited methods. This may be necessary when inherited methods need to be augmented or modified to serve the purposes of the inheriting class. For example, the class *Rare-Book* inherits the basic **Check-Out** method from the class *Item*. However, there may be special restrictions for borrowing a rare book as opposed to borrowing an ordinary book, video, or audiotape. It may be the case that rare books may only be checked out to libraries or museums.

To support method extension by a subclass, COBOL allows subclasses to override inherited methods by appending the reserved word **Override** to the **Method-Id** declaration. In effect, the subclass redefines the superclass method with a method of the same method-name.

| Quick Reference Map:
Method-Id paragraphs. | Identification Division.
Class-Id.
Environment Division.
Identification Division.
Factory.
Environment Division.
Data Division.
Procedure Division.
  {Methods.} ←
End Factory. | Identification Division.
Object.
Environment Division.
Data Division.
Procedure Division.
  {Methods.} ←
End Object.
End Class. |

Format: required entries for overriding an inherited method.

Method-Id. method-name-1 Override.
method statements
End Method method-name-1.

Example: the method Borrow overrides an inherited method of the same name.

Method-Id. "Borrow" Override.
method statements
End Method "Borrow".

The **Override** attribute notifies the compiler to use this method, as opposed to the inherited method. When using the **Override** attribute, a previously defined method of the same name must occur in a superclass or an error will occur.

MULTIPLE INHERITANCE

Object-Oriented COBOL allows for multiple as well as single inheritance. Multiple inheritance permits subclasses to inherit methods from more than one superclass. Multiple inheritance is used to extend the functionality of subclasses by mixing aspects of more than one superclass. Figure 5.8 shows a class *Child* inheriting from two superclasses, *Mother* and *Father*.

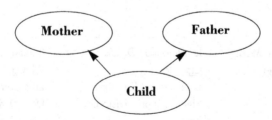

FIGURE 5.8. An example of multiple inheritance.

When a subclass inherits methods with the same name from different parent classes, inheritance proceeds in the order the name of the superclass appears in the **Class-Id** paragraph. Thus, if the *Mother* and *Father* classes both contain a method named **Call-Home,** the name of the first superclass encountered in the **Class-Id** of the class *Child* will be the method inherited.

Multiple inheritance is a double-edged sword. There are occasions when multiple inheritance is necessary and useful. Care should be taken when using multiple inheritance, however, because of its potential for increasing the complexity of an application.

Using Multiple Inheritance

A subclass inherits methods (class and object) from two or more superclasses by specifying the **Inherits** phrase in the **Class-Id** paragraph, followed by a list of the inherited classes. The inherited classes (superclasses) must also be specified in the **Repository** paragraph of the descendant class.

Quick Reference Map: Class-Id paragraph.	Identification Division.
	Class-Id. ←
	Environment Division.
	Identification Division.
	Factory.
	Environment Division.
	Data Division.
	Procedure Division.
	    {Methods.}
	End Factory.
		Identification Division.
		Object.
		Environment Division.
		Data Division.
		Procedure Division.
		    {Methods.}
		End Object.
		End Class.

Format: permitted and required entries for multiple inheritance.

Class-Id. class-name-3 Inherits class-name-2, class-name-1...
[Environment Division.]
Configuration Section.
Repository.
    class-name-1 Is Class "system-name"
    class-name-2 Is Class "system-name"
    class-name-3 Is Class "system-name".
[Factory Definition.]
[Object Definition.]
End Class class-name-3.

The following example illustrates *Child* inheriting from *Mother* and *Father* (where *Mother* and *Father* have been defined elsewhere). If both *Mother* and *Father* defined a Call-Home method, the method from the class *Mother* is the inherited method because it is the first superclass name encountered in the Class-Id paragraph.

Example: Child Inherits from Mother and Father classes.

```
Class-Id. Child Inherits Mother, Father.
Environment Division.
Configuration Section.
Repository.
    Mother    Is Class "Mother"
    Father    Is Class "Father"
    Child     Is Class "Child".
Factory Definition.
Object Definition.
End Class Child.
```

Figure 5.9 shows how a class, *Book*, may inherit from both class *Reorder* and class *Item*. Classes such as *Reorder* are known as mixin classes because they are mixed into an inheritance hierarchy to add additional functionality.

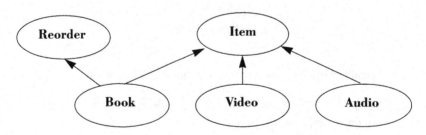

FIGURE 5.9. An example of a mixin class.

The class *Book* may be defined this way in order to add existing functionality supported by the class *Reorder* without having to burden the *Book* class with additional complexity and the possible change of data structures.

Example: Book inherits from the mixin class Reorder and from the class Item.

```
Class-Id. Book Inherits Item, Reorder.
Environment Division.
Configuration Section.
Repository.
     Item       Is Class "Item"
     Reorder   Is Class "Reorder"
     Book       Is Class "Book".
Factory Definition.
Object Definition.
End Class Book.
```

The Library Class Base

Object-Oriented COBOL includes a Class Library to supply essential functionality for user-defined classes. An important class in the Library is the class *Base*. Through inheritance, the class *Base* supplies user-defined classes with capabilities that are useful in doing object-oriented programming.

The syntax for inheriting the class *Base* is the same as inheriting from any class.

Format: required entries for inheriting the Base class (from Object-Oriented COBOL's Class Library).

```
[Identification Division.]
Class-Id. class-name-1 Inherits Base.
[Environment Division.]
Configuration Section.
Repository.
     Base              Is Class "Base"
     class-name-1    Is Class "system-name".
[Factory Definition.]
[Object Definition.]
End Class class-name-1.
```

Notice that *Base* is declared in the **Class-Id** paragraph as well as in the **Repository** paragraph.

The following is an example of the class *Item* inheriting from the class *Base*.

Example: Item inherits from the Base class.

```
Identification Division.
Class-Id. Item Inherits Base.
Environment Division.
Configuration Section.
Repository.
    Base    Is Class "Base"
    Item    Is Class "Item".
Factory Definition.
Object Definition.
End Class Item.
```

CLASS RELATIONSHIP DIAGRAMS

Although class diagrams depict the data and code associated with class definitions, they are only part of the complete picture of an object-oriented system. Relationships between classes define important system details necessary to model an application. Consider the following Unified Method representation for the class *Book*.

Book
attributes
methods

Although useful, it is important to know the relationships that *Book* has with other classes. In object-oriented systems there are three important relationships that are specified.

1. *Is-A*—also referred to as *A-Kind-Of, generalization/specialization,* or *gen/spec.* For example, a *Book* is-a(n) *Item* for check out.

2. *Has-A*—also referred to as *aggregation, whole-part,* or *composition.* For example, a *Lamp* has-a *Cord* and *Bulb.*

3. *Association*—the most general kind of relationship that can be augmented with a name that tells what kind of association is involved. For example, *Patrons* check out *Books* is an example of an association between two classes.

The *Is-A* relationship may be implemented with inheritance. In the library example, the fact that a *Book* object *Is-A*(n) *Item* object can be represented in Object-Oriented COBOL using the **Inherits** key word. Because the *Is-A* relationship models from the general to the specific it is often called *generalization/specialization*. Other examples of *Is-A* relationships include corn *Is-A* vegetable and Object-Oriented COBOL *Is-A* programming language.

Inheritance relationships are drawn with an arrow directed from the inheriting subclass to the inherited superclass. The following is a picture of the *Is-A relationship* between the class *Book* and the class *Item*.

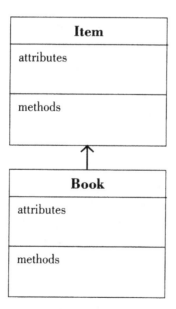

The second important relationship, *Has-A*, reflects a *whole/part* relationship between objects. *Has-A* models the fact that the *whole* is dependent on the *parts*. Examples of whole/part relationships are the parts making up a car or the parts making up a computer. For example, a *Car Has-A Windshield* and a *Computer Has-A Central Processing Unit*.

Has-A (aggregate) relationships are diagrammed with a diamond-tipped arrow placed near the *whole* object. The following is an example.

The third important relationship is *association. Associations* specify dependency relationships between classes. Associations are the most general form of relationships and are used to model relationships that are not either *Is-A* or *Has-A*. An example is the relationship between a company and its employees. The company and employee relationship is not modeled as a *Has-A* relationship because the existence of the company is not tied to the existence of the employees.

The association relationship is diagrammed with a line drawn between the classes. Below is an example.

Relationship diagrams may be embellished by providing additional information about the roles played by participating classes. The *role name* is written nearest the class that fulfills the role. Often a good descriptive name for a class may serve as a role name, making role names redundant. The following is an example.

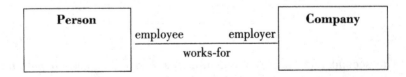

Additional detail about the relationship may be noted on an Association Diagram. Multiplicity indicates how many instances of one class may be associated with another.

The format of multiplicity is given by a range with a lower bound followed by two dots, followed by an upper bound. For example, the range "0..6" indicates there may be from 0 to 6 instances of one class associated with another. The star symbol "*" is used to show "many" (i.e., an unlimited number of instances). A single integer value is used when the exact number of instances in a relationship is known in advance (i.e., "1"). A one-to-one relationship is the default, in which case multiplicity does not need to be listed. The following is an example of explicit multiplicity.

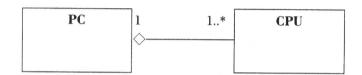

Relationship Considerations

Typically, in business applications, inheritance is not extended deeper than 7 ± 2 classes. In addition, composite objects are limited to 5 ± 2 objects and class associations generally are not wider than 7 ± 2 classes. At the upper limits, the result is a 7 x 7 matrix with some composite objects nested 5 deep.

Relationship Diagrams and Responsibility-Driven Design

During the early phases of responsibility-driven design, it is not necessary to capture specific relationships between classes. Relationships that are immediately obvious may be noted. However, it is a good idea to delay making relationship decisions that have a tendency to limit other design options.

During analysis, association, the most general relationship, should be used first to characterize the relationship between classes. Inheritance and aggregate relationships, more specific kinds of association, should be added later because they carry design and implementation implications. Of course, immediately visible inheritance relations, such as the library hierarchy of *Item* (superclass) and *Book*, *Video*, *Audio* (subclasses) should be expressed in diagrams as they are recognized.

Key Points

- Inheritance is implemented with the **Inherits** phrase in the **Class-Id** paragraph.

- Object-Oriented COBOL supports single and multiple inheritance.
- Inherited methods may be overridden with the **Override** option in the **Method-Id** paragraph.
- Mixin classes provide a means of augmenting functionality without sacrificing clarity.
- The *Base* class is Object-Oriented COBOL's Class Library.
- Three important relationships in object-oriented models are *Is-A, Has-A,* and *association.*

Suggested Readings

Halbert, P., & O'Brien, P. (1987). Using Types and Inheritance in Object-Oriented Programming. *IEEE Software, 4*(5), 71–79.

Ledbetter, L., & Cox, B. (1990). Software-ICs: A Plan for Building Reusable Software Components. In T. DeMarco & T. Lister (Eds.). *Software State-of-the-Art: Selected Papers.* New York: Dorset House.

Lovejoy, A. (1936). *The Great Chain of Being.* Cambridge, MA: Harvard University Press.

Parnas, D. (1979). On the Criteria to be Used in Decomposing Systems into Modules. In E. Yourdon (Ed.). *Classics in Software Engineering.* New York: Yourdon Press.

Review Questions

5.0 What is an abstract class? Give an example.

5.1 Name three hierarchical structures one might expect to find in a business or university.

5.2 Implement a program outline such that the subclasses *Automobile* and *Truck* inherit from the superclass *Vehicle.*

5.3 Yes or no—a subclass may choose not to inherit some of the methods defined in its superclass.

5.4 Describe the process used by Object-Oriented COBOL for finding methods in hierarchies.

5.5 How can inheritance be overridden? Implement an example.

5.6 Implement an example of multiple inheritance.

5.7 Describe a mixin class. What is another name for a mixin class?

5.8 How many levels of inheritance are typically considered good programming practice?

5.9 Diagram the following relationships:

    (a) a state has a capitol.

    (b) an employee is a salaried employee.

    (c) a pilot fish keeps a shark's gills clean.

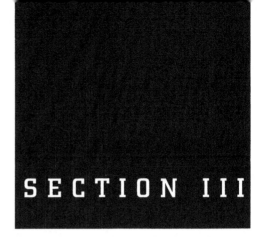

SECTION III

OBJECTS IN ACTION

CHAPTER 6

Messages

Object-oriented programming involves a duality often expressed in terms such as *clients* and *servers*, *class-builders* and *class-users*, *consumers* and *suppliers*, and *implementation* and *interface*. Working with objects means understanding this underlying duality.

From a client–server perspective, an object is known by its interface—the messages to which it will respond. Clients have no need to know an object's internal workings. Whether the client is another object or a separate program, only knowledge of the interface—the external view—is necessary.

In traditional programming one is "in for a penny, in for a pound." Programs must be seen in their entirety, without the benefit of different vantage points or platforms from which to view operations. Message passing frees the user from having to know a multiplicity of arcane and intricate implementation details. Messages are the means by which services are requested and operations are executed.

Focus and Format of This Chapter

This chapter focuses on the concepts and mechanisms of messages, clients, servers, and object interfaces. In addition, responsibility-driven design and object message diagrams are discussed.

- Reserved words
  Invoke
  Using
  Returning
  Self
- Concepts
  Interface
  Parameters
  Client
  Server
  Message

MESSAGES

Messages are the way objects communicate. Although this is a simple concept, some of the terminology can be confusing. Sending a message is often referred to as *requesting a service, message passing, invoking a method,* and *method resolution.* Message sending is all of these things.

In Object-Oriented COBOL sending a message involves

- An **Invoke** statement, followed by
- Message-specific information.

The message detail has three parts:

- An object identifier
- A method name
- An optional list of parameters and an optional returned parameter (reply)

Figure 6.1 illustrates message passing between a client (message sender) and server (message recipient). The objects involved may be factory objects, object instances, or any combination of the two. The basic message passing operation is the same.

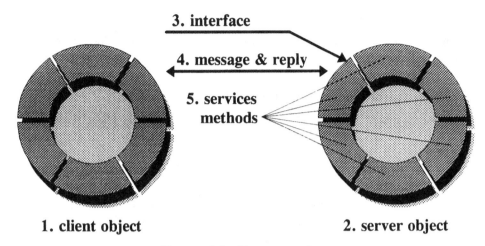

FIGURE 6.1. Message passing.

THE INVOKE STATEMENT

The **Invoke** statement is used to trigger a method within an object. The **Invoke** verb is analogous to a **Call** statement in that **Invoke** transfers control to a block of code similar to how a **Call** transfers control to a subprogram. The semantics of a **Call** and an **Invoke** are so similar that ANSI considered whether to simply extend the functionality of the **Call** statement to include methods. However, the decision to introduce the new verb, **Invoke,** was made to make it clear that objects, and not subprograms, were the target of the transfer of control.

Quick Reference Map:
Procedure Division.
Method-Id.

Identification Division.	Identification Division.
Class-Id.	Object.
Environment Division.	Environment Division.
Identification Division.	Data Division.
Factory.	Procedure Division.
Environment Division.	{Methods.} ←
Data Division.	End Object.
Procedure Division.	End Class.
{Methods.} ←	
End Factory.	

Methods are invoked (messages are sent) by using the reserved word Invoke followed by an object identifier, the method-name, and optionally the Using and Returning phrases and End-Invoke delimiter.

Format: a general form of the Invoke statement.

Invoke identifier-1 identifier-2 Using identifier-3 Returning identifier-4 End-Invoke.

where

> identifier-1 is the object identifier (the class name for a factory object),
> identifier-2 is the method-name,
> identifier-3 is an optional list of parameters passed to the method,
> identifier-4 is at most one optional parameter returned by the method, and
> End-Invoke delimits the operation.

Invoke statements may appear within the methods of objects or within the Procedure Division of conventional programs. This opens the door to using objects in two ways:

- as collaborators with other objects
- as service providers to conventional programs

Below are two classes, Class-1 and Class-2, in which Class-1 Invokes a method in Class-2.

Example: Class-1 Invokes a method of Class-2.

Invoking class	Invoked class
Class-Id. Class-1.	Class-Id. Class-2.
...	...
Method-Id. "Method-1".	Method-Id. "Method-2".
Procedure Division.	Procedure Division.
Invoke Class-2 "Method-2" End-Invoke.	procedure division statements
...	...

Parameters are used to pass information across an object boundary. To aid in program understanding, it is good practice to limit the number of parameters to five or fewer. Parameters may be specified with either the By Reference or By Content phrases.

Invoke By Reference makes the actual data available to the invoked method. The data may be changed by the invoked method and these changes will be reflected in the invoking program's data area.

Invoke By Content passes a *copy* of the data specified in the parameter list. Data passed to the invoked method may be changed, but only the copy is changed, not the original data. The By Reference and By Content phrases may be interleaved within the same Invoke statement. If neither By Reference or By Content is stipulated, the default is By Reference.

Format: a general form of the Invoke statement with By Reference and By Content.

$$\text{Invoke } \underline{\text{identifier-1}} \ \underline{\text{identifier-2}} \text{ Using } \begin{Bmatrix} \text{BY REFERENCE} \\ \text{BY CONTENT} \end{Bmatrix} \underline{\text{identifier-3}} \ \underline{\text{End-Invoke}}.$$

where

      identifier-1 is the object identifier,

      identifier-2 is the method-name,

      By Reference passes the address of the parameters to the invoked method,

      By Content passes a copy of the data to the invoked method,

      identifier-3 is an optional list of parameters passed to the method, and

      End-Invoke delimits the operation.

In the Invoke statement, the parameters of the Using and Returning phrases must be defined in the Data Division as level 01, level 77, or as an elementary item (not further subdivided). Objects may also be passed as parameters by using object handles. This will be discussed in Chapter 7.

Example: an Invoke statement with the phrase Using By Reference.

```
Method-Id. "Method-1".
Data Division.
Working-Storage Section.
01 A              Pic x(01) Value "Y".
Procedure Division.
    Invoke Class-2 "Method-2" Using By Reference A
    End-Invoke.
    ...
```

An Invoke statement that includes a Returning phrase will return data to the calling object or program. The Returning phrase allows at most one parameter of any valid data type (including objects) to be returned after the method has completed. The following is an example of an Invoke statement with a Returning parameter.

Example: an Invoke statement with the Returning phrase.

```
Method-Id. "Method-1".
Data Division.
Working-Storage Section.
01 B              Pic x(01) Value Spaces.
Procedure Division.
    Invoke Class-2 "Method-2" Returning B End-Invoke.
...
```

Variations on the Invoke statement include the options: On Exception and Not On Exception. If the method invoked is not available for execution, control will be returned to the On Exception phrase. Control will be returned to the Not On Exception phrase if the method being invoked is available for execution.

Format: a general form of the Invoke statement with On Exception and Not On Exception phrases.

Invoke identifier-1 identifier-2 Using identifier-3 Returning identifier-4
On Exception statement-1 Not On Exception statement-2 End-Invoke.

where

identifier-1 is the object identifier (the class for a factory object),
identifier-2 is the method-name,
identifier-3 is an optional list of parameters passed to the method,
identifier-4 is at most one optional parameter returned by the method,
statement-1 is an imperative statement,
statement-2 is an imperative statement, and
End-Invoke delimits the operation.

and where an imperative statement:

1. specifies an unconditional action (i.e., **Move**) or

2. is a conditional statement explicitly terminated by its delimiter (i.e., **If... End-If**)

3. An imperative statement may contain other imperative statements (i.e., **Compute X = Y + Z**

> On Size Error
>
>   If X > Z
>
>   ...
>
>   End-If
>
> ...
>
> End-Compute.)

Example: an Invoke statement with the phrases: On Exception and Not on Exception.

> Method-Id. "Method-1".
> Procedure Division.
>   Invoke Class-2 "Method-2"
>   On Exception Display "Error on Invocation"
>   Not On Exception Continue
>   End-Invoke.
>
> ...

Invoking Self

An object will often have two or more of its methods work together to accomplish some task. This means that a method must know the identity of the object to which it belongs. To facilitate referencing an object from within an object, the special identifier **Self** is used. This allows a method to reference the object it is part of quite easily.

Recall that when sending a message, via **Invoke**, the method name must be preceded by the object name. In Object-Oriented COBOL, the reserved word **Self** is used to refer to the object that holds a method so that a method can invoke another method *part of the same object*.

Figure 6.2 illustrates an object invoking one of its own methods using the reference to **Self**.

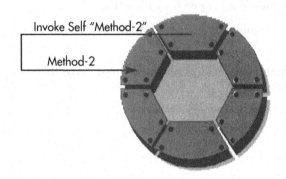

FIGURE 6.2. An object uses Self.

Self is a predefined object identifier. This means that it is predefined and automatically available to every object (factory and instance).

Format: a general form of the Invoke statement using Self.

Invoke <u>Self</u> identifier-2 Using identifier-3 Returning identifier-4 End-Invoke.

where

Self is the identity of the currently executing object.

Example: Class-1 invokes one of its methods, Method-2 by specifying Self.

Class-Id. Class-1.
...
Method-Id. "Method-1".
Procedure Division.
Invoke Self "Method-2"
End-Invoke.
Exit Method.
End Method "Method-1".

Method-Id. "Method-2".
Procedure Division.

```
statements
  Exit Method.
  End Method "Method-2".
End Class Class-1.
```

Self is borrowed from the Simula programming language. Smalltalk also uses the Self identifier. In C++ the same self-referential identifier is called "This" and in the programming language Eiffel it is called "Current."

The Procedure Division Header

The designers of Object-Oriented COBOL have tried to make the transition from procedural to object-oriented code as seamless as possible. As a result, the syntax for defining an object interface is almost identical to that which defines a subprogram interface. An interface is simply the set of parameters defined in a method's Procedure Division header and corresponding Linkage Section.

A Procedure Division header parameter list specifies the data items a method can receive along with the data item a method can return. In Object-Oriented COBOL, the Procedure Division header has been extended to include a Returning phrase. The Returning phrase allows at most one parameter of any valid data type to be returned from the invocation of a method (request for service).

Format: general format of a Procedure Division header showing the Using and Returning phrases.

Procedure Division Using data-name-1 Returning data-name-2.

where

data-name-1 is an optional list of parameters passed to a method, and
data-name-2 is an optional parameter returned by a method.

Example: a method's Procedure Division header with Using and Returning phrases (commas are optional).

Method-Id. "Method-1".
Procedure Division Using X, Y Returning Z.
  statements

Exit Method.
End Method "Method-1".

The list of arguments in the Using and Returning phrases are collectively called a method's parameter list. The data items specified in the *receiving* method's Procedure Division header parameter list must also be defined in the *receiving* method's Linkage Section.

Example: a receiving methods Procedure Division with Using and Returning phrases and corresponding definitions in the Linkage Section.

```
Method-Id. "Method-1".
Working-Storage Section.
Linkage Section.
01 X      Pic x(02).
01 Z      Pic 9(05).
Procedure Division Using X Returning Z.
    statements
End Method "Method-1".
```

A method's Procedure Division header specifies the parameters expected when a method is invoked. The parameters passed in an Invoke statement are matched by position (not by name) with the parameters listed in the Procedure Division header.

Example: an invoking and an invoked method.

Invoking method	Invoked method
Class-Id. Class-1.	Class-Id. Class-2.
...	...
Method-Id. "Method-1".	Method-Id. "Method-2".
Data Division.	Data Division.
Working-Storage Section.	Linkage Section.
01 X Pic 9(02) value 0.	01 A Pic 9(02).
01 Z Pic 9(02) value 2.	01 B Pic 9(02).
Procedure Division.	Procedure Division Using A Returning B.
Invoke Class-2 "Method-2"	Compute B = A * A.

Using X Returning Z   Exit Method.
End-Invoke.   End Method "Method-2".
If Z = 4

...

A common message-passing area is established to send and receive messages in the **Procedure Division** header and **Linkage Section**. In the following example, data names X and Z, declared in the invoking method (client) correspond to the names **A** and **B** in the invoked method (supplier). The names may be the same or different.

Example: Invoke Class-2 with Using and Returning parameters.

Invoke Class-2 "Method-2" Using X Returning Z End-Invoke.

Invoking method		Invoked method
Class-Id. Class-1.		Class-Id. Class-2.
...		...
Method-Id. "Method-1".		Method-Id. "Method-2".
Working-Storage Section.		Linkage Section.
01 X Pic 9(02) value 2.	common message-	01 A Pic 9(02).
01 Z Pic 9(02) value 0.	passing area	01 B Pic 9(02).
Procedure Division.		Procedure Division Using A
Invoke Class-2 "Method-2"		Returning B.
Using X Returning Z		Compute B = A * A
End-Invoke.		Exit Method.
If Z = 4		End Method "Method-2"
...		...

The parameters specified in the **Procedure Division** header must be declared in the **Linkage Section**. Initial values may not be defined in the **Linkage Section**.

The parameters passed from the invoking method must match the invoked method in

- number, the same number or fewer,
- data type (in the example above, data items X and A are both **Pic 9**),
- size (in the example above, data items X and A both have a size of (02).

SPECIFYING OBJECT BEHAVIOR

In the Unified Method classes are diagrammed using rectangles and objects are diagrammed using peaked hexagons. Class diagrams depict a static view of classes and their relationships. However, in object-oriented systems understanding object communication is a major aspect of program understanding, and it requires a dynamic system view.

Dynamic models have not been a part of structured methodologies. Structured analysis and design is primarily concerned with system partitioning. Data-flow diagrams (DFDs) make no attempt to capture the dynamics of a system being modeled.

In object-oriented design, dynamic models are just as important as static models. Object-message diagrams are an important dynamic model for describing the behavior of object-oriented systems. Object-message diagrams are used to describe the sequences of messages during program execution. Object-message diagrams trace the flow of interaction between objects, usually showing how the system responds to specific events.

Object-Message Diagrams

An object-message diagram traces the sequence of messages in response to an event. An object-message diagram shows the message (the method name), an optional list of parameters, an optional returned result, and the client and server (target) object. Figure 6.3 shows an object-message diagram showing a *Customer* object sending a message to a *Book* object. As a result of the original message, the *Book* object sends a message to itself.

In object-message diagrams, the names of the object methods and attributes are usually omitted for the sake of clarity. The purpose of an object-message diagram is to focus on the message sending. The static *class* or *object diagram* is used to show methods and attributes.

In Figure 6.3 an arrow is used to indicate the direction of the message. Each arrow has an associated sequence number, followed by the method name and, optionally, any parameters. The actual sequence of messages may be traced by following the nested numbering scheme. In the above example, the operation calculateDueDate is given a sequence number of 1.1 because it is triggered in response to the message checkOut.

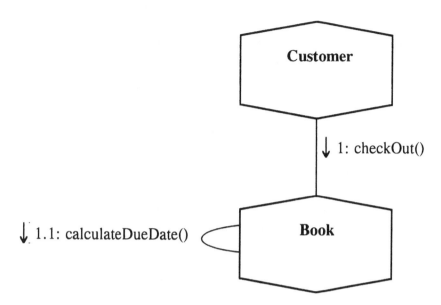

FIGURE 6.3. An example of an object-message diagram.

Return parameters are specified by an assignment sign (':='), following the parameter list. The following example shows that calculateDueDate returns a date value.

↓1.1:calculateDueDate():=date()

State and State Transition Diagrams

A state is the value or set of values of a system or of a component of the system at a given time. Changes to the state of the system are caused by events (messages). The model for depicting states and events are "state-transition diagrams." Many ordinary devices encountered every day are examples of state machines, in which a "state machine" is a system that has states and events.

The idea of state is very important in computer science and electrical engineering. State-transition diagrams are used to design system software, integrated circuits, and any number of devices that incorporate logic. Tools to model state are used in object-oriented analysis, object-oriented design, and object-oriented programming.

To show one example, a mouse button may be viewed as a state machine. The states are "On" and "Off," and an event is clicking the button. The mouse is modeled by

(continued on next page)

the state-transition diagram below. The circles represent the states, the arrows represent the events.

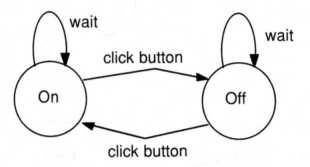

A state-transition diagram

Objects constrain state within their boundaries. The diagrams below depict how state is handled in object-oriented versus procedural programs. In the first diagram, the functions of procedural code operate within a domain of shared state, where any one of the functions may operate on and change the common state. The second diagram represents containment of states by objects. The squares represent objects with their state concealed. Because object data is local, objects maintain their own state.

| Function | Function | Function |

Functions with shared state.

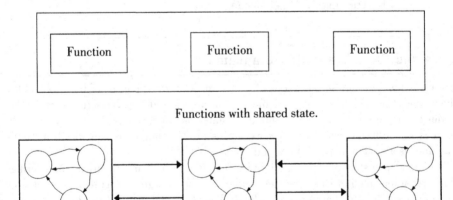

Objects with concealed state.

(continued on next page)

State diagrams are derived from *automata theory,* a branch of mathematics pioneered by Alan Turing. The finite refers to the fact that the automaton only has a finite number of memory locations. Lexical scanners in compilers and spelling checkers in text editors all use finite automata. Finite automata share more than a casual relationship to object-oriented languages. Alan Kay, one of the originators of Smalltalk, described his vision of Smalltalk as a collection of little automata all off doing their own thing.

APPLYING RESPONSIBILITY-DRIVEN DESIGN

Messages are the means by which *responsibility-driven* collaborations occur. The emphasis in object-oriented analysis and design is to discover, invent, define, and implement class and object responsibilities and the collaborations among the objects. Data plays a supporting role. Data exists to support responsibilities. Data does not drive the design of object-oriented systems.

In designing a system to support the sale of tickets at a baseball stadium, most programmers with a background in data-driven design would immediately start by thinking of the attributes (data) necessary to support such a system. In an object-oriented system, however, rather than becoming swamped in the details of data, the ticket operation can be modeled by identifying the system's classes/objects, responsibilities, and collaborations. As in all object-oriented design, some classes will be discovered, other classes will be invented. The discovered classes will reflect entities in the problem domain: such things as tickets, customers, seats, prices, and bleachers. The invented classes will reflect issues related to design and are usually found after the initial discovery phase is completed. Invented classes are there to support the design. They provide the classes required to implement a system. They are the "rubber couplings" that support the domain classes and allow object-oriented systems to more readily bend and flex.

Key Points

- There are two views to consider when speaking of objects: the view from the inside and the view from the outside.
- Invoking a method and sending a message are the same thing.

- Object-oriented applications consist of client and server objects sending and receiving messages.
- A new verb, **Invoke,** has been introduced to the COBOL syntax.
- **Self** is a predefined object identifier that may be stipulated as the target object of messages.
- Object-Oriented COBOL supports recursion.
- An object's interface is defined in the **Procedure Division** header of a **Method-Id** paragraph. An object may define many interfaces—one for each method.
- The nouns and noun phrases from the problem statement make an excellent starting point for discovering the candidate application domain classes.
- Object-message diagrams are one means of illustrating the operations in object-oriented applications.

Suggested Readings

Carmichael, A. (1994). Objects: Changing Software Production and Procurement. In *Object Development Methods.* New York: SIGS Books.

Carroll, J., & Long, D. (1989). *Theory of Finite Automata with an Introduction to Formal Languages.* Englewood Cliffs, NJ: Prentice Hall.

Hodges, A. (1983). *The Enigma.* New York: Simon & Schuster.

Parnas, D., Clements, P., & Weiss, D. (1983). Enhancing Reusability with Information Hiding. In *Proceedings of the Workshop on Reusability in Programming.* Stratford, CT: ITT Programming, pp. 240–247.

Review Questions

6.0   What are some other terms for invoking a method?

6.1   What are the two types of objects? Give a description of how each might be used.

6.2   What is the syntax for object-1 sending object-2 a message?

6.3   How many variables may be returned from the invocation of a method?

6.4   Discuss the object identifier **SELF.** What kinds of situations might **SELF** be used in?

6.5   Diagram a baseball team in which the players are the objects and the ball is the message.

CHAPTER 7

CREATING AND DESTROYING OBJECTS

C lasses provide the foundation for object-oriented programming, specifying blueprints for the objects that come to life and carry out the work of a program. Objects are dynamic: they are created and destroyed; they interact with one another; they provide the behavior.

Objects trace their heritage to Simula 67, the language that pioneered objects as an organizational technique for computer simulation. In computer simulation, the modeler describes entities and their interactions, then puts the model in motion. Businesses use simulation to study networks, queues, and purchasing patterns. With mature object-oriented languages, objects are now available to help model the world and to build systems that more accurately reflect how work is done. Objects bring a new dimension to COBOL. Procedural COBOL is a static brew. Object-Oriented COBOL is a dynamic, powerful brew for modeling business systems.

FOCUS AND FORMAT OF THIS CHAPTER

This chapter focuses on the creation and destruction of objects. Of importance for object creation is the factory object, which actually does the work of creating object instances for a class. In the context of object creation and destruction we will examine messages, interfaces, inheritance, and methods.

- Reserved words
    Finalize
    New
    Only
    Self
    Super

- Concepts
    Abstract class
    Accessor method
    Automatic garbage collection
    Conformance
    Constructor method
    Destructor method
    Dynamic object
    Interface
    Memory leakage
    Persistent object
    Polymorphism
    Typed object
    Untyped object

AN OBJECT'S LIFE SPAN

Objects have a life span; they are created and destroyed. The life span of an object, however, is not necessarily the same as the application. In Object-Oriented COBOL objects are created after an application begins. However, objects may be destroyed either

- before the application terminates,
- when the application terminates,
- after the application terminates.

Figure 7.1 is a timeline showing the beginning and ending points of an application, and the creation of an object.

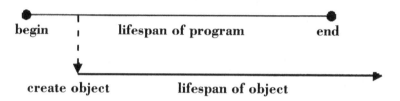

FIGURE 7.1. A timeline showing the beginning and ending points of an application.

The life span of an object begins when memory is allocated for it. An object's life span ends when its memory is returned to the system. Objects that exist past the execution of an application are called *persistent objects*. Objects that only exist for the duration (or less) of an application are called *dynamic objects*. *Persistent objects* are similar to records in a file or a database that are maintained after a program terminates.

Objects may be destroyed in one of two ways. First, an explicit method may be invoked to delete an object, or the run time environment may automatically delete objects when they are no longer accessible.

The deletion of inaccessible objects by the run time environment is called *automatic garbage collection*. *Automatic garbage collection* is an important feature of Object-Oriented COBOL, which reduces much of the complexity associated with memory allocation and deallocation. Not every object-oriented language provides automatic garbage collection: Smalltalk does, C++ does not.

Automatic garbage collection removes a major concern of many object-oriented applications called *memory leakage*. Memory leakage is a term that refers to creating and then failing to delete objects that are no longer necessary. During the running of an object-oriented program, thousands of objects may be generated. Memory leakage can easily corrupt a system by retaining memory that otherwise would be released to the system. It is not uncommon for COBOL applications to run for weeks or more at a time. Although minimal memory leakage may be tolerated in small applications, mission-critical business applications can *not* afford the possibility of application failure caused by inaccessible objects clogging the system.

CREATING OBJECTS

The factory object is responsible for creating object instances. Creating object instances is accomplished by invoking the method **New**. To facilitate object creation, the method **New** is defined in the class **Base**, which is specifically used for creating object instances.

The following is the format of an **Invoke** statement using the method **New**. **New** takes no parameters and returns the handle of the created object.

Format: a general form of the Invoke statement with New.

> Invoke identifier-1 "New" Returning identifier-4 End-Invoke.

where

> identifier-1 is the class-name (the class-name is also the factory object's name),
> New is the method-name,
> identifier-4 is the object identifier (handle returned by the New method), and
> End-Invoke delimits the operation.

Each class that inherits from the **Base** Class Library has **New** available to it. The following depicts the format for inheriting the Class **Base**.

Format: required entries for inheriting the Base class.

> Class-Id. class-name-1 Inherits Base.
>
> ...
>
> Repository.
> Base   Is Class "Base"
>   class-name-1 Is Class "system-name".
> [Factory Definition.]
> [Object Definition.]
> End Class class-name-1.

Typed Objects

In order to reference the object created by **New**, an object handle must be declared with the **Usage** clause. A class name is optionally included in the **Usage** clause. When a class name is specified, the handle may only reference objects of the declared type or class.

Format: a general format for defining an object identifier.

Ox data-name	Usage Is Object Reference [class-name].

where

> Ox is a level number 01 through 49 or 77,
>
> data-name is a user-defined object identifier (object's handle),
>
> Usage Is key phrase is optional,
>
> Object Reference is a required key phrase to declare a data type of object handle, and
>
> class-name is an optionally included type (a class).

When specifying the type of class in the **Usage** phrase, the system will ensure that the object will only be used in operations defined for similarly typed objects. Typing an object allows the compiler to guarantee the integrity of operations among objects and to generate warning messages when they are used inappropriately. Object-Oriented COBOL allows for typed as well as untyped objects, whereas Smalltalk is totally untyped, and C++ allows only typed objects.

Typed objects are afforded the same kind of protection other data types receive. For example, just as numeric data cannot be added to character data, typed objects are prevented from participating in certain user-defined operations. For example, typed objects may be specified as parameters in messages. When a message is sent, the type of object expected is compared with the type of object received, and unless they agree, an error will result. Type checking for objects is called *conformance checking*. The following is an example of conformance checking.

Example: a method of Class-1 passes an Object of type Class-1 to a method in Class-2.

Class-Id. Class-1.	Class-Id. Class-2.
...	...
Factory.	Factory.

```
Method-Id. "Pass-Object".              Method-Id. "Run".
Working-Storage Section.               Linkage Section.
01 anObject Object Reference Class-1.  01 aClass-1Object  Object Reference Class-1.
Procedure Division.                    Procedure Division Using aClass-1Object.
   Invoke Class-2 "Run" Using anObject     procedure division statements
...                                    ...
End Class Class-1.                     End Class Class-2.
```

The following is the syntax for declaring a handle to an object of class (type) *Book*.

Example: an object handle of class Book.

```
   01 Macbeth          Object Reference Book.
```

Creating an object is called a *constructor* operation. In the following example, the class *Book* creates an object instance with a handle called *Macbeth*.

Example: a class method, Create-Objects, creates an object, Macbeth, of type Book.

```
      Class-Id. Book Inherits Base.
      ...
      Repository.
         Base   Is Class "Base"
         Book   Is Class "Book".
      Factory.
      Data Division.
      Working-Storage Section.
      01 Macbeth      Object Reference Book.
      Method-Id. "Run".
      Procedure Division.
         Invoke Book "New" Returning Macbeth End-Invoke.
         Exit Method.
      End Method "Run".
      End Factory.
      <Object Definition>
      End Class Book.
```

A Driver Program

An object-oriented program is composed of objects that hold the program code. In order for an object-based program to get started, a starting message must be sent. In an Object-Oriented COBOL program that contains only methods, at least one procedural program is necessary to begin executing the application. We introduce a small procedural program called *Driver* for this purpose.

Integrating object constructs with procedural COBOL code is one of Object-Oriented COBOL's strong points, particularly for developers working with legacy applications. In order for a procedural program to send a message to an object, it must reference the class in its **Repository** paragraph. The following program references the class *Book* in its **Repository** paragraph and then invokes the **Run** method of the class *Book*.

Example: a procedural program with object-oriented constructs invokes a class method in Book.

```
Program-Id. Driver.
...
File-Control.
Repository.
     Book   Is Class "Book".
Procedure Division.
     Invoke Book "Run" End-Invoke.
End Program Driver.
```

Figure 7.2 illustrates the procedures involved in *Driver*.

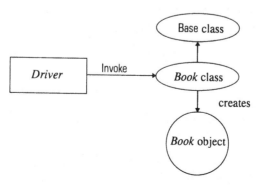

FIGURE 7.2. A visual representation of the procedures involved in *Driver*.

Object Methods—Working in the Object Paragraph

Quick Reference Map:
Object Paragraph
Object methods

Identification Division.	Identification Division.
Class-Id.	Object. ←
Environment Division.	Environment Division.
Identification Division.	Data Division.
Factory.	Procedure Division.
Environment Division.	{Methods.}
Data Division.	End Object.
Procedure Division.	End Class.
{Methods.} ←	
End Factory.	

Object methods serve as the workhorses of an application. All object instances created in a program rely on their object methods to get the work done. For example, a *Book* object with a handle called *Macbeth* might have a **Report-Status** method to indicate whether a book is checked "In" or "Out" of the library. We will assume *Macbeth* is "In" to start. The following is the definition of the *Book* object method called **Report-Status**.

Example: the Object paragraph of class Book implements an accessor method called Report-Status.

```
Object.
Data Division.
Working-Storage Section.
01 Status          Pic X(03).
Method-Id. "Report-Status".
Data Division.
Linkage Section.
01 Return-Status       Pic X(03).
Procedure Division Returning Return-Status.
    Move Status to Return-Status.
    Exit Method.
End Method "Report-Status".
End Object.
```

Notice in the above example that **Status** is defined as object data. This is because data defined as object data (in the **Data Division** of the **Object** paragraph) is permanent over the life span of the object, whereas data defined in methods is temporary to each invocation of the method.

Report-Status is an example of an *accessor method*. Accessor methods are methods that either read or write data values maintained by an object. The following list details some of the qualities of accessor methods.

- Accessor methods allow inquiries about the data values held by an object.

- Accessor methods permit the data values of an object to be modified.

Accessor methods are defined in the **Object** paragraph of the object and are necessary to get at an object's data. Remember, access to data in object-oriented systems is accomplished only through methods; direct access to an object's data is not permitted. An object, therefore, must define accessor methods to make its data visible and to allow its data to be changed. Not all objects must have accessor methods. Specialized objects such as those that only return error messages or objects responsible for displaying graphical user interfaces may not require accessor methods.

The following is a method called **Check-Out** that changes the value of **Status** from "**In**" to "**Out**." In this example, logic is kept to a minimum to help illustrate syntax. In a real application, there would be additional code to ensure the application's integrity.

Example: an accessor method, Check-Out, for changing the value of Status.

```
Object.
Data Division.
Working-Storage Section.
01 Status          Pic X(03).
< Method Report-Status would be defined here >
Method-Id. "Check-Out".
Procedure Division.
    Move "Out" to Status.
    Exit Method.
End Method "Check-Out".
End Object.
```

The following illustrates a **Check-In** method, for checking a book into the library.

Example: an accessor method, Check-In, to return a book to the library.

```
Object.
Data Division.
Working-Storage Section.
01 Status            Pic X(03).
< Method Report-Status would be defined here >
< Method Check-Out would be defined here >


Procedure Division.
  Move "In " to Status.
  Exit Method.


End Object.
```

Having defined the above three methods, our *Book* object *(Macbeth)* now has three object methods and one attribute, **Status**, defined as object data. This situation is represented pictorially in Figure 7.3.

Creating Multiple Book Objects

At this point our library only contains one book, *Macbeth*. The following example shows how a Factory object could be used to create several object instances with a

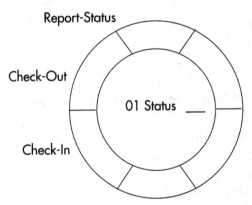

FIGURE 7.3. *Macbeth—Book* object.

method called *Create-Objects-1*. An approach of this kind is useful when an application needs to have specific object instances always available. Maintaining multiple objects is better done with tables of objects or collections; however, this information is presented later.

Example: the class method, Create-Objects-1, creates three book objects.

```
Class-Id. Book Inherits Base.
...
Factory.
Data Division.
Working-Storage Section.
01 Macbeth        Object Reference Book.
01 Hamlet         Object Reference Book.
01 Othello        Object Reference Book.
Method-Id. Create-Objects-1.
Procedure Division.
    Invoke Book "New" Returning Macbeth End-Invoke.
    Invoke Book "New" Returning Hamlet End-Invoke.
    Invoke Book "New" Returning Othello End-Invoke.
  Exit Method.
End Method Create-Objects-1.
End Factory.
<Object Definition>
Method-Id. "Report-Status".
Method-Id. "Check-In".
Method-Id. "Check-Out".
End Class Book.
```

Figure 7.4 illustrates the class *Book* creating the three *Book* objects.

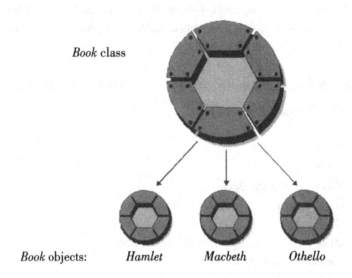

Book class

Book objects: *Hamlet* *Macbeth* *Othello*

FIGURE 7.4. The class *Book* creating *Book* objects.

Each *Book* object *(Hamlet, Macbeth,* and *Othello)* contains the same object methods, **Report-Status**, **Check-In**, and **Check-Out**, and the same attribute, **Status**. It is important to remember, however, that each object attribute does *not* necessarily contain the same value. Each object will have its own **Status** value depending on whether the book is checked out or not. Figure 7.5 describes the situation.

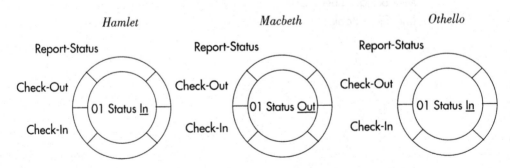

FIGURE 7.5. The *Book* objects and their **Status** values.

It is important to note that *Hamlet, Macbeth,* and *Othello* may each be invoked using the **Report-Status, Check-In,** and **Check-Out** methods. The following example invokes the **Check-Out** method for *Hamlet.*

Example: an Invoke statement for executing the Check-Out method for Hamlet.

Invoke Hamlet "Check-Out" End-Invoke.

Objects in Tables

When working with multiple objects, tables provide a useful organizational construct. Similar to tables in procedural COBOL, tables may be defined using the **Occurs** clause. Tables (also referred to as arrays) may be limited to objects of a given data type.

Format: a general form for defining an array of objects.

0x data-name   Occurs n Times Object Reference class-name.

where:

        0x is the level number (other than **01, 66, 77,** or **88**),
        data-name is the user-defined object identifier (object handle),
        Occurs is a required key word for defining an array,
        n is a literal integer greater than 0,
        Times is an optional key word,
        Object Reference is a required key phrase to declare a data type of
           object handle, and
        class-name is the type of object that will be created.

Example: an array of Book objects.

01 Book-Objects.
05 Book-Object   Occurs 500 Times Object Reference Book.

In the above example, **Book-Objects** declares the array **01** level, whereas **Book-Object,** at the **05** level, is the reference to an individual object in the array.

The rules regarding the **Occurs** clause are the same for declaring arrays of nonobject data elements. Tables may be indexed or subscripted and variable table lengths may be defined with the **Depending On** clause.

Example: the class Book defines a table of Book objects.

```
Class-Id. Book Inherits Base.
...
Factory.
Data Division.
Working-Storage Section.
01 Book-Objects.
  05 Book-Object      Occurs 500 Times
                      Object Reference Book.
01 Sub                Pic s9(04) Binary Value 0.
Method-Id. "Create-Objects-1".
Procedure Division.
    Add 1 to Sub.
    Invoke Book "New" Returning Book-Object (Sub) End-Invoke
    Exit Method.
End Method "Create-Objects-1".
End Factory.
<Object Definition>
End Class Book.
```

Objects and Identity

Storing groups of objects in arrays frees the programmer from having to assign unique names such as *Hamlet, Macbeth, Othello* to instances of a *Book* class. In such cases, an object attribute may be used to hold the title of the book. The following object accessor method, **Set-Title,** assigns a title to a *Book* object.

Example: an object method to store the book title in the object.

```
Object.
Data Division.
Working-Storage Section.
01 Status           Pic X(03).
01 Title-of-Book    Pic X(60).
< Method Report-Status would be defined here >
< Method Check-Out would be defined here >
```

```
< Method Check-In would be defined here >
Method-Id. "Set-Title".
Data Division.
Linkage Section.
01 In-Title              Pic X(60).
Procedure Division Using In-Title.
   Move In-Title to Title-of-Book.
   Exit Method.
End Method "Set-Title".
End Object.
```

Assign-Title stores the book's title in the object's **Data Division**. The temporary data item, In-Title, is defined in the method's **Linkage Section**.

In the following example, the class *Book* reads a file with book titles and creates a table of objects with the title from the file stored as an object attribute.

Example: class Book creates a table of Book objects.

```
Class-Id. Book Inherits Base.
...
Factory.
Input-Output Section.
File-Control.  Select Book-File Assign to "BookFile"
               Organization is Sequential
               Access is Sequential.
Data Division.
File Section.
FD Book-File Contains 60 characters.
01 Book-Title-Record       Pic x(60).
Working-Storage Section.
01 Book-Objects.
  05 Book-Object            Occurs 500 Times
                            Object Reference Book.
01 Book-Title              Pic x(60).
01 Sub                     Pic s9(04) Binary Value 0.
01 Eof-On                  Pic x(01) Value spaces.
Method-Id. "Read-File-1".
```

```
Procedure Division.
    Open Input Book-File.
    Perform Until Eof-On = "Y"
        Read Book-File Into Book-Title
            At End Move "Y" to Eof-On
            Not At End
                Invoke Book "Create-Objects-1" End-Invoke
                Invoke Book-Object (Sub) "Assign-Title" Using Book-Title
                End-Invoke
        End-Read
    End-Perform.
    Exit Method.
End Method "Read-File-1".
*>
Method-Id. "Create-Objects-1".
Procedure Division.
    Add 1 to Sub.
    Invoke Book "New" Returning Book-Object (Sub) End-Invoke
    Exit Method.
End Method "Create-Objects-1".
End Factory.
<Object Methods>
Assign-Title method defined here
End Class Book.
```

Figure 7.6 shows the class *Book* reading the **Book-Title** file, creating objects, and storing the book's title in the object.

Although tables may be used to hold many objects, *collection classes* are the preferred way to maintain and manipulate groups of objects. Collection classes provide a much more powerful and flexible structure for working with objects and will be covered in Chapter 9.

Untyped Objects

Object handles may either by typed or untyped. Typing is a way to control how objects are used but, at times, typing may be too restrictive. The type of object that can be

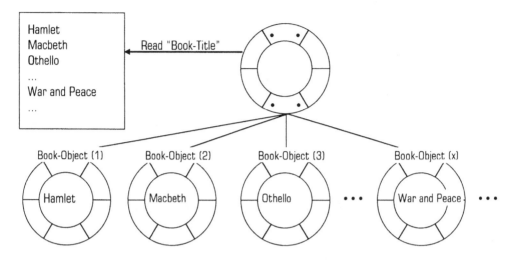

FIGURE 7.6. The class *Book* reads a **Book-Title** file, creates objects, and stores the titles.

referenced by an object-handle is determined by the class-name parameter specified in the **Usage** clause.

Format: a general format for defining an object identifier.

> **0x data-name   Usage Is Object Reference [class-name].**

where:

> **class-name** is an optionally included type (a class).

Note that **class-name** is an optional parameter. An object reference may be declared without specifying a class. The untyped object handle given below is capable of holding an object of any type. Here is the syntax.

> **01 anObject   Object Reference.**

An object handle without the restriction of a type (class name) may be used in an **Invoke "New"** statement, creating an untyped object. The code below gives an example.

Example: creating an untyped object.

> Class-Id. Book Inherits Base.
>
>   ...

```
Factory.
Data Division.
Working-Storage Section.
01 anObject          Object Reference.
Method-Id. "Create-Untyped-Object".
Procedure Division.
    Invoke Book "New" Returning anObject End-Invoke.
    Exit Method.
End Method "Create-Untyped-Object".
```

An untyped object such as *anObject* can hold objects of type *Book, Rare-Book, Video, Audio,* or any other type. Untyped objects effectively bypass *conformance checking.* With untyped objects, it is the programmer's responsibility to make certain the object is used correctly. Untyped objects, when used incorrectly, produce run time errors. Typed objects, when used incorrectly, may cause compile time errors.

CREATING OBJECTS WITH RESTRICTIONS

The **Usage** clause may also include the optional key word **Only**. When **Only** is specified the handle may only hold objects of the declared type. Here is the format.

Format: a general format for defining an object identifier.

```
0x data-name     Usage Is Object Reference class-name [Only].
```

where:

> **Only** is an optional key word that restricts the type of object a handle may hold to the declared type (class-name).

Example: an object handle is restricted to holding only objects of type Book.

```
01 Book-Object     Object Reference Book Only.
```

Other Techniques for Creating Objects

In previous examples we have seen how objects may be created by invoking a class method (i.e., **Create-Object**) from within the same class that defines the object. The following code offers an illustration of this.

Example: creating an object from within the defining class.

Class-Id. Book Inherits Base.
...
Factory.
Data Division.
Working-Storage Section.
01 anObject   Object Reference.
Method-Id. "Create-Object".
Procedure Division.
    Invoke Book "New" Returning anObject End-Invoke.
    Exit Method.
End Method "Create-Object".
Object.
<object to be created>
<object data>
<object methods (Report-Status, Check-In, Check-Out)>
End Object.
End Class Book.

The above **Create-Object** method then could be invoked by the following *Driver* program.

Example: Driver invokes Create-Object.

Program-Id. Driver.
...
Procedure Division.
    Invoke Book "Create-Object" End-Invoke.
End Program Driver.

Other techniques are available for object creation that permit more flexibility. One way is to allow other programs to create the object. Recall that procedural programs may use many of the Object-Oriented COBOL constructs. By declaring an object handle in a procedural program, the program itself can create *anObject* by sending a **New** message to a class. The following is an example of this.

Example: Driver creates anObject.

Program-Id. Driver.

...

Data Division.
Working-Storage Section.
01 anObject   Object Reference Book.
Procedure Division.

Invoke Book "New" Returning anObject End-Invoke.

...

End Program Driver.

The *Driver* program may now **invoke** the object methods of anObject. The following shows an example.

Example: Driver invokes the Report-Status method of anObject.

Program-Id. Driver.

...

Data Division.
Working-Storage Section.
01 anObject   Object Reference Book.
01 Status   Pic X(03).
Procedure Division.
   Invoke Book "New" Returning anObject End-Invoke.
   Invoke anObject "Report-Status" Returning Status End-Invoke.

...

End Program Driver.

The *Driver* program creates anObject by using the class *Book's* inherited **New** method. Here is a listing of the class *Book*.

Example: the class Book.

Class-Id. Book Inherits Base.

...

Factory.
Object.
Data Division.

```
Working-Storage Section.
01 Status              Pic X(03).
01 Title-of-Book       Pic X(60).
< Method Report-Status is defined here >
< Method Check-Out is defined here >
< Method Check-In is defined here >
< Method Set-Title is defined here >
End Object.
End Class Book.
```

In the above example, note that the class *Book* does not have a method **New** defined, yet the program sends the message **New** to *Book* to create an object instance. This is possible because **New** is available in the superclass of *Book* (the class **Base**) because methods defined in the superclass are considered to be methods of the subclass. Figure 7.7 illustrates how the method **New** may be considered to be a method in the factory object of *Book*.

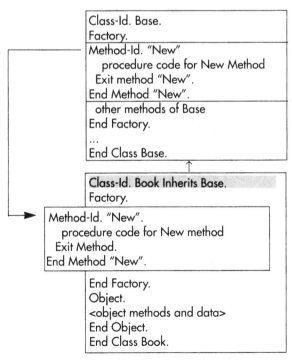

FIGURE 7.7. Class *Book* inherits **New** from **Base**.

The *Book* class need not declare a **Factory** paragraph to inherit class methods from the **Base** class. The class *Book* only needs to declare the **Inherits Base** phrase or to be part of an inheritance chain that **inherits** from **Base**. Figure 7.8 illustrates how the **New** method is available to all of the subclasses in an inheritance chain that originates from **Base**.

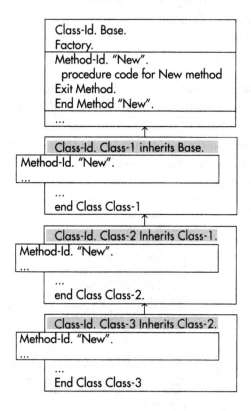

FIGURE 7.8. Method **New** available to subclasses in an inheritance chain.

Creating Objects with Self

The predefined object identifier **Self** may be used to create object instances. Earlier we showed how **Self** references the object that encapsulates a method. Figure 7.9 shows how **Self** is useful in allowing one method to call another method within the same object.

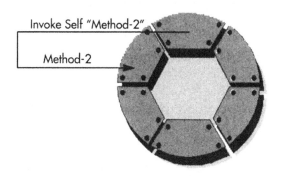

Invoke Self "Method-2"

Method-2

FIGURE 7.9. Self allows method interaction within an object.

Self may also be used as the identifier when creating object instances.

Example: using Self to create objects.

Invoke Self "New" Returning anObject.

Here is an example in the context of the class *Book*.

Example: the class Book creates anObject.

```
Class-Id. Book Inherits Base.
...
Factory.
Data Division.
Working-Storage Section.
01 anObject         Object Reference Book.
Method-Id. "Create-Object".
Procedure Division.
   Invoke Self "New" Returning anObject End-Invoke.
 Exit Method.
End Method "Create-Object".
End Factory.
Object.
```

```
< Method Report-Status is defined here >
< Method Check-Out is defined here >
< Method Check-In is defined here >
< Method Set-Title is defined here >
End Object.
End Class Book.
```

The Predefined Object Identifier Super

Super is a predefined object identifier that references the superclass of the currently executing object. **Self** and **Super** are generic forms for selecting methods for execution. With **Self** the search for the correct method to execute begins with the currently executing object. With **Super** the search for the correct method begins with the object's superclass. Figure 7.10 illustrates the invocation of the method **Create-Object** by the class *Rare-Book*, showing how the search begins in a different place when designating either **Self** or **Super**.

The following is a listing of the class *Book* using the identifier **Super**.

Example: the predefined object identifier Super.

Class-Id. Book Inherits Base.

```
...
Factory.
Data Division.
Working-Storage Section.
```

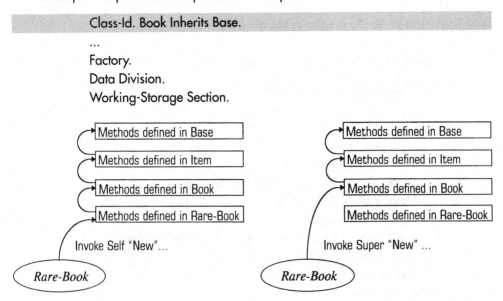

FIGURE 7.10. Invocation of **Create-Object** by the class *Rare-Book*.

```
01 anObject              Object Reference Book.
Method-Id. "Create-Object".
Procedure Division.
     Invoke Super "New" Returning anObject End-Invoke.
Exit Method.
End Method "Create-Object".
```

The use of **Super** means that any methods defined as part of the currently executing object will be ignored. In the above example, if a *Book* method **New** was declared it would be ignored and the method **New** defined in **Base** would instead be executed.

Super, rather than **Self,** is the preferred object identifier to use when invoking the **New** method from within a class method. This avoids recursive iteration when a **New** method has been defined within the subclass.

Self As a Class Name

In addition to using **Self** as the identifier in an **Invoke** statement, **Self** may be used as the class identifier in the **Usage** phrase of an object declaration.

Format: a general format for defining an object identifier.

```
0x data-name      Usage Is Object Reference [class-name].
```

where:

        class-name may specified as the identifier **Self** (only allowed in a class method).

Here is an example.

Example: specifying Self in an object declaration.

```
01 anObject      Object Reference Self.
```

Destroying Objects

The Object-Oriented COBOL standard does not currently specify a method for deleting objects. Explicit object deletion by destructor methods is an important topic, however. Because explicit object destruction may be specified in the final version of the language, we introduce the topic here by focusing on the approach to object deletion taken by Micro Focus.

The Micro Focus method for deleting objects is called **Finalize** and is inherited from the Class Library by specifying the **Inherits Base** phrase in the **Class-Id** paragraph. The following is the syntax for the **Finalize** method.

Format: a general format for destroying an object.

Invoke identifier-1 "Finalize" Returning nullObject End-Invoke.

where:

> identifier-1 is the object to be deleted (identified by its handle),
> **Finalize** is the method name, and
> nullObject is a user-defined object **set** to the **null** value.

The semantics of the **Set** statement have been extended and may be used to assign values to an object reference. **Null** is a predefined object identifier that always references the **Null** object. Here is the format for the **Set** statement used to assign an object reference of **Null**.

Format: a general format for using the set statement with objects.

Set object-identifier-1 To object-identifier2

where:

> object-identifier-1 is a usage object reference and
> object-identifier-2 is either a usage object reference or a predefined
>   object identifier (i.e., **Self, Null**).

Example: setting an object reference to Null.

Set anObject To Null

Setting an object to **Null** is analogous to moving **low-values** to a numeric item.

The following is an example of first creating and then deleting an object.

```
Class-Id. Book Inherits Base.
...
Factory.
Working-Storage Section.
01 Macbeth          Object Reference Book.
01 nullObject       Object Reference Book.
Method-Id. "Create-and-Destroy-Objects".
Procedure Division.
    Invoke Book "New" Returning Macbeth End-Invoke.
    set nullObject to null.
    Invoke Macbeth "Finalize" Returning nullObject End-Invoke.
    Exit Method.
End Method "Create-and-Destroy-Objects".
Object.
<Object Definition.>
End Class Book.
```

Persistent Objects

The objects we have been creating cease to exist at the conclusion of the application if they have not been explicitly destroyed. *Persistent objects* may exist before, during, and after the execution of an application, however.

An object becomes persistent by being "registered" or "named" (registered and named are synonymous) with the System-Object. System-Object is a predefined class (factory object) that provides methods to register the name of objects. System-Object provides methods in the same way the class Base provides methods that support the essential functionality required for working with objects. Here is an outline of the System-Object class.

```
Format: methods provided by the class System-Object.

    Class-Id. System-Object.
    Factory.
    Procedure Division.
    Method-Id. "Assign-Name".
    Method-Id. "Retrieve-Object" Invariant.
```

> Method-Id. "Remove-Name".
> End Factory.
> End Class System-Object.

There are no object methods associated with the **System-Object**. The two methods of interest for creating and destroying persistent objects are **Assign-Name** and **Remove-Name**.

The following is the format for registering an object name with the **System-Object**.

Format: a general format for making an object persistent.

> Invoke identifier-1 "Assign-Name" Using By Content data-name-1 By
> Reference object-identifier-1
> Returning name-flag
> End-Invoke.

where:

> identifier-1 is the **System-Object**,
> data-name-1 is a literal or a data-name containing a literal (maximum of 31 characters),
> **Assign-Name** is the method name,
> object-identifier-1 is the data-name defined as object reference, and
> name-flag is user-defined **88-level** condition.

Here is an example.

Example: making an object persistent.

> Invoke System-Object "Assign-Name" Using By Content "Book-1" By
> Reference anObject
> Returning name-flag
> End-Invoke.

Here is the same operation in the context of the class *Book*.

Example: an object contains the handle to another object.

```
Class-Id. Book.
...
Factory.
Data Division.
Working-Storage Section.
01 anObject    Object Reference Book.
01 name-flag              Pic X.
   88 name-flag-ok        Value "0".
   88 name-duplicate      Value "d".
   88 name-fail           Value "9".
Method-Id. "Create-Object".
Procedure Division.
    Invoke Book "New" Returning anObject
    Perform Self "Name-Object".
    Exit Method.
End Method "Create-Object".
*>
Method-Id. "Name-Object".
Procedure Division.
    Invoke System-Object "Assign-Name" Using "Book-1" anObject
        Returning name-flag
    End-Invoke.
    When name-flag-ok
        continue

        ...
    Exit Method.
End-Method "Name-Object".
End Factory.
End Class Book.
```

A named object is a persistent object. The name of a persistent object should be removed from the **System-Object** before it is destroyed. The **Remove-Name** method dissociates a previously named object from the **System-Object**. Here is the format.

Format: a general format for removing a persistent object from the System-Object.

Invoke <u>identifier-1</u> "<u>Remove-Name</u>" Using <u>data-name-1</u> End-Invoke.

where:

identifier-1 is the System-Object,
Remove-Name is the method name, and
data-name-1 is a literal or a data-name containing a literal (maximum
    of 31 characters).

Here is an example.

Example: removing an object's persistence.

Invoke System-Object "Remove-Name" Using "Book-1" End-Invoke.

An object that is no longer registered with the System-Object may be finalized in order to remove it from the system, or it may be automatically removed by the automatic garbage collector.

Although some kind of file-storage format for persistent objects seems natural, ANSI has given wide latitude to Object-Oriented COBOL vendors in implementing persistent objects. A vendor's implementation of the System-Object, and its ability to track objects across multiple run units and multiple users, will determine the practicability and usefulness of persistent objects.

Creating Static Objects

Object instances may be referenced in two ways. The first, which we have seen, is to define an object handle that refers to an object instance created by sending the message New to the factory object. The second is to declare an object directly, much like a conventional COBOL data item. Objects created this way are called static objects.

Static objects must reference a Simple class. A Simple class is defined with the new, reserved word Simple.

Format: the format for declaring a Simple class.

Class-Id. class-name-1 Simple.

where:

Simple is a reserved word attribute for use in the Class-Id paragraph.

The following is an example.

Example: declaring a Simple class, called Class-1.

Class-Id. Class-1 Simple.

Object instances of a **Simple** class are declared by omitting the reserved word **Reference** in the **Usage** clause of an object declaration.

Format: the format for declaring a static object.

0x data-name   Usage Is <u>Object</u> <u>class-name</u>.

where:
Object is a required key word to declare a static object, and
class-name is a Simple class.

Here is an example of declaring a static object using the previously defined **Simple** class Class-1.

Example: declaring a static object of type Class-1.

01 aStaticObject   Object Class-1.

A static object is found as part of a larger data structure and allocated by its declaration, *not* by invoking the method **New**. As an example, consider class, *Class-2*, which declares **aStaticObject** in its class **Data Division**.

Example: Class-2 declares aStaticObject.

Class-Id. Class-2.
Factory.
Data Division.
Working-Storage Section.

01 aStaticObject   Object Class-1.

...
End Factory.

Space is allocated in the class **Data Division** of *Class-2* for the data items defined in the **Object** paragraph of *Class-1*. A static object is, in a very limited sense, similar to a copylib although the data items in *Class-1* are encapsulated, and static objects, as we will see in Chapter 8, provide us with a strategic bridge to much more powerful possibilities.

A static object may be declared in a program, in class data, in object data, or in method data. A static object's life span is dependent on the life span of the declaring data structure. If a static object is declared in the **Data Division** of an object, the data items and values of the static object are allocated when the object that contains the static object is created, and the static object is destroyed when the object instance is destroyed.

The same is true for method data. Method data is discarded at the conclusion of a method's execution. Any static object declared within the **Data Division** of a method is created when the method begins execution and is automatically destroyed when the method terminates.

Because a static object is *not* declared as an **Object Reference**, it is not a handle to an object, but a direct reference to the object itself. Static objects bear a strong resemblance to conventional data declarations and as such serve a useful role in the transition from legacy systems to objects.

RESPONSIBILITY-DRIVEN DESIGN AND CREATING OBJECTS

One of the important issues in responsibility-driven design is assigning responsibility for object creation. Although objects are created by sending the message **New** to the class (factory), some program component, either an object instance, a driver program, or a class factory object, must assume responsibility for actually invoking the **New** message

Creating with Factory Objects

The following set of examples illustrates assigning responsibility to *Class-2* for the creation of instances of *Class-1*. First, *Class-1* inherits (directly or indirectly) from the **Base** class in order to have access to the method **New**.

Example: Class-1 inherits Base.

Class-Id. Class-1 Inherits Base.

...

Object.
Data Division.
Working-Storage Section.

...

<Object methods defined>
End Object.
End Class Class-1.

With the above definition, objects of type *Class-1* may be created and *Class-1* may be said to have fulfilled its responsibility by inheriting **New** from **Base**.

One of the questions CRC sessions and responsibility-driven design attempts to answer is which class should be responsible for invoking the constructor method (**New**) of *Class-1*. Figure 7.11 shows a CRC card giving *Class-2* the responsibility for creating instances of *Class-1*.

Class: Book	
(Responsibilities)	(Collaborators)
create instances of Class-1	Class-1
report title	
...	

Figure 7.11. CRC card giving *Class-2* the responsibility of creating instances of *Class-1*.

The CRC card specifies that *Class-2* has responsibility for creating instance objects of *Class-1* by collaborating with *Class-1*. The following is brief listing of the factory definition of *Class-2*.

Example: Class-2 creates an instance of Class-1.

```
Class-Id. Class-2
Factory.

...
01 aClass-1Object        Object reference Class-1.
Method-Id. "Create-Class-1-Object".
Procedure Division.
        Invoke Class-1 "New" Returning aClass-1Object.

...
End Factory.
Object.
Data Division.
Working-Storage Section.

...
<Object methods defined>
End Object.
End Class Class-2.
```

Creating with Object Instances

An object instance may also create other object instances. Before creating other instances, the first object must be created. The following example illustrates the creation of an object instance of *Class-1* by an object instance of *Class-2*.

Example: an instance of Class-2 creates an instance of Class-1.

```
Class-Id. Class-2.
Factory.

...
01 aClass-2Object        Object Reference Class-2.
Method-Id. "Create-Class-2-Object".
Procedure Division.
        Invoke Self "New" Returning aClass-2Object.
        Invoke aClass-2Object "Create-Class-1-Object".

...
End Factory.
```

```
Object.
...
01 aClass-1Object        Object Reference Class-1.
Method-Id. "Create-Class-1-Object".
Procedure Division.
        Invoke Class-1 "New" Returning aClass-1Object.
...
End Object.
End Class Class-2.
```

Constructor Methods

All concrete classes, which are classes designed for object-instance creation, must have access to the method **New** for class construction. Abstract classes do not need constructor methods because they are not intended to have object instances, only to provide a foundation for other subclasses.

A class automatically has access to the method **New** when it inherits from the class **Base**. It is useful for a class to define its own method **New** in order to handle initialization of its object instances, however. When a class defines its own method **New**, it must still invoke the method **New** in the class **Base** to actually create an object instance. Here is an example.

Example: Class-1 explicitly defines a constructor method called New.

```
Class-Id. Class-1 Inherits Base.
...
Factory.
Method-Id. "New".
Data Division.
Linkage Section
01 anObject           Object Reference Self.
Procedure Division Returning anObject.
      Invoke Super "New" Returning anObject.
<do some initialization on anObject >

End Method "New".
...
```

```
End Factory.
Object.
<Object methods defined>
End Object.
End Class Class-1.
```

Diagramming Object Creation

The Unified Method uses a dashed arrow to symbolize object creation. The dashed arrow points from the object to the creating entity. Object creation may be diagrammed showing either a class factory object or an object instance responsible for creating an object (see below). The following code illustrates *Class-1* creating an instance of *Book*.

Example: Class-1 creates an instance of Book.

```
Class-Id. Class-1
Factory.

...
01 anObject        Object Reference Book.
Method-Id. "Create-Book-Object".
Procedure Division.
    Invoke Book "New" Returning anObject.

...
End Factory.
Object.
<Object methods defined>
End Object.
End Class Class-1.
```

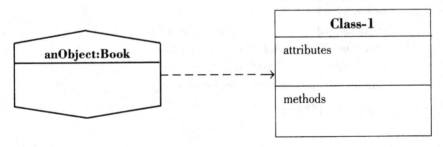

The following is the code and a diagram of an object of *Class-1* creating an instance of *Book*.

Example: a Class-1 object creates an instance of Book.

```
Class-Id. Class-1.
Factory.

...
01 class-1-Object          Object Reference Class-1.
Method-Id. "Create-Class-1-Object".
Procedure Division.
    Invoke Self "New" Returning class-1-Object.
    Invoke class-1-Object "Create-Book-Object".

...
End Factory.
Object.

...
01 anObject                Object reference Book.
Method-Id. "Create-Book-Object".
Procedure Division.
    Invoke Book "New" Returning anObject.

...
End Object.
End Class Class-1.
```

Key Points

- Objects are created by invoking the **New** method.

- Persistent objects can exist independent of an application's life span.

- Objects may be deleted automatically by the Object-Oriented COBOL garbage collector or manually by the programmer issuing the **Finalize** message.

- Abstract classes exist to provide common functionality to inheriting subclasses.

- Objects may be typed by declaring a class-name in the **Usage** phrase.

- Objects may provide accessor methods to provide information about the state of an object or to allow the object's state (variables) to be changed.

- The predefined object identifier **Self** may be used in place of a class-name in an **Invoke** statement and in an object handle declaration **Using** phrase.

- The predefined object identifier Super is in some ways a restricted form of **Self**.

- Conformance is a relationship between a class (and objects of that class) and an interface.

- Untyped objects may be created by excluding a type (class-name) in the **Using** phrase of an object handle's declaration.

- The **Set** statement may be used to assign the object reference (object handle) of one object to another.

- Object handles may be restricted to holding only objects of a given type by specifying the key word **Only** in the **Using** phrase.

Suggested Readings

Belcher, K. (1990). Object-Orientation: The COBOL Approach. *Object Magazine 1*(1).
Cattell, R. (1991). *Object Data Management: Object-Oriented and Extended Relational Database Systems.* Reading, MA: Addison-Wesley.
Graham, I. (1994). *Object-Oriented Methods*, 2nd ed. Reading, MA: Addison-Welsey.
Mandrioli, D., & Meyer, B. (1992). *Advances in Object-Oriented Software Engineering.* Englewood Cliffs, NJ: Prentice Hall.

Review Questions

7.0   What is memory leakage and how does Object-Oriented COBOL deal with it?

7.1   Create an object called *aCar* by invoking the proper message.

7.2   What is conformance checking and what does it provide in an application?

7.3   How might one use object-oriented constructs in procedural COBOL programs?

7.4   What is a constructor method and what is an accessor method? Give examples of both.

7.5   First create and then invoke a method called "**Report-Model**" for a table of objects of type *Vehicle*.

7.6   Create and invoke a method called "**Report-Job-Title**" for a table of untyped objects.

7.7   Describe how one might use the object identifier **Super**.

7.8   True or false—objects are invoked on methods.

7.9   What is one way in which a programmer might destroy an object? Give an example.

7.10   Implement a method that creates an unreachable object.

7.11   What is one purpose of the **System-Object**?

7.12   Implement a static object.

CHAPTER 8

WORKING WITH OBJECTS

The stored-program concept, developed by John von Neumann and others in 1945, marked the beginning of the "age of software." Storing instructions along with data opened up the world of computer programming, eliminating the need for thousands of manual switch settings and board wirings.

"Software," a term coined by Ashler Opler of the Computer Usage Company in the late 1950s, reflected the development medium (paper) and storage devices (tape and punched cards) in stark contrast to the "hard" physical characteristics of the machine.

Today, strands of wire have been replaced with strands of code that bind a computer more tightly than any wire ever invented. Programs are long loping sequences of instructions, stitched together like needlepoint. Maintenance requires unraveling threads of computation; a faulty pull on any one thread, and the program logic puckers in unforeseen ways. Objects hold the promise of breaking with the immediate past, returning the "soft" to "ware," and proving Mr. Opler correct once again.

FOCUS AND FORMAT OF THIS CHAPTER

This chapter continues the discussion of the scope of object data, a topic that is often troublesome to COBOL programmers. In addition, the various techniques for declaring object types are examined, and several constructs that simplify working with objects are presented.

- Reserved Words
  Property
  Set
  Simple

- Concepts
  In-line Invocation
  Invocation operator
  Property of Object
  Property reference
  Static objects

THE SCOPE OF VARIABLES

In procedural COBOL programs, all **Data Division** variables are visible to all **Procedure Division** operations. Because of this global visibility of data, the concept of *scope of variables* may be new to many programmers. In Object-Oriented COBOL data that is declared as part of an object is only visible to the methods of that object.

In the following example, the local variable **Counter** is defined as object data. As a result, all instances of class *Item* will have memory allocated for **Counter**. The method **Running-Count** is defined as an object method, meaning each instance of *Item* will be assigned its own **Counter** variable.

Example: the class Item defines an object method called Running-Count and an object variable Counter.

    Class-Id. Item Inherits Base.

    ...

    Factory.

```
...
End Factory.
*>
Object.
Data Division.
Working-Storage Section.
01 Counter              Pic 9(02) Value 0.
Method-Id. "Running-Count".
Linkage Section.
01 LS-Counter           Pic 9(02).
Procedure Division Returning LS-Counter.
    Add 1 to Counter
    Move Counter to LS-Counter.
    Exit Method.
End Method "Running-Count".
End Object.
End Class Item.
```

If both class *Book* and class *Rare-Book* inherit from *Item*, their instance objects will also inherit the Running-Count method and the variable Counter. For example, the instance objects *aBookObject1* of class *Book* and *aRareBookObject1* of class *Rare-Book*, shown in Figure 8.1, both support the method Running-Count.

Example: aBookObject1 invokes Running-Count.

```
Invoke aBookObject1 "Running-Count" Returning ...
```

Example: aRareBookObject1 invokes Running-Count.

```
Invoke aRareBookObject1 "Running-Count" Returning ...
```

Each object, *aBookObject1* and *aRareBookObject1*, will have its own unique Counter variable, as illustrated in Figure 8.1.

Even though the object instances *aBookObject1* and *aRareBookObject1* inherit the variable Counter from class *Item*, they cannot, through their own methods, access the variable Counter. Rather, they must use a method inherited from *Item* (in this example Running-Count). This encapsulation between superclasses and subclasses

aBookObject1   aRareBookObject1

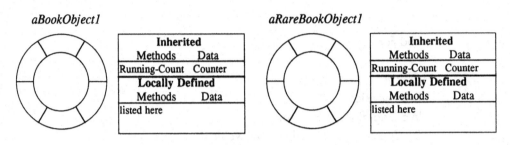

FIGURE 8.1. Objects with their unique Counter variables.

forces instances of the subclass to use the superclass interface to access superclass data, thereby fully encapsulating object data.

The following is a listing for class *Book* that defines a method called Book-Count. Notice that because *Book* inherits from *Item,* it inherits the method Running-Count, which allows the object instance *aBookObject1* to send itself the Running-Count message.

> Example: the class Book inherits Running-Count from Item.

>> Class-Id. Book Inherits Item.
>>
>> ...
>>
>> Factory.
>> Method-Id. "New".
>> Data Division.
>> Working-Storage Section.
>> 01 aBookObject1   Object Reference.
>> Procedure Division.
>>   Invoke Super "New" Returning aBookObject1.
>>   Invoke aBookObject1 "Book-Count".
>>   Exit Method.
>> End Method "New".
>> End Factory.
>> *>
>> Object.
>> Data Division.

```
Working-Storage Section.
01 Book-Counter        Pic 9(02) Value 0.
01 Running-Counter     Pic 9(02) Value 0.
Method-Id. "Book-Count".
Procedure Division.
    Add 1 to Book-Counter
    Invoke Self "Running-Count" Returning Running-Counter.
    Exit Method.
End Method "Book-Count".
End Object.
End Class Book.
```

The statement

```
Invoke Self "Running-Count" Returning Running-Counter.
```

in the **Object** paragraph allows *aBookObject1* indirect access to the variable **Counter**. The access is indirect because it must utilize the inherited method **Running-Count**, rather than directly access **Counter**. An error will occur if the **Book-Count** method attempts to use the variable **Counter**.

When a second Book object, *aBookObject2*, is created, it has its own local copy (and value) of **Counter**. The following listing shows the creation of *aBookObject1* and *aBookObject2*, showing the value of **Counter** associated with each object instance. In this example, the factory object invokes the method **Running-Count**.

Example: the class Item creates two Book objects and invokes the Running-Count method.

```
Class-Id. Book Inherits Item.
...
Factory.
Method-Id. "New".
Data Division.
Working-Storage Section.
01 aBookObject1     Object Reference.
01 aBookObject2     Object Reference.
```

```
01 Count-1          Pic 9(02).
01 Count-2          Pic 9(02).
Procedure Division.
    Invoke Super "New" Returning aBookObject1.
    Invoke aBookObject1 "Running-Count" Returning Count-1.
    Invoke Super "New" Returning aBookObject2.
    Invoke aBookObject2 "Running-Count" Returning Count-2.
  Exit Method.
  End Method "New".
  End Factory.
  *>
  Object.
  Data Division.
  Working-Storage Section.
  01 Book-Counter      Pic 9(02) Value 0.
  01 Running-Counter   Pic 9(02) Value 0.
  Method-Id. "Book-Count".
  Procedure Division.
     Add 1 to Book-Counter
   Exit Method.
   End Method "Book-Count".
   End Object.
   End Class Book.
```

Figure 8.2 gives the values of **Counter** for each *Book* object.

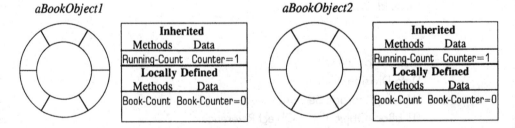

FIGURE 8.2. The values of **Counter** for each *Book* object.

The following is a listing in which *aBookObject2* invokes Running-Count twice and *aBookObject1* only invokes the method once.

Example: the class Item creates two Book objects and invokes the Running-Count method.

```
Class-Id. Book Inherits Item.
...
Factory.
Method-Id. "New".
Data Division.
Working-Storage Section.
01 aBookObject1      Object Reference.
01 aBookObject2      Object Reference.
01 Count-1           Pic 9(02).
01 Count-2           Pic 9(02).
Procedure Division.
    Invoke Super "New" Returning aBookObject1.
    Invoke aBookObject1 "Running-Count" Returning Count-1.
    Invoke Super "New" Returning aBookObject2.
    Invoke aBookObject2 "Running-Count" Returning Count-2.
    Invoke aBookObject2 "Running-Count" Returning Count-2.
    Exit Method.
End Method "New".
End Factory.
*>
Object.
<"Book-Count" defined here>.
End Object.
End Class Book.
```

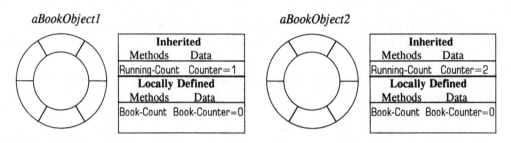

FIGURE 8.3. The value of Counter associated with each *Book* object.

In the above example, the value of Count is returned to the variables Count-1 and Count-2. The value of Counter, associated with each *Book* object, is indicated in Figure 8.3.

OBJECT-RELATION CONDITIONS

Objects may only be compared for equality and inequality. The syntax follows.

Format: object relation conditions (1) equality (2) inequality.

(1). object-identifier-1 Is = To object-identifier-2

(2). object-identifier-1 Is Not = To object-identifier-2

where:

object-identifier-1 is an object identifier (in which object identifier is a user-defined data item of Usage Object Reference or one of the predefined object identifiers and the Null object may not be compared to itself),

Is is an optional reserved word,

Not is an optional word to test for inequality,

= is the relation condition for equality (may also be written in long form "equal"),

To is an optional reserved word, and

object-identifier-2 is an object identifier.

The condition has a true value if and only if object-identifier-1 is the same object as object-identifier-2. Here are two examples.

Example: an object relation condition test for equality.

> If anObject = anotherObject

Example: an object relation condition test for inequality.

> If anObject Not = anotherObject

Do not confuse the **object-identifier** for the data name of the **object-identifier**. Two **objects-identifiers** are *not* equal even though they may have the same data name. The following offers an example.

Example: two objects that have the same data name (anObject) but are not equal.

Class-Id. Class-1 Inherits Base.	Class-Id. Class-2 Inherits Base.
...	...
Factory.	Factory.
Data Division.	Data Division.
Working-Storage Section.	Working-Storage Section.
01 anObject Object Reference.	01 anObject Object Reference.
Method-Id. "Create-Object".	Method-Id. "Create-Object".
Procedure Division.	Procedure Division.
Invoke Super "New" Returning anObject.	Invoke Super "New" Returning anObject.
...	...
End Class Class-1.	End Class Class-2.

CONFORMANCE

Objects may receive messages they do not understand. This occurs when a message (a method) is not supported by the receiving object. When a message is sent to an object, a search is made among all the methods defined in the object's class. If the method is not found at the level of the class, the search continues up the chain of superclasses. If the method cannot be found in the inheritance chain an error results.

Often, the cause of this error is that a programmer assumes that an object either defines or inherits a method when in fact it does not. To address this Object-Oriented COBOL provides a feature known as conformance, which, when used with typed objects, allows the compiler to check that certain objects will respond to certain messages (define or inherit certain methods).

For example, if class *Person* inherits from class *Mammal*, then one can expect instances of class *Person* to be able to respond to any messages defined for *Mammal*. The reason for this is inheritance, which makes all the methods of an inherited superclass available to instances of a subclass. The following is an illustration of this.

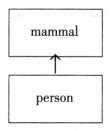

When a *person* class inherits from the *mammal* class, a *person* object is said to *conform* to the *mammal* interface. Therefore, any statement that expects an object of type *mammal* will work with an object of type *person*. Here is an example.

Invoke mammal "any-method-defined-in-mammal"

An object of type *person* may be substituted in the above **Invoke** statement as follows:

Invoke person "any-method-defined-in-mammal"

Because subclasses are considered *subtypes* of superclasses, a *person* object is considered a *subtype* of type *mammal*. Subtypes *conform* to the type of the superclass and may be used in place of the supertype.

Conformance and Polymorphism

Polymorphism allows different classes, unrelated by inheritance, to respond to the same message, provided they have implemented a method that corresponds to the message name. With inheritance, an object that is a subtype of another will always be able to respond to a message understood by its supertype. This is because inheritance is an all-or-nothing proposition. If a *person* object inherits from a *mammal* object, then any method defined in *mammal* is guaranteed to be inherited by *person*. A programmer cannot selectively exclude certain methods from inheritance by descendant classes.

With conformance, the compiler then makes certain assumptions about which methods are available to which objects. The result is an inheritance pyramid, which is wider at the bottom than at the top. The pyramid is wider at the bottom because descendant classes may implement their own methods. Figure 8.4 is based on three classes from our library application.

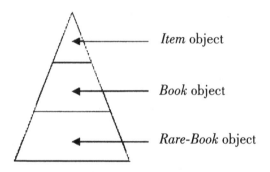

FIGURE 8.4. An inheritance pyramid.

Figure 8.5 shows the same picture inverted for convenience.

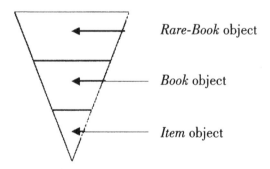

FIGURE 8.5. An inverted inheritance pyramid.

Object Handles and Conformance

Object handles may be declared with an associated class name as in the following:

| 01 Book-Object | Object-Reference Book. |
| 01 RareBook-Object | Object-Reference Rare-Book. |

The above declarations restrict the type of objects that may be held by the handles. Because of *conformance,* however, objects that are part of the inheritance hierarchy can also be referenced by the object handles. Thus, an object handle declared as **Object Reference Rare-Book** can hold objects of type *Rare-Book, Book,* and *Item.* This is because objects of type *Rare-Book* conform to the class interface of *Rare-Book, Book,* and *Item.* Figure 8.6 illustrates conformance in action.

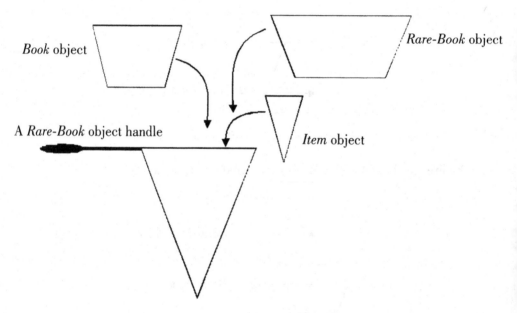

FIGURE 8.6. An example of conformance.

An object handle declared as **Object Reference Book** can hold objects of type *Book* and *Item,* but can *not* hold objects of type *Rare-Book,* as illustrated in Figure 8.7.

An object handle declared as **Object Reference Item** can only hold objects of type *Item.* It can *not* hold objects of type *Book* or *Rare-Book.* This is illustrated in Figure 8.8.

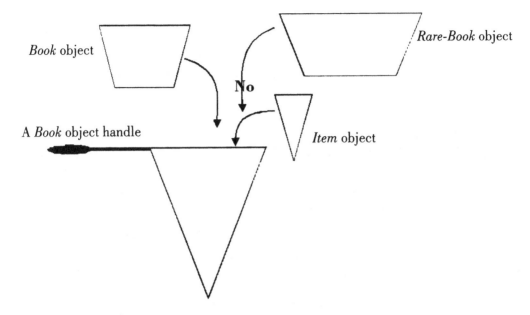

FIGURE 8.7. An object handle declared as Object Reference Book.

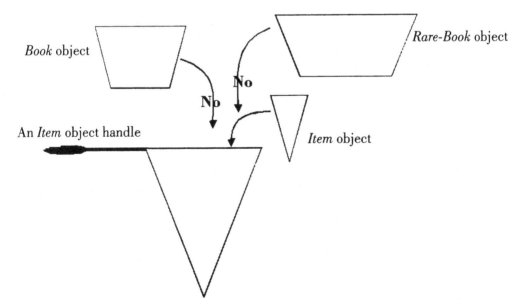

FIGURE 8.8. An object handle declared as Object Reference Item.

Conformance checking may be thought of as type checking applied to objects. Conformance ensures that an operation is valid before an operation is executed. Conformance is related to conventional arithmetic operations in which the compiler ensures that only numeric variables participate in numeric operations.

Typing and Binding

A data item declared as Pic 9(04) Binary may be considered a *subtype* of type Pic 9(04) Display in that it may be used in the same operations as Pic 9(04). Both are numbers. Binary is, however, a more efficient machine representation for certain operations. Adding a data item of type Binary and a data item of type Display is permitted.

Typing is a mechanism that attempts to ensure that the data items in operations are type consistent. Languages may be strongly typed (Pascal), weakly typed (the original C), or untyped (Smalltalk). Each has advantages and disadvantages. For example, a data item declared as Pic x(04) may contain a numeric value but is prevented from participating in numeric operations. A programmer is forced to either redefine the Pic x field, or move the variable to a Pic 9 field to perform addition.

Binding is a mechanism that binds a variable to a data type. Binding of data names to data types may occur at compile time, or at run time. When binding occurs at compile time the binding is called *static binding*. When the binding occurs at run time, the binding is called *dynamic binding*.

The concepts of typing and binding are orthogonal. A language may be implemented with varying degrees of typing and binding. Procedural COBOL is a strongly typed, statically bound language. OOCOBOL supports both weak and strong typing and static and dynamic binding for working with objects. Strong typing and static binding provide safety; untyped and dynamic binding provide flexibility.

Strongly Typed Object Handles

Object handles may be defined so that they reference only objects of a specific type; in effect this turns off conformance checking. This strong typing feature can be used by including the optional key word Only in the Usage clause. Only specifies that the handle may only hold objects of the declared type and may not hold conforming objects.

Example: an object handle is restricted to only holding objects of type Book.

01 Book-Object   Object Reference Book Only.

Figure 8.9 illustrates nonconformant strong typing.

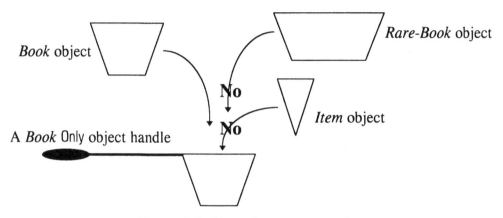

FIGURE 8.9. Nonconformant strong typing.

Untyped Objects

At times we do not want to restrict what types of objects an object handle can hold. An untyped object handle is declared as follows:

Example: an untyped object handle.

```
01 Object-1              Object Reference.
```

Figure 8.10 depicts an untyped object handle.

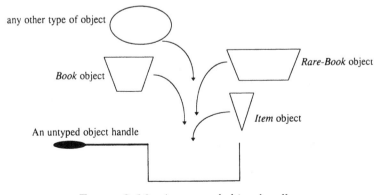

FIGURE 8.10. An untyped object handle.

Examples of Untyped Objects

An Invoke statement with parameters may pass data or objects. In Object-Oriented COBOL when passing objects, we pass an object handle, not the object itself. Often it is useful to declare parameters as untyped objects.

Consider a *Book* object with a data item of Status and two methods called Get-Status and Set-Status. Here is a listing of the code.

Example: the class Book defines an object data item and methods.

```
Class-Id. Book Inherits Base.
...
Factory.
Method-Id. "New".
Data Division.
Linkage Section.
01 aBookObject       Object Reference Self.
Procedure Division Returning aBookObject.
     Invoke Super "New" Returning aBookObject.
End Method "New".
End Factory.
*>
Object.
Data Division.
Working-Storage Section.
01 Status            Pic X(03).
Method-Id. "Get-Status".
Data Division.
Linkage Section.
01 Return-Status     Pic X(03).
Procedure Division Returning Return-Status.
  Move Status to Return-Status.
  Exit Method.
End Method "Get-Status".
*>
Method-Id. "Set-Status".
```

```
Data Division.
Linkage Section.
01 Return-Status      Pic X(03).
Procedure Division Using LS-Status.
    Move LS-Status to Status.
    Exit Method.
    End Method "Set-Status".
End Object.
```

Another class or program may invoke the *Book* class and create a *Book* object. Consider an inventory operation in which new books are checked into the library and their status is set to In. Another object, of class *Inventory,* is responsible for this operation. Here is a listing of the object methods and data of an *Inventory* object.

Example: an inventory object creates and manipulates Book objects.

```
Class-Id. Inventory.
...
*>
Object.
Data Division.
Working-Storage Section.
01 In-Status          Pic X(03) Value "In".
Method-Id. "Create-Manipulate-Book-Object".
Data Division.
Working-Storage Section.
01 anObject           Object Reference Book.
Procedure Division.
    Invoke Book "New" Returning anObject.
    Invoke anObject "Set-Status" Using In-Status.
    Exit Method.
End Method "Create-Manipulate-Book-Object".
*>
End Object.
End Class Inventory.
```

The **Create-Manipulate-Book-Object** method defines the object returned from invoking **New** on the class *Book* to be an object of type **Book**. Here is the line we are referring to.

> 01 anObject   Object Reference Book.

A declaration of type **Book** restricts this object handle (**anObject**) to only holding objects of type *Book* or subtypes of *Book*. The application may require the same operation to be performed on *Audio* and *Video* items. Currently implemented, the declaration prohibits **anObject** from holding objects of type *Audio* or *Video*.

To circumvent this limitation **anObject** may be declared as untyped. Declaring **anObject** as untyped provides the greatest flexibility while bypassing the safety of type checking.

Consider Figure 8.11: *Book* does not inherit from *Reorder*. An object handle defined as type *Book* would be unable to hold objects of type *Reorder*.

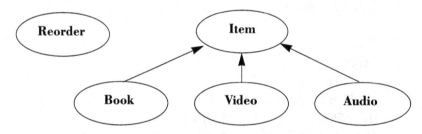

FIGURE 8.11. An object handle of type *Book* may not hold objects of type *Reorder*.

Suppose both *Item* and *Reorder* implement methods called **Get-Status** that return a **Pic X(03)** parameter. We would like to declare an object handle capable of holding a *Reorder* object, as well as any object that is a subtype of *Item (Book, Video, Audio)*.

Item subtypes understand the **Get-Status** message. *Reorder* objects also understand the **Get-Status** message. When the invoked object was a *Book* object the **Get-Status** method inherited from *Item* would be executed; when the invoked object was a *Reorder* object, the *Reorder* **Get-Status** method would execute. By declaring an untyped object, the class *Inventory* could process and **Invoke** *Book, Video, Audio,* and *Reorder* objects using the same statements. The following code is an example of this.

Example: an inventory object creates and manipulates Book and Reorder objects.

```
Class-Id. Inventory.
...
Object.
Method-Id. "Create-Manipulate-Object".
Data Division.
Working-Storage Section.
01 anObject          Object Reference.
Procedure Division.
   Evaluate True
      When <some condition>
         Invoke Book "New" Returning anObject
      When <some condition>
         Invoke Reorder "New" Returning anObject
   End-Evaluate.
   Invoke anObject "Get-Status" Using In-Status.
   Exit Method.
End Method "Create-Manipulate-Object".
...
End Class Inventory.
```

One technique for ensuring that only the correct methods are invoked on a given object is to use a variable to hold the method name. Consider that an object of type *Item* implements a method called Get-Status and a object of type *Reorder* implements a method called Put-Status. anObject is declared untyped so that it may hold *Book, Video, Audio,* and *Reorder* objects. At run time the correct method to Invoke is determined based on the object type. Here is an example of this.

Example: a variable used in the Invoke statement.

```
01 Method-Name      Pic X(10) Value Spaces.
01 anObject          Object Reference.
...
Procedure Division.
   Evaluate True
      When <a Book, Video, or Audio object>
```

```
        Move "Get-Status" to Method-Name
    When <a Reorder object>
        Move "Put-Status" to Method-Name
    End-Evaluate
    Invoke anObject Method-Name ...
```

We will discuss determining an object's type (class) later in the chapter.

The Set Statement

Object-Oriented COBOL has extended the semantics of the **Set** statement to include objects. One use of the **Set** statement is assigning the value of indexes as in the following:

```
    Set Index-1 to 5.
```

When two names are used in a **Set** statement, the receiving fields are named first. The following example sets **Index-2** to the value of **Index-1**.

```
    Set Index-2 to Index-1.
```

Similarly, object handles may be assigned using the **Set** statement as in the following:

```
    Set Object-2 to Object-1.
```

After the **Set** statement, **Object-2** refers to the same object as **Object-1**. **Object-1** is unaffected by the operation. **Object-1** and **Object-2** are equal and a condition test for equality (=) will be true.

The Set Statement and Conformance

There are rules to follow when using the **Set** statement for indexes and there are rules to follow when using the **Set** statement with objects. The rules of conformance must be followed when setting one object identifier (handle) to another.

Consider the hierarchy of *Item, Book,* and *Rare-Book.* Object handles of type *Rare-Book* may be **Set** to object handles of type *Book* and *Item.* Object handles of type *Book* may be **Set** to object handles of type *Item.* Object handles of type *Item* may *not* be **Set** to object handles of type *Book* or *Rare-Book,* however. Stated another way, object types lower in the inheritance chain may be **Set** to object types higher in the inheritance chain (hierarchy). An example of this is shown in Figure 8.12.

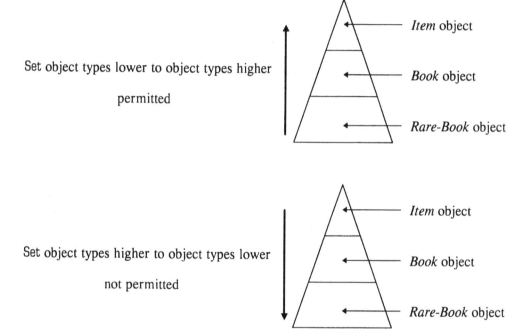

FIGURE 8.12. Object types may be **Set** only to object types higher in the inheritance chain.

Here are some examples.

Example: an object type lower in the hierarchy is Set to an object type higher in the hierarchy. Permitted

```
01 aRareBookObject      Object Reference Rare-Book.
01 aBookObject          Object Reference Book.
```

Set aRareBookObject to aBookObject

Example: an object type lower in the hierarchy is Set to an object type higher in the hierarchy. Permitted

01 aRareBookObject   Object Reference Rare-Book.
01 anItemObject   Object Reference Item.

Set aRareBookObject to anItemObject

This next example will cause an error during compilation.

Example: an object type higher in the hierarchy is Set to an object type lower in the hierarchy. Not permitted

01 aRareBookObject   Object Reference Rare-Book.
01 anItemObject   Object Reference Item.

Set anItemObject to aRareBookObject	will cause an error

The reason for this restriction is simple. Because inheritance guarantees that descendant objects will contain the methods defined in ascendant classes, an object lower in the hierarchy will always be able to invoke methods defined higher in the hierarchy. For example, if *Item* defines a **Get-Status** method, objects of type *Book* and *Rare-Book* will also understand the message **Get-Status**.

The reverse is not necessarily true, however. If *Rare-Book* defines a method called **Get-Rare-Book**, objects of type *Book* and *Item* do *not* inherit the **Get-Rare-Book** method. Consequently, objects of type *Book* and *Item* do *not* understand the message and sending the message **Get-Rare-Book** to a *Book* object causes an error.

It should be noted that there are occasions when the assumptions made by conformance checking are not correct and unnecessarily prohibit valid operations. For example, if person is a subclass of mammal, and both support the same method, conformance checking will *not* allow an object of type *mammal* to be substituted for an object of type *person*, even when the programmer knows that both *mammal* and *person* support a given method and the invocation will work.

Figure 8.13 offers another way to depict inheritance.

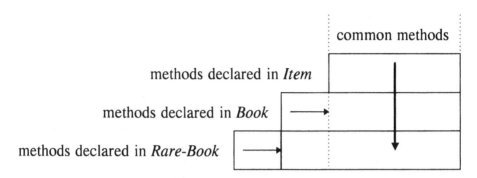

common methods

methods declared in *Item*

methods declared in *Book*

methods declared in *Rare-Book*

FIGURE 8.13. Viewing inheritance as a staircase.

Methods defined at the top of the staircase are declared in *Item*, those of the middle stair are declared in *Book*, and at the lowest stair are the methods declared in *Rare-Book*. Any object in the inheritance chain understands the messages between the dotted lines: the common methods. When the purpose is to invoke a common method, objects lower in the hierarchy should be allowed to be Set to object types higher in the hierarchy without causing an error.

The "As" Object Modifier

Untyped object handles may be too permissive. For safety, some degree of conformance checking may be necessary. Object-Oriented COBOL provides the **As** object-modifier to selectively restrict, relax, or remove conformance checking. The **As** modifier is used to change (modify) an object's type. Here is the way the syntax looks.

Format: a general form of the object-modifier As.

$$
\text{object-identifier-1 As} \left\{ \begin{array}{l} \text{class-name-1 [Only]} \\ \text{Universal} \end{array} \right\}
$$

where:

object-identifier-1 is an object identifier, but not the predefined object identifier **Super**;

As is the reserved word object-modifier;

class-name-1 is a user-defined class-name;

Only is a reserved word attribute that limits the interface to class-name; and

Universal is a reserved word that removes conformance checking (similar in effect to declaring an untyped object identifier).

The following is an example of setting anItemObject of type *Item*, to aBookObject of type *Book*.

Example: using the As modifier to bypass normal conformance checking.

```
01 aBookObject     Object Reference Book.
01 anItemObject    Object Reference Item.
```

```
Set anItemObject To aBookObject As Book.
```

The object handle anItemObject may hold objects of type *Book*. It is the programmer's responsibility to ensure anItemObject only invokes common methods. Should anItemObject attempt to invoke methods declared only in the *Book* object, an error will occur.

The object handle anItemObject may be returned to its original type by first saving the object handle. Here is an example of this.

Example: saving then restoring an object's type.

```
01 aBookObject       Object Reference Book.
01 aTempItemObject   Object Reference Item.
01 anItemObject      Object Reference Item.
```

```
Set aTempItemObject To anItemObject          save anItemObject
Set anItemObject To aBookObject As Book.
Set anItemObject To aTempBookObject As Item   restore anItemObject
```

The As modifier may also be used with the Invoke statement. The following offers an example.

Example: using the As modifier with Invoke.

```
01 anItemObject      Object Reference Item.
```

```
Invoke anItemObject As Book "common-method"
```

The "As Universal" Object Modifier

The object modifier **As Universal** may be used to completely eliminate conformance checking. Below is an example of changing an object of type *Book* to an untyped object.

Example: using the As modifier Universal.

```
01 aBookObject      Object Reference Book.
01 anObject         Object Reference.
```

Set aBookObject to anObject As Universal.

The **As Universal** object modifier may also be used in an **Invoke** statement.

Example: the As Universal modifier with Invoke.

```
01 aBookObject      Object Reference Book.
```

Invoke aBookObject As Universal ...

Consider our library example with a variety of classes, some of which are related by inheritance. We would like to declare a dispatcher method capable of receiving an object of any type along with a message and then send (dispatch) the message to that object. Here is a general-purpose dispatcher method.

Example: a general-purpose Dispatcher method.

```
Method-Id. "Dispatcher".
Data Division.
Linkage Section.
01 A-Method         Pic X(31).
01 anObject         Object Reference.
Procedure Division Using A-Method anObject.
   Invoke anObject A-Method
  Exit Method.
End Method "Dispatcher".
```

Working with Types

The object modifier **As** and untyped objects are useful in implementing extremely flexible systems. Gradations of conformance checking (**As** class-name) permit a programmer to fine tune a system based on performance and extendibility considerations. Systems without a great deal of conformance checking can be developed very quickly. As the prototype evolves and more is learned about the system under construction, type checking can be increased or decreased as needed.

The Object Identifier Null

The predefined object identifier **Null** conforms to every class. **Null** is used as a placeholder when an object reference isn't meant to actually refer to a real object. When an object identifier is **Null**, no messages can be sent. The following is an example of setting an object identifier to **Null**.

```
Set anObject to Null.
```

Null facilitates working with objects in that the programmer can check whether an object reference is valid. The **Null** object may be used anywhere an object identifier (handle) is allowed. A reference to the reserved word **Null** always references the same **Null** object.

An object identifier (handle) may be interrogated for equality or inequality to the **Null** object. For example, the following statement checks to see if the value of **anObject** is equal to **Null**.

Example: comparing anObject with the Null object

```
If anObject = Null
Then
    statements
End-If.
```

or

```
If anObject Not = Null
Then
    statements
End-If.
```

Operations involving the Null object are similar to those involving figurative constants. Many operations in COBOL involve comparing and assigning **Low-Values,** **High-Values, Zeros,** and **Spaces** to data items. The Null object provides the same kind of convenience for assigning, comparing, and selecting objects based on equality or inequality to the Null object.

More on Object Reference

The **Object Reference** clause is used to specify an object handle. When the optional phrase is omitted, the object handle is untyped, which means it is capable of referring to any object. When a class-name is provided, the object reference becomes typed, and is only able to refer to a particular class or its descendants (based on conformance).

Format: a general form for the Usage-Object Reference clause.

Object Reference [optional phrase]

However, the optional phrase of an **Object Reference** clause may specify the following entries.

Format: an expanded form for the Usage-Object Reference clause.

$$\underline{\text{Object}}\ \underline{\text{Reference}}\ \left[\ \begin{bmatrix} \begin{Bmatrix} \underline{\text{Factory}} \\ \underline{\text{Class}} \end{Bmatrix}\ \text{Of} \end{bmatrix}\ \underline{\text{Self}}\ \right]\ \\ [\underline{\text{Factory}}\ \text{Of}]\ \text{class-name-1}\ [\underline{\text{Only}}]$$

where:

Factory Of Self is the factory object identified by Self or a reference to the Null object;

Class Of Self is an object created by the factory object that created the object; identified as Self or a reference to the Null object;

Factory Of class-name-1 is the factory object of class-name-1 or factory object of a class that inherits from class-name-1 or a reference to the Null object; and

Factory Of class-name-1 Only is the factory object of class-name-1 or a reference to the Null object.

Here are some examples.

Example: Factory Of Self.

> 01 aFactoryObject   Object Reference Factory Of Self

The **Factory Of Self** object identifier may only be used in an object method; it may not be used in a class method. The identifier refers to the factory object used to create the currently executing class.

Example: Class Of Self.

> 01 aClassObject   Object Reference Class Of Self.

The **Class Of Self** identifier may be used in an object method or a class method. The identifier refers to the object of the class used to create the currently executing class.

Example: Factory Of class-name-1.

> 01 aFactoryObjectItem   Object Reference Factory Of Item.

The **Factory Of class-name-1** object identifier may be used in an object or in a class method. The identifier refers to the named class. It may also be used to reference the factory object of any of *Item's* subclasses *(Book, Video, Audio)*.

Example: Factory Of class-name-1 Only.

> 01 aFactoryObjectItem   Object Reference Factory Of Item Only.

The **Factory Of class-name-1 Only** object identifier may be used in an object or in a class method. The identifier may only refer to the named class.

The GetClass Method

It is often useful to be able to ask an object its class. In programs with untyped object handles this can be very useful. The class **Base** provides a method called **GetClass** that returns the factory object identifier of the invoking object. Any class that inherits from **Base** will have this method available.

Format: the GetClass syntax.

Invoke object-identifier-1 "GetClass" Returning object-identifier-2

where:
object-identifier-1 is the invoking object,
GetClass is a predefined method supplied in the **Base** class, and
object-identifier-2 is the returned factory object identifier of the class
used to create object-identifier-1.

Here is an example.

Example: the GetClass method.

01 aFactoryObject   Object Reference Factory Of Self.
...

Invoke Self "GetClass" Returning aFactoryObject.

Consider an application that must determine dynamically the class of an object before invoking a method. The **Dispatcher** method is passed **anObject**. **anObject** may be of type *Book* or it may be an object of a different type. In order to interrogate the objects it receives, **Dispatcher** can send the message **GetClass** to help it decide what action to take.

The method as shown below determines the factory object for *Book* and compares that object identifier with the factory object identifier of **anObject**. When the comparison is equal **anObject** is of type *Book*. Remember, there is only one factory object per class.

Example: Dispatcher determines at run time the factory object of a received object for comparison.

Method-Id. "Dispatcher".
Working-Storage Section.
01 aBookFactoryObject   Object Reference Factory of Book Only.
01 aBookObject   Object Reference Book Only.
Linkage Section.

01 anObject   Object Reference.

```
...
Procedure Division Using anObject.
    Invoke Book          "New"       Returning aBookObject
    Invoke aBookObject "GetClass" Returning aBookFactoryObject
    Invoke anObject        "GetClass" Returning anObjectFactoryObject
    Evaluate True
        When aBookFactoryObject = anObjectFactoryObject
            Move "Get-Status" to Method-Name
            Invoke anObject Method-Name ...
        When other
            Perform ...
    End-Evaluate
```

The GetClass method is also useful for creating an object of the same type as the object that is currently executing. If a *Book* object is executing we want to create an object of type *Book;* if an *Audio* object is executing we want to create an *Audio* type object, and so on. The method should be inheritance-ready, that is to say, usable by every class in the *Item* hierarchy.

Books, videos, and audiotapes are often part of a larger set. Encyclopedias and reference manuals are two examples of this. A method called Multiple-Volumes is responsible for creating other objects of the same type as the one currently executing.

Example: Multiple-Volume, at run time, determines and creates objects of the same type (class) as the currently executing object.

```
        Class-Id. Item.
        ...
        Object.
        Data Division
        Method-Id. "Multiple-Volumes".
        Data Division.
        Working-Storage Section.
          01 aFactoryObject     Object Reference Factory Of Self.
          01 anotherObject      Object Reference Class Of Self.
        Procedure Division.
            Invoke Self "GetClass" Returning aFactoryObject
```

Invoke aFactoryObject "New" Returning anotherObject
End-Perform.

...

End-Method "Multiple-Volumes".

IN-LINE METHOD INVOCATION

Object-Oriented COBOL provides a shorthand notation for invoking methods called *in-line invocation*. Methods invoked using in-line invocations must return a parameter. The general format of an in-line method invocation is as follows:

Format: a form of an in-line invocation.

Move <u>object-identifier-1</u> <u>::</u> <u>method-1</u> to <u>data-name-1</u>

where:

object-identifier-1 is the object identifier (the class name for the factory object);

:: is the in-line invocation operator (must immediately be preceded and followed by a separator space);

method-1 is the alphanumeric literal method-name; and

data-name-1 is the receiving field from the invocation of the method defined as a level 01, 77, or elementary data item in the File Section, Working-Storage Section, or Linkage Section.

The behavior of an in-line method invocation is the same as if an object identified by object-identifier-1 invoked a method defined as method-1 and returned a parameter defined as data-name-1. Figure 8.14 shows how it works.

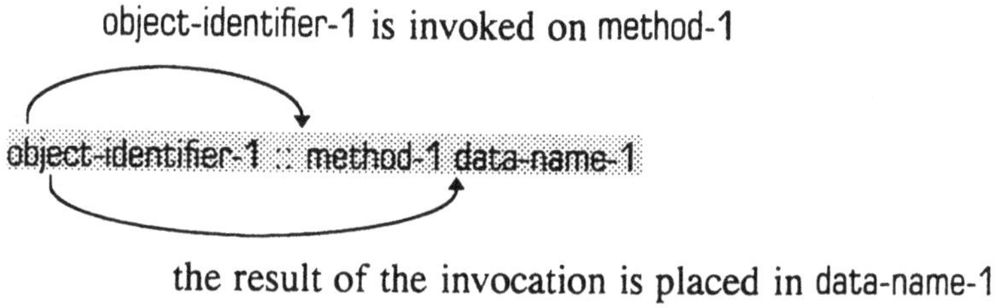

object-identifier-1 is invoked on method-1

object-identifier-1 :: method-1 data-name-1

the result of the invocation is placed in data-name-1

FIGURE 8.14. An in-line method invocation.

Here is another form of an in-line method invocation.

Format: a form of an in-line invocation.

If object-identifier-1 :: method-1 <u>relational-operator</u> data-name-1

where:

> relational-operator is a relation condition (=, >=, <=, and the negating not, i.e., not =); a class condition (Numeric, Alphabetic, Alphabetic-Upper, Alphabetic-Lower; note that class condition in this context refers to the standard class condition, *not* an object-oriented construct); a sign condition (positive, negative, zero, and the negating not, i.e., not positive); a condition-name condition (88-level conditions).

Example: a form of an in-line invocation.

If object-identifier-1 :: method-1 = data-name-1

If aBookObject :: "Get-Status" = "In"

The key to working with in-line method invocations is to realize their extreme versatility and compatibility with existing COBOL-type syntax. In-line method invocation may be used anywhere a data item is used, provided that the method invoked returns a parameter. The compiler is responsible for generating the necessary temporary data items and picture clauses to accomplish the requested operation.

For example, consider the two in-line method invocations below:

1. Move aBookObject :: "Get-Status" to Book-Status

2. If aBookObject :: "Get-Status" = "In"

The first (1.) in-line invocation requires the programmer to define a data name called Book-Status of the proper Picture to receive the parameter returned by the Get-Status method.

The second (2.) in-line invocation does not require the programmer to define a data name for the returning parameter. It is the responsibility of the compiler, behind the scenes and without programmer intervention, to generate the necessary temporary data items such that the If statement is executed correctly.

Compatibility is the driving force behind the versatility of the in-line invocation. The in-line syntax allows COBOL programmers to modify legacy code, replacing data references with object method calls as in the following:

Move (object) :: (method) to

If (object) :: (method) > 0

This shorthand notation for method invocation preserves the flavor of COBOL syntax, limits the proliferation of **Invoke** statements, and eases the programmer into objects and methods.

USING IN-LINE INVOCATION

For the next few sections we will be referring to the **Get-Status, Set-Status, Overdue,** and **Calculate-Fine** methods. The methods are listed for reference below. The classes *Book*, *Video*, and *Audio* inherit the methods. Consider *aBookObject* has been created.

```
Class-Id. Item.
...
Object.
Data Division.
Working-Storage Section.
01 Status          Pic X(03)
01 Date-Due        Pic X(08)
*>
Method-Id. "Get-Status".
Data Division.
Linkage Section.
01 LS-Get-Status     Pic X(03).
Procedure Division Returning LS-Get-Status.
    Move Status to LS-Get-Status
  Exit Method.
End Method "Get-Status".
*>
Method-Id. "Set-Status".
```

```
Data Division.
Linkage Section.
01 LS-Set-Status        Pic X(03).
Procedure Division Using LS-Set-Status.
      Move LS-Set-Status to Status
   Exit Method.
End Method "Set-Status".
*>
Method-Id. "Overdue".
Data Division.
Linkage Section.
01 A-Date              Pic X(08).
01 Days-Late           Pic 9(05).
Procedure Division Using A-Date Returning Yes-Or-No.
      this method is passed A-Date and calculates based on the Due-Date
      how many days the Item is overdue. If the item is not overdue a 0 is
      placed in the Days-Late field.
   Exit Method.
End Method "Overdue".
*>
Method-Id. "Calculate-Fine".
Data Division.
Linkage Section.
01 Days-Late           Pic 9(05).
01 Fine-Amount         Pic s9(04)V99.
Procedure Division Using Days-Late Returning Fine-Amount.
      this method is passed Days-Late and calculates a Fine-Amount. If there
      is no fine (i.e. Days-Late = 0) the method returns a 0; otherwise the
      method returns the amount of the fine.
   Exit Method.
End Method "Calculate-Fine".
End Object.
```

The following examples illustrate some additional aspects of in-line invocations. Below is a standard Invoke operation involving a *Book* object called *aBookObject*.

Example: a standard Invoke statement with a returning parameter.

> Invoke aBookObject "Get-Status" Returning Status

The Invoke statement above may be rewritten as an in-line invocation as follows:

Example: an in-line invocation of the Get-Status method.

> Move aBookObject :: "Get-Status" to Status

In-line invocation allows a method invocation to be used as an identifier with the restriction that the identifier is not a receiving item (where an identifier is a data name that uniquely identifies a data item). For example, the Get-Status in-line invocation is used as a sending item and is permitted. The following is the general format of an in-line invocation used as a sending item and is allowed.

Format: an in-line invocation used as a sending item. Permitted.

> Move (result of the in-line invocation) to data-name-1

where:

> result of the in-line invocation is the returned parameter from the invoked method, and
> data-name-1 is a receiving field.

The following example shows an incorrect use of in-line invocation used as a receiving item and is *not* permitted.

Example: an invalid in-line invocation.

> Move Status to aBookObject :: "Set-Status"

Because in-line invocations may be used anywhere identifiers are permitted (with the sending-item restriction as noted), the following three operations are allowed.

1	If aBookObject :: "Get-Status" = "In"
2	Evaluate True
	When aBookObject :: "Get-Status" = "In"

3	Evaluate aBookObject :: "Get-Status"
	When "In" ...

In-line invocations may also be used in arithmetic statements. Assume for a moment that there is a method called **Report-Fine** defined in the class *Book* that returns a numeric value. The following in-line invocation may then be used to add the value returned by the method **Report-Fine** to a data item called **Running-Total**.

```
01 Running-Total      Pic 9(04).
...
```

> Add aBookObject :: "Report-Fine" to Running-Total

Objects may be created using in-line invocation. Here is an example of creating an object of class *Book* and returning its handle to the data name *aBookObject1*.

> Move Book :: "New" to aBookObject1

In-Line Method Invocations with Input Parameters

In-line invocation, in addition to receiving an output parameter, may also supply any required input parameters to the invoked method. Here is the format.

Format: a form of an in-line invocation with an input parameter.

> object-identifier-1 :: method-1 data-name-1 (input-parameter-1 ...)

where:

> input-parameter-1 is a data item (including objects) expected by the invoked method or another in-line method invocation.

The method **Overdue** requires an input parameter and returns a parameter. Here is the format of an in-line invocation of the **Overdue** method supplying an input parameter. Note that the code fragment below uses the **Current-Date** intrinsic function, which returns a date that includes the century. For more information on intrinsic functions see Appendix E.

```
01 Todays-Date      Pic X(08).
..
```

> Move Function Current-Date to Todays-Date
> If aBookObject :: "Overdue" (Todays-Date) >= 0

Assume the **Overdue** method requires not one but two input parameters. The second input parameter is a variable of some kind we will simply call **A-Flag**. Below is the syntax of an in-line invocation using two parameters.

```
01 Todays-Date      Pic X(08).
01 A-Flag           Pic X(01) Value "1".
  ..
```

> Move Function Current-Date to Todays-Date

> If aBookObject :: "Overdue" (Todays-Date, A-Flag) >= 0

Nesting In-Line Invocations: In-Line Method Invocations as Input Parameters

In-line method invocations may be nested in two ways. First, the input parameter of an in-line invocation may itself be another in-line method invocation.

> Format: an in-line method invocation with an in-line invocation input parameter.

> object-identifier-1 :: method-1 data-name-1 (in-line-invocation)

where:

> in-line-invocation is another in-line method invocation.

The in-line invocation within the parenthesis is operated on first. The returning parameter is then used as input to the outer in-line method invocation. The outer in-line invocation must require an input parameter and return an output parameter. Here is how it works.

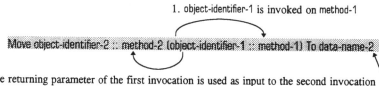

1. object-identifier-1 is invoked on method-1

> Move object-identifier-2 :: method-2 (object-identifier-1 :: method-1) To data-name-2

2. the returning parameter of the first invocation is used as input to the second invocation

3. the returning parameter from the second invocation is placed in data-name-2

The **Calculate-Fine** method takes as an input parameter for the number of days a *Book, Video,* or *Audio* object is late and calculates a fine amount. If there is no fine the method returns a 0.

Example: an in-line invocation using an in-line invocation as an input parameter.

01 Customer-Fine   Pic s9(04)V99.

...

Move aBookObject :: "Calculate-Fine" (aBookObject :: "Overdue"(Todays-Date)) To
    Customer-Fine

If aBookObject :: "Calculate-Fine" (aBookObject :: "Overdue"(Todays-Date)) > 0

Nesting In-Line Invocations: In-Line Method Invocations as the Object

The second technique for nesting in-line method invocations substitutes the object with another in-line invocation, subject to the restriction that the nested invocation returns an object. Here is a syntax diagram for nesting in-line method invocations.

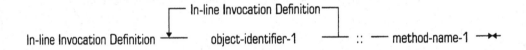

The object identifier to the left of the invocation operator may itself be an in-line invocation.

Expansion is accomplished by substituting the object on the left of the invocation operator with another in-line invocation. An illustration of in-line invocations substituted for the left-most object follows. The curved arrow indicates the method that is invoked.

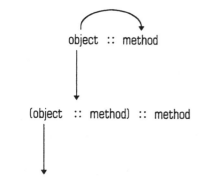

each invocation, with the exception of the last method invoked, must return an object

the object is replaced by an in-line invocation

the object is replaced by an in-line invocation

The object that results from the left-most method invocation is passed as input to the next method and so on until the last method (listed on the right) is applied, which returns the final result. Here is an example of repeated in-line invocations returning a value to **data-name-1**.

Move object-1 :: "method-1" :: "method-2" :: "method-3" to data-name-1

The invocation above proceeds as follows: **object-1** is invoked on **method-1**. The returning parameter must be an object, which is then invoked on **method-2**. The returning parameter again must be an object that is invoked on **method-3**. The returning parameter from the invocation of **method-3** may return a parameter of any data type that is placed in **data-name-1**.

THE PROPERTY CLAUSE

Object-Oriented COBOL's **Property** clause provides controlled access and visibility to class and object data without the need for writing accessor methods. Normally the data is only accessible to methods of the declaring object (factory or instance).

Programmer-written accessor methods are one means of providing encapsulated data to other classes and programs; the **Property** clause provides another. The syntax is as follows.

Format: the Property clause syntax.

<u>0x</u> data-name <Usage clause> <<u>Property</u>> <<u>Property attributes</u>>

where:

0x is a level 01, 77, or elementary data item *only* allowed in the **Data Division Working-Storage Section** of a **Factory** or **Object** paragraph;

Property is a reserved word declaring the data item a property of an object (where property is read as belongs to); and

Property attributes are optional qualifiers and may be either **No Get** or **No Set**.

With the two optional attributes, **No Set** and **No Get**, the **Property** clause may be specified in one of three ways with three different effects on the declared data item.

1. **Property** (no attributes specified)—the data item may be viewed and changed.

2. **Property No Set**—the data item may only be viewed.

3. **Property No Get**—the data item may only be changed.

The following example specifies the **Property** clause without attributes on the data item **Status** from the class *Item*.

Example: class Item specifies the Property clause on the variable Status.

01 Status   Pic X(03) Property.

Declaring **Property** on the data item **Status** grants other methods (methods and programs defined outside of the containing object) access to view and change the value of the data item. For example, the value of **Status** currently may only be viewed by invoking the method **Get-Status**, or changed by invoking **Set-Status**.

Specifying **Property** allows the data item **Status** to be accessed in much the same manner as other data items are accessed. For example, standard COBOL syntax permits the following:

Move (literal-1|data-name-1) to data-name-2 <u>Of</u> <u>Record</u>

where:

| means the logical operator **Or**, and

Of Record uniquely identifies the receiving field of a Record.

Object-Oriented COBOL allows data items of objects declared with the **Property** clause to be operated on using the same syntax. Here is a general format.

> Move (literal-1|data-name-1) to <u>data-name-2</u> <u>Of</u> <u>Object</u>

where:

> | means the logical operator **Or**, and
> **data-name-2 Of Object** uniquely identifies the property of an object, when **data-name-2** is declared with the **Property** clause.

To recognize a statement that relies on the prior declaration of a **Property** clause the syntax may be reduced to the form (where property reads as belongs to, or property of):

> <u>Property</u> <u>Of</u> <u>Object</u>

where:

> **Property** refers to a data item declared with the **Property** clause,
> **Of** is a reserved word,
> **Object** is the object in which the data item is defined, and the entire statement is referred to as a Property Reference.

The following examples illustrate how a *Driver* program (or other classes or programs) may access **Status** when it is declared with **Property**.

Example: the value of Status is interrogated.

> If Status Of aBookObject = "In"

Example: "Out" is moved to Status.

> Move "Out" to Status Of aBookObject

Example: the value of Status is moved to data-name-1.

> Move Status Of aBookObject to data-name-1.

THE NO-SET ATTRIBUTE

The **No Set** attribute of the **Property** clause allows the value of a data item to be viewed but not changed. In database terminology this is equivalent to granting "read-only" access or in a **Call** statement is similar to **Call** ... **by Content**. Here is the format.

Format: the No-Set-Property clause syntax.

> 01 data-name <Usage clause> Property No Set

The following example illustrates declaring the **Property** clause with the **No Set** attribute on **Status**.

Example: class Item specifies the Property clause on the variable Status.

> 01 Status   Pic X(03) Property No Set.

The following syntax permits the **No Set** attribute to be specified.

Example: the value of Status is interrogated.

> If Status Of aBookObject = "In"

Here is an example that is *not* permitted when the **No Set** attribute is specified.

Example: "Out" is not allowed to be moved to Status when the data item specifies the No-Set option.

> Move "Out" to Status Of aBookObject   will cause an error

Here is an example that is permitted with the **No Set** attribute specified.

Example: the value of Status is moved to data-name-1.

> Move Status Of aBookObject to data-name-1.

THE NO-GET ATTRIBUTE

The **No Get** attribute of the **Property** clause allows the value of a data item to be changed but not viewed. This attribute differs from its database cousin. In database terminology a "write" capability usually grants a "read" capability. This is not the case for the **Property** clause **No Get** attribute. The **No Get** option of the **Property** clause may be useful in situations in which an application is granted an update capability only, such as updating an employee's pay record. Here is the format.

Format: the No-Get-Property clause syntax.

> 01 data-name <Usage clause> <u>Property</u> <u>No</u> <u>Get</u>

The following is an example of declaring the **Property** clause with the **No Get** attribute on **Status**.

Example: class Item specifies the Property clause on the variable Status.

> 01 Status   Pic X(03) Property No Get.

The following example is *not* permitted when the **No Get** attribute is specified.

Example: the value of Status is not allowed to be viewed when the data item specifies the No-Get option.

> If Status of aBookObject = "In"   will cause an error

Here is an example that is permitted when the **No Get** attribute is specified.

Example: "Out" is moved to Status.

> Move "Out" to Status of aBookObject

NESTED PROPERTIES

Property references may be nested, subject to the restriction that the nested reference returns an object. Thus, an object in a property reference may be replaced with another property reference, where a property reference takes the form:

> Property Of Object

Here is a syntax diagram.

Below is an example of a nested property in which the nested property reference is in parentheses.

> **Property Of (Property Of Object)**

The nesting of property references is very similar in form to the nesting of in-line invocations. Expansion is accomplished by substituting the object with another property reference. Below is an illustration of property references being repeatedly substituted for the object.

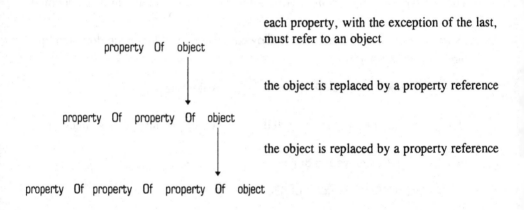

The following example illustrates nested property references, in which the innermost nested property reference (**data-name-2 Of Object-2**) returns an object, and both **data-name-1** and **data-name-2** are declared with a **Property** clause.

> **Move data-name-1 Of (data-name-2 Of Object-2) to data-name-3**

This example is rewritten using in-line invocation in the sidebar.

Sidebar

Although the encapsulation firewall may appear to have been breached by allowing object data to be accessed without writing accessor methods, accessor methods are in fact used. Accessor methods are automatically generated by the compiler when a

Property clause is declared. When encountering a property reference (Property of Object) the compiler uses the generated method to access the requested data.

Consider what occurs when the following statements are encountered by a COBOL compiler.

```
01 variable-1      Pic s99 Packed-Decimal  Value 1.
01 variable-2      Pic s99 Binary          Value 2.
01 variable-3      Pic s99                 Value 0.
Procedure Division.
    Compute variable-3 = variable-1 + variable-2.
```

The Compute statement causes the compiler to automatically generate the instructions necessary to add data items stored as different data types. Modern languages, unlike assembler languages, recognize and operate on a single domain of numbers that include real and integers. Assembler languages divide the domain of numbers into many smaller domains that requires the programmer to convert from one domain to another before an addition operation is performed.

A simple calculation then becomes a mind-numbing experience of loading, storing, converting, restoring, ad infinitum, until 20 statements later the operation is complete. Modern language theory emphasizes that a language should clearly and succinctly address the problem at hand. The statement:

```
Compute Total-Pay = Normal-Pay + Overtime-Pay
```

is clear and succinct. The corresponding assembler instructions necessary to perform the calculation would fill half a page.

The statement:

```
Move data-name-1 Of object to data-name-2
```

is also clear and succinct. The number of statements required to write the supporting accessor methods would also fill half a page.

The philosophy behind both compiler-generated methods for data access and compiler-generated instructions for calculations is the same: an increased ability to express solutions clearly and succinctly.

Here is how it works. Consider the **Get-Status** method. Instead of requiring the programmer to write the accessor method **Report-Status**, the **Property** clause may be declared on the data name **Status** as shown below.

```
Object.
Data Division.
Working-Storage Section.
01 Status            Pic X(03) Property.
```

When encountering the **Property** clause without attributes (**No Get** or **No Set**), the compiler generates two accessor methods. The first is called **getStatus**; the second is called **setStatus**. The following two methods are generated by the compiler.

```
1.      Method-Id. getStatus.
        Data Division.
        Linkage Section.
        01 ls-status     Pic X(03).
        Procedure Division Returning ls-status.
           Move Status to ls-status.
           Exit Method.
        End Method getStatus.

2.      Method-Id. setStatus.
        Data Division.
        Linkage Section.
        01 ls-status     Pic X(03).
        Procedure Division Using ls-status.
           Move ls-status to Status.
           Exit Method.

        End Method setStatus.
```

To arrive at the method-name, the compiler concatenates **set** and/or **get** with the data-name. When the **No Get** attribute is specified only the **setData-name** method is generated. Here is an example using the data-name **Title-Information**.

```
Object.
Data Division.
```

```
Working-Storage Section.
01 Date-Due          Pic X(08) Property No Get.
   ...
```

Remember the No Get attribute means the data item may only be changed. The following set method is therefore generated.

```
Method-Id. setDue-Date.
Data Division.
Linkage Section.
01 LS-Due-Date        Pic X(08).
Procedure Division Using LS-Due-Date.
   Move LS-Due-Date to Due-Date.
   Exit Method.
End Method setDue-Date.
```

When the No Set attribute is specified only the getData-name method is generated. Here is an example using Due-Date again.

```
Object.
Data Division.
Working-Storage Section.
01 Due-Date          Pic X(08) Property No Set.
   ...
```

Here is the generated method.

```
Method-Id. getDue-Date.
Data Division.
Linkage Section.
01 LS-Due-Date        Pic X(08).
Procedure Division Returning LS-Due-Date.
   Move Due-Date to LS-Due-Date.
   Exit Method.
End Method getDue-Date.
```

The automatically generated accessor methods are available for use in other statements. For example, either of the following statements could be used after generating the getDue-Date method.

```
01 Date-Due      Pic X(08).
      ...
```

| (1.) | Invoke aBookObject "getDue-Date" Returning Date-Due |
| (2.) | If Due-Date Of aBookObject > Function current-date |

Statement (1.) above uses a standard **Invoke** statement with the compiler-generated getDue-Date method. Statement (2.) also uses the compiler-generated getDue-Date method. The method is not apparent from the syntax. When encountering a property reference (**Property Of Object**), the compiler hides the details to promote a more concise and succinct solution.

This example of nested property references was given previously.

Move data-name-1 Of (data-name-2 Of Object-2) to data-name-3

The example may be rewritten as an in-line invocation explicitly using the compiler-generated accessor methods (where data-name-1 and data-name-2 are declared with a **Property** clause) as:

Move Object-2 :: "getData-Name-2" :: "getData-Name-1" to data-name-3

APPLYING IN-LINE INVOCATIONS AND PROPERTIES

Declaring a **Property** clause generates the appropriate accessor methods. Utilizing the **Property** clause to generate the necessary accessor methods, the class *Item* no longer needs to have the **Get-Status** and **Set-Status** methods. Simply declaring the **Property** clause on **Status** is sufficient.

Example: Status declared with Property.

01 Status   Pic X(03) Property.

Another class or program may retrieve or change the value of **Status** by explicitly using the compiler-generated method. Here is an example.

```
01 Status-1          Pic X(03).
    ...
    Invoke aBookObject "getStatus" Returning Status-1
```

An alternative would be to use an in-line invocation as follows.

```
01 Status-1          Pic X(03).
    ...
    Move aBookObject :: "getStatus" to Status-1
```

Another way would be to use Property-of-Object syntax as follows.

```
01 Status-1          Pic X(03).
    ...
    Move Status Of aBookObject to Status-1
```

WORKING WITH STATIC OBJECTS

In Chapter 7 we discussed static objects and **Simple** classes as a means of bringing the power of objects to bear on legacy applications.

Example: a static object declaration

```
01 aStaticObject     Object Class-1.
```

Notice the **Usage Object** phrase. The word **Reference** is *not* used. By omitting the reserved word **Reference**, a static object is declared. The class name, **Class-1**, refers to a **Simple** class.

Static objects are used with **Simple** classes. A **Simple** class is a class declared with the reserved word **Simple** in the **Class-Id** header. A **Simple** class is subject to the following restrictions:

1. The object definition may not contain a **File Section.**

2. The object definition may not declare tables with indexes.

3. The object definition must contain, at most, one **01-level** data-description entry.

4. The class may only inherit another **Simple** class.

5. The object definition may only use the word **Self** for method invocation and it must be on the right side of an **As** modifier.

The following is an example of a **Simple** class called *Class-1* that we will be developing and working with.

Example: a Simple class.

```
Class-Id. Class-1 Is Simple.
..
Factory.
...
End Factory.
*>
Object.
Data Division.
Working-Storage Section.
01 Validated-Name
    05 Last-Name      Pic X(20).
    05 First-Name     Pic X(12).
    05 Middle-Initial Pic X(01).
Method-Id. <to be defined>
Procedure Division.
...
End Object.
End Class Class-1.
```

A Credit Application

To demonstrate the utility of **Simple** classes, we will integrate the class *Class-1* into a legacy system called *Credit*. *Credit* is an application program developed by a company called TRX, which supplies credit reports on individuals to other companies. TRX develops a credit report on an individual by integrating the information it receives about the person from other companies.

TRX receives credit information from thousands of other companies. Correctly merging the information about an individual is critical to the accuracy of the credit report. When TRX began, it only served a local area. Since that time the company has grown and the original routines to validate a person's name are no longer adequate.

More sophisticated routines to verify and validate names before attempting to merge associated data from different sources are needed. Currently *Credit* only verifies that the name field is not blank. The following code shows a portion of the current legacy system that reads the input-file and checks the name field.

Example: a program called Credit.

```
Identification Division.
Program-Id. Credit.
...
Input-Output Section.
File-Control.
    Select Customer-File                        Assign Filein.
    Select Validated-Customer-File              Assign Fileout.
Data Division.
File Section.
FD Customer-File
    Label Records Are Omitted
    Record Contains 100 Characters
    Block Contains 0 Records
    Recording Mode is F
    Data Record Is Input-Record.
01 Input-Record                 Pic X(100).
*>
FD Validated-Customer-File
    Label Records Are Omitted
    Record Contains 120 Characters
    Block Contains 0 Records
    Recording Mode is F
    Data Record Is Output-Record.
01 Output-Record                Pic X(120).
```

```
...
Working-Storage Section.
01 WS-Record.
  03 WS-Name.
    05 WS-Last-Name              Pic X(20).
    05 WS-First-Name            Pic X(12).
    05 WS-Middle-Initial        Pic X(01).
  03 WS-Input-Address.

  ...
01 Validated-Record.
  03 Validated-Name.
    05 Last-Name                Pic X(20).
    05 First-Name              Pic X(12).
    05 Middle-Initial          Pic X(01).
  03 Validated-Address.

  ...
01 WS-Output-Record.
  03 WS-Output-Code             Pic X(04).
  03 WS-Output-Name.
    05 WS-Output-Last-Name      Pic X(20).
    05 WS-Output-First-Name     Pic X(12).
    05 WS-Output-Middle-Initial Pic X(01).

  ...
Procedure Division.

  ...
  Read Customer-File Into WS-Record
  ...

B100-Verify-Input-Record.
    If WS-Name Not = Spaces
        Move WS-Name To Validated-Name
    Process all the fields of the input record
    ...
        Perform C100-Output-Validated-Record.
*>- - - - - - - - - - - - - - - - - - - - - - - - - - - - - - - - - *
*> The WS-Output-Record has a different order of fields than     *
*> the WS-Input-Record. The WS-Output-Record also contains       *
```

```
*> additional fields (date-stamp and counts of acceptable fields).*
*> Contributors of data are paid according to how much of the  *
*> data from each record is acceptable.                        *
*>- - - - - - - - - - - - - - - - - - - - - - - - - - - - - - -*
C100-Output-Validated-Record.
        Move Validated-Contributor-Code to WS-Output-Code
        Move Validated-Name to WS-Output-Name
        ...
        Write Output-Record From WS-Output-Record.
        ...
End-Program Credit.
```

Rather than completely rewriting the existing code to conform to new name-checking requirements, we can declare a **Simple** class to seamlessly insert additional processing on the **Validated-Name** field without altering the existing program.

The following are the lines we need to insert, change, and remove in the *Credit* application:

#1.	03 objectName.		to be inserted
#2.	03 Validated-Name.		to be removed
	05 Last-Name	Pic X(20).	to be removed
	05 First-Name	Pic X(12).	to be removed
	05 Middle-Initial	Pic X(01).	to be removed
#3.	Move WS-Name To Validated-Name		to be changed
#4.	Move Validated-Name to WS-Output-Name		to be changed

Example: the Credit program with the changes applied.

```
Identification Division.
Program-Id. Credit.
...
Working-Storage Section.
01 WS-Input-Record.
 03 WS-Name.
  05 WS-Last-Name        Pic X(20).
```

```
           05 WS-First-Name        Pic X(12).
           05 WS-Middle-Initial    Pic X(01).
           03 WS-Input-Address.

           ...
           01 Validated-Record.
```
#1 and #2.   `03 objectName        Object Class-1.`
```
           03 Validated-Address.

           ...
           Procedure Division.

           ...
           Read Customer-File Into WS-Record

           ...
           B100-Verify-Input-Record.
              If WS-Name Not = Spaces
```

#3.   `Move WS-Name To Validated-Name Of objectName`
```
              Perform C100-Output-Validated-Record.
           *>- - - - - - - - - - - - - - - - - - - - - - - - - - - - - - - - - - - - - - *
           *> The WS-Output-Record has a different order of fields than   *
           *> the WS-Input-Record. The WS-Output-Record also contains     *
           *> additional fields (date-stamp and counts of acceptable fields). *
           *> Contributors of data are paid according to how much of the   *
           *> data from each record is acceptable.                         *
           *>- - - - - - - - - - - - - - - - - - - - - - - - - - - - - - - - - - - - - - *
           C100-Output-Validated-Record.
              Move Validated-Contributor-Code to WS-Output-Code
```
#4.   `Move Validated-Name Of objectName to WS-Output-Name`
```
              ...
              Write Output-Record From WS-Output-Record.
           End-Program Credit.
```

Here is what is happening with changes #1 and #2. The Validated-Name field is removed and replaced with a static object called *objectName* by specifying the reserved word Object along with the Simple class called *Class-1*.

For the program to work as before the data description of the previous entries (those we removed from *Credit*) must match the data description entries in the Simple class. The data items in *Class-1* are inserted in the program *Credit* at the point the static object is declared. The static object is treated as an elementary data item when it is not involved in an object operation (i.e., an **Invoke** statement or Propertylike syntax). We will treat *objectName* as an object by using Propertylike syntax.

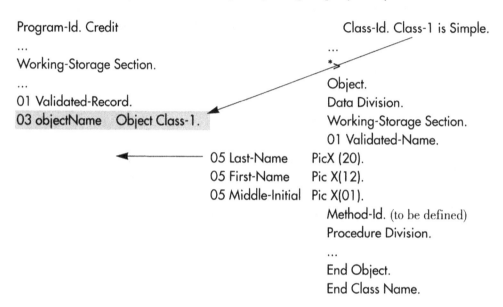

```
Program-Id. Credit                              Class-Id. Class-1 is Simple.
...                                             ...
Working-Storage Section.
...                                             Object.
01 Validated-Record.                            Data Division.
03 objectName   Object Class-1.                 Working-Storage Section.
                                                01 Validated-Name.
                      05 Last-Name      PicX (20).
                      05 First-Name     Pic X(12).
                      05 Middle-Initial Pic X(01).
                                                Method-Id. (to be defined)
                                                Procedure Division.

                                                ...
                                                End Object.
                                                End Class Name.
```

Change #3 involves the manner in which the **Property** clause works. Recall that the **Property** clause automatically generates accessor methods for any object data item that declares the reserved word **Property**. The accessor method generated has the same name as the name of the data item (preceded by the word **get** or **set**). The method may then be invoked by a statement in the following form:

> **data-item Of object**

When the compiler encounters a similar phrase (a data name followed by **Of** followed by the name of an object) as in:

> **Validated-Name Of objectName**

and finds:

> **Move WS-Name To Validated-Name Of objectName**

the compiler looks for a class associated with the object called *objectName*. Finding the declaration associating *Class-1* with *objectName*, the compiler next looks for an accessor method with the same name as the data name specified (Validated-Name), preceded by the word set.

The compiler looks for a set method instead of a get method because of the form of the Move statement. The Property-Of phrase (the words Validated-Name Of objectName) acts as a receiving item in the Move statement.

If the compiler encountered the statement:

```
Move Validated-Name Of objectName to WS-Name
```

the compiler looks for a get method. In this case the Property-Of phrase acts as a sending field. Validated-Name Of objectName is being sent to WS-Name.

Currently there is no setValidated-Name method. We will define one in *Class-1*. Here is the class *Class-1* with the setValidated-Name method.

Example: the setValidated-Name method.

```
Class-Id. Class-1 Is Simple.

..

*>
Object.
Data Division.
Working-Storage Section.
01 Validated-Name.
    05 Last-Name       Pic X(20).
    05 First-Name      Pic X(12).
    05 Middle-Initial  Pic X(01).
Method-Id. "setValidated-Name".
Data Division.
Linkage Section.
01 LS-Validated-Name    Pic X(33).
Procedure Division Using LS-Validated-Name.
    Move LS-Validated-Name to Validated-Name
    Exit Method.
End Method "setValidated-Name".
```

End Object.
End Class Class-1.

The statement **Move WS-Name To Validated-Name Of objectName** "invokes" the **setValidated-Name** method and sends the data item **WS-Name** to the **Validated-Name** field in *objectName*.

The fourth and final change to the *Credit* program is listed below.

#4.	Move Validated-Name Of objectName to WS-Output-Name

The compiler, encountering the **Move** statement above, searches for a **getValidated-Name** method. Again we will define the method in *Class-1*. Here is the method.

Example: the getValidated-Name method.

```
Class-Id. Class-1 Is Simple.
  ..
  *>
  Object.
  Data Division.
  Working-Storage Section.
  01 Validated-Name.
     05 Last-Name        Pic X(20).
     05 First-Name       Pic X(12).
     05 Middle-Initial   Pic X(01).
  <the setValidated-Name method is defined here>
  Method-Id. "getValidated-Name".
  Data Division.
  Linkage Section.
  01 LS-Validated-Name       Pic X(33).
  Procedure Division Returning LS-Validated-Name.
      we can add whatever additional validation and name clean-up here.
      Move Validated-Name to LS-Validated-Name
      Exit Method.
  End Method "getValidated-Name".
  End Object.
  End Class Class-1.
```

The statement Move Validated-Name Of objectName To WS-Name "invokes" the getValidated-Name method and sends the data item Validated-Name in the static object to the WS-Name field.

The getValidated-Name method may be as sophisticated as desired without needing to disturb the existing application. Other data items in the *Credit* program may be dealt with similarly. Simple classes and static objects provide a strategic bridge for companies migrating to Object-Oriented COBOL.

Key Points

- The semantics of the Set statement have been expanded to include objects.

- Object-Oriented COBOL provides a Null object for testing equivalence and nonequivalence.

- In-line invocation provides a shorthand notation for invoking objects.

- In-line invocations may be nested to any depth.

- A Property clause may be specified on data items, causing accessor methods to automatically be generated.

- Property-of-Object syntax may be used to invoke objects when a Property clause has been declared.

- Static objects and Simple classes provide a means of using objects with minimal impact on existing applications.

Suggested Readings

Bulman, D. (1991). Refining Candidate Objects. *Computer Language,* January, pp. 30–39.

Kirkerud, B. (1989). *Object-Oriented Programming with Simula.* Reading, MA: Addison-Wesley.

McGregor, J., & Sykes, D. (1992). *Object-Oriented Software Development: Engineering Software for Reuse.* New York: Van Nostrand.

Shlaer, S., & Mellor, S. (1992). *Object Lifecycles: Modeling the World in States.* Englewood Cliffs, NJ: Yourdon Press.

Review Questions

8.0   What are the relation conditions for which objects may be tested?

8.1   What is meant by the term local scope? Give an example of a data item with local scope.

8.2   Give an example of a hierarchy of classes and discuss which classes conform to which classes.

8.3   Compare and contrast the ideas of typing and binding.

8.4   What does the reserved word **Only** provide?

8.5   Give an example of correctly using the **Set** statement for the classes defined in question 8.2.

8.6   Show how the modifier **AS** is used.

8.7   How might one use the **Null** object?

8.8   Implement a method that uses **Object Reference Factory of Self**.

8.9   Write an in-line invocation.

8.10 What is the purpose of the **Property** clause?

8.11 Implement an example of a **Simple** class and a static object.

CHAPTER 9

COLLECTIONS

B ooks, motorcycles, baseball players, and Van Gogh's paintings are all examples of objects. Objects denote not only physical entities but also behavior. A story of adventure, the sound of a Harley, a grand-slam, the view of a starry night.

Grouping these objects should not fall to something as mundane as a table or record—and it does not: it falls to a structure that itself has behavior—a collection. Collections are smart containers for objects. A collection is a group of objects, either the same or different. Sometimes we only want one kind of object to be grouped together, like the players on a baseball team. Other times we might want different kinds of objects to be together, like books, videos, and audiotapes.

Collections preserve the harmony of groupings by allowing higher-level decisions to be more directly captured and implemented. The rhyme and reason of analysis and design is often lost amid the crush of detail when one is forced to work with tables and other static data structures. We frequently must declare table sizes without a clue to their actual or expected dimensions; a time bomb, silently waiting for the day when loads exceed limits and the application responds, not with a gentle reminder, but with a force requiring white-knuckle, dead-of-night recoding, recompiling, and other hand-wringing exercises.

FOCUS AND FORMAT OF THIS CHAPTER

Object-Oriented COBOL supports several types of collections. Collections are part of the class libraries supplied with Object-Oriented COBOL compilers. Our work here addresses the collection classes supplied with Micro Focus COBOL, and is, therefore, specific to the Micro Focus class library. However, the ideas and concepts are germane to Object-Oriented COBOL in general (see Appendix A for more information concerning other vendor's class libraries).

In the following sections we focus on the following three collection classes:

- Bag
- CharacterArray
- Dictionary

There are several other issues we will deal with in our discussion of collection classes. They are:

- Associations
- Callbacks
- Intrinsic data
- Intrinsic classes

COLLECTION CLASSES—A HIERARCHY

Collections provide user-ready, smart containers for grouping and managing objects and data. The terms collection class and container class are synonymous. Collections present a uniform interface to the class-user, significantly reducing the amount of code that must be written and maintained.

The 12 collection classes of the Micro Focus class library inherit common behavior from an abstract class called **Collection**. In some cases a subclass of

Collection will redefine a method or not offer it. Two of the 12 classes are abstract classes and 1 is private.

Below is a hierarchy of the Micro Focus class library, showing the collection classes. The collection class name is listed with the system name in parenthesis. The classes listed in boldface (Bag, SequencedCollection, and ValueSet) are the three major categories of collection classes. Instances of the abstract classes and private class should not be created (Collection, SequencedCollection, ArrayedCollection, and DynamicArrayedCollection).

Class Library Hierarchy

```
Base (Base)
    Behavior (Behavior)
    DelegateManager (Delegate)
    Dependent (Dependnt)
        Alarm (Alarm)
        Clipboard (Clipbrd)
        Collection (Collectn)—abstract class                    Begin collection classes
1.)         Bag (Bag)
            SequencedCollection (Sequence)—private class
                ArrayedCollection (Arrayed)—abstract class
2.)             Array (Array)
3.)                 CharacterArray (Chararry)
                DynamicArrayedCollection (Dynarray)—abstract class
4.)                 OrderedCollection (Ordrdcll)
5.)                 SortedCollection (Srtdclln)
6.)         ValueSet (Valueset)
7.)             Dictionary (Dictinry)
8.)                 IdentityDictionary (Idictnry)
9.)             IdentitySet (Iset)                              End collection classes
        other classes
```

Content of Collections

Collection classes may contain objects (the same kind or different) or they may contain intrinsic data (with the exception of the class CharacterArray, which may only contain intrinsic data). Collection classes are capable of holding the following elements:

- Objects
- Intrinsic data—(Pic X, Comp-x, Comp-5: where Comp-x and Comp-5 are Micro Focus data types).

From a collection standpoint, the objects and/or intrinsic data that make up a collection are called *elements*. Figure 9.1 shows one collection containing objects, the other collection containing intrinsic data.

Intrinsic data may be converted to objects, allowing intrinsic data to be stored alongside other objects. This concept is depicted in Figure 9.2.

Categories of Collection Classes

In prior chapters we have focused more on creating classes than in using the services of predefined classes. The one exception to this has been the class Base and the method New. It is time to switch roles from class builder to class user.

There are three major categories of collection classes, Bag, SequencedCollection, and ValueSet. The following is a list of the nine collection classes, along with a summary of their properties.

1. Bag—a subclass of Collection and the most general kind of collection. A Bag is unordered, allows duplicate entries, and is not indexed. Bags automatically increase in size when their capacity is exceeded.

2. Array—a subclass of SequencedCollection. An Array is indexed, allows duplicate entries, and its size increases by sending a message when the capacity is exceeded.

3. CharacterArray—a subclass of SequencedCollection. A CharacterArray is indexed, allows duplicate entries, and its size increases by sending a message when the capacity is exceeded.

4. OrderedCollection—a subclass of SequencedCollection. An OrderedCollection is indexed by the order of entry insertion, and allows duplicate entries. Ordered-Collection automatically increases in size when the original capacity is exceeded.

5. SortedCollection—a subclass of SequencedCollection. A SortedCollection is indexed by sort order, and allows duplicate entries. A SortedCollection automatically increases in size when the original capacity is exceeded.

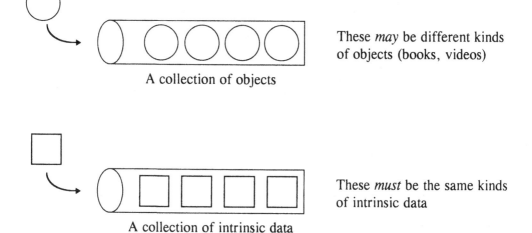

A collection of objects

These *may* be different kinds of objects (books, videos)

A collection of intrinsic data

These *must* be the same kinds of intrinsic data

FIGURE 9.1. Two types of collections.

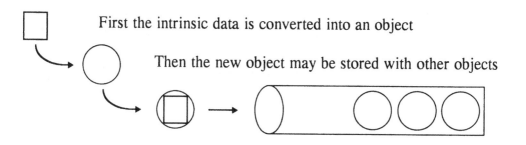

First the intrinsic data is converted into an object

Then the new object may be stored with other objects

producing:

A collection of objects - one of which previously was intrinsic data

FIGURE 9.2. Intrinsic data stored with objects.

6. ValueSet—a subclass of Collection. The class ValueSet and its subclasses share the same class membership principle as mathematical sets—duplicate entries are not allowed. A ValueSet is not indexed, and automatically increases in size when the capacity is exceeded.

7. Dictionary—a subclass of ValueSet. Duplicate entries are not allowed. A Dictionary is indexed by key values and automatically increases in size when its capacity is exceeded.

8. IdentityDictionary—a subclass of ValueSet. Duplicate entries are not allowed. An IdentityDictionary is indexed by key object handles and automatically increases in size when the capacity is exceeded.

9. IdentitySet—a subclass of ValueSet. Duplicate entries are not allowed. ValueSets are not indexed and automatically increase in size when their capacity is exceeded.

The first two categories of collection classes, Bag and SequencedCollection (including Array, CharacterArray, OrderedCollection, and SortedCollection), allow duplicate entries. The third category, ValueSet (including Dictionary, IdentityDictionary, and IdentitySet), does not allow duplicates.

Every collection class, with the exception of Array and CharacterArray, automatically increases in size to accommodate additional elements. Instances of Array and CharacterArray must be sent a message, typically "grow," to increase their capacity.

Only Bag, ValueSet, and IdentitySet are not indexed. The indexed collections, with the exception of Dictionary and IdentityDictionary, may be accessed by supplying a position, much like accessing a table. Entries in a Dictionary and an IdentityDictionary are accessed by key value.

Collection Class Methods

There are many different methods associated with collection classes. Bag alone has 40; CharacterArray has 89, with other collection classes falling within this range. Collection class methods may be divided into nine basic categories based on their behavior. A summary of the categories and methods is given below.

Instance Methods and Categories

- Adding—used to add elements to a collection. Methods include: add, atPut.
- Changing—used to change the size of a collection. Methods include: grow, growTo.

- Converting—used to convert one type of collection into another type of collection. Methods include: **asBag, asArray.**
- Copying—used for copying collections. Methods include: **copy, copyEmpty.**
- Inquiring—used to inquire about the condition of a collection. Methods include: **capacity, size.**
- Iterating—used to iterate through every element in a collection, passing each element as a parameter, generally based on some user-defined criteria. Methods include: **do, select.**
- Removing—used to remove elements from a collection or to remove the entire collection. Methods include: **deepFinalize, finalize, remove.**
- Retrieving—used to retrieve elements from a collection. Methods include: **at, getValue.**
- Testing—used for testing the emptiness of a collection, presence of an element, or number of occurrences of an element in the collection. Methods include: **equal, equalsIgnoreCase, isEmpty, occurencesOf.**

Important Collections

We will examine three collection classes: **Bag, CharacterArray,** and **Dictionary.** Table 9.1 lists the methods organized by class.

Not every method is available to every collection. For example, the method **equal** is only available to instances of the classes **Array, CharacterArray, OrderedCollection,** and **Sorted-Collection.** Table 9.2 shows which of the methods are available to which classes.

Collection Class Constructor Methods

The collection classes provide several methods for creating instances. The two we will examine are:

ofReferences—These are used to create collection class instances for holding objects.

ofValues—These are used to create collection class instances for holding intrinsic data.

TABLE 9.1. Methods Organized by Class

Methods	Bag	CharacterArray	Dictionary
add			
asArray			
asBag			
atPut			
capacity			
copy			
copyEmpty			
do			
equal			
equalsIgnoreCase			
equalByLengthValue			
finalize			
getValue			
grow			
growTo			
includes			
occurencesOf			
remove			
removeAll			
size			

CREATING BAG INSTANCES: OFREFERENCES

Creating collection class instances differs from other class construction in that the method *New* cannot be used. To avoid an error in collection creation use the following syntactic form:

Format: syntax for creating instances of the class Bag.

Invoke object-identifier-1 "method-name" Using size Returning object-identifier-2 End-Invoke

TABLE 9.2. Method Availability

Methods	Bag	CharacterArray	Dictionary
add	•		•
asArray	•	•	•
asBag	•	•	•
atPut		•	•
capacity	•	•	•
copy	•	•	
copyEmpty	•	•	•
do	•	•	•
equal		•	
equalsIgnoreCase		•	
equalByLengthValue		•	
finalize	•	•	
getValue		•	
grow		•	•
growTo		•	
includes	•	•	•
occurencesOf	•	•	•
remove	•		
removeAll	•	•	•
size	•	•	•

where:

object-identifier-1 is the name of the collection class being created;
method-name is either ofReferences or ofValues;
size is a data-name declared as Pic X(4) Comp-5 (a Micro Focus data type similar to unsigned binary, where the number of "x"s equals the length in bytes); and
object-identifier-2 is a user-declared object handle.

Format: a general form for creating instances of Bag.

Invoke Bag "of References" Using PicX4Comp5 Returning a Bag End-Invoke

The following example shows the creation of a **Bag** instance, *aBag*, capable of holding 10 objects. The object *aBag* can hold 10 objects because the **Using** parameter, PicX4Comp5 is given an initial value of 10. Note that the class **Bag** is declared in the **Repository** paragraph.

Example: creating a Bag object.

    Class-Id. BagManager.

    ...

    Repository.
        Bag   Is Class "Bag"
        BagManager   Is Class "BManager".
    Factory.
    Data Division.
    Working-Storage Section.
    01 PicX4Comp5   Pic X(04) Comp-5 Value 10.
    01 aBag   Object Reference.
    Method-Id. "Create-a-Bag".
    Procedure Division.
        Invoke Bag "ofReferences" Using PicX4Comp5 Returning aBag End-Invoke.
        Exit Method.
        End Method "Create-a-Bag".
        End Factory.

We have created an object instance of the class **Bag**, called *aBag*, capable of holding 10 object instances. This is depicted in Figure 9.3.

Bag-Adding Method: Add

Earlier we looked at tables as a structure for storing objects. Instead of using a table, however, we can manage our objects much more effectively using collections.

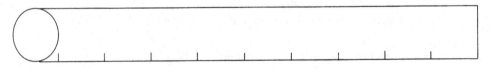

FIGURE 9.3. *aBag* capable of holding 10 objects, currently empty.

Let's make *aBag* responsible for holding *Book* objects. Below is a class program that supports *Book* creation.

Example: a class program called Book.

```
Class-Id. Book Inherits Base.
Environment Division.
Repository.
   Class Book Is "Book"
   Class Base Is "Base".
Object.
Data Division.
Working-Storage Section.
01 ws-Title          Pic X(20).
* -----------------------------------------------------------------*
Method-Id. "Set-Title".
Linkage Section.
01 ls-Title          Pic X(20).
Procedure Division Using ls-Title.
   move ls-Title to ws-Title.
   exit method.
End Method "Set-Title".
* -----------------------------------------------------------------*
Method-Id. "Report-Title".
Procedure Division.
   Display "Title: " ws-Title
   exit method.
End Method "Report-Title".
End Object.
End Class Book.
```

The class *Book* has two object methods, **Set-Title** and **Report-Title,** and one object data item, **ws-Title**. The program responsible for creating the *Book* objects as well as for creating *aBag* object is called **BookMgr** (short for BookManager). The following is the **BookMgr** program.

Example: a program called BookMgr.

```
Program-Id. BookMgr.
Environment Division.
Repository.
 Class Book Is "Book".
Data Division.
Working-Storage Section.
01 aBag          Object Reference.
01 aBook         Object Reference.
01 PicX4Comp5    Pic X(04) Comp-5 Value 10.
Procedure Division.
```

Invoke Bag "ofReferences" Using PicX4Comp5 Returning aBag

Invoke Book "New" Returning aBook

```
End Program BookMgr.
```

When *Book* objects are created they will be added to *aBag*. As each *Book* object is created, **BookMgr** is responsible for storing the *Book* objects in *aBag*. Only one statement is necessary.

Example: adding a Book object to aBag.

Invoke aBag "add" Using aBook

The **add** method has been defined for instances of *Bag*. Our instance of a *Bag*, called *aBag*, understands the **add** message. The following is the **add** syntax.

Format: syntax for adding an object to an instance of a Bag collection.

Invoke object-identifier-1 "method-name" Using object-identifier-2 End-Invoke

where:

object-identifier-1 is the name of the **Bag** instance,
add is the method-name, and
object-identifier-2 is the object being added to the collection.

Below the **BookMgr** program adds five *Book* objects to *aBag*. Each time *aBook* is created it is a unique object, with a unique value returned to the object handle. Although the same object handle (*aBook*) is used in the **Returning** phrase, **New** returns a unique instance. It is the responsibility of the creator to ensure that the object handles are not lost by capturing them in some permanent manner.

Example: a program called BookMgr creates and manages Book objects.

```
Program-Id. BookMgr.
Environment Division.
Repository.
    Class Book Is "Book".
Data Division.
Working-Storage Section.
01 aBag              Object Reference.
01 aBook             Object Reference.
01 PicX4Comp5        Pic X(04) Comp-5 Value 5.
01 i                 Pic X(04) Comp-5 Value 5.
Procedure Division.
* ----------------------------------------------------------------------*
* Create aBag to hold Book objects                                      *
* ----------------------------------------------------------------------*
        Invoke Bag "ofReferences" Using PicX4Comp5 Returning aBag
* ----------------------------------------------------------------------*
* Create 5 Book objects and add them to aBag                            *
* ----------------------------------------------------------------------*
    Perform 5 Times
        Invoke Book "new" Returning aBook
        Invoke aBag "add" Using aBook
    End-Perform
```

Bag-Converting Method: asArray

Some of the most useful methods provided by the collection classes are methods that convert one type of collection into another. The conversion methods support the identity operation. Any collection of a given type may be converted into the same type.

For example, an instance of **Bag** may always be converted into a **Bag** (in which case the returning instance is **Self**).

Conversion methods change one type of collection instance into a different type of collection instance. For example, converting a **Bag** into an **Array** is accomplished as follows:

Format: syntax for converting a collection class to another type of collection class.

Invoke <u>object-identifier-1</u> "<u>method-name</u>" Returning <u>object-identifier-2</u> End-Invoke

where:

object-identifier-1 is the name of the **Bag** instance,
asArray is the method-name, and
object-identifier-2 is the object handle of the new collection instance.

Below is an example, where *aBag* has been created and is converted into an instance of the collection class **Array**.

Example: converting aBag into an instance of an Array.

    01 aBag   Object Reference.
    01 anArray   Object Reference.

    ...

Invoke aBag "asArray" Returning anArray

Bag-Copying Method: Copy

Making copies of collections can be useful in a variety of situations. There are numerous methods for copying collections. One of the most common is the method **copy**. **Copy** returns another instance of the specified object. The following code shows the syntax.

Format: syntax for copying a Bag collection.

Invoke <u>object-identifier-1</u> "<u>method-name</u>" Returning <u>object-identifier-2</u> End-Invoke

where:

object-identifier-1 is the name of the **Bag** instance,

copy is the method-name, and
object-identifier-2 is the object handle of the new collection instance.

Below is an example, where *aBag* has been created.

Example: copying aBag.

01 aBag	Object Reference.
01 anotherBag	Object Reference.

...

Invoke aBag "copy" Returning anotherBag

Bag-Inquiry Methods: Capacity and Size

The key to successfully using predefined collection classes is in understanding the interfaces and messages to which a collection class responds. Figure 9.4 shows the same picture of *aBag* as seen in Figure 9.3, but it is now reduced in size so that we can show it in the familiar figure of a circle. In the picture, the *Bag* object is asked its capacity.

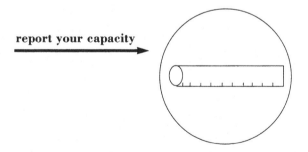

report your capacity

FIGURE 9.4. An example of *aBag* being asked to report its capacity.

Of course the syntax is not "report your capacity," but the idea is the same. The syntax for asking an instance of Bag (in this case *aBag*) its capacity is:

Format: syntax for finding the capacity of an instance of a Bag.

Invoke object-identifier-1 "method-name" Returning data-name-1 End-Invoke

where:

> object-identifier-1 is the name of the **Bag** instance,
> capacity is the method-name, and
> data-name-1 is a data-name declared as **Pic s9(9) Comp-5** (a Micro
>   Focus data type similar to signed binary).

The following is an example of asking *aBag* (its "**Capacity**") how many objects it can hold.

> 01 Bag-Capacity   Pic s9(9) Comp-5.
> ...

Invoke aBag "Capacity" Returning Bag-Capacity End-Invoke

Every collection class can understand and respond to the **Capacity** message. Thus, any collection class instance may be substituted for *aBag* in the above example. The message **Capacity** sent to this *aBag* returns the response "10," because *aBag* has been initialized with the capacity to hold 10 objects.

Size is another message every collection class understands. **Size** returns the number of elements currently stored in the collection. The syntax is identical to **Capacity** with the exception of the method name. The following is the syntax.

Format: syntax for finding the capacity of a Bag instance.

Invoke object-identifier-1 "method-name" Returning data-name-1 End-Invoke

where:

> object-identifier-1 is the name of the **Bag** instance,
> size is the method-name, and
> data-name-1 is a data-name declared as **Pic s9(9) Comp-5** (a Micro
>   Focus data type similar to signed binary).

The following is an example of asking *aBag* (its "**Size**") how many objects it currently holds.

Example: syntax for finding the size of an instance of aBag.

> 01 Bag-Size   Pic s9(9) Comp-5.

...

Invoke aBag "Size" Returning Bag-Size End-Invoke

Because we have not put any objects in the collection, the above message returns a value of 0.

Below the **BookMgr** program adds five *Book* objects to *aBag* and then inquires about its size and capacity.

Example: BookMgr creates aBag, Book objects, and inquires about the size and capacity of aBag.

```
Program-Id. BookMgr.
Environment Division.
Repository.
    Class Book Is "Book".
Data Division.
Working-Storage Section.
01 aBag            Object Reference.
01 aBook           Object Reference.
01 PicX4Comp5      Pic X(04) Comp-5 Value 5.
01 i               Pic X(04) Comp-5 Value 5.
Procedure Division.
* -----------------------------------------------------------------------*
* Create aBag to hold Book objects                                       *
* -----------------------------------------------------------------------*
```

Invoke Bag "ofReferences" Using PicX4Comp5 Returning aBag

```
* -----------------------------------------------------------------------*
* Create 5 Book objects and add them to aBag                             *
* -----------------------------------------------------------------------*
    Perform 5 Times
        Invoke Book "new" Returning aBook
        Invoke aBag "add" Using aBook
    End-Perform
* -----------------------------------------------------------------------*
* Inquire about different aspects of aBag                                *
* -----------------------------------------------------------------------*
```

> Invoke aBag "Capacity" Returning i End-Invoke
> Display "capacity of aBag: " i

> Invoke aBag "Size" Returning i End-Invoke
> Display "size of aBag: " i

End Program BookMgr.

In the above example, the first display statement (asking for the **Capacity**) will display "5" because that is the value used when *aBag* was created. The second display statement (asking for the **Size**) also returns "5" because we looped five times creating and adding *Book* objects.

Bag instances have a distinct advantage over tables in that they automatically grow when their capacity is exceeded. For example, *aBag* in the above class program is currently at the limit of its capacity. It was created to hold five objects and it contains five objects. If another object is added, *aBag* will accommodate, without complaint, the new object.

Figure 9.5 shows a picture of *aBag* with two interfaces, **Capacity** and **Size**, labeled.

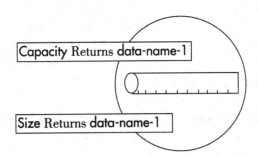

FIGURE 9.5. *aBag* is capable of understanding and responding to **Capacity** and **Size** messages.

The methods **Capacity** and **Size**, which are labeled in Figure 9.5, are only two of the more than 60 instance methods available to **Bag** objects. To effectively use collection classes the programmer must become familiar with the methods (both class and object) and parameters of collections.

Bag-Iterator Method: Do

Collections are more than static repositories of data. Collections know how to iterate over their elements. Two of the most powerful and commonly used iterator methods are *select* and *do*. Both are used to visit each member of a collection and do something.

Do simply visits each element and does something. *Select* visits each element and creates another collection based on user-defined criteria. The following is the syntax for *do*.

Format: the do syntax.

Invoke <u>object-identifier-1</u> "<u>method-name</u>" Using <u>object-identifier-2</u> End-Invoke

where:
> object-identifier-1 is the name of the **Bag** instance,
> do is the method-name, and
> object-identifier-2 is a user-defined message sent to every object of the collection.

Remember, sending a message and invoking a method are the same thing. The message required by the **do** method is the name of a method that must be understood by the objects contained within the collection. For example, assume that *Book* objects contain the following called **Report-Title** method.

Example: the Book object method, Report-Title.

```
Class-Id. Book Inherits Base.
...
Object.
Data Division.
Working-Storage Section.
01 ws-Title Pic X(20).
...
*-------------------------------------------------------------*
Method-Id. "Report-Title".
Procedure Division.
    Display "Title: " ws-Title
```

exit method.
End Method "Report-Title".
End Object.
End Class Book.

Assume three *Book* objects with the names *Hamlet, Macbeth,* and *Othello* in the ws-Title field, each having been placed into *aBag*. Figure 9.6 illustrates this idea.

FIGURE 9.6. Three book objects in *aBag*.

Figure 9.7 shows the imaging in Figure 9.6 at a reduced size, so we can more easily show it as an object with the **do** method interface.

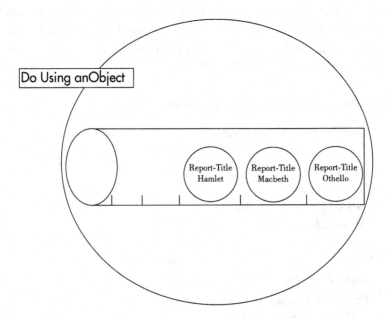

FIGURE 9.7. *aBag* with three Book objects and the **do** method.

If we wish to **invoke** the **Report-Title** method on all the books in the *aBag* collection, we can send the collection the **do** message; however, the message name must be stored in an object. **Do** will be responsible for sending the message (**Report-Title**) to every object in the collection, but first the message must be objectified as a text string as in "**Report-Title**." Figure 9.8 shows a picture of what we must accomplish.

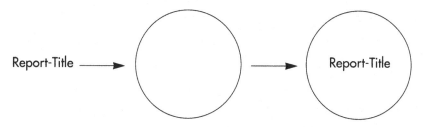

FIGURE 9.8. Objectifying a text string.

To accomplish this, we will use the services of another library class named **Callback** to turn our text string into an object. The following code turns the message into an object.

Format: creating a message encapsulated in an object, using Callback.

> Invoke <u>Callback</u> "<u>New</u>" Using <u>object-identifier-1</u> <u>text-string</u> Returning <u>object-identifier-2</u> End-Invoke

where:

> **Callback** is the name of the library class,
> **New** is the method name,
> **object-identifier-1** is an object handle set to null,
> **text-string** is either a literal or data item with a value of the message
>   (with a maximum length of 80 characters), and
> **object-identifier-2** is the object that will contain the text string.

The following is an example of putting the text string "**Report-Title**" into an object called *aMessage*.

Example: putting a string of text in an object.

> Program-Id. BookMgr.

```
Environment Division.
Repository.
   Class Book Is "Book"
   Class Callback Is "Callback".
   ...
   01 text-string      Pic X (12) Value "Report-Title".
   01 aMessage         Object Reference.
   01 aNullObject      Object Reference.
   ...
Procedure Division.
   Set aNullObject to Null
   Invoke Callback "New" Using aNullObject, text-string Returning
       aMessage End-Invoke
   ...
```

The object *aMessage* now contains the message "Report-Title" and can be used in the do method. The following is an example of the do method using *aMessage*.

Example: invoking the do method on aBag using aMessage.

```
Invoke aBag "do" Using aMessage End-Invoke
```

The method do sends every object in *aBag* the message Report-Title. Figure 9.9 shows a picture of *aBag* sending the message to each object in the collection.

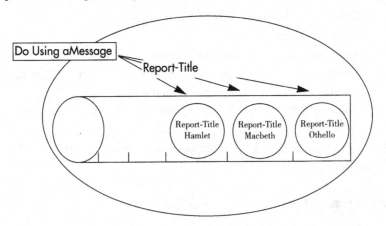

FIGURE 9.9. The objects of *aBag* being sent the Report-Title message.

Each object, will in turn, report its title. For methods that require parameters, the parameters must be objects; the **Callback** is created with the required objects as part of the argument list.

Bag-Removing Method: Remove

Remove, as the name implies, eliminates a selected element from a collection. The following is the syntax.

Format: syntax for the remove method.

Invoke <u>object-identifier-1</u> "<u>method-name</u>" Using <u>object-identifier-2</u> End-Invoke

where:
object-identifier-1 is the name of the **Bag** instance,
remove is the method name, and
object-identifier-2 is the object being removed from the collection.

The following is an example of removing *aBook* from *aBag*.

Example: removing an object from a collection.

Invoke aBag "<u>remove</u>" Using aBook End-Invoke

The following is an example of the **remove** method in the **BookMgr** program. First the collection is tested to determine if the object is present and based on a true condition, then the object is removed.

Example: a program called BookMgr creates and manages Book objects.

```
Program-Id. BookMgr.
   ...
*--------------------------------------------------------------------*
* Search aBag using anotherBook—if the object is found remove the
     object from the collection                                      *
*--------------------------------------------------------------------*
   Invoke aBag "includes" Using anotherBook Returning YesOrNo End-Invoke
   Evaluate True
```

When isYes
> Invoke aBag "remove" Using anotherBook

When isNo
> Display "aBag does not contain the object searched for"

End-Evaluate

End Program BookMgr.

Bag-Testing Method: Includes

Bags do not allow objects to be retrieved based on a subscript or an index. One can *not* retrieve the fourth object added to *aBag* based on position. Instead, *Bags* are queried to find specific objects. One kind of search is based on the value of an object identifier. To perform the search a method called includes is used. The following is the includes syntax.

Format: syntax for the includes method (an iterator method).

> Invoke <u>object-identifier-1</u> <u>"method-name"</u> Using <u>object-identifier-2</u>
> Returning aBoolean End-Invoke

where:
> object-identifier-1 is the name of the Bag instance,
> includes is the method-name,
> object-identifier-2 is the object being searched for in the collection, and
> aBoolean is a pseudo-Boolean defined as Pic X Comp-5.

The following is an example of asking *aBag* if it holds a particular *Book* object.

Example: searching for aBook.

```
01 YesOrNo      Pic X Comp-5.
   88 isYes     value 1.
   88 isNo      value 0.
   ...
```

> Invoke aBag "includes" Using aBook Returning YesOrNo End-Invoke

The following is an example of the includes method in the **BookMgr** program. Notice that the third *Book* object created is captured by setting another object handle to the same value with the **set** statement. This object handle (representing the third *Book* object) is then used as the search criterion.

Example: a program called BookMgr shown using the includes method.

```
Program-Id. BookMgr.
Environment Division.
Repository.
    Class Book Is "Book".
Data Division.
Working-Storage Section.
01 aBag            Object Reference.
01 aBook           Object Reference.
01 anotherBook     Object Reference.
01 PicX4Comp5      Pic X(04) Comp-5 Value 5.
01 i               Pic X(04) Comp-5 Value 0.
01 YesOrNo         Pic X Comp-5.
   88 isYes        Value 1.
   88 isNo         Value 0.
Procedure Division.
*---------------------------------------------------------------*
* Create aBag to hold Book objects                              *
*---------------------------------------------------------------*
    Invoke Bag "ofReferences" Using PicX4Comp5 Returning aBag
*---------------------------------------------------------------*
* Create 5 Book objects and add them to aBag—set the third Book object
    created to anotherBook *
*---------------------------------------------------------------*
    Perform 5 Times
        Invoke Book "new" Returning aBook
        Invoke aBag "add" Using aBook
        add 1 to i
        Evaluate i
          When 3
             set anotherBook to aBook
```

```
        End-Evaluate
        End-Perform
*----------------------------------------------------------------------*
* Search aBag using anotherBook                                        *
*----------------------------------------------------------------------*
```

Invoke aBag "includes" Using anotherBook Returning YesOrNo End-Invoke

```
Evaluate True
    When isYes
        Display "aBag contains the object searched for"
    When isNo
        Display "aBag does not contain the object searched for"
End-Evaluate
```

End Program BookMgr.

CREATING CHARACTERARRAY INSTANCES

CharacterArray stores strings as objects. Unlike Bag, CharacterArray is indexed and does not automatically increase in capacity. CharacterArray is a subclass of SequencedCollection, an example of the second of our three collection class types (Bag, SequencedCollection, ValueSet). CharacterArray allows duplicate entries.

Instances of CharacterArray may be created using a variety of methods, including ofValues. The ofReferences method may *not* be used. One useful method for creating CharacterArray instances is withLengthValue. WithLengthValue creates and initializes an object in one step.

The following is the syntax for creating an object of class CharacterArray initialized to a value.

Format: creating an object initialized to a string using the withlengthValue of CharacterArray.

Invoke object-identifier-1 "method-name" Using size text-string Returning object-identifier-2 End-Invoke

where:

object-identifier-1 is the name of the collection class being created, method-name is withLengthValue,

size is the length of the string in bytes defined as Pic s9(9) Comp-5 (a Micro Focus data type comparable to signed binary),

text-string is either a literal or data item with a string value,

object-identifier-2 is the object that will contain the text string.

The following is an example of creating an object called *aString* that contains the string *Hamlet*.

Example: creating an object using the class CharacterArray.

```
01 text-string       Pic X(06) value "Hamlet".
01 Pics9Comp5        Pic s9(9) Comp-5 value 6.
01 aString           Object Reference.
   ...
```

Invoke CharacterArray "withLengthValue" Using Pics9Comp5 text-string Returning aString End-Invoke

Below is an example of withLengthValue in the program BookMgr. Notice the class CharacterArray is declared in the Repository section.

Example: using the method withLengthValue.

```
Class-Id. BagManager.
   ...
Repository.
    CharacterArray  Is Class "CharArry"
    BagManager      Is Class "BManager".
Factory.
Data Division.
Working-Storage Section.
01 text-string       Pic X(06) value "Hamlet".
01 Pics9Comp5        Pic s9(9) Comp-5 value 6.
01 aString           Object Reference.
Method-Id. "Create-a-String".
Procedure Division.
    Invoke CharacterArray "withLengthValue" Using Pics9Comp5 text-string
```

Returning aString End-Invoke

    Exit Method.
    End Method "Create-a-String".
    End Factory.

Adding Characters to Instances of CharacterArray

Characters are added to instances of CharacterArray by using the atPut method. atPut is similar to the add method used for Bags. Unlike Bags that are not indexed, atPut adds an element at a programmer-defined position. The following is the atPut syntax.

Format: the atPut method of CharacterArray.

Invoke <u>object-identifier-1</u> "<u>method-name</u>" Using <u>atPosition</u> <u>data-item</u> End-Invoke

where:
        object-identifier-1 is the name of the CharacterArray instance,
        method-name is atPut,
        atPosition is the programmer-defined location declared as Pic s9(09)
          Comp-5, and
        data-item is the data-name or literal containing a character.

Below is an example of putting the character "A" at position 22 in *aString*. Note that the capacity of the instance must be large enough to accommodate the declared position, otherwise an error will result. A good rule to follow is to place atPut within an Evaluate or If statement to ensure the position is within the bounds of the instance capacity.

Example: using the atPut message on aString.

```
01 i              Pic s9(09) Comp-5.
01 atPosition     Pic s9(09) Comp-5 Value 22.
...
Invoke aString "Capacity" returning i
Evaluate True
```

> When i >= atPosition
>> Invoke aString "atPut" Using atPosition, "A"
> End-Evaluate

CharacterArray-Changing Methods: grow, growTo

The **grow** method is used to increase the capacity of a CharacterArray instance. Unlike a **Bag** an instance of CharacterArray does not automatically increase its capacity.

The following is the syntax used to increase the capacity of an instance of CharacterArray.

Format: the grow method of CharacterArray.

Invoke <u>object-identifier-1</u> "<u>method-name</u>"

where:

object-identifier-1 is the name of the CharacterArray instance and method-name is grow.

The following is an example of increasing the capacity of *aString*, by sending it the **grow** message.

Example: sending the grow method to aString.

Invoke aString "grow"

The capacity of *aString* after receiving the **grow** message is platform dependent. In other words, depending on the platform (Unix, DOS, OS/2, or other) the capacity will vary.

The **growTo** method, on the other hand, is programmer defined. **growTo** will increase as well as decrease the capacity of an instance. The following is the **growTo** syntax.

Format: the growTo method of CharacterArray.

Invoke <u>object-identifier-1</u> "<u>method-name</u>" Using <u>size</u> Returning <u>object-identifier-2</u> End-Invoke

where:

object-identifier-1 is the name of the CharacterArray instance,

method-name is growTo,

size is the programmer-defined capacity declared as Pic X(04) Comp-5, and

object-identifier-2 is an object handle set to null.

The following is an example of sending *aString* the growTo message.

Example: sending the growTo method to aString.

```
01 PicXComp5      Pic X(04) Comp-5 Value 100.
01 nullObject     Object Reference.
...
Set nullObject to null
```
Invoke aString "growTo" Using PicXComp5 Returning nullObject End-Invoke

Below is an example of decreasing the capacity of *aString*.

```
move 100 to PicXComp5
Invoke aString "growTo" Using PicXComp5 Returning nullObject End-Invoke

move 20 to PicXComp5
```

Invoke aString "growTo" Using PicXComp5 Returning nullObject End-Invoke

CharacterArray-Converting Method: asBag

An instance of a CharacterArray may be converted into an instance of a Bag. The following shows the syntax.

Format: syntax for converting a collection class to another type of collection class.

Invoke object-identifier-1 "method-name" Returning object-identifier-2 End-Invoke

where:

object-identifier-1 is the name of the Bag instance,

asBag is the method name, and
object-identifier-2 is the object handle of the new collection instance.

Below is an example wherein *aString* has been created and is converted to an instance of the class Bag.

Example: converting aString into an instance of a Bag.

```
01 aBag        Object Reference.
01 aString     Object Reference.
...
```

Invoke aString "asBag" Returning aBag

CharacterArray-Copying Method: copyEmpty

The copy method examined for the collection class Bag works equally well on instances of CharacterArray. Another method for copying is copyEmpty. CopyEmpty returns an empty instance of the same type of collection class. The following code shows the syntax.

Format: syntax for copyEmpty.

Invoke <u>object-identifier-1</u> "<u>method-name</u>" Returning <u>object-identifier-2</u> End-Invoke

where:

object-identifier-1 is the name of the CharacterArray instance,
copyEmpty is the method-name, and
object-identifier-2 is the object handle of the new collection instance
(the same type as object-identifier-1).

In the following example *aString* has already been created and a new instance, *aString1*, is created.

Example: copyEmpty returning aString1.

```
01 aString     Object Reference.
01 aString1    Object Reference.
...
```

Invoke aString "copyEmpty" Returning aString1

CharacterArray-Inquiry Methods: Capacity and Size

Like Bag, CharacterArray provides methods for determining the capacity and size of an instance. The following is the syntax for finding the capacity of a CharacterArray object.

Format: syntax for finding the capacity of an instance of a CharacterArray.

Invoke <u>object-identifier-1</u> "<u>method-name</u>" Returning <u>data-name-1</u> End-Invoke

where:
>   object-identifier-1 is the name of the CharacterArray instance,
>   capacity is the method-name, and
>   data-name-1 is a data-name declared as Pic s9(9) Comp-5 (a Micro
>   Focus data type similar to signed binary).

The following is an example of asking *aString* (its "Capacity") how many bytes it can hold.

Example: finding the capacity of an instance of a CharacterArray.

>   01 String-Capacity   Pic s9(9) Comp-5.
>   ...

Invoke aString "Capacity" Returning String-Capacity End-Invoke

The following is the syntax for the size method of a CharacterArray instance.

Format: syntax for finding the size of an instance of CharacterArray.

Invoke <u>object-identifier-1</u> "<u>method-name</u>" Returning <u>data-name-1</u> End-Invoke

where:
>   object-identifier-1 is the name of the CharacterArray instance,
>   size is the method-name,
>   data-name-1 is a data-name declared as Pic s9(9) Comp-5 (a Micro
>   Focus data type similar to signed binary).

The following is an example of asking *aString* how many characters it currently holds (its "Size").

Example: finding the size of an instance of a CharacterArray.

01 String-Size   Pic s9(9) Comp-5.

...

Invoke aString "Size" Returning String-Size End-Invoke

CharacterArray-Retrieving Methods: at and getValue

CharacterArray, unlike Bag, is a type of SequencedCollection, which means elements may be retrieved based on position. At is the reciprocal method to atPut (the method that adds elements to a Sequenced-Collection). The following is the syntax for the at method.

Format: syntax for retrieving an element from an instance of CharacterArray.

Invoke object-identifier-1 "method-name" Using atPosition Returning data-item End-Invoke

where:

object-identifier-1 is the name of the CharacterArray instance,
method-name is at,
atPosition is the programmer-defined location declared as Pic s9(09) Comp-5, and
data-item is the data-name that will contain the returned character.

Below is an example of returning the third character from *aString*. The size of the instance must be within the range of the declared position; otherwise an error will result. A good rule to follow is to place at within an Evaluate or If statement to ensure the position is within the bounds of the instance capacity.

Example: using the atPut message on aString.

01 i   Pic s9(09) Comp-5.
01 atPosition   Pic s9(09) Comp-5 Value 22.
01 aCharacter   Pic X(01).

...

Invoke aString "size" returning i

```
Evaluate True
    When atPosition < = i
        Invoke aString "at" Using atPosition Returning aCharacter
End-Evaluate
```

The method **getValue** returns a string from an instance of **CharacterArray**. The following is the syntax.

Format: syntax for retrieving a string from an instance of CharacterArray.

Invoke object-identifier-1 "method-name" Returning data-item End-Invoke

where:

object-identifier-1 is the name of the **CharacterArray** instance,
method-name is **getValue**, and
data-item is the data-name that will contain the returned string.

In a previous example, we created an instance of **CharacterArray** called *aString* that contained the value *Hamlet*. The **getValue** method may be used to retrieve the string from the object as follows.

Example: using the method getValue.

```
Class-Id. BagManager.
...
Factory.
Data Division.
Working-Storage Section.
01 text-string        Pic X(06) value "Hamlet".
01 return-string      Pic X(06).
01 Pics9Comp5         Pic s9(9) Comp-5 value 6.
01 aString            Object Reference.
Method-Id. "Create-and-Return-String".
Procedure Division.
    Invoke CharacterArray "withLengthValue" Using Pics9Comp5 text-string
        Returning aString End-Invoke
```

Invoke aString "getValue" Returning return-string End-Invoke
> Exit Method.
> End Method "Create-and-Return-String".
> End Factory.

CharacterArray-Testing Methods: equal, equalsIgnoreCase, equalByLengthValue

CharacterArray provides a number of methods for comparing the contents of the collection to other objects or strings. We examine equal, equalsIgnoreCase, and equalByLengthValue. Equal is used to compare one object to another. The following is the syntax.

> Format: comparing an object containing a string to another object containing a string using equal.

Invoke object-identifier-1 "method-name" Using object-identifier-2
Returning result End-Invoke

where:
> object-identifier-1 is a CharacterArray instance containing a string;
> method-name is equal;
> object-identifier-2 is a CharacterArray instance containing a string; and
> result is either 1 for equal or 0 for not equal declared using Pic X
> > Comp-5 (a Micro Focus data type comparable to unsigned binary).
> > May be treated as a pseudo-Boolean.

The following is an example of using equal to compare *aString* to *aString1*, both of which have been previously created.

> Example: using equal to compare objects containing strings.
> 01 PicXComp5   Pic X Comp-5.
> ...

Invoke aString "equal" Using aString1 Returning PicXComp5 End-Invoke

Below is an example of using **equal** in the program **BookMgr**. First *aString* is created with the value *Hamlet,* then *aString1* is created with the value *Macbeth,* then the objects are compared using **equal**. In this case, a "0" is returned because the two objects are not equal.

Example: comparing two objects using equal.

```
Class-Id. BagManager.
...
Repository.
    CharacterArray    Is Class "CharArry"
    BagManager        Is Class "BManager".
Factory.
Data Division.
Working-Storage Section.
01 text-string       Pic X(10) value "Hamlet".
01 text-string1      Pic X(10) value "Macbeth".
01 Pics9Comp5        Pic s9(9) Comp-5 value 10.
01 PicXComp5         Pic X Comp-5 value 0.
01 aString           Object Reference.
01 aString1          Object Reference.
Method-Id. "Create-and-Compare".
Procedure Division.
    Invoke CharacterArray "withLengthValue" Using Pics9Comp5 text-string
        Returning aString End-Invoke
    Invoke CharacterArray "withLengthValue" Using Pics9Comp5 text-string1
        Returning aString1 End-Invoke

    Invoke aString "equal" Using aString1 Returning aResult
    Evaluate aResult
        When 1
        ...
    Exit Method.
End Method "Create-a-String".
End Factory.
```

EqualsIgnoreCase compares objects, ignoring the case. The **equalsIgnoreCase** syntax is identical to **equal** with the exception of the method-name.

Format: comparing objects containing strings using equalsIgnoreCase.

Invoke <u>object-identifier-1</u> <u>"method-name"</u> Using <u>object-identifier-2</u>
Returning <u>result</u> End-Invoke

where:

object-identifier-1 is a CharacterArray instance containing a string;
method-name is equalsIgnoreCase;
object-identifier-2 is a CharacterArray instance containing a string; and
result is either 1 for equal or 0 for not equal declared using Pic X
Comp-5 (a Micro Focus data type comparable to unsigned binary).

The following is an example comparing "Hamlet" to "HAMLET". The comparison in this case returns a "1" because the values, except for the case, are equal.

Example: comparing two objects using equalsIgnoreCase.

```
Class-Id. BagManager.
   ...
01 text-string        Pic X(10) value "Hamlet".
01 text-string1       Pic X(10) value "HAMLET".
01 Pics9Comp5         Pic s9(9) Comp-5 value 10.
01 PicXComp5          Pic X Comp-5 value 0.
01 aString            Object Reference.
01 aString1           Object Reference.
Method-Id. "Create-and-Compare".
Procedure Division.
   Invoke CharacterArray "withLengthValue" Using Pics9Comp5 text-string
      Returning aString End-Invoke
   Invoke CharacterArray "withLengthValue" Using Pics9Comp5 text-string1
      Returning aString1 End-Invoke

   Invoke aString "equalsIgnoreCase" Using aString1 Returning aResult
   Evaluate aResult
      When 1
         ...
```

EqualByLengthValue compares an object to a string. Unlike the previous two methods, equal and equalsIgnoreCase, the string compared to an object does not need to be in an object. The following is the syntax for equalByLengthValue.

Format: comparing an object containing a string to a string (not in an object) using equalByLengthValue.

> Invoke <u>object-identifier</u> "<u>method-name</u>" Using <u>length</u> <u>data-item</u> Returning <u>result</u> End-Invoke

where:

> object-identifier is a CharacterArray instance containing a string;
> method-name is equalByLengthValue;
> length is the number of bytes compared given as Pic X(04) Comp-5;
> data-item is the data-name or literal containing a string; and
> result is either 1 for equal or 0 for not equal declared using Pic X
> Comp-5 (a Micro Focus data type comparable to unsigned binary).

EqualByLengthValue compares not only the values but also the length of the strings. For example, if the string within the object contains a value of "Hamlet" and it was created with a length of 10, and the string being compared to the object has a value of "Hamlet" but a length of only 6 (given in the Using parameter length), the comparison will return a "0", an unequal condition. The following is an example that returns an unequal condition due to the difference in lengths.

Example: comparing two objects using equalByLengthValue.

```
Class-Id. BagManager.
...
01 text-string        Pic X(10) value "Hamlet".
01 text-string1       Pic X(06) value "Hamlet".
01 Pics9Comp5         Pic s9(9) Comp-5 value 10.
01 PicXComp5          Pic X Comp-5 value 0.
01 PicXCompX          Pic X Comp-X value 6.
01 aString            Object Reference.
Method-Id. "Create-and-Compare".
Procedure Division.
```

Invoke CharacterArray "withLengthValue" Using Pics9Comp5 text-string
Returning aString End-Invoke

Invoke aString "equalByLengthValue" Using PicXCompX text-string1
Returning aResult

Evaluate aResult
When 1

...

The following example returns an equal condition.

Example: comparing two objects using equalByLengthValue.

Class-Id. BagManager.

...

```
01 text-string        Pic X(10) value "Hamlet".
01 text-string1       Pic X(10) value "Hamlet".
01 Pics9Comp5         Pic s9(9) Comp-5 value 10.
01 aResult            Pic X Comp-X value 0.
01 aLength            Pic X(04) Comp-5 value 10.
01 aString            Object Reference.
```
Method-Id. "Create-and-Compare".
Procedure Division.

Invoke CharacterArray "withLengthValue" Using Pics9Comp5 text-string
Returning aString End-Invoke

Invoke aString "equalByLengthValue" Using aLength text-string1 Returning
aResult

Evaluate aResult
When 1

...

Storing CharacterArray Instances in a Bag

A useful technique for working with strings as objects is to use a **Bag** object to store
Character Array instances. For example, consider the following input file of names.

Barbara   Bennet
Kathy   Franklin
Theodore   Gowers
Sandra   Nguyen
Victor   Sanchez
...

The file could be read and the values stored in an instance of **CharacterArray** as follows.

Example: storing input records in an instance of CharacterArray.

```
01 i                    Pic s9(09) Comp-5.
01 Pics9Comp5           Pic s9(9) Comp-5 Value 10000.
01 text-string          Pic X(10000) Value Spaces.
01 atPosition           Pic s9(09) Comp-5 Value 1.
01 Input-Record         Pic X(20).
01 aString              Object Reference.
    ...
Method-Id. "Create-aString".
Procedure Division.
    Invoke CharacterArray "withLengthValue" Using Pics9Comp5 text-string
        Returning aString End-Invoke
    Invoke Self "Read-and-Store-Record"
  Exit Method.
End Method "Create-aString".
  * -------------------------------------------------------
Method-Id. "Read-and-Store-Record".
Procedure Division.
    Read Input-File into Input-Record
        At End ....
    Not At End
        Invoke aString "atPut" Using atPosition, Input-Record End-Invoke
        Compute atPosition = atPosition + 21
    End-Read
    Exit Method.
End Method "Read-and-Store-Record".
```

In the above example, the method **Create-aString** creates a string of 10,000 empty spaces. The method **Read-and-Store-Record** puts each input record into *aString* at the location indicated by **atPosition**. *AString* would look as follows (Figure 9.10).

FIGURE 9.10. An example of a string.

CharacterArray methods for manipulating records are limited because they generally depend on strings of equal length. For example, *aString* with a capacity of 10 containing *Hamlet* and *aString1* containing *Hamlet* with a capacity of 8 are not considered equal because of the difference in string capacities.

Rather than creating one large instance of **CharacterArray**, many smaller instances can be created, each one containing an input record. The individual instances may then be placed in a **Bag** object. Figure 9.11 depicts this.

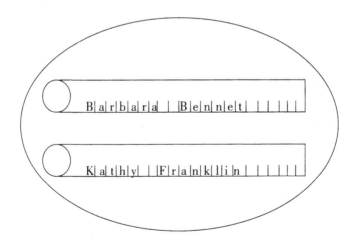

FIGURE 9.11. A **Bag** object containing **CharacterArray** instances.

The following is a routine for reading an input file, converting the records to instances of **CharacterArray**, and then placing each instance into *aBag*.

Example: storing instances of CharacterArray in aBag.

```
01 i                   Pic s9(09) Comp-5.
01 Pics9Comp5          Pic s9(9) Comp-5 Value 20.
01 PicX4Comp5          Pic X(04) Comp-5 Value 100.
01 text-string         Pic X(10000) Value Spaces.
01 atPosition          Pic s9(09) Comp-5 Value 1.
01 Input-Record        Pic X(20).
01 aString             Object Reference.
01 aBag                Object Reference.
    ...
Method-Id. "Create-aBag".
Procedure Division.
    Invoke Bag "ofReferences" Using PicX4Comp5 Returning aBag End-Invoke
    Invoke Self "Read-and-Store-Record"
  Exit Method.
End Method "Create-aBag".
  * -------------------------------------------------------
Method-Id. "Read-and-Store-Record".
Procedure Division.
    Read Input-File into Input-Record
        At End ....
        Not At End
      Invoke CharacterArray "withLengthValue" Using Pics9Comp5 Input-Record
        Returning aString End-Invoke

      Invoke aBag "add" Using aString
    End-Read
  Exit Method.
End Method "Read-and-Store-Record".
```

Searching for a particular record may be accomplished by using the **includes** message. Finding duplicate entries is accomplished by sending the **occurencesOf** message to *aBag*. **OccurencesOf** is covered later in the chapter.

CREATING DICTIONARY INSTANCES

Dictionary is a keyed collection class that does not allow duplicate keys. Instances of **Dictionary** automatically grow to accept additional elements. **Dictionary** stores data in

strings as objects. Dictionary is a subclass of ValueSet, an example of the third of our three collection class types (Bag, SequencedCollection, and ValueSet).

Instances of Dictionary are slightly more complicated to create than instances of either CharacterArray or Bag. A template, describing the key and element portions of the instance, must be created before creating the Dictionary instance. The template defines what type of elements will be stored in the Dictionary.

There are a number of methods to create the template, depending on what type of key/element combination is required. Dictionary allows both the key and the element portions of the template to be intrinsic data, or both portions to be objects, or it allows the key to be intrinsic data and the element to be an object or vice versa. Figure 9.12 depicts the possible template combinations.

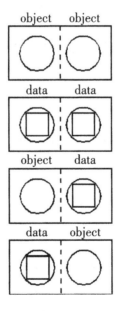

FIGURE 9.12. Possible template combinations key/component.

Creating the template requires the assistance of two other classes in the class library. The two classes are subclasses of the class Intrinsic. The first is Association, the second is CobolPicX. The following is a hierarchy showing the relationship of the three classes.

>   Intrinsic (Intrnsic)—abstract class
>   Association (Associtn)
>
>   ...
>
>   CobolPicX (PicX)

The class **Intrinsic** provides behavior that is common to all COBOL intrinsic data. The class **Association** stores two elements as a key/component pair, and is commonly used to store the elements of a **Dictionary**. The class **CobolPicX** enables **Pic X** data to be treated as an object.

NewClass is inherited from **Intrinsic** and implements slightly different behaviors in **Association** and **CobolPicX**. **CobolPicX** is used to define the key portion of the key/component combination.

We will create the fourth type of template shown above, a key of intrinsic data and an object as the component. The following is the syntax for creating the key portion.

Format: the newClass method for creating a key.

> Invoke <u>object-identifier-1</u> "<u>method-name</u>" Using <u>length</u> Returning <u>object-identifier-2</u> End-Invoke

where:

>   object-identifier-1 is the class **CobolPicX**,
>   method-name is newClass,
>   length is the key size in bytes given as **Pic s9(09) Comp-5**, and
>   object-identifier-2 is the key portion of the template.

The following example indicates how to create a key of five bytes.

Example: using the newClass method to create a key five bytes in length.

>   01 a-length   Pic s9(09) Comp-5.
>   01 aKey   Object Reference.
>
>   ...
>
>   move 5 to a-length

> Invoke CobolPicX "newClass" Using a-length Returning aKey

The type of key created (in this case **CobolPicX**, for holding **Pic X** data) is used as input to the **Association** method **newClass**. The following is the syntax for **newClass** applied to the class **Association**.

Format: the newClass method for creating a key.

> Invoke <u>object-identifier-1</u> "<u>method-name</u>" Using <u>aKey</u> <u>object-identifier-2</u>
> Returning <u>object-identifier-3</u>

where:

> object-identifier-1 is the class Association,
> method-name is newClass,
> aKey is a previously defined key,
> object-identifier-2 is a nullObject, and
> object-identifier-3 is the template.

The following is an example of creating a template with a key of five bytes (aKey defined above) and an object as the component.

Example: using the newClass method to create a data/object combination template.

> 01 aKey   Object Reference.
> 01 aNullObject   Object Reference.
> 01 aTemPlate   Object Reference.
> ...
> set aNullObject to null

> Invoke Association "newClass" Using aKey, aNullObject Returning aTemPlate

The final step in the creation of a Dictionary instance uses the method ofAssociations to create the instance. The created template is used as input to ofAssociations. The following shows the syntax.

Format: the ofAssociation method for creating an instance of Dictionary.

> Invoke <u>object-identifier-1</u> "<u>method-name</u>" Using <u>aTemPlate</u> <u>a-capacity</u>
> Returning <u>object-identifier-2</u>

where:

> object-identifier-1 is the class Dictionary,
> method-name is ofAssociations,
> aTemPlate is a previously defined template,

a-capacity is the capacity of the Dictionary instance given as Pic s9(09)
Comp-5, and

object-identifier-2 is the instance of Dictionary.

The following is an example of creating a Dictionary instance capable of holding
10 objects.

Example: using ofAssociations to create an instance of Dictionary.

```
01 aDictionary     Object Reference.
01 a-capacity      Pic S9(09) Comp-5.
01 aTemPlate       Object Reference.
...
move 10 to a-capacity
Invoke Dictionary "ofAssociations" Using aTemPlate, a-capacity Returning
    aDictionary
```

The steps are fairly straightforward; first create the key, then create the template,
then create an instance of Dictionary. The following is an example of this. Notice
CobolPicX, Association, and Dictionary are declared in the Repository section.

Example: creating an instance of Dictionary.

```
        Program-Id. BookMgr.
        Environment Division.
        Repository.
            CobolPicX      Is Class "PicX"
            Association    Is Class "Associtn"
            Dictionary     Is Class "Dictinry"
            BagManager     Is Class "BManager".
        Data Division.
        Working-Storage Section.
        01 aKey                Object Reference.
        01 a-length            Pic s9(09) Comp-5.
        01 a-capacity          Pic s9(09) Comp-5.
        01 aNullObject         Object Reference.
        01 aTemPlate           Object Reference.
```

```
01 aDictionary              Object Reference.
Procedure Division.
* -----------------------------------------------------------------*
* Create aKey                                                       *
* -----------------------------------------------------------------*
    move 5 to a-Length
    Invoke CobolPicX "newClass" Using a-length Returning aKey
* -----------------------------------------------------------------*
* Create aTemPlate                                                  *
* -----------------------------------------------------------------*
    set aNullObject to null
    Invoke Association "newClass" Using aKey, aNullObject Returning
        aTemPlate
* -----------------------------------------------------------------*
* Create aDictionary                                                *
* -----------------------------------------------------------------*
    move 5 to a-capacity
    Invoke Dictionary "ofAssociations" Using aTemPlate, a-capacity
        Returning aDictionary
    ...
```

Adding Elements to Instances of Dictionary

One technique of adding elements to instances of Dictionary is atPut. AtPut for Dictionary is very similar to the atPut method used for CharacterArray. The primary difference is the key value. CharacterArray uses a numeric key, Dictionary allows a user-defined key. The instance of Dictionary created above called *aDictionary* uses Pic X data, five bytes long. The following is the atPut syntax.

Format: the atPut method of CharacterArray.

Invoke <u>object-identifier-1</u> "<u>method-name</u>" Using <u>aKey</u> <u>object-identifier-2</u> End-Invoke

where:

      object-identifier-1 is the name of the Dictionary instance,
      method-name is atPut,

aKey is the programmer-defined key, and

object-identifier-2 is the object to be stored at aKey position.

Below is an example of storing a previously created *Book* object at a key value of "123AB."

Example: storing an object at a key value in aDictionary with atPut.

    01 keyValue   Pic X(05).
    01 aBook   Object Reference.
    01 aDictionary   Object Reference.
    ...
    move "123AB" to keyValue

Invoke aDictionary "atPut" Using keyValue, aBook End-Invoke

A Dictionary object does not allow duplicate keys. The component element, however, can be duplicated. For instance, the following example is allowed.

Example: the same object stored at different key values.

    move "123AB" to keyValue
    Invoke aDictionary "atPut" Using keyValue, aBook End-Invoke
    move "123CD" to keyValue

Invoke aDictionary "atPut" Using keyValue, aBook End-Invoke

An attempt to store an object at an existing key value will fail. The following is an example of this.

Example: an attempt to store different objects using the same key value. This will fail.

    move "123AB" to keyValue
    Invoke aDictionary "atPut" Using keyValue, aBook End-Invoke

Invoke aDictionary "atPut" Using keyValue, anotherBook End-Invoke

Dictionary-Changing Method: grow

The grow method is used to increase the capacity of a Dictionary. A Dictionary will automatically increase in capacity to accommodate additional entries. The method growTo is *not* supported for Dictionary instances. The **grow** syntax for Dictionary is identical to the syntax for CharacterArray. The following code offers an example.

Example: sending the grow method to aDictionary.

Invoke aDictionary "grow" End-Invoke

Again, the resulting capacity of a Dictionary instance after receiving the **grow** message is both implementor and platform dependent.

Dictionary-Converting Method: asBag

Instances of a Dictionary may be converted into instances of the other collection classes, including a Bag. The syntax is identical for converting from a Dictionary to a Bag as it is for converting from a CharacterArray to a Bag. The following is an example of the syntax.

Example: converting a Dictionary into an instance of a Bag.

```
01 aBag          Object Reference.
01 aDictionary   Object Reference.
...
```

Invoke aDictionary "asBag" Returning aBag

Dictionary-Copying Method: deepCopy

Dictionary does *not* support either **copy** or **copyEmpty**, the two copying methods previously examined. Instead, to copy instances of Dictionary a method called **deepCopy** is used. The syntax, with the exception of the method name, is identical to the method copy. The following is the **deepCopy** syntax.

Format: syntax for deepCopy.

Invoke <u>object-identifier-1</u> "<u>method-name</u>" Returning <u>object-identifier-2</u> End-Invoke

where:

object-identifier-1 is the name of the Dictionary instance,

deepCopy is the method-name, and
object-identifier-2 is the object handle of the new collection instance
(the same type as object-identifier-1).

The following is an example in which *aDictionary* has previously been created, and a new instance, called *aDictionary2,* containing the same keys and components is created.

Example: deepCopy returning aDictionary2.

```
01 aDictionary     Object Reference.
01 aDictionary2    Object Reference.
...
```

Invoke aDictionary "deepCopy" Returning aDictionary2

Dictionary-Inquiry Methods: Capacity and Size

Like CharacterArray, the methods capacity and size work equally well for Dictionary instances. The syntax is identical. Below are two examples showing the capacity and size messages sent to *aDictionary.*

Example: finding the capacity of an instance of a Dictionary.

```
01 a-capacity      Pic s9(9) Comp-5.
...
```

Invoke aDictionary "Capacity" Returning a-capacity End-Invoke

Example: finding the size of an instance of a Dictionary.

```
01 a-size          Pic s9(9) Comp-5.
...
```

Invoke aDictionary "Size" Returning a-size End-Invoke

Dictionary-Retrieving Method: at

Retrieving elements from a Dictionary is accomplished by using the at method. Dictionary is a user-defined indexed collection, which means elements may be retrieved based on key value. The following is the syntax for the **at** method applied to **Dictionary** with an object as the component.

Format: syntax for retrieving an element from an instance of Dictionary.

Invoke <u>object-identifier-1</u> "<u>method-name</u>" Using <u>aKey</u> Returning <u>object-identifier-2</u> End-Invoke

where:

object-identifier-1 is the name of the **Dictionary** instance,
method-name is **at**,
aKey is the programmer-defined key, and
object-identifier-2 is the handle of the returned instance.

The following is an example of returning the object stored at a key defined as Pic X(05) with a value of "123AB." Note, a key value of "123AB" is different from the value "123ab." If the **Dictionary** does not contain the requested key, an error will result. The **includesKey** method may be used to ensure a collection does contain a key value.

Example: returning the object at the key value "123AB" from aDictionary.

01 anObject   Object Reference.
...

Invoke aDictionary "at" Using "123AB" Returning anObject

Dictionary-Removing Methods: associationAt, removeAssociation, deepFinalize

The method **remove** is not supported by **Dictionary**. Instead, the method **remove-Association** is used to remove selected elements. Removing an element is a two-part process. First, the handle of the association (the key/component) is determined. Second, the handle of the association is used to remove both the key and the component. Finding the handle to the association is done by using a method called **associationAt**. The following is the syntax for **associationAt**.

Format: syntax for the associationAt method.

Invoke <u>object-identifier-1</u> "<u>method-name</u>" Using <u>a-Key</u> Returning <u>object-identifier-2</u> End-Invoke

where:

> object-identifier-1 is the name of the Dictionary instance,
> method-name is associationAt,
> a-Key is a data item or literal containing the value of the key, and
> object-identifier-2 is the handle of the key/component combination.

The following is an example of finding the association handle to the key value "123AB" in *aDictionary*.

Example: return the association handle in aDictionary.

> 01 anAssociation   Object Reference.
> ...

Invoke aDictionary "associationAt" Using "123AB" Returning anAssociation

RemoveAssociation uses the handle to the requested key/component combination as the Using parameter. The following is the removeAssociation syntax.

Format: syntax for the removeAssociation method.

Invoke <u>object-identifier-1</u> "<u>rmethod-name</u>" Using <u>object-identifier-2</u> End-Invoke

where:

> object-identifier-1 is the name of the Dictionary instance,
> method-name is removeAssociation, and
> object-identifier-2 is the association handle representing the key/com-
> ponent being removed from the collection.

The following is an example of removing *aBook* from *aDictionary*, after getting the association handle.

Example: removing an object from a collection using removeAssociation.

Invoke aDictionary "<u>removeAssociation</u>" Using anAssociation End-Invoke

Dictionary does not support the method finalize. To delete an instance of a Dictionary the method deepFinalize must be used. The syntax is shown below.

Format: syntax for deepFinalize.

Invoke object-identifier-1 "method-name" Returning object-identifier-2 End-Invoke

where:

        object-identifier-1 is the name of the Dictionary instance,
        method-name is deepFinalize, and
        object-identifier-2 is the object identifier set to null.

The following is an example of deleting *aDictionary*.

Example: deleting a Dictionary instance.

Invoke aDictionary "deepFinalize" Returning aNullObject End-Invoke

Dictionary-Testing Method: includesKey, occurencesOf

IncludesKey is a method used to determine if a keyed collection contains a particular key value. The following shows the syntax.

Format: syntax for includesKey.

Invoke object-identifier-1 "method-name" Using aKey Returning a-Bool End-Invoke

where:

        object-identifier-1 is the name of the Dictionary instance,
        method-name is includesKey,
        aKey is a data item or literal containing the value of the key, and
        a-Bool is a pseudo-Boolean data item defined as Pic X Comp-5.

The following is an example of code that asks *aDictionary* if the collection contains the key value "11111."

Example: searching for a key.

```
01 a-Boolean      Pic X Comp-5.
88 isYes          value 1.
88 isNo           value 0.
```

...

> Invoke aDictionary "includesKey" Using "11111" Returning a-Boolean

The method **occurencesOf** returns the number of selected elements in a collection. A **Dictionary** permits duplicate component entries, it does not permit duplicate key entries. For example, *aDictionary* may contain two occurrences of *aBook*, each stored under a different key value. The following is the **occurencesOf** syntax.

Format: syntax for occurencesOf.

> Invoke <u>object-identifier-1</u> "<u>method-name</u>" Using <u>object-identifier-2</u>
> Returning <u>data-name</u> End-Invoke

where:

object-identifier-1 is the name of the **Dictionary** instance,
method-name is occurencesOf,
object-identifier-2 is component being searched for, and
data-item is a data-name defined as **Pic s9(09) Comp-5**.

The following is an example that asks *aDictionary* how many times *aBook* is in the collection.

Example: return the number of time aBook is found in aDictionary.

01 book-count   Pic s9(09) Comp-5.

...

> Invoke aDictionary "occurencesOf" Using aBook Returning book-count

COLLECTIONS IN ACTION

This chapter has only begun to present the power and versatility of collections. Knowing which situation requires what kind of collection class distinguishes the beginner from the seasoned veteran and makes the application easier to code and maintain.

Collection classes provide a wide range of options. Although collection classes require a certain overhead, they more than make up for it in their ability to free the programmer of many size-related headaches. In many ways, collections manage themselves if properly constructed. This self-managing capability presents humans the opportunity to make trade-off decisions at their convenience, not the machine's.

The source code (when supplied) of collection classes provides an excellent workshop on how to construct classes for reuse. For the functionality provided, there is very little actual code in a collection class, thanks to inheritance. Code is not duplicated, it is inherited. One of the keys to this reuse is taking advantage of the dynamic (run time) capabilities of Object-Oriented COBOL.

Key Points

- The three major classifications of collection classes are **Bag, SequencedCollection,** and **ValueSet.**
- Objects and intrinsic data may be stored in collections.
- Collection classes provide client objects to be used by the programmer.
- The types of operations that may be performed on collection classes generally fall within one of nine categories.
- Some instances of collection classes automatically grow, others must be sent a message.
- Most collections may be converted to other types of collections.
- Dictionaries provide the ability to store an object along with a key.

Suggested Readings

Kernighan, B., & Plauger, P. (1974). *The Elements of Programming Style.* New York: McGraw-Hill.

Knuth, D. (1992). *Literate Programming.* Stanford, CA: CSLI, Leland Stanford Junior University.

LaLonde, W. (1994). *Discovering Smalltalk.* Menlo Park, CA: Benjamin/Cummings.

Pinson, L., & Weiner, R. (1988). *An Introduction to Object-Oriented Programming and Smalltalk.* Reading, MA: Addison-Wesley.

Wirfs-Brock, R. (1991). Object-Oriented Frameworks. *American Programmer, 4*(10).

Review Questions

9.0   Characterize a collection class.

9.1   What are the three major categories of collection classes? Give an example of each.

9.2   How are instances of collection classes created?

9.3   What is one method used to store objects in a collection class?

9.4   What does "automatically growable" mean?

9.5   How might one store intrinsic data types as objects?

9.6   Implement a method for searching an instance of **Bag**.

9.7   Implement an instance of **Dictionary** to store vehicle registration numbers and car owners.

9.8   How is an instance removed from a **Dictionary**?

9.9   Implement an instance of **Dictionary**, fill it with gift objects, then convert it to a **Bag**.

SECTION IV

PUTTING OBJECTS TO WORK

CHAPTER 10

OBJECT-ORIENTED ANALYSIS AND DESIGN

O bject-oriented analysis and design (OOA&D), like its predecessor structured analysis and design, attempts to provide a path for developers to follow as they strive to build usable systems. Analysis and design methods do not arise in a vacuum, however. Methods only surface after developers wrestle with the capabilities and limitations of programming languages, discovering what works and what does not. Methods are collective wisdom—the fruits of experience. Although Fred Brooks pointed out, "There is no silver bullet," methods at least help keep the target in range.

FOCUS AND FORMAT OF THIS CHAPTER

The purpose of this chapter is twofold. First, to introduce a context called the Rolling Lifecycle Perspective as a tool to understand the phases of object-oriented software development in terms of product and process. Second, to walk through a worked example and apply the Rolling Lifecycle Perspective to the library application.

Concepts

- Candidate classes
- Object-message diagrams
- Object-oriented analysis
- Object-oriented design
- Object sequence chart
- Rolling Lifecycle
- Scenarios

ANALYSIS AND DESIGN

OOA&D methods differ from structured methods in several important ways. First, object-oriented methods focus on objects throughout the entire software development life cycle. Second, object-oriented methods support incremental development, which allows applications to be tested earlier in the life cycle than with conventional methods. In object-oriented development functionality is gradually accrued as a working system is constructed.

Although OOA&D differs in approach from traditional methods, object-oriented analysis is still analysis, object-oriented design is still design, and the objective is still to go from the often fuzzy world of user expectations to the concrete world of programs. The task of analysis is to define "what" the system is expected to do in contrast to "how" it gets accomplished, which is the task of design.

The "what" of analysis involves working with customers, end-users, marketing personnel, sales people, anyone else who may shed light on what the system is expected to do. Designers then structure an architecture around which a solution may be built. In object-oriented development analysis is very much a modeling activity concerned with identifying business classes/objects. The fact that the business objects can be implemented in object-oriented languages establishes a continuity between analysis and design where end-users and designers speak the same language.

In design, the class and object definitions developed from analysis are often refined to meet the constraints of the implementation. Designers make trade-offs in the context of an object-oriented solution to satisfy system requirements. In addition classes are introduced that serve as rubber couplings to isolate the business logic from certain necessary machine dependencies. The output of design is a specification of class descriptions that becomes a roadmap for implementors.

When making changes during systems development, it is important that the reasons for the changes are recorded and maintained as part of the system documentation. Programmers coming along later, in the maintenance phase, should be able to reconstruct the rationale for why the system exists as it does. Unfortunately, many design decisions fall through the cracks and are lost forever, making it extremely difficult and costly for those trying to fix or enhance the system.

The classes and objects introduced during design often have names that reflect their function, such as coordinator, scheduler, dispatcher, or policy manager. These objects provide an infrastructure for an application, often referred to as design patterns, frameworks, or software architectures. These assemblies are often crucial to the success of an application because they address important systems issues, such as performance, reliability, and portability.

Patterns are an important emerging topic in the object-oriented world. One of the more influential books on the subject is *Design Patterns: Elements of Reusable Object-Oriented Software* by Gamma, Helm, Johnson, and Vlissides (1995) (known as the Gang of Four). Patterns represent reuse at a very high level of abstraction, a level that transcends applications and addresses entire systems and common solutions across industries. More information on patterns can be obtained at the patterns home page at http://st-www.cs.uiuc.edu/users/patterns/patterns.html.

Object-Oriented Methods

There are a variety of object-oriented methods that provide guidelines for performing object-oriented development. Currently, several are widely used, including Booch (1994); Coad/Yourdon (1990); Rumbaugh, Blaha, Premerlani, Eddy, and Lorensen

(1991); Jacobson, Christerson, Jonsson, and Overgaard (1992); Shlaer/Mellor (1988); and Wirfs-Brock, Wilkerson, and Wiener (1990). Although the field is still relatively young, the Unified Method (a combination of many of the best techniques from Booch, Rumbaugh, Jacobson, and others) is quickly becoming a standard. OOA&D has matured to the point where useful graphical notational techniques have emerged and found their way into almost all methods. The notations include:

- Class diagrams
- CRC Cards (Class–Responsibility–Collaboration)
- Object-message diagrams
- Use-case scenarios

To help the reader navigate we provide a generic view of object-oriented development rather than focus on any one method and its associated processes and notation. Important to this perspective is how the different notational forms fit into a generalized object-oriented life cycle and what deliverables are associated with different aspects of object-oriented development. The Unified notation, CRC cards, and responsibility-driven design presented in earlier chapters are still used. It is the context of how to properly apply these techniques and notations we address.

The Role of Iteration

A major difference between structured and object-oriented development is the emphasis on iteration. Iteration is possible because objects provide a unifying theme throughout the development life cycle. As a result, ideas can be moved forward from analysis, through design, and tested in code before an entire project is complete. By incrementally testing software components, it is possible to reduce risk by validating the feasibility of different architectures.

Figure 10.1 illustrates the iterative cycle of analysis, design, and code. Because class descriptions are the fundamental units of object-oriented construction, iteration provides early testing and feedback. As Peter Coad describes it, one does some analysis, some design, and some coding, then stands back to assess progress and repeats the cycle. However, the generalized maxim "go forth and iterate" will not get one very far on an actual project. Developers need more detail in order to know where to begin, how to proceed, and what deliverables to generate.

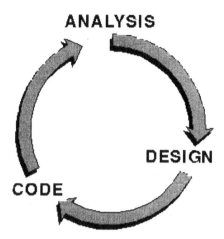

FIGURE 10.1. The cycle of analysis, design, and code.

ROLLING LIFECYCLE PERSPECTIVE

To help understand how OOA&D is actually done, the idea of iterative development is extended into a view we call the Rolling Lifecycle Perspective (RLP). The purpose of the Rolling Lifecycle Perspective is used to connect the fundamental software phases of analysis, high-level design, and low-level design with the iterative cycle of analysis, design, and coding characteristic of object-oriented systems. The Rolling Lifecycle Perspective rolls the iterative triad across time and associates it with deliverables for each phase. The three phases of the RLP are shown in Figure 10.2.

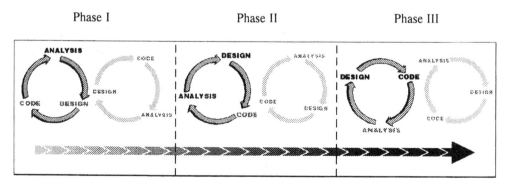

FIGURE 10.2. The three phases of the Rolling Lifecycle.

The RLP is intended to illustrate how object-oriented development is both different from and similar to conventional development. Object-oriented development does not abandon established software practice. There is still analysis and modeling at the front end to capture the business model, there is still high-level design to establish a framework for development, and there is still low-level design to fill in the details needed to actually build the software. The following sections describe each of the three Rolling Lifecycle phases with their associated notational components.

Phase I: Analysis and Modeling

Phase I of an object-oriented development effort is concerned with modeling the business application. The deliverables of Phase I are

- a problem description that defines what the intended software is expected to do
- usage scenarios that will be used to drive design and establish a basis for later testing
- class diagram—a list of candidate classes that are part of the problem domain

Because Phase I is "pure" analysis or modeling, emphasis is on defining the problem and the entities associated with the problem domain. The conventional wisdom for the early stages of analysis is not to spend too much time trying to get objects "just right." Rather, the focus is on laying a foundation for design and additional analysis that will follow in Phases II and III. Contributors to Phase I should include individuals who can take an end-user perspective as well as more technical people.

Problem Description

Phase I involves brainstorming about the problem domain. The initial session should begin with a problem statement, if one exists. If there is no problem statement, then the group should construct one. The problem statement is important in establishing requirements and useful in finding candidate classes.

Candidate Classes

For many, finding the right classes in an application is the hardest part of OOA&D. One technique for getting started is to focus on the nouns and noun phrases in the problem statement. Have a team member write items down on a white board as individuals call out candidate classes. At this early stage of analysis, classes shouldn't be analyzed, only listed.

While listing classes, it may be obvious that certain entities have attributes of importance for the application. If attributes are readily identifiable, then they should be listed along with their classes. For example, the candidate class *Customer* may have readily identifiable attributes of name, address, and telephone number. Record such information but do not spend time trying to list attributes of every candidate class.

Class Diagrams

At the end of an analysis session the candidate classes may be mapped into a class diagram to provide some visual perspective on the system or subsystem being developed. The notation for these classes are the diagrams introduced in Chapter 3. Figure 10.3 provides a very simple diagram showing two classes.

FIGURE 10.3. A class diagram.

The relationship between the classes is an association, which is the simplest relationship. It is better, during this phase, to leave the relationships open (simple) and not become locked into any preconceived aggregate or inheritance relationships.

Candidate classes may include not only physical objects but more abstract entities, such as roles and incidents that are part of an application. Physical objects are, of course, the easiest to identify as they represent actual things such as customers, automatic teller machines (ATM), and accounts. However, more abstract entities, such as coordinators and managers, also qualify as objects. Also important are incident objects that track the occurrence of events and are responsible for holding and maintaining the data associated with events. Examples of incident objects include banking transactions, flights in airline reservations systems, or an alarm event in a security system. Incident objects derive from events occurring within the domain and have responsibility for maintaining the associated data structures.

Scenarios

Use-case scenarios describe instances of system usage. Use cases take an external system view describing the interactions between an actor external to the system and the system itself. Use cases were first described by Ivar Jacobson who had the keen insight that use cases could serve as the basis for system requirements. Since then, use cases have found their way into almost all object-oriented methods and are becoming part of common object-oriented design practice.

The advantages of use cases are

- they correspond to how users view the system
- they are text-based and easy to understand
- they can be constructed iteratively, matching the way object-oriented development is done

After listing candidate classes taken from the problem statement, simple scenarios can be constructed to discover other possible classes. The word scenario as used in object-oriented terminology is in keeping with its more general usage. A scenario is like a small play, act, or sequence of events. As events in the scenario unfold (are carried forward) other actors (potential classes—participants in the mini-series) are unearthed. For example, a scenario for developing a library application would be, "What happens when Rachel Wilson goes to check out a book?" Another scenario would trace the steps and discuss the interactions needed by a system when Rachel returned the book.

A list of scenarios is developed. Keep the scenarios simple. In many cases, complex scenarios are combinations of more simple scenarios. For example, a scenario that begins by asking, "What happens when John Doe goes to check out a book and has too many fines and is checking out too many books and has a number of books overdue?" quickly loses sight of the interaction of a system and an actor. It is better to pose a series of scenarios, such as, "What happens when John goes to check out a book and has overdue books?" "What happens when John goes to check out a book and has too many fines?"

The list of scenarios serves three purposes. First they uncover information about the system under development, second they serve as input to CRC sessions, and third they provide test cases to validate the system's operation.

It is important to stress that in Phase I of OOA&D, the objective is to describe the domain, not design or build an implementation. The scenarios and classes outlined in Phase I should be seen as foundational and subject to change as development proceeds. Some candidate objects will evolve into actual class definitions within the implementation, whereas others may appear as data elements (attributes), and others will disappear.

Classes or Objects?

Sometimes object-oriented terminology can be confusing. It is important to note that while we are looking for entities or objects within the problem domain, the accepted notational form for describing the objects is the class diagram. In object-oriented systems, classes describe the general form of individual objects. Thus, although we talk about finding objects, technically we are finding classes, that is, general descriptions of objects. The descriptions we come up with—customers, accounts, and transactions—represent classes of individual object instances, such as customer Joe Smith, account #212, or transaction-8373.

Iterating in Phase I

Iterative object-oriented development means constantly updating viewpoints and perspectives. As development proceeds, insights occur that may mean reworking or changing classes and scenarios. This is a natural part of object-oriented development. It may be useful, however, to ask questions to stimulate thinking about domain objects. Some questions that may help in eliciting additional facts about the problem domain are:

- What is a more general name for the object? (to identify potential superclasses)
- What is a more specific name for the object? (to identify potential subclasses)
- What is the object composed of? (to identify subparts of a class)
- Is the object part of another object? (to identify subparts of a class)

Phase II: High-Level Design

Phase II builds on the scenarios and candidate classes delivered from Phase I by allocating responsibilities to individual classes. The primary high-level design activity of Phase II centers around CRC cards. In addition, the decisions reached during CRC sessions may be captured in class diagrams. The deliverables of this phase are therefore the CRC cards and class diagrams, which set the stage for the more detailed design work of Phase III.

CRC Cards

As mentioned, CRC cards are an inexpensive, easy-to-use notational technique for identifying classes and assigning responsibilities to those classes. Originally CRC cards were used to help people begin thinking in object-oriented terms. More recently, CRC cards have been recognized as a useful technique in their own right for actually doing object-oriented design.

The typical CRC card is a 3 x 5 (or 4 x 6) index card. The top of the card is used for the class name and any superclasses of the class. The remainder of the front of the card is divided into two columns: one for listing class responsibilities and the other for listing the collaborators needed to help carry out the responsibilities (see Figure 10.4). The reverse side of the card is used to give a brief description of the class and class attributes as they are uncovered during the design process.

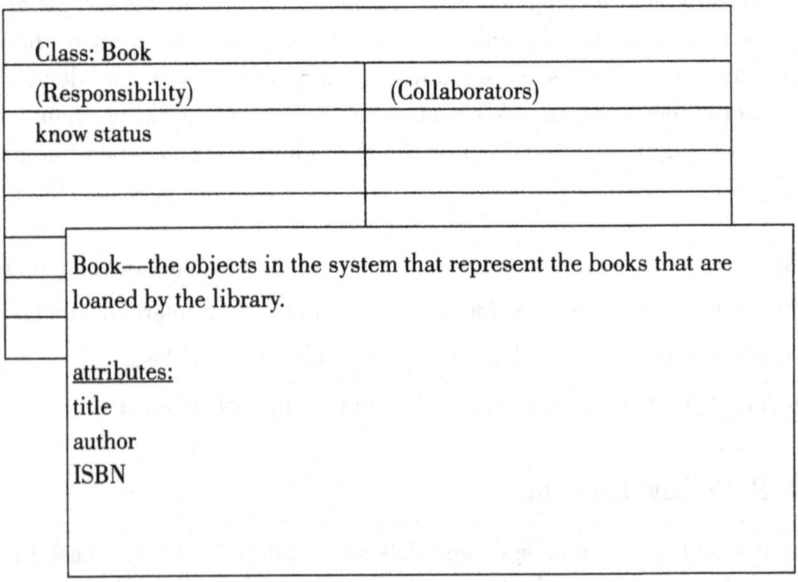

Class: Book	
(Responsibility)	(Collaborators)
know status	

Book—the objects in the system that represent the books that are loaned by the library.

attributes:
title
author
ISBN

FIGURE 10.4. A CRC card.

The scenarios serve as input to the CRC sessions. For example, one scenario is "What happens when Rachel Wilson goes to check out a book?" By constructing the sequence of events that must occur to support this system functionality, the classes discovered during high-level and low-level design are assigned responsibilities. In addition, other candidate classes necessary to support the scenario become apparent.

The word *"know"* in the phrase "know due date" in the responsibility column of the *Book* class above is a key element in how we seal ourselves off from the design of the application, the unnecessary details of data structures, data representation, and a host of other related data questions. We do not ignore data but do not dwell on it. By saying an object "knows" something we indicate that the particular attribute is either maintained by the object or the object will be responsible for obtaining the data. We do not allow the underlying details of machine dependency to creep into design decisions during the early stages.

Later, in low-level design, we will introduce a class that will be responsible for interacting with whatever type of data structure we must deal with. In this way, should our data repository change from, let's say, an indexed file to a database, it does not impact our system. The only class that would need to be modified would be the class responsible for interacting with the data structure. We could even change the location of our data structure to reside on a remote client–server with minimal impact.

Class Diagrams

During high-level design, the relationships between classes begin to emerge. Class visibility, the requirements that one class knows or doesn't know about another class, also begins to take form. We want to constrain the visibility each class has to others in the system. In this way we limit the possible couplings between classes, simplify our implementation, and increase the likelihood that certain classes may be reused in other applications. We will more fully cover this issue in Phase III.

Figure 10.5 offers a simple example of the inheritance relationships between the classes *Item, Book, Video,* and *Audio.*

Phase III: Low-Level Design

Phase III adds the necessary details to turn a design into an application. Class definitions must have a sufficient level of detail to describe messages, attributes, object creation, object destruction, inheritance relationships, and class/object visibility. The deliverables of Phase III include:

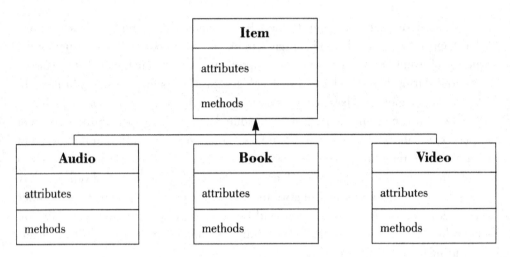

FIGURE 10.5. A class diagram.

- class diagrams
- CRC cards
- data dictionary
- object-message diagrams (message-trace diagram, optional)

Together, these deliverables specify sufficient detail so that an implementor can generate code that tests both usability and performance. Users can validate whether the software actually meets expectations and designers can test early deliverables against critical assumptions. This feedback helps reduce life cycle costs because faulty assumptions are much less costly to change if discovered early.

Object-Message Diagram

Object-message diagrams provide additional detailed information about collaborating objects by graphically specifying the sequence of messages used to get a particular job done. Message sequencing specifies how different objects in the system communicate. Object-message diagrams document object interaction by graphically specifying:

- the sender of the message
- the receiver of the message
- the name, parameters, and return value, if any, of the message

Depending on the amount of documentation required, there may be an object-message diagram for each major function of the system. Figure 10.6 shows a partial object-message diagram showing the collaboration of a customer, book, and date object in support of the book check-out operation.

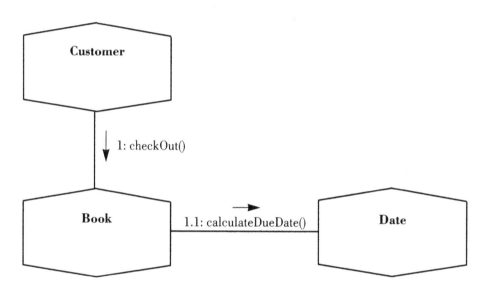

FIGURE 10.6. An object-message diagram.

Message-Trace Diagram

Message-trace diagrams provide an alternative method of describing the same set of interactions that are depicted in object-message diagrams. In message-trace diagrams, the objects are represented as vertical lines and the messages sent between objects are indicated by arrows between the lines. Message-trace diagrams are read from top to bottom, reflecting the sequence of messages over time. Figure 10.7 illustrates a message-trace diagram.

One benefit in using message-trace diagrams in lieu of or in combination with object-message diagrams is the script column that allows more explanation about the operation. Figure 10.8 shows the object-message diagram of Figure 10.6 shown as a message-trace diagram.

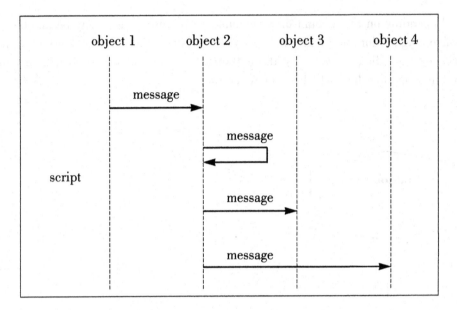

FIGURE 10.7. A message-trace diagram.

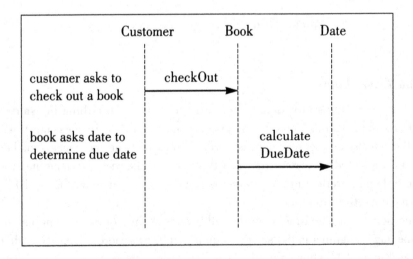

FIGURE 10.8. A message-trace diagram.

Object Visibility

In object-oriented systems, in order for one object to send another object a message, the receiving object must be visible to the sending object. Visibility options include global visibility, visibility maintained as part of an object's internal data store, or visibility resulting from passing an object reference as a parameter with a message.

For example, consider a high-level design that specifies object A sends a message to object B. To program this, there are three possibilities:

1. B must be global to A.
2. B must be defined as part of A.
3. B must be passed as a parameter to A.

Table 10.1 lists the alternatives with their associated pros and cons.

TABLE 10.1. Options for Object Visibility

Alternatives	Pros	Cons
B is global	Easy to program	B is potentially coupled to all other objects, making change difficult
B is part of A	Useful when there is a natural association between two classes	Makes it more difficult to decouple A and B for reuse in other systems
B is passed as a parameter to A	Easy to reuse A and B separately in different systems	Design strategy must allocate responsibility for A passing B as a parameter

Those classes in an application that are only sent messages by other classes (and by classes we mean classes and objects) are more likely candidates for reuse because their function is strictly as server classes, supplying requests and information. These classes do not themselves maintain knowledge about the rest of the application.

Class Diagrams

In addition the responsibilities assigned during CRC sessions can begin to be assigned as class methods. Responsibilities do not necessarily map one-for-one to methods, so care must be exercised. For example, during implementation one responsibility may require several methods and/or several responsibilities may be handled by one method.

Data Dictionary

The data dictionary is a description of the important terms and entries that define an application. When developing using CRC cards, a data dictionary can be constructed by listing all the CRC card classes and their attributes. In addition, superclasses, methods, and invariants* may also be included. Table 10.2 shows a data dictionary that can be a useful component of the system documentation.

The Set of Documents

The documents described (a problem statement, scenarios, class diagrams, object-message diagrams, CRC cards, message-trace diagrams, and a data dictionary), in total, are a complete description for developing an application. A programmer should be able to look at the package of specifications and directly code the system.

A good designer works defensively, operating under the assumption that a relatively inexperienced programmer will handle the coding. A good design specification should omit as little as possible because coding for an object-oriented system should not be a creative act.

A WORKED EXAMPLE OF OBJECT-ORIENTED ANALYSIS AND DESIGN

The following section describes how OOA&D is actually carried out by stepping through an example of object-oriented system building. The three phases of the Rolling Lifecycle are tracked to see how a system is actually constructed from the deliverables due in each stage.

The Problem

Our target application is the automation of a corporate library. Company employees check out and return materials as well as do searches. Currently, the system is partially

---

* Invariants are a form of assertion-based programming that guarantee specified data items will not be changed during the execution of an invariant method. Invariants are specified in the proposed COBOL 97 standard.

TABLE 10.2. A Data Dictionary

Item	Kind	Description
Customer	Class	Responsible for maintaining customer data and computing monthly deductions
Person	Superclass	Defines attributes common to subclasses of Customer and Client
computeAge	Method	Code that computes age based on birthday and current date
Name	Attribute	Text
Address	Attribute	Text
Transaction	Class	Responsible for maintaining type of transaction and start date

computerized based on a batch-processing operation that generates reports at the end of each day. The reports are used by librarians to determine whether a borrower can check out materials based on whether fines over $10 are owed or too many books are checked out.

The Players

Experience with object-oriented software construction has found that teams of about 5 or 6 participants are good-sized working groups. Although the actual composition of teams will vary, members should be drawn from the following categories:

- a facilitator skilled in object-oriented methods
- systems people, knowledgeable about computer operations
- end-user representatives, knowledgeable about how the system will be used

Phase I: Analysis

The objective of Phase I is to produce the following deliverables:

- a problem statement

- scenarios of usage
- a list of candidate classes

Problem Statement

Because the software system is intended to replace an existing semi-automated system, we will assume that the following problem statement has already been formulated.

> Develop software for a corporate library system to automate the checkout and return of library materials, which include books, videos, and audiotapes. The system should also support on-line search based on author, title, and keywords.
>
> An important aspect of the system will be a mechanism for restricting the checkout of materials based on an employee's overdue fines and unreturned materials. Employees who have accumulated over \$10 in unpaid fines or who have more than 5 library items checked out will not be able to check out additional materials. Fines are accrued as follows: books are \$1, audiotapes \$2, and videos \$3 a day for every day the item is overdue.

Scenarios

With the problem statement formulated, the team assembles for a brainstorming session to identify scenarios of usage. Scenarios will be used later to drive the high-level design effort in Phase II. When formulating scenarios it is important to focus on the most common cases and not worry about exceptions until later.

For clarity we are limiting the dialogues to three participants. In an actual development situation, however, one would expect additional contributors. In our example the participants include Alex, the facilitator, with experience in building object-oriented systems; Brenda, the librarian, who has worked in the library for several years and is knowledgeable about library procedures; and Nick, the systems analyst, who has been responsible for maintaining the database that is used to generate reports for the current library system.

Figure 10.9 is a picture of our players going to work.

Scene 1.   Initial Brainstorming.

Alex: Let's try and identify the major scenarios that will occur in the library. Brenda, as you are most familiar with the day-to-day library operations, please tell us what the most common library scenarios are.

Brenda: The most common scenario is checking out books. An employee comes up

Library Application
Book
Video
Audio

FIGURE 10.9.   Alex standing, Brenda and Nick sitting.

to the desk and presents an ID card and a book. I look up the employee on the computer printout that Nick sends me each morning to see if the employee owes over $10 or has more than 5 books checked out. If not, I let her check out the book. I remove the card from the back, stamp it with the due date, write the employee number on it, and put the card in a box for the data-entry clerk.

Alex: OK, that gives us an idea about how things are done with the manual system. What we need is a scenario that can be used to drive our efforts to automate the process. The key is to focus on the basic, most common scenario before dealing with exceptional conditions.

Nick: Like just checking out a book without considering delinquent employees?

Alex: Yes.

Nick: Well, an employee comes up to the desk and presents an ID card and a book. Both employee ID and book ID are entered into the system. The system approves the checkout and prints a receipt for the employee indicating the due date.

Alex: Good. That captures the basic checkout scenario. Are there any other scenarios that describe what the system needs to be able to support?

Brenda: Checking a book in and querying the library database.
Alex: All right, shall we try and formulate our scenario deliverables?

After some discussion, the team comes up with the following scenarios.

Scenario 1: Check Out
An employee comes up to the desk and presents an ID card and a book. Both employee ID and book ID are entered into the system. The system approves the checkout and prints a receipt for the employee indicating the due date.

Scenario 2: Return
An employee comes up to the desk with an item to be returned. The book ID is entered into the system.

Scenario 3: Query
An employee comes up to the desk requesting information based on author, title, or keyword. The request is entered into the system and a printout is generated with title, author, and call number for materials satisfying the criteria.

Candidate Class List

After the problem statement and important scenarios have been formulated, the facilitator can go to the front of the room and ask for the candidate classes that are part of the problem description and scenarios. As participants come up with candidate classes, the facilitator should write them all down on a white board or flip chart.

After a bit of brainstorming the group comes up with the following list:

book	database
video	search
employee	book ID
employee ID	ISBN
librarian	audiotape

Phase II: High-Level Design

Scene: *Defining CRC cards.*

Alex: Now that we have defined several scenarios and candidate classes, let's begin with book checkout and try to identify classes involved in the scenario. Which of the candidate classes should we make responsible for handling the book checkout?

Brenda: How about the Librarian, just the way it is now?

Alex: Yes, that's fine. In fact it is often useful to define a class that parallels roles in the real world. Remember that our class definitions can represent not only things but roles and events.

Nick: But if the Librarian class is responsible for checking out books, does that mean it has to keep all the employee data?

Alex: No, that's where collaboration comes in. The Librarian can rely on other objects to help check out books. What other classes do we need?

Nick: The database I maintain can deliver information about who checked out what book when, but we rely on Brenda to hand-calculate overdue fines. Should we continue to make the Librarian responsible for fine calculation?

Brenda: That seems like too much to ask of the Librarian, just like now.

Alex: There's some truth to that. Often it makes sense to let the calculation occur where the data is.

Nick: The book?

Alex: Yes, since checkin and checkout data are associated with the book, let the book compute the overdue fines, if any. Remember, we need to get away from thinking of data as passive entities. We're in the world of objects now.

Nick: But there may be more than one book checked out. A book doesn't know about other books checked out.

Brenda: Why don't we put the individual's outstanding books into a collection and let the collection do our computation for us?

Alex: That's what collections are for. If the items within the collection can do individual calculations, the collection can iterate over the collection and compute things like sums, averages, and counts quite easily.

Brenda: OK. So if the Librarian is responsible for book checkout, then it can do its job with help from Books and the database.

Alex: Instead of making a direct connection to a database, it's common to set up a DataBase Manager Class to handle communication between the application and the database. This decouples the application from a dependence on a particular database or database language.

Nick: So we don't have to write SQL code right now!!

Alex: Right. All we need to do is specify what responsibility we expect of the DataBase Manager class. If we get the interface right, implementing it can be done later.

Nick: Aren't we forgetting the data that triggers all of this? Who's responsible for getting the Employee ID and the ID of the book that's being checked out? Do we need to worry about a scan code or data-input screen?

Alex: No, we can just declare a User Interface Manager class that will ultimately deal with the GUI or scan codes or whatever. Just like our strategy for the database, we can talk to an intermediary and free ourselves from getting bogged down in detail that's better left until later.

The team develops the following CRC cards from their high-level design session (Figures 10.10, 10.11).

Class: Librarian

(Responsibilities)	(Collaborators)
check out book	Employee, Book
	Database Manager,
	User Interface Manager

Class: DataBase Manager

(Responsibilities)	(Collaborators)
return Employee object	

FIGURE 10.10. Some CRC cards resulting from the team's session.

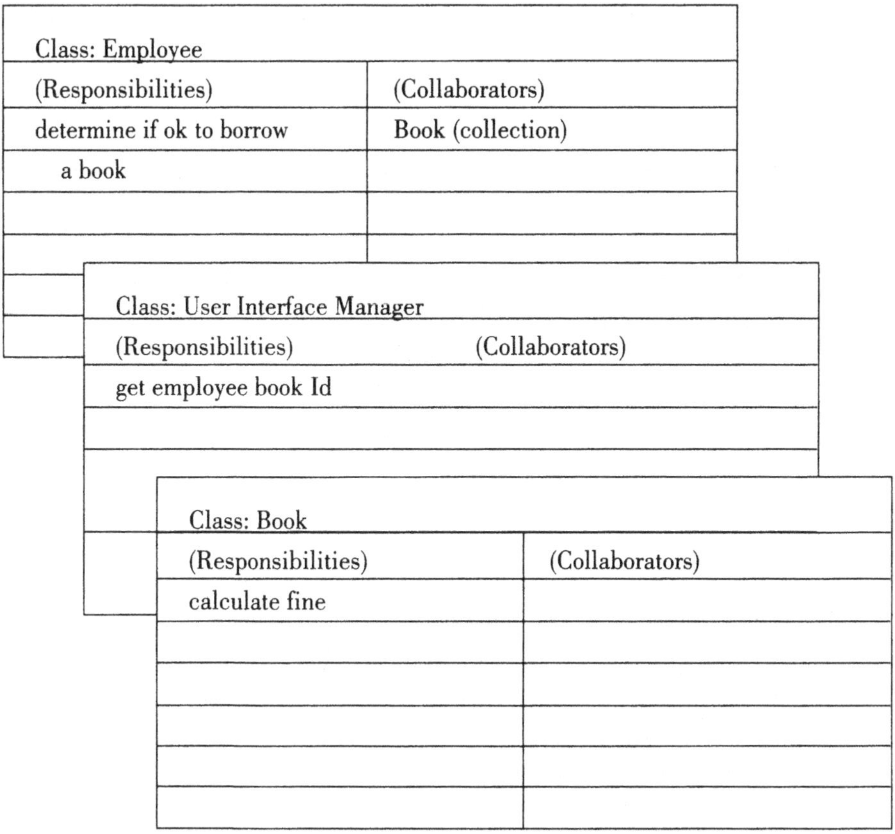

Class: Employee	
(Responsibilities)	(Collaborators)
determine if ok to borrow	Book (collection)
a book	

Class: User Interface Manager	
(Responsibilities)	(Collaborators)
get employee book Id	

Class: Book	
(Responsibilities)	(Collaborators)
calculate fine	

FIGURE 10.11. More CRC cards from the team's design session.

Phase III: Detailed Design

Scene: *Filling in lower-level details.*

Alex: OK. Let's try and take the checkout scenario to a lower level of detail by trying to specify messages that can be used to communicate between collaborating objects. It may be that we'll discover some new design objects in the process.

Nick: I've got a dumb question. Where does this all start since there is no main program?

Alex: That's a good question. The kind of program we're looking at is event driven.

Actually nothing much happens until someone tries to check out a book. If we assume we have some kind of GUI that gets the employee ID and book ID, then we can start things off by waking up the librarian and asking for an OK to check out the book since it's the Librarian's responsibility. Our job in Phase III is to specify messages, parameters, and return values or objects.

Brenda: OK. Let me try.

1. GUI sends ConfirmCheckOut(EmployeeID, BookID) to Librarian expects return value of OK or NOT OK
2. Librarian sends GetEmployee (EmployeeID) to DataBaseManager expects Employee object back
3. Librarian sends AreYouOverdue () to Employee expects Yes or No back

That's it.

Nick: Wait. How does the Employee know whether it's overdue?

Brenda: The Employee knows what books have been checked out so it sends a ComputeFine message to each book and tallies them.

Nick: Wait. How does a Book know whether it's overdue? All it knows is the checkout date, but I don't think we need to provide books with calendars.

Brenda: Hmmm. Hadn't thought of that.

Alex: Well, dates are a problem and maybe it's time to introduce a new class—a design class called Date. The Date class is quite useful. Whenever you want the date, just ask it.

Brenda: So Date collaborates with Book to help compute the current fine!

Alex: Right.

Nick: I hate to be a party pooper but nobody has said anything yet about who is responsible for keeping track of what the fines are per day. The book needs to know that in order to compute the fine, so I say let's make that part of every book.

Brenda: I think the librarian should keep track of the fine rate. That's who does it now in the manual system. It's listed in the Rolodex.

Alex: That raises an interesting issue. What we're talking about here is a policy that can and does change over time. Rather than lock a specific set of values into an arbitrary object, developers have found it useful to build Policy classes that hold data that may change over time. This is an example of another design object.

Nick: Oh, so the Book asks Date for the current date, figures out how many days it's overdue, asks the Policy object for the fine per day, computes the fine, and passes the fine to the Employee who originally asked for it.

Brenda: This is like a mini-drama.

Alex: That's right. That's what responsibility-driven design is all about.

Nick: Didn't we say originally that the Employee class maintained a collection of books? What's the role of the collection in all of this?

Alex: Collections are quite powerful and in object-oriented systems are very nice replacements for arrays and linked lists, if you've ever used those.

         If an Employee uses the aBag collection for holding all the books currently checked out, the Employee can simply ask the bag how many books are in it and ask the bag to iterate over all its books and come up with the total fines owed. Collection classes come built with these capabilities. As long as the items in the collection can compute values on their own, like overdue fines for one book, the collection can manage summing all the fines. It comes for free with collections.

Nick: OK, so what we end up with is a checkout scenario that must be supported by the classes we define.

Brenda: And we make the following changes to the CRC cards (Figure 10.12).

Alex: Very good. Notice that we can actually start to code this scenario right now. We have our class definitions and the methods that we need to support book checkout.

Brenda: Where do we go next?

Alex: We run through scenarios that support all the operations stated in the problem statement. The next scenario we tackle could be the checkin scenario or a scenario to support searching for a book.

Nick: We also have to do scenarios that support exceptions. Like when a customer has too many overdue books and tries to check one out. Look how many responsibilities we found just for checking out a book. It seems we're going to have an awful lot of responsibilities.

Alex: Good point, Nick. Yes, we do need to walk-through exception scenarios, but as we add certain responsibilities, like finding how many books a customer has checked out, we reach a point where the responsibilities already in place are able, with a little refinement, to handle the exceptions.

Brenda: I get it. Only the major functions of the system will substantially add responsibilities. One responsibility will handle the exceptions when some-

Class: Book	
(Responsibilities)	(Collaborators)
know status	
check-in	
check-out	
calculate fine	Date, Policy

Class: Policy	
(Responsibilities)	(Collaborators)
know per diem fines	
know book limits	
for employees	
know fine dollar limits	
for employees	

Class: Date	
(Responsibilities)	(Collaborators)
know current date	
calculate future dates	
calculate past dates	

FIGURE 10.12. CRC card changes.

one has $20, $40, or $80 in fines. Also only one responsibility will be needed no matter how many overdue books an employee might have.

Alex: Exactly, Brenda. And should a requirement to extend the functionality of the system be needed some time in the future, to send notices to folks who have outstanding fines over a certain limit, we could add a Notices class to take care of that.

As the team launches into the next scenario other responsibilities are added and existing responsibilities refined. The group discovers the same responsibilities will handle checking in and out books, as well as videos and audiotapes. Team member are assigned responsibilities for writing certain class programs. Nick, the database expert, is given the task of writing the class program (DataBase Manager) to interface with the data repositories. Alex writes the Date and User Interface Manager class programs. Other members of the programming staff are similarly assigned classes to complete. In this manner the functionality of the entire system is evenly and clearly managed.

For a complete listing of CRC cards, class diagrams, object-message diagrams, and program listings, see Appendix B.

Key Points

- The Rolling Lifecycle Perspective shows when and what deliverables are required in each step of an object-oriented software development project.

- Analysis, high-level design, and low-level design start and end with the same focus: classes and objects.

- Analysis and high-level design are focused on the system from the users' point of view.

- Low-level design focuses on the system from the implementors' point of view.

Suggested Readings

Berard, E. (1993). *Essays on Object-Oriented Software Engineering.* Englewood Cliffs, NJ: Prentice Hall.

Booch, G. (1994). *Object-Oriented Analysis and Design with Applications*, 2nd ed. Redwood City, CA: Benjamin/Cummings.

Coad, P., & Yourdon, E. (1990). *Object-Oriented Analysis.* Englewood Cliffs, NJ: Yourdon Press.

Gamma, E., Helm, R., Johnson, R., & Vlissides, J. (1995). *Design Patterns: Elements of Reusable Object-Oriented Software.* Reading, MA: Addison-Wesley.

Jacobson, I., Christerson, M., Jonsson, P., & Overgaard, G. (1992). *Object-Oriented Software Engineering.* Workingham, England: Addison-Wesley.

Rumbaugh, J., Blaha, M., Premerlani, W., Eddy, F., & Lorensen, W. (1991). *Object-Oriented Modeling and Design.* Englewood Cliffs, NJ: Prentice-Hall.

Shlaer, S., & Mellor, S. (1988). *Object-Oriented Analysis: Modeling the World in Data.* Englewood Cliffs, NJ: Yourdon Press.

Wilkerson, N. (1995). *Using CRC Cards.* New York: SIGS Books.

Wirfs-Brock, R., Wilkerson, B., & Wiener, L. (1990). *Designing Object-Oriented Software.* Englewood Cliffs, NJ: Prentice Hall.

Wyder, T. (1996). Capturing Requirements with Use Cases. *Software Development,* February, 36–40.

Review Questions

10.0 How does object-oriented analysis and design differ from conventional analysis and design?

10.1 What notational forms are part of OOA&D?

10.3 What role does iteration play in object-oriented software development?

10.4 What are CRC cards and how can they be used to support object-oriented design?

CHAPTER 11

MIGRATING LEGACY SYSTEMS

O ne of the biggest challenges facing organizations today is the integration of existing applications with new technologies and architectures. Companies looking to reengineer or restructure their operations must address how to connect their established base of legacy code with the desktop world of personal computers (PCs), workstations, graphical user interfaces (GUIs), and local area networks (LANs). Important in this regard is how to leverage the rise of high-speed networks to connect the diverse islands of data and applications that have proliferated over the past decades.

FOCUS AND FORMAT OF THIS CHAPTER

The purpose of this chapter is to provide alternative strategies for moving from legacy code to Object-Oriented COBOL. We present several alternatives, from doing nothing to wrapping existing code in COBOL objects for reuse and interoperability across a network.

Concepts

- Legacy code
- Wrappers
- SOM (System Object Model)
- CORBA (Common Object Request Broker Architecture)

LEGACY OPTIONS

Because COBOL supports both conventional and object-oriented features, there are several alternatives for those with legacy COBOL systems, each with a different level of commitment to object technology.

1. Do nothing object oriented—use COBOL 97 as a better COBOL than COBOL 85.
2. Add GUI interfaces to existing applications.
3. Add additional functionality to an application using object-oriented features.
4. Wrap legacy code for reuse and network integration.

Figure 11.1 depicts the four major options for organizations with legacy code.

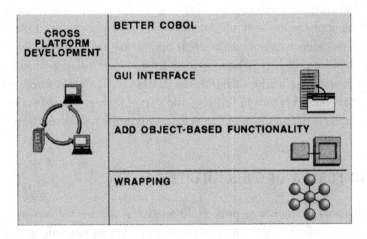

FIGURE 11.1. Four options for legacy code with multiplatforms.

Multiplatform Support

COBOL's multiplatform availability opens up the option of moving legacy applications from the mainframe to more cost-effective platforms. Applications requiring mainframe horsepower can take advantage of workstation and PC availability by offloading costly test and debug cycles to less expensive, more productive hardware. Mainframe code can be downloaded to PCs, debugged and tested interactively, and returned to the mainframe for compilation and delivery. Even if final delivery must be in a mainframe environment, the multiplatform support for COBOL allows the leveraging of graphical desktop environments by developing, testing, and debugging on workstations while targeting the mainframe for delivery.

OPTION 1: DO NOTHING OBJECT ORIENTED

It is possible to totally bypass objects and simply use COBOL 97 as a better language. Upward compatibility from COBOL 85, COBOL 74, and COBOL 68 allows the new features of COBOL 97 to be introduced without forcing changes to existing code. The following are some of the new conventional additions to the language:

- *Common exception processing* has been extended for COBOL 97.
- *Bit and Boolean data types* have been introduced to COBOL 97.
- *Free format source code* has been introduced in COBOL 97 to remove column restrictions.
- *In-line comments* are new to COBOL 97, allowing programmers to comment on specific lines of code.
- *Table sorts* have been improved.
- *Recursion* has been introduced, removing the need for vendors to supply non-standard extensions for reentrant code.
- *Call . . . Return parameter* for subroutines has been introduced in the COBOL 97 standard to allow a returning value from a call to a subprogram.
- *Set condition-name . . . False* has been introduced to the COBOL 97 standard, removing the previous limitation of only allowing condition-names to be set to True.
- *Strong Typing* for data items has been introduced using a new context-sensitive

key word, **Type**, for ensuring type compatibility as well as allowing user-defined type names.

- *Standard arithmetic* has been introduced for ensuring intermediate and final results.

- *Sixteen new intrinsic functions* have been added. There are now 58 intrinsic functions, including new exception processing, numeric, and character functions that can be used to speed up development.

COBOL 97 thus extends its range by including many well-established programming language constructs that may alone justify its adoption.

OPTION 2: GUI INTERFACES FOR LEGACY CODE

One of the reasons for the success of the PC in corporate environments has been the compelling, graphical front-ends on desktop applications. Users have come to expect consistent graphical interfaces for their applications and these expectations are now carrying over to mainframe applications. Until recently the interface has been the most neglected aspect of mainframe computing. However, that is changing. Legacy applications can now take on new dimensions of interactivity without the risk associated with changing business logic that has accrued over years of development and testing. Tools such as IBM's VisualAge for COBOL, Micro Focus' Visual Object COBOL, and Hitachi's Object-Oriented COBOL allow developers to replace conventional text screens with interactive graphical controls that include pull-down menus, buttons, and dialog boxes that can be arranged as graphical front-ends for legacy applications (Figure 11.2).

GUI Front-Ends

The process of attaching a GUI front-end to existing code can, in itself, serve as an avenue for moving legacy programmers to objects. GUI tools create objects that may be connected to a legacy application. In using OOCOBOL's new verb **Invoke** to access GUI services, programmers come to recognize objects and object services without actually having to program objects. This is an important first step in the transition to more ambitious object-oriented applications.

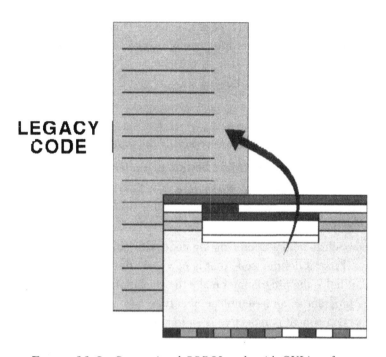

FIGURE 11.2. Conventional COBOL code with GUI interface.

OPTION 3: ADDING OBJECT-BASED FUNCTIONALITY TO AN APPLICATION

Very few applications remain static over their lifetimes. Successful applications go beyond their original scope, adding layers of functionality and features to meet the changing needs of users. With OOCOBOL, objects can augment legacy-code functionality.

OOCOBOL's object-oriented features do not sacrifice the essential structure of the COBOL language. OOCOBOL remains a combination of **Identification, Environment, Procedure,** and **Data** Divisions. Object-oriented features are added to the language by encapsulating the four classical COBOL divisions in a new section and class paragraph. This syntactic similarity between conventional and Object-Oriented COBOL enables a gradual transition to objects for those already familiar with the language.

In conventional COBOL, new functionality typically means new paragraphs that are accessed with either a **Perform** or **Call** statement. In OOCOBOL, however, an object must be created to encapsulate the new code. Then, instead of performing the paragraphs or calling a subroutine, the code is invoked by sending a message to the newly created object.

The process consists of the following steps:

- writing the paragraphs,
- defining an object responsible for executing the paragraphs,
- adding a line in the **Configuration Section** that references the new object, and
- adding a line in the program's **Procedure Division** that results in sending a message to the new object to execute its code.

This approach to augmenting existing code with object-based functionality pays off in two ways. First, it defines code that is now potentially reusable by other applications. Second, it helps the programmer make the transition to object-think; that is, conceptualizing a program as an assemblage of service providers and consumers. Such a client–server or component perspective is an important step to understanding objects.

OPTION 4: WRAPPING PROGRAMS

> Client server systems is the area where objects will realize their
> greatest potential; in the process they will become the new
> mainstream computing model.
>
> —Robert Orfali et al.
> *Essential Client Server Survival Guide*

Many believe that objects working together across system boundaries will define the next generation of computing technology. Object-Oriented COBOL can help transform, integrate, and access legacy functionality in ways that turn it into a strategic resource for the organization. The challenge for many organizations is how to expand the scope of their legacy applications to take advantage of advances in networking technologies without completely reworking tested code. The technique for making this happen is called wrapping.

A wrapper is an object that encapsulates code and data. Wrappers act as intermediaries between service providers and clients. Clients may include other objects, other COBOL programs, or even objects residing elsewhere on a network.

Wrapping in OOCOBOL is straightforward because the structure of an object resembles that of a conventional COBOL program complete with Identification, Environment, Data, and Procedure Divisions.

Wrapping Strategies

Wrapping can be done in one of two ways depending on the structure of the application, its modularity and system requirements.

1. Wrap an entire program as a single service.
2. Partition a program into individual services.

The Big Wrapper

The easiest strategy to use is the big wrap, which creates a wrapper object responsible for executing the program in its entirety. The strategy consists of

- surrounding a conventional COBOL program with an object definition
- providing a method or methods to execute all or part of the wrapped code

This strategy is effective when a program's functionality can be viewed as a single service. Figure 11.3 illustrates the big-wrapper technique. The original program is simply engulfed by the wrapper object. Data and procedures of the original program are local to the wrapped object with minimal code modification.

Wrapping Parts

A more involved strategy involves wrapping individual program components. Although more ambitious, this approach has a higher potential payoff if the individually wrapped components can be used by other applications and the program can be partitioned along functional lines. In this approach, each functional component is mapped to individual methods of the wrapper object. The longer-term payoff is that individual services can be reused and made available to other applications.

Figure 11.4 shows a program that has been wrapped in parts. The basic strategy is to package code and data referenced by the code into a single object. However, the steps to follow in piecewise program wrapping will depend on program structure. To

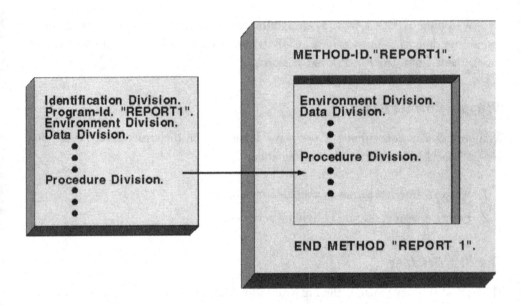

FIGURE 11.3. Wrapping a COBOL program with one access method.

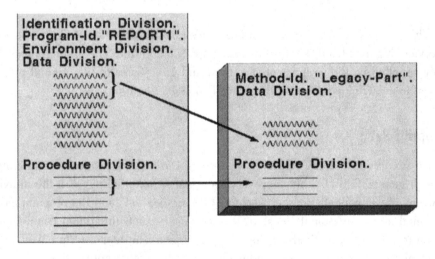

FIGURE 11.4. Partial wrap.

successfully partition and wrap a program the relationship between code and data must be understood.

The steps for wrapping are as follows:

1. **Partition the code along fault lines.** Performed paragraphs are good starting points for identifying code for wrapping, particularly if the code can be described by a simple phrase or verb. This is a sign of a highly cohesive block. Paragraphs that do several things are probably better off being further broken down.

2. **Identify data referenced by the code.** Code can reference files, records, or individual fields—potentially anything in the Data Division.

3. **Locate other code that references the data identified in step 2.** If the data is not referenced elsewhere you have a candidate for a self-contained object. Go on to step 5. If the data *is* referenced elsewhere in the code then the situation is more complex and you have to make some decisions about where to actually house the data. Go to step 4.

4. **Associate shared data with appropriate code.** If data is referenced by more than one block of code that you are wrapping, there are two alternatives. The first is to let one of the wrappers assume responsibility for the data. For example, if object A and object B both refer to data item X, then let either A or B encapsulate X. This means that if A, for example, holds onto X then B must access the data through A.

The other strategy is to define an additional wrapper object C that encapsulates X. When A or B require access to X, they then must go through C. A good rule of thumb to follow is to determine to which object the attribute (data) most naturally falls. The partitioning of attributes and code across an application is a design issue in object-oriented programming and can be resolved by doing a mini-CRC session to determine the object's attributes.

5. **Build class definitions for code and associated data.** The code and data associated with each of the steps 1–4 are used as the basis for COBOL class definitions. The data is moved to the wrapper object's Data Division and the code to the wrapper object's Procedure Division.

LEGACY APPLICATIONS AND DISTRIBUTED COMPUTING

Object-Oriented COBOL is in a unique position to help bridge the gap between legacy applications and distributed computing (Figure 11.5). Adding object-based functionality to legacy programs, either by wrapping existing pieces or adding new object services, opens the door to network computing, which is increasingly focusing on object-based strategies for distribution.

The CORBA standard for distributed computing provides a mechanism for allowing objects written in any language and operating on any platform to communicate. CORBA (the Common Object Request Broker Architecture) is the result of efforts by the Object Management Group (OMG), a consortium of over 300 of the leading hardware and software companies. The CORBA specification is currently being implemented by many vendors for a wide range of systems. Of particular interest to organizations with legacy code is the effort by IBM to provide a common foundation for all their object-oriented languages, including Object-Oriented COBOL. By wrapping legacy code in OOCOBOL, connection to the universe of objects is possible.

IBM's implementation of the CORBA specification is based on its System Object Model (SOM). SOM allows applications written or wrapped in one object-oriented language to access or be a service provider for objects in other languages. IBM's Distributed System Object Model (DSOM) supports the distribution of SOM-compliant objects on other platforms. This distributed object technology opens the door that allows legacy applications to be extended beyond their current scope.

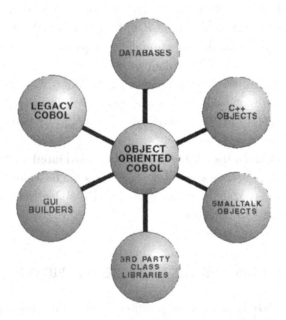

FIGURE 11.5. The role of Object-Oriented COBOL.

Key Points

- With its object-oriented features, COBOL 97 provides new options for organizations with an investment in legacy software.
- The multiplatform availability for COBOL supports cross-platform development.
- It is possible to add GUI interfaces to existing COBOL code without upsetting business logic.
- Object-based functionality can be added to existing applications.
- Wrapping provides a mechanism for converting existing code to object-oriented code.
- Legacy code can be extended to include network integration through the use of SOM- and DSOM-compatible wrappers.

Suggested Readings

McGibbon, B. (1995). *Managing Your Move to Object Technology.* New York: SIGS Books.
Lewis, T. (1995). *Delivering Reliable Client/Server Software.* New York: SIGS Books.
Otte, R., Patrick, P., & Roy, M. (1995). *Understanding CORBA, The Common Object Request Broker Architecture.* Englewood Cliffs, NJ: Prentice Hall.

Review Questions

11.0   Describe the new conventional features of COBOL 97.

11.1   How can an organization with significant investment in legacy code leverage Object-Oriented COBOL?

11.2   What is a wrapper and how can it be used to extend the life of legacy code?

11.3   How can Object-Oriented COBOL be used in a distributed-computing environment?

OBJECT-ORIENTED COBOL VENDORS: HITACHI, IBM, AND MICRO FOCUS

Three vendors currently offer Object-Oriented COBOL (OOCOBOL): Hitachi, IBM, and Micro Focus. Their offerings vary in degrees of compliance to the proposed standard as defined by the ANSI/ISO October 1995, Working Draft 1.1. Except in limited cases (collection classes, the **Finalize** method) the book adheres to the standard. There will be some changes made before the final version is published in 1997. These changes, however, should be minimal and limited to syntax.

Hitachi, IBM, Micro Focus, and others will be, over the next several months and years, releasing compilers that are 100% compatible with the standard. Table A.1 highlights some of the major differences among the vendors' versions and the proposed standard.

TABLE A.1. OOCOBOL: Vendor's Versions

Vendors	Hitachi	IBM	Micro Focus
Automatic garbage collection	✔		
Classes			
Class	✔	✔	✔
Parameterized class (c)			
Simple class			
Dynamic binding	✔	✔	✔
Encapsulation	✔	✔	✔
Inheritance			
Single	✔	✔	✔
Multiple	✔	✔	
Interface (h)	✔		
Methods			
Methods	✔	✔	✔
Methods—invariant (h)	✔		
Methods—prototype (h)	✔		
Objects			
Dynamic objects	✔	✔	✔
Factory object	✔		✔
Object modifiers	✔		
Persistent objects			✔
Property of object	✔		
Static objects			
Typed objects	✔	✔	
Untyped objects	✔	✔	✔
Repository	✔	✔	(s)
Reuses (c)			

(c) = See pp. 361–362 for the definition.
(h) = See the section on Hitachi.
(s) = Different syntax used to implement OOCOBOL.

HITACHI

Hitachi offers Object-Oriented COBOL as part of its COBOL 85 product. At this point, of the three vendors, the Hitachi offering most closely parallels the proposed standard. Hitachi's COBOL 85 runs on Windows NT, Windows 95, and various Unix platforms, including HP UX.

Class Program Outline

Here is the basic outline of a Hitachi class program.

Format: Hitachi class program outline showing permitted and required entries for defining a class.

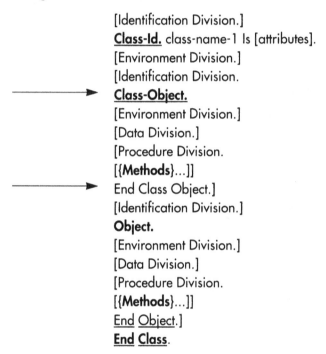

[Identification Division.]
Class-Id. class-name-1 Is [attributes].
[Environment Division.]
[Identification Division.
Class-Object.
[Environment Division.]
[Data Division.]
[Procedure Division.
[{**Methods**}...]]
End Class Object.]
[Identification Division.]
Object.
[Environment Division.]
[Data Division.]
[Procedure Division.
[{**Methods**}...]]
<u>End</u> <u>Object</u>.]
<u>End</u> <u>Class</u>.

Hitachi uses the term **Class-Object** rather than **Factory**. The term **Class-Object** was part of an earlier Object-Oriented COBOL–proposed ANSI standard. ANSI changed the term from **Class-Object** to the more descriptive **Factory** to avoid confusion between the terms **Class**, **Class-Object**, and **Object**.

A **Class-Object** is used in exactly the same manner as a **Factory** object. The **Class-Object** paragraph is delimited by the term **End Class-Object**.

Library

Hitachi supplies a Tool Class Library that is divided into a Basic Class Library and a Sample Class Library. The Basic Class Library provides essential and supplementary functionality for creating and working with objects. The root of the Class Library is the class **CBL-Base,** from which all classes inherit. The prefix **CBL** is again a throwback to an earlier ANSI version of the proposed standard. Every other class is prefixed with **HCB,** an abbreviation for Hitachi COBOL. Below is the Hitachi Basic Class Library hierarchy, followed by Table A.2, which defines the items in the Class Library hierarchy.

Class Library Hierarchy

```
CBL-Base
 HCB-Env
  HCB-Object
   HCB-String
   HCB-Association
   HCB-Collection
    HCB-Seq-Cltn
     HCB-Stack
     HCB-Order-Cltn
      HCB-Sort-Cltn
       HCB-Assoc-Sort
    HCB-Array
    HCB-Noseq-Cltn
     HCB-Hash-Array
     HCB-Bag
     HCB-Ident-Set
      HCB-Set
      HCB-Ident-Dict
       HCB-Dictionary
   HCB-List
    HCB-Ring
  HCB-Llnk
```

TABLE A.2. **Hitachi Basic Class Library Components**

Component	Function
HCB-Env	Initializes and manages the Basic Class Library
HCB-Object	Handles errors, evaluates classes, and compares objects
HCB-String	Performs basic string operations
HCB-Association	Operates on associative arrays. Manages key/value pairs
HCB-Seq-Cltn	Abstract classes. Elements stored in sequential order
HCB-Stack	Operates on stacks. Duplicate elements are permitted.
HCB-Order-Cltn	Operates on arrays. Elements are stored in sequential order. Duplicate elements are permitted.
HCB-Sort-Cltn	Operates on arrays. Elements are sorted when additions and deletions are made. Duplicate elements are permitted.
HCB-Assoc-Sort	Operates on arrays. Elements are stored in ascending order and sorted when additions and deletions are made. Duplicate elements are permitted.
HCB-Array	Operates on arrays. Elements are stored in sequential order and are referenced using subscripts. Duplicate elements are not permitted.
HCB-Noseq-Cltn	Abstract class. Elements stored in no predefined order.
HCB-Hash-Array	Operates on arrays using hash values. Duplicate elements are permitted.
HCB-Bag	Operates on arrays. Duplicate elements are permitted.
HCB-Ident-Set	Operates on arrays. Duplicate elements are not permitted.
HCB-Set	Operates on arrays. Duplicate elements are not permitted.
HCB-Ident-Dict	Operates on associative arrays using key/value pairs. Duplicate elements are not permitted.
HCB-Dictionary	Operates on associative arrays using key/value pairs. Duplicate elements are not permitted.
HCB-List	Operates on double-linked lists using head-and-tail pointers. Duplicate elements are not permitted.
HCB-Ring	Operates on ring list. Duplicate elements are permitted.
HCB-Link	Defines links to lists and rings. Duplicate elements are permitted.

Creating and Destroying Objects

Creating an object using Hitachi's compiler diverges from the standard in one detail. The name of the method invoked is **CBL-New**. In addition, the class must directly or indirectly inherit from **CBL-Base**. Here is the format.

Format: creating an object.

> Class-Id. Book Inherits CBL-Base.
>
> ...
>
> 01 anObject   Object Reference Book.
>
> ...

> Invoke Book "CBL-New" Returning anObject.

Destroying an object using Hitachi's compiler involves a method called **CBL-Discard**. Here is the format.

Format: deleting an object.

> Invoke anObject "CBL-Discard".

Invariant Methods

Two features, proposed by the standard and partially supported by Hitachi, that are not discussed in this book are **invariant** methods and interfaces as a language construct.

Invariant methods are not allowed to change object data. A method is defined as invariant by specifying the reserved word **invariant**. Here is the format.

Format: declaring an invariant method.

> Method-Id. "Method-1" <u>Invariant</u>.

Interfaces As a Language Construct

An interface as a language construct is a grouping of method prototypes, in which a method **prototype** is the outline of a method specifying only the method-name and any parameters. An interface is defined by the **Interface-Id** paragraph. Here is the format.

Format: declaring an Interface-Id paragraph.

> <u>Interface-Id</u>. interface-name-1

Method prototypes are defined by using the reserved word **prototype** in the Method-Id paragraph. Below is the format.

Format: declaring a prototype method.

Method-Id. "Method-1" <u>Prototype</u>.

Method prototypes are useful in large class programs. Method prototypes may be included in a class program, whereas the implementation of the method (a method with the same method-name, but containing the procedural code) is separately compiled. Below is a method **prototype** called **Method-1** and the implementation method of **Method-1**. The prototype is compiled as part of a larger class program (for instance, **class-name-1**) while the implementation method is compiled separately at a later date.

```
* ---------------------------------------*
* Method prototype -             *
* compiled with a class          *
* program (class-name-1).         *
* ---------------------------------------*
```
Method-Id. "Method-1" <u>Prototype</u>.
Data Division.
Linkage Section.
01 aParameter   Object Reference.
Procedure Division Using aParameter.
    no procedural statements allowed
End Method "Method-1".

```
* ---------------------------------------*
* Method implementation -        *
* may be compiled separately     *
* from the rest of class-name-1   *
* ---------------------------------------*
```
Method-Id. "Method-1" of class-name-1.
Environment Division.
Configuration Section.
Repository.
    Class class-name-1 is system-name.
Data Division.
Linkage Section.

```
01 aParameter
Procedure Division Using aParameter.
    procedural statements
End Method "Method-1".
```

IBM

IBM's Object-Oriented COBOL is marketed under a variety of names depending on the platform used. For OS/2 platforms the product is called VisualAge for COBOL, for AIX platforms the product is called COBOL Set for AIX, and for MVS the product is COBOL for MVS.

IBM's Object-Oriented COBOL makes uses of IBM's SOM (System Object Model) and DSOM (Distributed SOM) technology. SOM is the enabling framework for many of IBM's offerings, including C++ and Smalltalk. SOM and DSOM both support the OMG's (Object Management Group) CORBA (Common Object Request Broker Architecture) specification.

Class Program Outline

Here is the basic outline of an IBM class program.

Format: IBM class program outline showing permitted and required entries for defining a class.

```
[Identification Division.]
Class-Id. class-name-1 Is [attributes].
[Environment Division.]
[Data Division.]
[{Methods}...]]
End Class Object.]
End Class.
```

IBM does not, at this point, directly support the factory object. In this regard the IBM implementation is more like C++ than Smalltalk. IBM does support a class object that must specifically be created using a metaclass operation.

Library

Working with IBM's base class primarily involves inheriting SOMObject or SOMClass. For a complete list of SOM methods the reader is directed to the *IBM SOM User's Guide* reference.

Creating and Destroying Objects

Creating an object using IBM's compiler involves inheriting from SOMObject and invoking the SOMNew method. Here is an example.

Example: creating an object.

```
Class-Id. Book Inherits SOMObject.
...
01 anObject        Object Reference Book.
...
```
Invoke Book "SOMNew" Returning anObject.

Destroying an object involves a method called SOMFree. Here is the format.

Example: deleting an object.

Invoke anObject "SOMFree".

MICRO FOCUS

The Micro Focus Object-Oriented COBOL compiler is included in their Workbench product. Micro Focus uses the proprietary name Object COBOL when referring to any of their compilers that include the object-oriented constructs.

Class Program Outline

Here is the basic outline of a Micro Focus class program.

Format: Micro Focus class program outline showing permitted and required entries for defining a class.

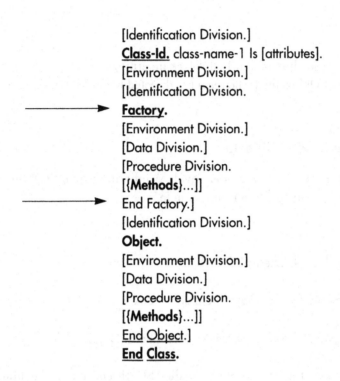

```
[Identification Division.]
Class-Id. class-name-1 Is [attributes].
[Environment Division.]
[Identification Division.
Factory.
[Environment Division.]
[Data Division.]
[Procedure Division.
[{Methods}...]]
End Factory.]
[Identification Division.]
Object.
[Environment Division.]
[Data Division.]
[Procedure Division.
[{Methods}...]]
End Object.]
End Class.
```

Micro Focus does not support the Repository paragraph and instead uses an Object Section and Class-Control paragraph to connect the program name to a system name. Here is the format.

Format: Micro Focus class program specifying Object Section and Class-Control.

```
Class-Id. class-name-1.
Object Section.
Class-Control.
    class-name-1 is system-name.
```

Micro Focus permits a Procedure Division to be declared in a class program that is not declared in a Method-Id paragraph. This Procedure Division is executed only one time when the class program is first invoked. Below is an outline of this.

Format: Micro Focus class program specifying a free-standing Procedure Division.

```
Class-Id. class-name-1.
```

```
         ..
         Procedure Division.
         ..
         Factory.
         ...
         Object.
         ...
         End Class.
```

In addition, Micro Focus allows a **Data Division** that is not part of a Factory or an Object. Here is an example.

Format: Micro Focus class program specifying a free-standing Data Division.

```
         Class-Id. class-name-1.
         ..
         Data Division.
         Procedure Division.
         ..
         Factory.
         ...
         Object.
         ...
         End Class.
```

Micro Focus is the most liberal of the vendors when it comes to data encapsulation. Micro Focus allows data to be inherited from superclasses by specifying the **Inherits with Data** phrase in the **Class-Id** paragraph. Below is the format.

Format: Micro Focus class program specifying a free-standing Procedure Division.

```
         Class-Id. class-name-2 Inherits from class-name-1 with Data.
```

The superclass the data is inherited from must specify and correspond with the **Data is Protected** phrase in its **Class-Id** paragraph. To prevent subclasses from inheriting data, a superclass may alternately specify the **Data is Private** phrase. Following is an example showing **Data is Protected**.

Format: Micro Focus class program specifying a free-standing Procedure Division.

Class-Id. class-name-1 <u>**Data is Protected**</u>.

There are a number of **Data Division** entries offered by Micro Focus that are not defined in the standard, specifically, an **Object-Storage Section** and a **Local-Storage Section**. Data in the **Object-Storage Section** is inherited by subclasses, and data declared in the **Local-Storage Section** is unique to each invocation of the declaring method. **Local-Storage Section** data may be used for recursive routines. Here is an outline showing only the **Object-Storage** and **Local-Storage Sections** in a class program.

Format: Object-Storage and Local-Storage Sections.

Class-Id. class-name-1.

..

Data Division.

Object-Storage Section.   data declared is available to all class methods
Procedure Division.

..

Factory.
Data Division.
Object-Storage Section.   data declared here may be inherited by subclass factory objects
*>
Method-Id.
Data Division.
Local-Storage Section.   data declared here is unique to each method invocation
Procedure Division.

...

End Factory.
*>
Object.
Data Division.
Object-Storage Section.   data declared here may be inherited by subclass object instances
*>
Method-Id.
Data Division.
Local-Storage Section.   data declared here is unique to each invocation of the method

Procedure Division.

...

End Object.
End Class class-name.

Library

Micro Focus follows the standard and names its class library **Base**. For a detailed look at the Micro Focus Class Library, specifically the collection classes, see Chapter 9.

Creating and Destroying Objects

Micro Focus does not, at this time, support typed objects. All objects must be created as untyped using the method **New**. Here is an example.

Example: creating an object.

Class-Id. Book Inherits Base.

...

01 anObject   Object Reference.

...

Invoke Book "New" Returning anObject.

Destroying an object involves a method called **Finalize**.

Example: deleting an object.

Invoke anObject "Finalize".

OTHER FEATURES NOT SUPPORTED BY THE VENDORS

Reuses

The **Reuses** clause is specified in the **Class-Id** paragraph. Declaring **Reuses** allows a class to incorporate the methods of the reused class as part of its definition without the rules of conformance. Here is the format.

Format: declaring Reuses.

Class-Id. class-name-1 <u>Reuses</u> class-name-2.

Parameterized Classes

Parameterized classes use class types as parameters. The ability to parameterize class descriptions allows the type of one class to be used as the specification to determine the type of another. The type of class being determined is a parameterized class and is specified by the Using phrase in the Class-Id paragraph. Here is the format.

Format: declaring a parameterized class.

Class-Id. class-name-1 Using class-name-2.

The class that instantiates the parameterized class is specified in the Repository paragraph of the instantiating class. Below is the format.

Format: instantiating a parameterized class.

Repository. class-name-1 Of class-name2 Using class-name-2.

Here is an example in which the class *Book* becomes the type of instantiated parameterized class.

Class-Id. Container Using AType.

Repository. AContainer Of Container Using Book.

Parameterized classes are also called templates or generic modules. Generally, parameterized classes are used to declare container classes.

THE LIBRARY APPLICATION

The Library application is a working example of a system that checks books, videos, and audiotapes into and out of a library. There are 10 class programs and one procedural program that comprise the application.

Audio	class program
Book	class program
Customer	class program
Dateclass	class program
DBMgr	class program
Driver	procedural program
Item	class program
Librarian	class program
Policy	class program
UIMgr	class program
Video	class program

NOTES ON STYLE

To facilitate navigating the application the following conventions are used:

1. Class methods begin in uppercase (i.e., New).

2. Object methods are all lowercase (i.e., check-out).

3. Object handles use camelback. Camelback concatenates multiple words, capitalizing all but the first word (i.e., aCustomerHandle). The only exception to this rule is in the Linkage Section where the name of the object is prefaced with an ls- (i.e., ls-CustomerHandle).

4. FACTORY, END FACTORY, OBJECT, END OBJECT, and END CLASS are in uppercase.

THE COMPILER

The example adheres to the ANSI standard as closely as possible. Where the example differs from the standard it does so out of necessity. The Library example was written using Micro Focus Workbench v4.0.

At this point the Micro Focus compiler does not support typed objects. The objects are therefore untyped.

The application does not destroy objects that become inaccessible; for example, customer and book objects. When Micro Focus supports automatic garbage collection, these objects will be destroyed by the automatic garbage collector. It is usually better programming practice to let the garbage collector destroy unneeded objects than to manually destroy them.

Two compiler directives are needed:

$set ooctrl(+n)—enables the use of Factory and End Factory syntax.

$set ooctrl(+w)—enables the Working-Storage Section to be used in place of the Micro Focus Object-Storage Section. This directive can not be used in subclasses (those classes that inherit from a user-defined superclass, i.e. Book, Video, and Audio).

Subclasses must include the Object-Storage Section in the Factory paragraph.

CRC Cards

Class: Book (subclass of Item)	
(Responsibility)	(Collaborators)
know due-date	Policy, Dateclass
calculate any fines incurred	Policy, Dateclass

Book—the objects in the system that represent the books that are loaned by the library.

attributes:
check-out period
fine-per-day

Class: Audio (subclass of Item)	
(Responsibility)	(Collaborators)
know due-date	Policy, Dateclass
calculate any fines incurred	Policy, Dateclass

Audio—the objects in the system that represent the audiotapes that are loaned by the library.

attributes:
check-out period
fine-per-day

Class: Video (subclass of Item)

(Responsibility)	(Collaborators)
know due-date	Policy, Dateclass
calculate any fines incurred	Policy, Dateclass

Video—the objects in the system that represent the videotapes that are loaned by the library.

attributes:
check-out period
fine-per-day

Class: Item (subclass of Item)

(Responsibility)	(Collaborators)
check-out	Librarian
check-in	Librarian
provide status	Librarian
provide item information	DBMgr

Item—the objects in the system that represent the items that are loaned by the library.

attributes:
item-type (book, video, audio)
item-status (in or out)
item-empid (the customer's empid)
item-due-date (the date the item is due back)
item-title (the title of the item)
item-ISBN (only books have an ISBN)

Class: Dateclass	
(Responsibility)	(Collaborators)
know current date	
calculate future dates	Policy

Date—the object that represents the current date in the system.

attributes:
todays-date (the current date)

Class: DBMgr	
(Responsibility)	(Collaborators)
get/put-item	Librarian, Policy, Dateclass
get/put-customer	Librarian, Policy, Dateclass

DBMgr—the object that interfaces with the data structures in the system.

attributes:
aLibrarianHandle (object that represents the librarian)
aCustomerHandle (object that represents the customer)
anItemHandle (object that represents an item)

Class: Librarian	
get/display information	UIMgr
check-in	Item, DBMgr
check-out	Customer, Item, DBMgr
get-status	Item
get-due-date	Item
get-borrowed-item-count	Customer
get-fine	Item
get-outstanding-fines	Customer
know-if-customer-has-over- due-items	Customer

Librarian—the object that checks items in and out of the library for a customer.

attributes:
aUIMgrHandle (object that represents the user interface)
aCustomerHandle (object that represents the customer)
anItemHandle (object that represents an item)
aDBMgrHandle (object that interfaces with the system data structures)

Class: Customer	
(Responsibility)	(Collaborators)
know if have overdue items	Item
know outstanding fines	
know how many items currently borrowed	

Customer—the objects that represent employees who borrow items from the library.

attributes:
anArray (object that holds currently borrowed items)
empid (the employee's empid)
itemid (the id of the item being borrowed or returned)
outstanding-fines (the amount of fines owed to the library by the customer)

Class: Policy	
(Responsibility)	(Collaborators)
check-due-status	Librarian, Dateclass
calculate-due-date	(Book, Video, or Audio),
	Dateclass
calculate-fine	(Book, Video, or Audio),
	Dateclass

Policy—the object that maintains library policy.

attributes:
aDateHandle (the object that represents the Dateclass)

Class: UIMgr	
(Responsibility)	(Collaborators)
display selection menu	
display messages	
send information	Librarian

UIMgr—the object that interfaces with the customer of the library system.

attributes:
selection (1= check-out, 2 = check-in)
empid (the employee empid for a customer)
itemid (the itemid of the item being borrowed or returned)
message-display (messages displayed to the customer)

DIAGRAMS

The diagrams below use the Unified notation.

Class Diagram (showing roles and relationships)

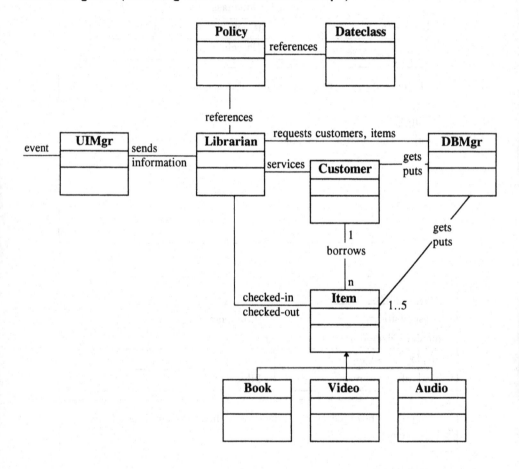

A Class Diagram (showing the interesting attributes and methods)

Audio
check-out-period fine-per-day
calculate-due-date calculate-fine

Customer
anArray customer-information
create-a-bag-of-items add-to-bag get-fines get-borrowed-items-count are-any-of-your-items-overdue

Dateclass
todays-date
is-this-item-overdue calculate-due-date get-todays-date

DBMgr
aLibrarianHandle aCustomerHandle anItemHandle
get-item get-customer update-employee-database update-item-database

Item
item-type item-status item-due-date item-title
get-empid get-status check-out check-in are-you-overdue

Librarian
aUIMgrHandle aDBMgrHandle aCustomerHandle aPolicyHandle
are-you-overdue check-in get-due-date calculate-fine update-employee-database get-item-status get-customer-handle get-outstanding-fines get-borrowed-items-count determine-if-any-items-overdue check-out calculate-due-date update-item-database

Policy
aDateHandle
check-due-status calculate-due-date calculate-fine

UIMgr
message-information
begin library-menu display-message

Note: Book and Video contain the same attributes and methods as Audio.

An Object-Message Diagram

An object-message diagram showing the creation of aUIMgrHandle, aLibrarianHandle, aDBMgrHandle, aPolicyHandle, and aDateHandle objects.

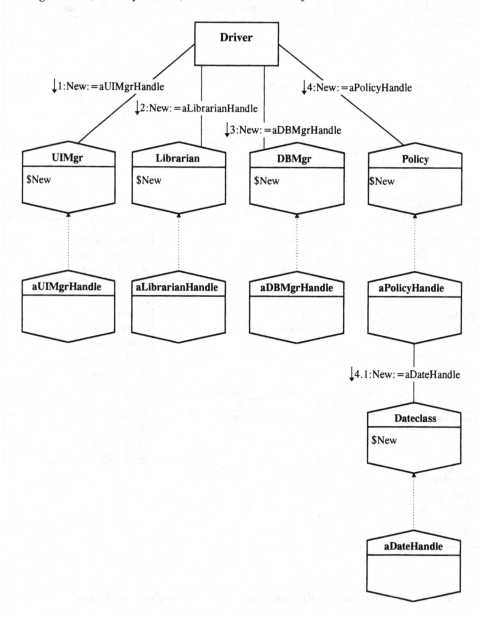

THE LIBRARY APPLICATION CODE

Program: Driver

```
* -----------------------------------------------------------------------------*
* Driver:                                                                       *
* Responsible for creating four of the objects that will exist for the duration of the application. *
* 1. an object of the class DBMgr called aDBMgrHandle                           *
* 2. an object of the class Librarian called aLibrarianHandle                   *
* 3. an object of the class Policy called aPolicyHandle                         *
* 4. an object of the class UIMgr called aUIMgrHandle                           *
* The Driver program executes first creating the above-named four objects and passes the handle *
* of the created objects to the other objects that have need of their services. *
* -----------------------------------------------------------------------------*

Program-Id. Driver.

Class-Control.
      UIMgr      is Class "UIMgr"
      Customer   is Class "Customer"
      Item       is Class "Item"
      Librarian  is Class "Librarian"
      DBMgr      is Class "DBMgr"
      Policy     is Class "Policy"
      .

Working-Storage Section.
01 aUIMgrHandle              Object Reference.
01 aLibrarianHandle          Object Reference.
01 aDBMgrHandle              Object Reference.
01 aPolicyHandle             Object Reference.
* -----------------------------------------------------------------------------*
Procedure Division.

      Invoke UIMgr        "New" Returning aUIMgrHandle
      Invoke Librarian    "New" Returning aLibrarianHandle
      Invoke DBMgr        "New" Returning aDBMgrHandle
      Invoke Policy       "New" Returning aPolicyHandle
*-- Pass the handle of the UIManager to the Librarian
          Invoke aLibrarianHandle "pass-handle" Using aUIMgrHandle
```

*-- Pass the handle of the DBManager to the Librarian
      Invoke aLibrarianHandle "pass-handle" Using aDBMgrHandle

*-- Pass the handle of the Librarian to the UIManager
      Invoke aUIMgrHandle "pass-handle" Using aLibrarianHandle

*-- Pass the handle of the Policy to the Librarian
      Invoke aLibrarianHandle "pass-handle" Using aPolicyHandle

*-- Begin processing in the object method "library-menu" of aLibrarianHandle
      Invoke aUIMgrHandle "library-menu"

      Stop Run
      .

End Program Driver.

Class program: UIMgr

```
$set ooctrl(+n)
$set ooctrl(+w)
* ------------------------------------------------------------------------------------------------------*
* UIMgr:                                                                                                 *
* Responsible for displaying the two selections: check-out or check-in an item. UIMgr is                *
* also responsible for displaying the messages to a customer. In a GUI application UIMgr would           *
* collaborate with the various screens and screen painters.                                             *
*                                                                                                        *
* aUIMgrHandle the object of class UIMgr is first invoked by the Driver program. After a customer         *
* enters their selections aUIMgrHandle invokes aLibrarianHandle to begin processing the request.         *
* ------------------------------------------------------------------------------------------------------*

Class-Id. UIMgr
      data is private
      inherits from Base.

Class-Control.
      UIMgr is class "UIMgr"
      Base  is class "Base"
      .
*-------------------------------- FACTORY OBJECT DEFINITION -----------------------------------*
FACTORY.
Working-Storage Section.
* -----------------------------------------------------------------------------------------------*
```

```
* New: is invoked by Driver to create an instance of UIMgr.                          *
* -------------------------------------------------------------------------------- *
Method-Id. "New".
Linkage Section.
01 aUIMgrHandle      Object Reference.
Procedure Division Returning aUIMgrHandle.

        Invoke Super "New" Returning aUIMgrHandle

        .

End Method "New".
END FACTORY.
*-------------------------------- INSTANCE OBJECT DEFINITION --------------------------------*
OBJECT.
Working-Storage Section.
01 aLibrarianHandle           Object Reference.
01 message-information.
   05 message-center          Pic x(40).
   05 message-date            Pic 9(08).
   05 message-fine            Pic 9(03)v99.
01 message-information-1.
   05 message-center-1        Pic x(40).
   05 message-fine-display    Pic $zz9.99.
* -------------------------------------------------------------------------------- *
* library-menu: displays choices to the customer—invoked by Driver.                  *
* -------------------------------------------------------------------------------- *
Method-Id. "library-menu".
Working-Storage Section.
01 user-selections.
   05 user-selection          Pic x(01) value spaces.
   05 empid                   Pic x(05) value spaces.
   05 itemid                  Pic x(06) value spaces.
   05 item-title              Pic x(07) value spaces.
01 end-of-time-switch         Pic x value "N".
   88 end-of-time             value "Y".
Linkage Section.

Procedure Division.

        Perform until end-of-time
```

Move spaces to user-selections
Initialize message-information

    Display "   Library System   "
    Display "   "
    Display "   1. Check-Out   "
    Display "   2. Check-In   "
    Display "   "
    Display "   Please select 1,2, or 3   "
      with no advancing
    Accept user-selection

    Evaluate user-selection
      When "1"
          Display "   "
          Display "   Check-Out   "
          Display "   "
          Display "   Please enter Employee Id: "
             with no advancing
          Accept empid
          Display "   "
          Display "   Please enter Item Id: "
             with no advancing
          Accept itemid

      When "2"
          Display "   "
          Display "   Check-In   "
          Display "   "
          Display "   Please enter Item Id: "
             with no advancing
          Accept itemid

      When "9"
          stop run

      When other
          Display "   "
          Display "   Invalid request   "
          Display "   choose 1 or 2   "
          Invoke Self "display-message"

```
                End-Evaluate

        Invoke aLibrarianHandle "begin"
            Using     user-selections
            Returning  message-information
        End-Invoke

        Invoke Self "display-message"

    End-Perform

    .

End Method "library-menu".
```
* --- *
* display-message: displays to the customer messages regarding the outcome of their selection. *
* --- *
```
Method-Id. "display-message".

Procedure Division.

    Evaluate message-fine
      When > 0
          Move message-fine    to message-fine-display
          Move message-center to message-center-1
          Display message-information-1
      When other
          Display message-information
    End-Evaluate

    Display " "

    .

End Method "display-message".
```
* --- *
* pass-handle: receives aLibrarianHandle passed from Driver.   *
* --- *
```
Method-Id. "pass-handle".
Linkage Section.
01 ls-LibrarianHandle            Object Reference.

Procedure Division Using ls-LibrarianHandle.

    Set aLibrarianHandle to ls-LibrarianHandle
```

End Method "pass-handle".

* ---*

END OBJECT.
END CLASS UIMgr.

Class program: Librarian

$set ooctrl(+n)
$set ooctrl(+w)

* ---*
* Librarian: *
* Responsible for collaborating with the DBMgr (aDBMgrHandle), Item (anItemHandle), and with *
* Customer (aCustomerHandle) to process a customer's request.   *
* ---*

Class-Id. Librarian
        data is private
        inherits from Base.

Class-Control.
        Librarian is class "Librarian"
        Base is class "Base"

* ------------------------------- FACTORY OBJECT DEFINITION ----------------------------*
FACTORY.
Working-Storage Section.

* ---*
* New: is invoked by Driver—creates an instance of the class Librarian.   *
* ---*

Method-Id. "New".
Linkage Section.
01 ls-LibrarianHandle   Object Reference.

Procedure Division Returning ls-LibrarianHandle.

        Invoke Super "New" Returning ls-LibrarianHandle

End Method "New".
END FACTORY.

```
*------------------------------------ INSTANCE OBJECT DEFINITION ------------------------------------*
OBJECT.
Working-Storage Section.
01 aUIMgrHandle              Object Reference.
01 aDBMgrHandle              Object Reference.
01 aPolicyHandle             Object Reference.
01 aCustomerHandle           Object Reference.
01 anItemHandle              Object Reference.
01 transaction-count         Pic 9(05) value 0.
01 first-invoke-indicator    Pic x(01) value "0".
01 user-selections.
   05 user-request           Pic x(01) value spaces.
   05 empid                  Pic x(05) value spaces.
   05 itemid                 Pic x(06) value spaces.
   05 item-title             Pic x(07) value spaces.
01 message-information.
   05 message-center         Pic x(40).
   05 message-center-date    Pic 9(08).
   05 message-fine           Pic 9(03)v99.
* ------------------------------------------------------------------------------------------------*
* begin: invoked by aUIMgrHandle.                                                                  *
* ------------------------------------------------------------------------------------------------*
Method-Id. "begin".
Working-Storage Section.
Linkage Section.
01 ls-user-selections.
   05 ls-user-request        Pic x(01) value spaces.
   05 ls-empid               Pic x(05) value spaces.
   05 ls-itemid              Pic x(06) value spaces.
   05 ls-item-title          Pic x(07) value spaces.
01 ls-message-information.
   05 ls-message-center      Pic x(40).
   05 ls-message-center-date Pic 9(08).
   05 ls-message-fine        Pic 9(03)v99.

Procedure Division Using ls-user-selections Returning ls-message-information.

    Move ls-user-selections to user-selections
    Initialize message-information
```

```
Evaluate ls-user-request
     When "1"
          Invoke aDBMgrHandle "get-item"
               Using        ls-user-selections
               Returning    anItemHandle
          End-Invoke

          Evaluate anItemHandle
               When Null
                    Move "invalid item id" to message center
               When other
                    Invoke Self "get-item-status"
          End-Evaluate
     When "2"
          Invoke aDBMgrHandle "get-item"
               Using        ls-user-selections
               Returning    anItemHandle
          End-Invoke

          Evaluate anItemHandle
               When Null
                    Move "invalid item id"
                    to message-center
               When other
                    Invoke Self "are-you-overdue"
          End-Evaluate

     End-Evaluate

     Move message-information to ls-message-information

End Method "begin".
* ----------------------------------------------------------------------------------- *
* are-you-overdue: collaborates with anItemHandle—invoked by Self.                    *
* ----------------------------------------------------------------------------------- *
Method-Id. "are-you-overdue".
Working-Storage Section.
01 item-due-date                    Pic 9(08).
01 item-yes-or-no-switch            Pic x comp-5.
     88 item-is-not-overdue         value 1.
     88 item-is-overdue             value 0.
```

```
Procedure Division.

    Invoke anItemHandle "are-you-overdue"
        Using    aPolicyHandle
        Returning item-yes-or-no-switch
    End-Invoke

    Evaluate true
        When item-is-overdue
            Invoke Self "get-due-date"
        When other
            Invoke Self "check-in"

    End-Evaluate

    .

End Method "are-you-overdue".
```
```
* --------------------------------------------------------------------------- *
* check-in: collaborates with anItemHandle—invoked by Self.                   *
* --------------------------------------------------------------------------- *
```
```
Method-Id. "check-in".
Working-Storage Section.
01 item-due-date                 Pic 9(08).

Procedure Division.

    Move zeros to item-due-date

    Invoke anItemHandle "check-in"
        Using item-due-date
    End-Invoke

    Invoke Self "update-item-database"
        Using item-due-date
    End-Invoke

    .

End Method "check-in".
```
```
* --------------------------------------------------------------------------- *
* get-due-date: collaborates with anItemHandle—invoked by Self.               *
* --------------------------------------------------------------------------- *
```
```
Method-Id. "get-due-date".
Working-Storage Section.
```

```
01 item-due-date                  Pic 9(08).

Procedure Division.

      Invoke anItemHandle "get-due-date"
         Returning item-due-date
      End-Invoke

      Invoke Self "calculate-fine"
         Using item-due-date
      End-Invoke

      .

End Method "get-due-date".
```

```
* ------------------------------------------------------------------------------------------------- *
* calculate-fine: collaborates with anItemHandle—passes aPolicyHandle to anItemHandle—invoked *
* by Self.                                                                                       *
* ------------------------------------------------------------------------------------------------- *
Method-Id. "calculate-fine".
Working-Storage Section.
01 fine-amount                    Pic 9(03)v99.
Linkage Section.
01 ls-item-due-date               Pic 9(08).

Procedure Division Using ls-item-due-date.

      Invoke anItemHandle "calculate-fine"
         Using    aPolicyHandle
                  ls-item-due-date
         Returning fine-amount
      End-Invoke

      Move "There is a late fine on the item of: " to message-center

      Move fine-amount to message-fine

      Invoke Self "update-employee-database"
         Using fine-amount
      End-Invoke

      .

End Method "calculate-fine".
* ------------------------------------------------------------------------------------------------- *
```

```
* update-employee-database: collaborates with aDBMgrHandle—invoked by Self.         *
* -------------------------------------------------------------------------------------- *
Method-Id. "update-employee-database".
Working-Storage Section.
01 item-empid                   Pic x(05).
Linkage Section.
01 ls-fine-amount               Pic 9(03)v99.

Procedure Division Using ls-fine-amount.

      Invoke anItemHandle "get-empid"
         Returning item-empid
      End-Invoke

      Invoke aDBMgrHandle "update-employee-database"
         Using    item-empid
                  ls-fine-amount
      End-Invoke

      Invoke Self "check-in"

      .

End Method "update-employee-database".
* -------------------------------------------------------------------------------------- *
* get-item-status: collaborates with anItemHandle to return item status—invoked by Self. *
* -------------------------------------------------------------------------------------- *
Method-Id. "get-item-status".
Working-Storage Section.
01 item-status                  Pic x(01).
Linkage Section.
01 ls-itemHandle                Object Reference.

Procedure Division.

      Invoke anItemHandle "get-status" Returning item-status

      Evaluate item-status
        When "I"
            Invoke Self "get-customer-handle"
        When "O"
            Move "item is currently checked out" to message-center
            Invoke Self "transaction-complete"
```

```
        End-Evaluate

   .

End Method "get-item-status".
* --------------------------------------------------------------------------------------*
* get-customer-handle: collaborates with aDBMgrHandle to return aCustomerHandle—invoked by*
* Self.                                                                                   *
* --------------------------------------------------------------------------------------*
Method-Id. "get-customer-handle".

Procedure Division.

        Invoke aDBMgrHandle "get-customer"
            Using    empid
                     itemid
            Returning aCustomerHandle
        End-Invoke

        Evaluate aCustomerHandle
            When Null
                Move "invalid employee id" to message-center
                Invoke Self "transaction-complete"
            When other
                Invoke Self "get-outstanding-fines"
        End-Evaluate

   .

End Method "get-customer-handle".
* --------------------------------------------------------------------------------------*
* get-outstanding-fines: collaborates with aCustomerHandle to get customer fines—invoked by Self. *
* --------------------------------------------------------------------------------------*
Method-Id. "get-outstanding-fines".
Working-Storage Section.
01 outstanding-fines              Pic 9(03)v99 value 0.

Procedure Division.

        Invoke aCustomerHandle "get-fines"
            Returning outstanding-fines
        End-Invoke

        Evaluate true
            When outstanding-fines >= 10.00
```

```
        Move "outstanding fines are over the limit" to message-center
        Invoke Self "transaction-complete"
    When other
        Invoke Self "get-borrowed-items-count"
End-Evaluate
.


End Method "get-outstanding-fines".
* ---------------------------------------------------------------------------------------*
* get-borrowed-items-count: collaborates with aCustomerHandle to get the number of items a   *
* customer has currently checked out of the library—invoked by Self.                         *
* ---------------------------------------------------------------------------------------*
Method-Id. "get-borrowed-items-count".
Working-Storage Section.
01 borrowed-items-count          Pic s9(09) comp-5.

Procedure Division.

    Invoke aCustomerHandle "get-borrowed-items-count"
        Returning borrowed-items-count
    End-Invoke

    Evaluate true
        When borrowed-items-count >= 5
            Move "too many items currently checked out"
                to message-center
            Invoke Self "transaction-complete"
        When other
            Invoke Self "determine-if-any-items-overdue"
    End-Evaluate
    .


End Method "get-borrowed-items-count".
* ---------------------------------------------------------------------------------------*
* determine-if-any-items-overdue: collaborates with aCustomerHandle to determine if any of the *
* currently checked out items are overdue—passes aPolicyHandle to aCustomerHandle—invoked*
* by Self.                                                                                    *
* ---------------------------------------------------------------------------------------*
Method-Id. "determine-if-any-items-overdue".
Working-Storage Section.
01 yes-or-no                     Pic x(01).
```

Procedure Division.

```
    Invoke aCustomerHandle "are-any-of-your-items-overdue"
        Using    aPolicyHandle
        Returning yes-or-no
    End-Invoke

    Evaluate yes-or-no
        When "Y"
            Move "items checked out are currently overdue"
                to message-center
            Invoke Self "transaction-complete"
        When "N"
            Invoke Self "check-out"
    End-Evaluate

    .

    End Method "determine-if-any-items-overdue".
```

```
* --------------------------------------------------------------------------------------------- *
* check-out: collaborates with anItemHandle to check item out—invoked by Self.                  *
* --------------------------------------------------------------------------------------------- *
```

Method-Id. "check-out".

Procedure Division.

```
    Invoke anItemHandle "check-out"

    Invoke Self "calculate-due-date"

    .
```

End Method "check-out".

```
* --------------------------------------------------------------------------------------------- *
* calculate-due-date: collaborates with anItemHandle to calculate a due date for an item being  *
* checked out—passes aPolicyHandle to anItemHandle—invoked by Self.                             *
* --------------------------------------------------------------------------------------------- *
```

Method-Id. "calculate-due-date".
Working-Storage Section.
01 item-due-date   Pic 9(08).

Procedure Division.

```
    Invoke anItemHandle "calculate-due-date"
        Using    aPolicyHandle
```

```
        Returning item-due-date
     End-Invoke

     Move "item due back:" to message-center
     Move item-due-date to message-center-date

     Invoke Self "update-item-database"
        Using item-due-date
     End-Invoke

     .

End Method "calculate-due-date".
* -------------------------------------------------------------------------------------------------------*
* update-item-database: collaborates with aDBMgrHandle to update the item database—invoked *
* by Self.                                                                                 *
* -------------------------------------------------------------------------------------------------------*
Method-Id. "update-item-database".
Linkage Section.
01 ls-item-due-date              Pic 9(08).

Procedure Division Using ls-item-due-date.

     Invoke aDBMgrHandle "update-item-database"
        Using   ls-item-due-date
                anItemHandle
     End-Invoke

     Invoke Self "transaction-complete"

     .

End Method "update-item-database".
* -------------------------------------------------------------------------------------------------------*
* pass-handle:                                                                             *
*    the first handle passed is for the UIMgr.                                             *
*    the second handle passed is for the DBMgr.                                            *
* -------------------------------------------------------------------------------------------------------*
Method-Id. "pass-handle".
Linkage Section.
01 ls-Handle                     Object Reference.
Procedure Division Using ls-Handle.

     Evaluate first-invoke-indicator
```

```
        When "0"
                Set aUIMgrHandle to ls-Handle
                Move "1" to first-invoke-indicator
        When "1"
                Set aDBMgrHandle to ls-Handle
                Move "2" to first-invoke-indicator
        When "2"
                Set aPolicyHandle to ls-Handle
    End-Evaluate


End Method "pass-handle".
* --------------------------------------------------------------------------------------------- *
* transaction-complete: tabulates the total number of transactions—invoked by Self.             *
* --------------------------------------------------------------------------------------------- *
Method-Id. "transaction-complete".
Procedure Division.

        Add 1 to transaction-count


End Method "transaction-complete".
* --------------------------------------------------------------------------------------------- *
END OBJECT.
END CLASS Librarian.
```

Class program: DBMgr

```
$set ooctrl(+n)
$set ooctrl(+w)
* --------------------------------------------------------------------------------------------- *
* DBMgr:                                                                                         *
* Responsible for creating the following two objects                                            *
* 1. an object of the class Customer called aCustomerHandle                                     *
* 2. an object of the subclass Item (Book, Video, or Audio) called anItemHandle                 *
*                                                                                               *
* Also responsible for interfacing with the data structures used by the application. In this case *
* we are using tables. To capture the changes to the item and employee tables in a permanent    *
* manner the tables would need to be changed to files or databases. The best solution would be  *
* to work with object-oriented databases that store objects. Currently object-oriented databases *
```

```
* are not available for Object-Oriented COBOL although this will change over the next year.    *
* -------------------------------------------------------------------------------------------- *
Class-Id. DBMgr
        data is private
        inherits from Base.

Class-Control.
        DBMgr     is class "DBMgr"
        Customer  is class "Customer"
        Item      is class "Item"
        Base      is class "Base"
        Book      is class "Book"
        Video     is class "Video"
        Audio     is class "Audio"
        .


*------------------------------- FACTORY OBJECT DEFINITION ------------------------------*
FACTORY.
Working-Storage Section.
* -------------------------------------------------------------------------------------------- *
* New: creates a new instance of the class DBMgr called a DBMgrHandle—invoked by Driver.    *
* -------------------------------------------------------------------------------------------- *
Method-Id. "New".
Linkage Section.
01 aDBMgrHandle              Object Reference.

Procedure Division Returning aDBMgrHandle.

    Invoke Super "New" Returning aDBMgrHandle
    .

End Method "New".
END FACTORY.
*------------------------------ INSTANCE OBJECT DEFINITION ------------------------------*
OBJECT.
Working-Storage Section.
01 aLibrarianHandle          Object Reference.
01 aCustomerHandle           Object Reference.
01 anItemHandle              Object Reference.
01 outstanding-fines         Pic 9(03)v99.
01 empid                     Pic x(05) value spaces.
```

```
01 employee-data.
    05    pic x(10) value "e000100300".
    05    pic x(10) value "e000200100".
    05    pic x(10) value "e000300900".
    05    pic x(10) value "e000400100".
    05    pic x(10) value "e000501500".
01 redefines employee-data.
    05 employee-data-table occurs 5 times
                indexed by emp-idx
                ascending key is table-empid.
        07 table-empid    Pic x(05).
        07 table-fines    Pic 9(03)v99.
* ----------------------------------------------------------------------------------------------------- *
* Position   element                                                                                     *
*   1-6      itemid                                                                                       *
*    7       item type: A = audio, B = book, V = video                                                    *
*    8       item status: I = in, O = out                                                                 *
*  9-16      due date: ccyymmdd                                                                           *
* 17-23      item title: the title of the item                                                           *
* 24-25      ISBN (only books have an ISBN)                                                               *
* 26-30      borrower's empid                                                                             *
* ----------------------------------------------------------------------------------------------------- *
01 item-data.
    05    Pic x(30) value "000001BI00000000Book-1 22      ".
    05    Pic x(30) value "000002VI00000000Video-1        ".
    05    Pic x(30) value "000003BO19960612Book-2 45e0002".
    05    Pic x(30) value "000004AO19960604Audio-1  e0004".
    05    Pic x(30) value "000005AI00000000Audio-2        ".
    05    Pic x(30) value "000006BI00000000Book-3 37      ".
    05    Pic x(30) value "000007VO19960606Video-2  e0004".
    05    Pic x(30) value "000008VO19960606Video-3  e0004".
    05    Pic x(30) value "000009BO19960219Book-4 78e0002".
    05    Pic x(30) value "000010BO19960611Book-5 39e0002".
01 redefines item-data.
    05 item-data-table occurs 10 times
                indexed by item-idx
                ascending key is table-itemid.
        07 table-itemid    Pic x(06).
        07 table-type      Pic x(01).
```

```
07 table-status       Pic x(01).
07 table-due-date     Pic 9(08).
07 table-title        Pic x(07).
07 table-ISBN         Pic x(02).
07 item-table-empid   Pic x(05).
```

```
* --------------------------------------------------------------------------*
* get-item: searches for the requested item in the item-data-table—invoked by the method "begin"*
* in Librarian.                                                              *
* --------------------------------------------------------------------------*
Method-Id. "get-item".
Working-Storage Section.
01 item-data-table-sub       Pic 9(02).
Linkage Section.
01 ls-user-selections.
   05 ls-user-request        Pic x(01) value spaces.
   05 ls-empid               Pic x(05) value spaces.
   05 ls-itemid              Pic x(06) value spaces.
   05 ls-item-title          Pic x(07) value spaces.
01 ls-ItemHandle             Object Reference.
Procedure Division Using ls-user-selections Returning ls-ItemHandle.

    Search all item-data-table
       at end
          Set ls-ItemHandle to Null
      when table-itemid(item-idx) = ls-itemid
          Set item-data-table-sub to item-idx
          Invoke Self "get-item-1"
             Using    ls-empid ls-itemid
                      item-data-table-sub
             Returning ls-ItemHandle
          End-Invoke
    End-Search
    .

End Method "get-item".
* --------------------------------------------------------------------------*
* get-item-1: creates the type of item requested (Book, Video, or Audio)—invoked by Self.  *
* --------------------------------------------------------------------------*
Method-Id. "get-item-1".
```

```
Working-Storage Section.
01 item-information.
    05 item-customer-empid        Pic x(05).
    05 item-itemid                Pic x(06).
    05 item-type                  Pic x(01).
    05 item-status                Pic x(01).
    05 item-due-date              Pic 9(08).
    05 item-title                 Pic x(07).
    05 item-ISBN                  Pic x(02).
Linkage Section.
01 ls-empid                       Pic x(05).
01 ls-itemid                      Pic x(06).
01 ls-sub                         Pic 9(02).
01 ls-ItemHandle                  Object Reference.

Procedure Division Using ls-empid ls-itemid ls-sub Returning ls-ItemHandle.

        Move item-table-empid(ls-sub)     to item-customer-empid
        Move ls-itemid                    to item-itemid
        Move table-type(ls-sub)           to item-type
        Move table-status(ls-sub)         to item-status
        Move table-due-date(ls-sub)       to item-due-date
        Move table-title(ls-sub)          to item-title
        Move table-ISBN(ls-sub)           to item-ISBN

        Evaluate table-type(ls-sub)
            When "B"
                Invoke Book "New"
                    Using      item-information
                    Returning  ls-ItemHandle
                End-Invoke
            When "V"
                Invoke Video "New"
                    Using      item-information
                    Returning  ls-ItemHandle
                End-Invoke
            When "A"
                Invoke Audio "New"
                    Using      item-information
                    Returning  ls-ItemHandle
```

```
            End-Invoke

        End-Evaluate
           .

End Method "get-item-1".
* ----------------------------------------------------------------------------*
* get-customer: creates an instance of the class Customer. Also responsible to find all the items  *
* in the item-data-table currently loaned to the customer and filling the customer's bag with the  *
* items checked out.                                                                               *
* ----------------------------------------------------------------------------*
Method-Id. "get-customer".
Working-Storage Section.
01 item-sub                 Pic 9(02) value 0.
01 pass-to-customer.
   05 an-empid              Pic x(05).
   05 an-itemid             Pic x(06).
   05 outstanding-fines     Pic 9(03)v99.
01 end-of-table             Pic x(01).
01 aBorrowedItemHandle      Object Reference.
Linkage Section.
01 ls-user-selections.
   05 ls-empid              Pic x(05).
   05 ls-itemid             Pic x(06).
01 ls-CustomerHandle        Object Reference.

Procedure Division Using ls-user-selections Returning ls-CustomerHandle.

    Search all employee-data-table
       at end
            Set ls-CustomerHandle to Null
      when table-empid(emp-idx) = ls-empid
            Move table-fines(emp-idx) to outstanding-fines
            Move ls-empid to an-empid
            Move ls-itemid to an-itemid

            Invoke Customer "New"
                Using       pass-to-customer
                Returning   aCustomerHandle
            End-Invoke
```

```
              Set ls-CustomerHandle to aCustomerHandle
      End-Search

      Evaluate true
         When aCustomerHandle not = null
              Move "N" to end-of-table
              Set item-idx to 1
              Perform until end-of-table = "Y"
                   Search item-data-table
                        at end
                             Move "Y" to end-of-table
                             When item-table-empid(item-idx) =
                                  ls-empid
                                  Set item-sub to item-idx
                                  Set item-idx up by 1
                                  Invoke Self "get-item-1"
                                       Using        ls-empid
                                                    ls-itemid
                                                    item-sub
                                       Returning aBorrowedItemHandle
                                  End-Invoke
                                  Invoke aCustomerHandle "add-to-bag"
                                       Using aBorrowedItemHandle
                                  End-Invoke
                   End-Search
              End-Perform
      End-Evaluate

      .

End Method "get-customer".
* ---------------------------------------------------------------------------------------------------*
* update-employee-database: updates the employee-data-table with the total fines owed by a    *
* customer—invoked by the method "update-employee-database" in Librarian.                     *
* ---------------------------------------------------------------------------------------------------*
Method-Id. "update-employee-database".
Linkage Section.
01 ls-item-empid                Pic x(05).
01 ls-fine-amount               Pic 9(03)v99.

Procedure Division Using ls-item-empid ls-fine-amount.
```

```
Search all employee-data-table
     at end
         display "error during employee update"
   When table-empid(emp-idx) = ls-item-empid
       compute ls-fine-amount =
               table-fines(emp-idx) + ls-fine-amount
       end-compute
   End-Search
```

.

End Method "update-employee-database".

```
* -----------------------------------------------------------------------------------*
* update-item-database: updates the item-data-table—invoked by the method of the same name in *
* Librarian.                                                                          *
* -----------------------------------------------------------------------------------*
Method-Id. "update-item-database".
Working-Storage Section.
01 item-information.
   05 item-empid            Pic x(05).
   05 item-itemid           Pic x(06).
   05 item-status           Pic x(01).
Linkage Section.
01 ls-due-date              Pic 9(08).
01 ls-ItemHandle            Object Reference.

Procedure Division Using ls-due-date ls-ItemHandle.

   Invoke ls-ItemHandle "get-item-information"
        Returning item-information
   End-Invoke

   Search all item-data-table
        at end
          Display "error during update"
     When table-itemid(item-idx) = item-itemid
          Move item-empid  to item-table-empid(item-idx)
          Move item-status  to table-status(item-idx)
          Move ls-due-date  to table-due-date(item-idx)
   End-Search
```

.

End Method "update-item-database".
* --- *
END OBJECT.
END CLASS DBMgr.

Class program: Customer

```
$set ooctrl(+n)
$set ooctrl(+w)
```
* --- *
* Customer: *
* Responsible for knowing the amount of fines owed to the library and how many items are checked *
* out by this customer.   *
* --- *

```
Class-Id. Customer
        data is private
        inherits from Base.

Class-Control.
        Customer          is class "Customer"
        Array             is class "Array"
        Base              is class "Base"
        Callback          is class "Callback"
        OrderedCollection is class "Ordrddcll"
```

* ---------------------------- FACTORY OBJECT DEFINITION ---------------------------- *
```
FACTORY.
Working-Storage Section.
```
* --- *
* New: creates an instance of the customer class called aCustomerHandle—invoked by the method *
* "get-customer" in Driver.   *
* --- *
```
Method-Id. "New".
Linkage Section.
01 ls-customer-information.
    05 ls-empid               Pic x(05).
    05 ls-item-id             Pic x(06).
    05 ls-outstanding-fines   Pic 9(03)v99.
```

```
01 ls-CustomerHandle              Object Reference.

Procedure Division   Using     ls-customer-information
                     Returning  ls-CustomerHandle.

    Invoke Super "New" Returning ls-CustomerHandle

    Invoke ls-CustomerHandle "initialize"
       Using ls-customer-information
    End-Invoke

    Invoke ls-CustomerHandle "create-a-bag-of-items"

    .

End Method "New".
END FACTORY.
*---------------------------------- INSTANCE OBJECT DEFINITION ----------------------------------*
OBJECT.
Working-Storage Section.
01 i                          Pic x(4) comp-5 value 0.
01 anArray                    Object Reference.
01 customer-information.
   05 empid                   Pic x(05).
   05 itemid                  Pic x(06).
   05 outstanding-fines       Pic 9(03)v99.
* ----------------------------------------------------------------------------------------------*
* initialize: saves the data supplied with the creation of a customer in the object data division—   *
* invoked by Self.                                                                               *
* ----------------------------------------------------------------------------------------------*
Method-Id. "initialize".
Linkage Section.
01 ls-customer-information.
   05 ls-empid                Pic x(05).
   05 ls-itemid               Pic x(06).
   05 ls-outstanding-fines    Pic 9(03)v99.

Procedure Division Using ls-customer-information.

    Move ls-customer-information to customer-information

    .

End Method "initialize".
```

```
* ----------------------------------------------------------------------- *
* create-a-bag-of-items: create an array to store the items currently checked out to this customer *
* —invoked by Self.                                                          *
* ----------------------------------------------------------------------- *
Method-Id. "create-a-bag-of-items".

Procedure Division.

      Move 5 to i

      Invoke Array "ofReferences" Using i
          Returning anArray
      End-Invoke

      Move 0 to i

      .

End Method "create-a-bag-of-items".
* ----------------------------------------------------------------------- *
* add-to-bag: put the items checked out to this customer in the array—invoked by the method *
* "get-customer" in Driver.                                                  *
* ----------------------------------------------------------------------- *
Method-Id. "add-to-bag".
Working-Storage Section.
Linkage Section.
01 ls-ItemHandle                     Object Reference.
Procedure Division Using ls-ItemHandle.

      Add 1 to i

      Invoke anArray "atPut" Using i ls-itemhandle
                            Returning ls-itemhandle
      End-Invoke

      .

End Method "add-to-bag".
* ----------------------------------------------------------------------- *
* get-fines: returns the outstanding fines owed by this customer to the method "get-outstanding- *
* fines" in Librarian.                                                        *
* ----------------------------------------------------------------------- *
Method-Id. "get-fines".
Linkage Section.
```

```
01 ls-outstanding-fines              Pic 9(03)v99.

Procedure Division Returning ls-outstanding-fines.

    Move outstanding-fines to ls-outstanding-fines

.

End Method "get-fines".
```

```
* --------------------------------------------------------------------------------------*
* get-borrowed-items-count: returns the number of items in the array (the items checked out to  *
* this customer) to the "get-borrowed-items-count" in Librarian.                         *
* --------------------------------------------------------------------------------------*
```

```
Method-Id. "get-borrowed-items-count".
Linkage Section.
01 ls-borrowed-items-count           Pic s9(09) comp-5.

Procedure Division Returning ls-borrowed-items-count.

    Invoke anArray "size" Returning ls-borrowed-items-count

.

End Method "get-borrowed-items-count".
```

```
* --------------------------------------------------------------------------------------*
* are-any-of-your-items-overdue: creates a Callback called getOverdue that contains the message *
* "get-overdue". The iterator method "select" sends the "get-overdue" message to every object    *
* stored in anArray. "get-overdue" uses aPolicyHandle as input. When the Callback is created ls- *
* PolicyHandle (aPolicyHandle) is supplied as a Using parameter. This allows aPolicyHandle to be *
* supplied to the "get-overdue" message.                                                 *
*                                                                                         *
* The iterator method "select" creates a subcollection for every object in anArray that returns a  *
* value of 1. anAnswer is the object that collects the objects in anArray that return a value of 1. *
* anAnswer is converted to anOrderedCollection. anOrderedCollection is then queried using the *
* "isEmpty" method. "isEmpty" returns a value of 1 when there is nothing stored in the collection;*
* otherwise it returns a 0.                                                              *
*                                                                                         *
* Invoked by the method "determine-if-any-items-overdue" in the class Librarian.          *
* --------------------------------------------------------------------------------------*
```

```
Method-Id. "are-any-of-your-items-overdue".
Working-Storage Section.
01 nullObject                        Object Reference.
01 anAnswer                          Object Reference.
```

```
01 object1                      Object Reference.
01 getOverdue                   Object Reference.
01 anOrderedCollection          Object Reference.
01 true-or-false                Pic X comp-5.
01 new-size                     Pic x(4) comp-5.
Linkage Section.
01 ls-PolicyHandle              Object Reference.
01 ls-yes-or-no                 Pic X(01).
```

Procedure Division Using ls-PolicyHandle Returning ls-yes-or-no.

```
    Set nullObject to null

    Invoke Callback "New"    *> put the string get-overdue into an object called getOverdue
            Using    nullObject "get-overdue"
                     ls-PolicyHandle     *> the get-overdue method requires aPolicyHandle as a
            Returning getOverdue         *> Using parameter
    End-Invoke

    Invoke anArray "select" Using getOverdue *> send the get-overdue message to every object
        Returning anAnswer                   *> stored in anArray
    End-Invoke

    Invoke anAnswer "asOrderedCollection" *> convert anAnswer to anOrderedCollection so
        Returning anOrderedCollection       *> that the method "isEmpty" may be used
    End-Invoke

    Invoke anOrderedCollection "isEmpty"
        Returning true-or-false
    End-Invoke

    Evaluate true-or-false
        When 0
            Move "Y" to ls-yes-or-no
        When 1
            Move "N" to ls-yes-or-no
    End-Evaluate

    .
```

End Method "are-any-of-your-items-overdue".
```
* ----------------------------------------------------------------------------------------------*
END OBJECT.
END CLASS Customer.
```

Class program: Item

```
$set ooctrl(+n)
$set ooctrl(+w)
* ----------------------------------------------------------------------------------------------- *
* Item: superclass                                                                                *
* Responsible for maintaining and getting information regarding a Book, Video, or Audio.          *
* ----------------------------------------------------------------------------------------------- *

Class-Id. Item
        data is private
        inherits from Base.

Class-Control.
        Base is Class "Base"
        Item is Class "Item"

    .


*---------------------------------------- FACTORY OBJECT DEFINITION ----------------------------------*
FACTORY.
Working-Storage Section.

* --------------------------------------------------------------------------------------------------- *
* New: inherited by Book, Video, and Audio. Item is an abstract class—invoked by the method "get- *
* item" in the class DBMgr.                                                                          *
* --------------------------------------------------------------------------------------------------- *

Method-Id. "New".
Working-Storage Section.
Linkage Section.
01 ls-item-information.
    05 ls-empid            Pic x(05).
    05 ls-itemid           Pic x(06).
    05 ls-item-type        Pic x(01).
    05 ls-item-status      Pic x(01).
    05 ls-item-due-date    Pic 9(08).
    05 ls-item-title       Pic x(07).
    05 ls-item-ISBN        Pic x(02).
01 ls-ItemHandle           Object Reference.

Procedure Division Using ls-item-information Returning ls-ItemHandle.

        Invoke Super "New" Returning ls-ItemHandle
```

```
        Invoke Is-ItemHandle "initialize"
            Using Is-item-information
        End-Invoke


        .

End Method "New".
END FACTORY.
```

-------------------------------- INSTANCE OBJECT DEFINITION -----------------------------------

```
OBJECT.
Working-Storage Section.
01 item-information.
    05 empid                    Pic x(05).
    05 item-itemid              Pic x(06).
    05 item-type                Pic x(01).
    05 item-status              Pic x(01).
    05 item-due-date            Pic 9(08).
    05 item-title               Pic x(07).
    05 item-ISBN                Pic x(02).
```
---
* initialize: saves the information about an item as object data—invoked by Self.   *
* --- *
```
Method-Id. "initialize".
Linkage Section.
01 Is-item-information.
    05 Is-empid                 Pic x(05).
    05 Is-item-itemid           Pic x(06).
    05 Is-item-type             Pic x(01).
    05 Is-item-status           Pic x(01).
    05 Is-item-due-date         Pic 9(08).
    05 Is-item-title            Pic x(07).
    05 Is-item-ISBN             Pic x(02).

Procedure Division Using Is-item-information.

    Move Is-item-information to item-information


    .

End Method "initialize".
```
* --*
* get-empid: returns the borrower's empid to the method "update-employee-database" in the class*

```
* Librarian.                                                                    *
* --------------------------------------------------------------------------- *
Method-Id. "get-empid".
Linkage Section.
01 ls-empid                      Pic x(05).

Procedure Division Returning ls-empid.

    Move empid to ls-empid

    .

End Method "get-empid".
* --------------------------------------------------------------------------- *
* get-status: returns the status ("I"—in or "O"—out ) to the method "get-item-status" in the *
* class Librarian.                                                            *
* --------------------------------------------------------------------------- *
Method-Id. "get-status".
Linkage Section.
01 ls-status                     Pic x(01).

Procedure Division Returning ls-status.

    Move item-status to ls-status

    .

End Method "get-status".
* --------------------------------------------------------------------------- *
* check-out: sets the status of the item to "O"—invoked by the method "check-out" in the class *
* Librarian.                                                                  *
* --------------------------------------------------------------------------- *
Method-Id. "check-out".

Procedure Division.

    Move "O" to item-status

    .

End Method "check-out".
* --------------------------------------------------------------------------- *
* check-in: sets the status, empid, and due-date to original values—invoked by the method "check- *
* in" in the class Librarian.                                                 *
* --------------------------------------------------------------------------- *
Method-Id. "check-in".
```

```
Linkage Section.
01 ls-item-due-date              Pic 9(08).

Procedure Division Using ls-item-due-date.

    Move "I"              to item-status
    Move spaces           to empid
    Move ls-item-due-date to item-due-date
    .

End Method "check-in".
```
* --- *
* are-you-overdue: collaborates with aPolicyHandle to determine if the item is overdue—invoked by*
* the method "are-you-overdue" in the class Librarian.   *
* --- *

```
Method-Id. "are-you-overdue".
Linkage Section.
01 ls-PolicyHandle               Object Reference.
01 ls-Boolean                    Pic x comp-5.
    88 ls-match                  value 1.
    88 ls-nomatch                value 0.

Procedure Division Using ls-PolicyHandle Returning ls-Boolean.

    Invoke ls-PolicyHandle "check-due-status"
        Using      item-due-date
        Returning  ls-Boolean
    End-Invoke
    .

End Method "are-you-overdue".
```
* --- *
* get-due-date: returns the item due-date to the method "get-due-date" in the class Librarian.   *
* --- *

```
Method-Id. "get-due-date".
Linkage Section.
01 ls-item-due-date              Pic 9(08).

Procedure Division Returning ls-item-due-date.

    Move item-due-date to ls-item-due-date
```

End Method "get-due-date".

```
* ---------------------------------------------------------------------------------------------------*
* get-overdue: collaborates with aPolicyHandle to determine if the item is overdue—this is the     *
* method that is invoked by the statement Invoke anArray "select"...in the class Customer. Notice  *
* the input parameter ls-PolicyHandle. The method "are-any-of-your-items-overdue" in the class     *
* Customer creates the getOverdue Callback using the ls-PolicyHandle. The same ls-PolicyHandle*
* required by the "get-overdue" method.                                                             *
* ---------------------------------------------------------------------------------------------------*

Method-Id. "get-overdue".
Working-Storage Section.
01 overdue-status              Pic x(01).
Linkage Section.
01 ls-PolicyHandle             Object Reference.
01 ls-Boolean                  Pic x comp-5.
   88 ls-match                 value 1.
   88 ls-nomatch               value 0.

Procedure Division Using ls-PolicyHandle Returning ls-Boolean.

     Invoke ls-PolicyHandle "check-due-status"
          Using      item-due-date
          Returning  ls-Boolean
     End-Invoke
     .

End Method "get-overdue".
```

```
* ---------------------------------------------------------------------------------------------------*
* get-item-information: returns item information to the method "update-item-database" in the class*
* DBMgr.                                                                                              *
* ---------------------------------------------------------------------------------------------------*

Method-Id. "get-item-information".
Linkage Section.
01 ls-information.
   05 ls-empid                 Pic x(05).
   05 ls-itemid                Pic x(06).
   05 ls-status                Pic x(01).

Procedure Division Returning ls-information.

     Move empid       to ls-empid
     Move item-itemid to ls-itemid
```

```
        Move item-status    to ls-status
        .

End Method "get-item-information".
* ------------------------------------------------------------------------------------------------- *
END OBJECT.
END CLASS Item.
```

Class program: Book

```
$set ooctrl(+n)
* ------------------------------------------------------------------------------------------------- *
* Book: subclass of class Item                                                                      *
* Responsible for calculating the book's due date and any fines for returning the book late.        *
* ------------------------------------------------------------------------------------------------- *

Class-Id. Book
        data is private
        inherits from Item.

Class-Control.
        Item is Class "Item"
        Book is Class "Book"
        .


*------------------------------------- FACTORY OBJECT DEFINITION ------------------------------------*
* Notice the declaration of the Object-Storage Section in the Factory paragraph below. This is a   *
* Micro Focus (not an ANSI) requirement for Book to inherit from its superclass Item.               *
* ------------------------------------------------------------------------------------------------- *
FACTORY.
Working-Storage Section.
Object-Storage Section.
END FACTORY.

*------------------------------------- INSTANCE OBJECT DEFINITION -----------------------------------*
OBJECT.
Working-Storage Section.
01 check-out-period             Pic 9(02).
01 fine-per-day                 Pic 9(03)v99.
* ------------------------------------------------------------------------------------------------- *
* calculate-due-date: collaborates with aPolicyHandle to calculate the book's due-date—the method*
```

```
* is declared in Book rather than in Item because Book, Video, and Audio all implement the method*
* using a different check-out period—invoked by the method "calculate-due-date" in the class    *
* Librarian.                                                                                     *
* -----------------------------------------------------------------------------------------------*
Method-Id. "calculate-due-date".
Linkage Section.
01 ls-PolicyHandle              Object Reference.
01 ls-due-date                  Pic 9(08).

Procedure Division Using ls-PolicyHandle Returning ls-due-date.

      Move 14 to check-out-period

      Invoke ls-PolicyHandle "calculate-due-date"
            Using      check-out-period
            Returning  ls-due-date
      End-Invoke

      .

End Method "calculate-due-date".
* -----------------------------------------------------------------------------------------------*
* calculate-fine: collaborates with aPolicyHandle to calculate the fines incurred when returning a *
* book late. The method is declared as a Book method rather than an Item method because Book,      *
* Video, and Audio all use a different daily fine-amount—invoked by the method "calculate-fine" in*
* the class Librarian.                                                                            *
* -----------------------------------------------------------------------------------------------*
Method-Id. "calculate-fine".
Linkage Section.
01 ls-PolicyHandle              Object Reference.
01 ls-item-due-date             Pic 9(08).
01 ls-fine-amount               Pic 9(03)v99.

Procedure Division    Using      ls-PolicyHandle ls-item-due-date
                      Returning  ls-fine-amount.

      Move 1 to fine-per-day

      Invoke ls-PolicyHandle "calculate-fine"
            Using      ls-item-due-date
                       fine-per-day
            Returning  ls-fine-amount
```

```
        End-Invoke

End Method "calculate-fine".
*-----------------------------------------------------------------------*
END OBJECT.
END CLASS Book.
```

Class Program: Video

```
$set ooctrl(+n)
*-----------------------------------------------------------------------*
* Video: subclass of class Item                                         *
* Responsible for calculating the video's due date and any fines for returning the video late.  *
*-----------------------------------------------------------------------*
Class-Id. Video
        data is private
        inherits from Item.

Class-Control.
        Item    is Class "Item"
        Video   is Class "Video"


*---------------------------- FACTORY OBJECT DEFINITION ----------------------------*
* Notice the declaration of the Object-Storage Section in the Factory paragraph below. This is a *
* Micro Focus (not an ANSI) requirement for Video to inherit from its superclass Item.  *
*-----------------------------------------------------------------------*
FACTORY.
Working-Storage Section.
Object-Storage Section.
END FACTORY.

*---------------------------- INSTANCE OBJECT DEFINITION ----------------------------*
OBJECT.
Working-Storage Section.
01 check-out-period        Pic 9(02).
01 fine-per-day            Pic 9(03)v99.
*-----------------------------------------------------------------------*
* calculate-due-date: invoked by the method "calculate-due-date" in the class Librarian.  *
```

```
* ------------------------------------------------------------------------------------ *
Method-Id. "calculate-due-date".
Linkage Section.
01 ls-PolicyHandle                    Object Reference.
01 ls-due-date                        Pic 9(08).

Procedure Division Using ls-PolicyHandle Returning ls-due-date.

      Move 7 to check-out-period

      Invoke ls-PolicyHandle "calculate-due-date"
           Using      check-out-period
           Returning  ls-due-date
      End-Invoke

      .

End Method "calculate-due-date".
* ------------------------------------------------------------------------------------ *
* calculate-fine: invoked by the method "calculate-fine" in the class Librarian.      *
* ------------------------------------------------------------------------------------ *
Method-Id. "calculate-fine".
Linkage Section.
01 ls-PolicyHandle                    Object Reference.
01 ls-item-due-date                   Pic 9(08).
01 ls-fine-amount                     Pic 9(03)v99.

Procedure Division    Using      ls-PolicyHandle ls-item-due-date
                      Returning  ls-fine-amount.

      Move 3 to fine-per-day

      Invoke ls-PolicyHandle "calculate-fine"
           Using      ls-item-due-date
                      fine-per-day
           Returning  ls-fine-amount
      End-Invoke

      .

End Method "calculate-fine".
* ------------------------------------------------------------------------------------ *
END OBJECT.
END CLASS Video.
```

Class Program: Audio

```
$set ooctrl(+n)
* ---------------------------------------------------------------------------------------------- *
* Audio: subclass of class Item                                                                  *
* Responsible for calculating the audio's due date and any fines for returning the audio late.   *
* ---------------------------------------------------------------------------------------------- *
Class-Id. Audio
        data is private
        inherits from Item.

Class-Control.
        Item    is Class "Item"
        Audio is Class "Audio"
        .


*--------------------------------- FACTORY OBJECT DEFINITION ----------------------------------*
* Notice the declaration of the Object-Storage Section in the Factory paragraph below. This is a *
* Micro Focus (not an ANSI) requirement for Audio to inherit from its superclass Item.           *
* ---------------------------------------------------------------------------------------------- *
FACTORY.
Working-Storage Section.
Object-Storage Section.
END FACTORY.

*--------------------------------- INSTANCE OBJECT DEFINITION ---------------------------------*
OBJECT.
Working-Storage Section.
01 check-out-period         Pic 9(02).
01 fine-per-day             Pic 9(03)v99.
* ---------------------------------------------------------------------------------------------- *
* calculate-due-date: invoked by the method "calculate-due-date" in the class Librarian.         *
* ---------------------------------------------------------------------------------------------- *
Method-Id. "calculate-due-date".
Linkage Section.
01 ls-PolicyHandle          Object Reference.
01 ls-due-date              Pic 9(08).

Procedure Division Using ls-PolicyHandle Returning ls-due-date.

        Move 7 to check-out-period
```

```
        Invoke ls-PolicyHandle "calculate-due-date"
                Using      check-out-period
                Returning  ls-due-date
        End-Invoke

        .

End Method "calculate-due-date".
*  ---------------------------------------------------------------------------*
* calculate-fine: invoked by the method "calculate-fine" in the class Librarian.   *
*  ---------------------------------------------------------------------------*
Method-Id. "calculate-fine".
Linkage Section.
01 ls-PolicyHandle              Object Reference.
01 ls-item-due-date             Pic 9(08).
01 ls-fine-amount               Pic 9(03)v99.

Procedure Division  Using      ls-PolicyHandle ls-item-due-date
                    Returning  ls-fine-amount.

        Move 2 to fine-per-day

        Invoke ls-PolicyHandle "calculate-fine"
                Using      ls-item-due-date
                           fine-per-day
                Returning  ls-fine-amount
        End-Invoke

        .

End Method "calculate-fine".
*  ---------------------------------------------------------------------------*
END OBJECT.
END CLASS Audio.
```

Class Program: Policy

```
$set ooctrl(+n)
$set ooctrl(+w)
*  ---------------------------------------------------------------------------*
* Policy:                                                                      *
* Responsible for creating an object of the class Dateclass called aDateHandle. The Policy class is *
* the only class in the application to directly collaborate with aDateHandle.   *
```

```
* -----------------------------------------------------------------------------*
Class-Id. Policy
        data is private
        inherits from Base.

Class-Control.
        Policy      is Class "Policy"
        Dateclass   is Class "Dateclass"
        Base        is Class "Base"
        .


*----------------------------- FACTORY OBJECT DEFINITION -----------------------*
FACTORY.
Working-Storage Section.
* -----------------------------------------------------------------------------*
* New: creates an instance of the class Policy and an instance of the class Dateclass—invoked by*
* the program Driver.                                                           *
* -----------------------------------------------------------------------------*
Method-Id. "New".
Working-Storage Section.
01 aDateHandle                  Object Reference.
Linkage Section.
01 aPolicyHandle                Object Reference.

Procedure Division Returning aPolicyHandle.

    Invoke Super "New" Returning aPolicyHandle

    Invoke Dateclass "New" Returning aDateHandle

    Invoke aPolicyHandle "initialize" using aDateHandle


    .

End Method "New".
END FACTORY.
*----------------------------- INSTANCE OBJECT DEFINITION ----------------------*
OBJECT.
Working-Storage Section.
01 aDateHandle                  Object Reference.
* -----------------------------------------------------------------------------*
* initialize: sets the handle to an instance of the Dateclass as object data (aDateHandle). *
* -----------------------------------------------------------------------------*
```

```
Method-Id. "initialize".
Linkage Section.
01 ls-DateHandle                    Object Reference.

Procedure Division Using ls-DateHandle.

    Set aDateHandle to ls-DateHandle

    .

End Method "initialize".
```
* --*
* check-due-status: collaborates with aDateHandle to determine if an item is overdue—invoked by*
* the methods "are-you-overdue" and "get-overdue" in the class Item.   *
* --*
```
Method-Id. "check-due-status".
Working-Storage Section.
01 overdue-status                   Pic x(01).
Linkage Section.
01 ls-item-due-date                 Pic 9(08).
01 ls-Boolean                       Pic X comp-5.
   88 ls-match                      value 1.
   88 ls-nomatch                    value 0.

Procedure Division Using ls-item-due-date Returning ls-Boolean.

    Invoke aDateHandle "is-this-item-overdue"
        Using       ls-item-due-date
        Returning   ls-Boolean
    End-Invoke

    .

End Method "check-due-status".
```
* --*
* calculate-due-date: collaborates with aDateHandle to calculate the due-date of an item when an*
* item is checked-out—invoked by the method "calculate-due-date" of the classes Book, Video, and*
* Audio.   *
* --*
```
Method-Id. "calculate-due-date".
Linkage Section.
01 ls-check-out-period              Pic 9(02).
01 ls-item-due-date                 Pic 9(08).
```

Procedure Division Using ls-check-out-period Returning ls-item-due-date.

    Invoke aDateHandle "calculate-due-date"
        Using   ls-check-out-period
        Returning ls-item-due-date
    End-Invoke

    .

End Method "calculate-due-date".

```
* --------------------------------------------------------------------------------------- *
* calculate-fine: collaborates with aDateHandle to calculate the due-date of an item when an item *
* is checked-out—invoked by the method "calculate-fine" of the classes Book, Video, and Audio. *
*                                                                                          *
* Uses the ANSI intrinsic function Integer-of-Date. See the intrinsic function appendix for more *
* information.                                                                              *
* --------------------------------------------------------------------------------------- *
```

Method-Id. "calculate-fine".
Working-Storage Section.
01 todays-date   Pic 9(08).
01 days-item-overdue   Pic 9(04).
Linkage Section.
01 ls-item-due-date   Pic 9(08).
01 ls-fine-per-day   Pic 9(03)v99.
01 ls-fine-amount   Pic 9(03)v99.

Procedure Division Using   ls-item-due-date ls-fine-per-day
              Returning ls-fine-amount.

    Invoke aDateHandle "get-todays-date"
        Returning todays-date
    End-Invoke

    Compute days-item-overdue =
        Function Integer-of-Date(ls-item-due-date) -
        Function Integer-of-Date(todays-date)
    End-Compute

    Initialize ls-fine-amount

    Compute ls-fine-amount =

        days-item-overdue * ls-fine-per-day
    End-Compute

End Method "calculate-fine".
* ---*
END OBJECT.
END CLASS Policy.

Class program: Dateclass

```
$set ooctrl(+n)
$set ooctrl(+w)
* -----------------------------------------------------------------------------------------------*
* Dateclass:                                                                                      *
* Responsible for maintaining todays date and determining if an item is overdue and the date an  *
* item is due back.                                                                               *
* -----------------------------------------------------------------------------------------------*

Class-Id. Dateclass
        data is private
        inherits from Base.

Class-Control.
        Base       is Class "Base"
        Dateclass  is Class "Dateclass"

          .

*--------------------------------- FACTORY OBJECT DEFINITION ---------------------------------*
FACTORY.
Working-Storage Section.
* -----------------------------------------------------------------------------------------------*
* New: creates an instance of the class Dateclass—invoked by the method "New" in the class        *
* Policy.                                                                                          *
* Uses the ANSI intrinsic function Current-Date that includes the century. See Appendix E on      *
* intrinsic functions for more information.                                                       *
* -----------------------------------------------------------------------------------------------*
Method-Id. "New".
Working-Storage Section.
01 todays-date-x            Pic x(08).
01 todays-date              Pic 9(08).
Linkage Section.
01 aDateHandle              Object Reference.

Procedure Division Returning aDateHandle.
```

```
        Invoke Super "New" Returning aDateHandle

        Move Function Current-Date    to todays-date-x
        Move todays-date-x            to todays-date

        Invoke aDateHandle "initialize" Using todays-date

        .

End Method "New".
END FACTORY.
*------------------------------------ INSTANCE OBJECT DEFINITION --------------------------------*
OBJECT.
Working-Storage Section.
01 todays-date                Pic 9(08).
* ----------------------------------------------------------------------------------------------------*
* initialize: saves the current date in ccyymmdd format as object data in the field todays-date.    *
* ----------------------------------------------------------------------------------------------------*
Method-Id. "initialize".
Linkage Section.
01 ls-todays-date             Pic 9(08).

Procedure Division Using ls-todays-date.

        Move ls-todays-date to todays-date

        .

End Method "initialize".
* ----------------------------------------------------------------------------------------------------*
* is-this-item-overdue: returns a match or nomatch value to the method "is-this-item-overdue" in    *
* the class Policy.                                                                                   *
* ----------------------------------------------------------------------------------------------------*
Method-Id. "is-this-item-overdue".
Linkage Section.
01 ls-item-due-date           Pic 9(08).
01 ls-Boolean                 Pic X comp-5.
    88 ls-match               value 1.
    88 ls-nomatch             value 0.

Procedure Division Using ls-item-due-date Returning ls-Boolean.

        Evaluate true
            When ls-item-due-date < todays-date
```

```
              Set ls-nomatch     to true
          When other
              Set ls-match       to true
       End-Evaluate

       .

End Method "is-this-item-overdue".
* ----------------------------------------------------------------------------------------*
* calculate-due-date: returns the due-date of an item to the method "calculate-due-date" in the  *
* classes Book, Video, and Audio.                                                         *
*                                                                                         *
* Uses the ANSI intrinsic functions Date-of-Integer and Integer-of-Date. See the intrinsic function  *
* Appendix E for more information.                                                        *
* ----------------------------------------------------------------------------------------*
Method-Id. "calculate-due-date".
Working-Storage Section.
01 item-due-date                 Pic 9(08) value 0.
Linkage Section.
01 ls-check-out-period                  Pic 9(02).
01 ls-item-due-date                     Pic 9(08).

Procedure Division Using ls-check-out-period Returning ls-item-due-date.

       Compute ls-item-due-date =
          Function Date-of-Integer(Function Integer-of-Date
               (todays-date) + ls-check-out-period)
       End-Compute

       .

End Method "calculate-due-date".
* ----------------------------------------------------------------------------------------*
* get-todays-date: returns todays-date to the method "calculate-fine" in the class Policy.   *
* ----------------------------------------------------------------------------------------*
Method-Id. "get-todays-date".
Linkage Section.
01 ls-todays-date                Pic 9(08).

Procedure Division Returning ls-todays-date.

       Move todays-date to ls-todays-date

       .
```

End Method "get-todays-date".

* ---*

END OBJECT.
END CLASS Dateclass.

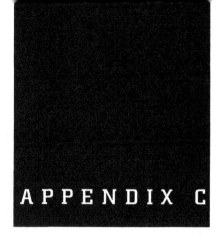

COBOL Reserved Words

Absent	Also	B-Xor
Accept	Alternate	Before
Access	And	Binary
Add	Any	Bit
Advancing	Are	Blank
After	Area	Block
Align	Areas	Boolean
All	As	Bottom
Allow	Ascending	By
Alphabet	Assign	
Alphabetic	At	Call
Alphabetic-Lower		Cancel
Alphabetic-Upper	B-And	CD
Alphanumeric	B-Not	CF
Alphanumeric-Edited	B-Or	CH

Character

Characters

Class

Class-Id

Close

Code

Code-Set

Col

Collating

Cols

Column

Comma

Common

Communication

Comp

Computational

Compute

Configuration

Conforming

Contains

Content

Continue

Control

Controls

Converting

Copy

Corr

Corresponding

Count

CRT

Currency

Cursor

Data

Date

Day

Day-Of-Week

DE

Debugging

Decimal-Point

Declaratives

Default

Delete

Delimited

Delimiter

Depending

Descending

Destination

Detail

Disable

Display

Divide

Division

Down

Duplicates

Dynamic

EGI

Else

EMI

Enable

End

End-Accept

End-Add

End-Call

End-Compute

End-Delete

End-Display

End-Divide

End-Evaluate

End-If

End-Invoke

End-Multiply

End-Of-Page

End-Perform

End-Read

End-Receive

End-Return

End-Rewrite

End-Search

End-Start

End-String

End-Subtract

End-Unstring

End-Write

Environment

EOP

Equal

Error

ESI

Evaluate

Exception

Exception-Object

Exit

Extend

External

Factory

False

FD

File

File-Control

Filler

Final

First

Footing

For

From

Function

Generate
Get
Giving
Global
Go
Greater
Group

Heading
High-Value
High-Values

Identification
If
In
Index
Indexed
Indicate
Inherits
Initial
Initialize
Initiate
Input
Input-Output
Inspect
Interface
Interface-Old
Into
Invalid
Invariant
Invoke
I-O
I-O-Control
Is

Just
Justified

Key

Last
Leading
Left
Length
Less
Limit
Limits
Linage
Linage-Counter
Line
Line-Counter
Lines
Linkage
Lock
Low-Value
Low-Values

Merge
Message
Method
Method-Id
Mode
Move
Multiply

National
National-Edited
Native
Negative
Next
No

Not
Null
Number
Numeric
Numeric-Edited

Object
Object-Computer
Occurs
Of
Off
Omitted
On
Only
Open
Optional
Or
Order
Organization
Other
Output
Overflow
Override

Packed-Decimal
Padding
Page
Page-Counter
Perform
PF
PH
Pic
Picture
Plus
Pointer
Position

Positive
Present
Printing
Procedure
Procedures
Proceed
Program
Program-Id
Property
Prototype
Purge

Queue
Quote
Quotes

Raise
Random
RD
Read
Receive
Record
Records
Redefines
Reel
Reference
References
Relative
Release
Remainder
Removal
Renames
Replace
Replacing
Report
Reporting

Reports
Repository
Reserved
Reset
Return
Returning
Reuses
Rewind
Rewrite
RF
RH
Right
Rounded
Run

Same
Screen
SD
Search
Section
Segment
Select
Self
Send
Sentence
Separate
Sequence
Sequential
Set
Sign
Simple
Size
Sort
Sort-Merge
Source
Source-Computer

Sources
Space
Spaces
Special-Names
Standard
Standard-1
Standard-2
Start
Status
Stop
String
Sub-Queue-1
Sub-Queue-2
Sub-Queue-3
Subtract
Sum
Super
Suppress
Symbolic
Sync
Synchronized
System-Object

Table
Tallying
Terminal
Terminate
Test
Text
Than
Then
Through
Thru
Time
Times
To

Top	Valid	+
Trailing	Validate	-
True	Value	*
Type	Values	/
Typedef	Varying	**
		>
Unit	When	<
Universal	With	=
Unstring	Working-Storage	>=
Until	Write	<=
Up		&
Upon	Zero	*>
Usage	Zeroes	::
Use	Zeros	
Using		

NEW **COBOL** RESERVED WORDS

The following COBOL reserved words have been added to the language.

Absent	Cols	Get
Align	Columns	
Allow	Conforming	Inherits
As	CRT	Interface
	Cursor	Interface-Id
Bit		Invariant
Boolean	Default	Invoke
B-And		
B-Not	End-Accept	Method
B-Or	End-Display	Method-Id
B-Xor	End-Invoke	
	Exception-Object	National
Class-Id		National-Edited
Col	Factory	Null

Object

Only

Override

Present

Property

Prototype

Raise

Repository

Returning

Reuses

Self

Screen

Simple

Sources

Super

System-Object

Typedef

Universal

Valid

Validate

INTRINSIC FUNCTIONS

For information on using intrinsic functions see COBOL 85 Features.

In the arguments column:

A means alphabetic.

B means Boolean.

I means integer.

N means numeric.

NL means national.

T means a type declaration.

X means alphanumeric.

... means the function takes multiple arguments.

| means or. (permitted data types—note: data types must not be intermingled. For a series of arguments they must all be of the same type: numeric or alphanumeric. Alphanumeric and alphabetic may be mixed.)

argument, argument means the function specifically takes the number and type of arguments listed, separated by a comma.

Function Name	Arguments	Returns
ABS	I1,N1	Absolute value of argument
ACOS	N1	Arccosine of argument
Allocated-Occurrences	A1|B1|N1|NL1|X1	Number of occurrences currently allocated for a dynamic table
Annuity	N1,I2	Ratio of annuity paid for I2 periods at interest of N1 to initial investment of one
ASIN	N1	Arcsine of N1
ATAN	N1	Arctangent of N1
Char	I1	Character in position I1 of the alphanumeric program collating sequence
Char-National	I1	Character position I1 of the national program collating sequence
COS	N1	Cosine of N1
Current-Date	none	Current date and time, and difference in time from Greenwich Mean Time (GMT)
Date-Of-Integer	I1	Standard date equivalent (YYYYMMDD) of integer date
Day-Of-Integer	I1	Julian date equivalent (YYYYDDD) of integer date
Display-Of	NL1,N1	Usage display representation of N1
E	none	The value of e, the natural base
Exception-File	none	Information about the file exception that caused the exception
Exception-Location	none	Implementor-defined location of statement causing an exception

Function Name	Arguments	Returns
Exception-Statement	none	Name of statement causing an exception
Exception-Status	none	Exception-name identifying last exception
EXP	N1	e raised to the power of N1
EXP10	N1	10 raised to the power of N1
Factorial	I1	Factorial of I1
Fraction-Part	N1	Fraction part of N1
Integer	N1	The greatest integer not greater than N1
Integer-Of-Date	I1	Integer date equivalent of standard date (YYYYMMDD)
Integer-Of-Day	I1	Integer date equivalent of Julian date (YYYYDDD)
Integer-Part	N1	Integer part of N1
Length	A1｜B1｜N1｜NL1｜T1｜X1	Length of argument in number of character positions or number of Boolean positions
Length-An	A1｜B1｜N1｜NL1｜T1｜X1	Length of argument in number of alphanumeric character positions
Log	N1	Natural logarithm of N1
Log10	N1	Natural logarithm to base 10 of N1
Lower-Case	A1｜NL1｜X1	All letters in the argument are set lowercase
Max	A1...｜I1...｜N1...｜NL1...｜X1...	The value of maximum argument
Mean	N1	Arithmetic mean of arguments
Median	N1	Median of arguments

Function Name	Arguments	Returns
Midrange	N1	Mean of minimum and maximum arguments
Min	A1... | I1... | N1... | NL1... | X1...	The value of minimum argument
Mod	I1,I2	I1 modulo I2
National-Of	X1,NL1	**Usage** national representation of X1
Numval	NL1 | X1	Numeric value of simple numeric string
Numval-C	X1,X2 | NL1,NL2	Numeric value of numeric string with optional commas and currency sign
Ord	A1 | N1 | X1	Ordinal position of argument in collating sequence
Ord-Max	A1... | N1... | NL1... | X1...	Ordinal position of maximum argument
Ord-Min	A1... | N1... | NL1... | X1...	Ordinal position of minimum argument
Pi	none	The value of pi
Present-Value	N1,N2...	Present value of a series of future period-end amounts, N2 at a discount rate of N1
Random	I1	Random number
Range	I1... | N1...	Value of maximum argument minus value of minimum argument
Rem	N1,N2	Remainder of N1/N2
Reverse	A1 | B1 | NL1 | X1	Reverse the order of the characters in the argument
Sign	N1	The sign of N1
SIN	N1	Sine of N1

Function Name	Arguments	Returns
SQRT	N1	Square root of N1
Standard-Deviation	N1...	Standard deviation of arguments
TAN	N1	Tangent of N1
Upper-Case	A1 | NL1 | X1	All letters in the argument are set uppercase
Variance	N1...	Variance of argument
When-Compiled	none	Date and time program was compiled

COBOL 85/89 FEATURES

COBOL 85 and the COBOL 89 addendum introduced many useful features to the language. This section, while not exhaustive, presents some of the more commonly used features and intrinsic functions.

NESTED PROGRAMS

COBOL 85 allows programs to be nested. The following is an example of a nested program.

```
* ---------------------------------
* start of Prog-1
* ---------------------------------
  Identification Division.
  Program-Id. Prog-1.
  ...
  Data Division.
  ...
```

```
Procedure Division
    Call Prog-2.
    ...
    Stop Run.
*   ----------------------------
*       start of Prog-2
*   ----------------------------
Identification Division.
Program-Id. Prog-2.
...
Data Division.
...
Procedure Division
    Call Prog-3.
...
Exit Program.
    *   ---------------------------------
    *       start of Prog-3
    *   ---------------------------------
    Identification Division.
    Program-Id. Prog-3.
    ...
    Data Division.
    ...
    Procedure Division
    ...
    Exit Program.
    End Program Prog-3.
End Program Prog-2.
End Program Prog-1.
```

Nesting programs are of limited value, although they provided COBOL with the ability, albeit a contrived one, to define variables with local scope. Data items are local to their defining program. Although the concept of nesting programs is limited, several ideas developed to enhance data sharing among nested programs are applicable and beneficial to Object-Oriented COBOL.

Data Sharing

To enhance data sharing between nested programs, COBOL 85 introduced the new reserved word Global. Global is an attribute that is coded at the FD or 01 level. All subordinate elements of the Global declared file or record also become Global. Global data items may be declared at the nesting program level (higher-level) and accessed at the nested program level. The code below provides an example. Global may *not* be used in the Linkage Section.

```
FD 100-Input-File      Global.

...

Working-Storage Section.
01 WS-Input-Record    Global.
```

Global may be used with class programs to allow subclasses access to data files or records at the superclass level. Although helpful in certain situations it should be used with caution to avoid unnecessarily introducing complexity into an application. Data items that may only be changed by one class ease the task of maintaining a system.

Another way to share data is by using the External attribute. The External attribute declares a file or record external to any particular program and allows all programs, subprograms, classes and objects in a run unit access to the data. External is coded the same as Global. Here is an example of the code.

```
FD 100-Input-File      External.

...

Working-Storage Section.
01 WS-Input-Record    External.
```

Flow of Control

COBOL 85 improved a programmer's control over the Perform statement by introducing a Do-Until loop. Perform statements may test a condition before or after the body of the loop with the reserved words Test Before or Test After. The following code provides an example.

Perform A100-Routine With Test Before   (the default, Do-While)

...

End-Perform.

Perform A100-Routine With Test After   (Do-Until)

...

End-Perform.

There is also an in-line **Perform** statement that eliminates specifying a procedure name. Here is an example.

Perform With Test Before Until (some condition)

imperative statements....
End-Perform.

COBOL 85 supports a case statement. It is implemented using the verb **Evaluate**. Below is an example of a case statement.

01 Input-Month   Pic X(03).

...

Evaluate Input-Month
    When "Jan"
        imperative statements
    ...
    When other
        imperative statements
End-Evaluate.

The **Evaluate** statement may be used with the reserved words **True** or **False** as the selectión subject rather than specifying a data name or literal. For example:

Evaluate True
    When Input-Month = "Jan"
        imperative statements
    When Input-Month = "Feb"
        imperative statements

```
...
When other
    imperative statements
End-Evaluate.
```

The **Set** statement may be used to set the value of an **88** level condition. The following is an example.

```
01 File-Eof-Sw      Pic X(01) Value "N".
    88 File-Eof-On            Value "Y".
    88 File-Eof-Off           Value "N".
...
Read 100-Input-File
    At End
        Set File-Eof-On to True
    Not At End
        imperative statements
End-Read.
```

COBOL 97 allows the **Set** statement to set a condition-name to **False** (previously not supported).

Reference modification brings the power of substrings to COBOL 85. Reference modification is very useful for working with variable length and other records whose structure is highly volatile. Reference modification is used by giving a starting position and length values. The format is shown below.

data-item (starting-position:length)

Here is an example.

```
01 Months-in-Year      Pic X(36) Value "JanFebMarApr...".
01 First-Month Pic X(03).
..
```

Move Months-in-Year (1:3) to First-Month. moves **Jan to First-Month**

The starting position and length can be expressions as long as they evaluate to an integer.

The Class clause (no relation to object-oriented concepts) of the Special-Names paragraph brings enumerated data types to COBOL. Here is an example.

```
Environment Division.
...
Special-Names.
        Class Desired-Color "Red" "Green" "Blue".
...
01 Input-Color      Pic X(05).
...
If Input-Color Desired-Color
...
```

INTRINSIC FUNCTIONS

Intrinsic functions were added to the COBOL language by way of the 89 addendum. For a list see Appendix E.

An intrinsic function is specified by the reserved word Function followed by the function name and any required parameters. Functions may be used anywhere a data type, as returned by the function, is allowed with the restriction that a function can not serve as a receiving field. Functions are recursive and one function may be used as the input to another function.

NUMERIC FUNCTIONS: FACTORIAL AND SUM

Here is an example of the Function Factorial.

```
01 A-Value      Pic 9(05).
...
Compute A-Value = Function Factorial (3). returns 6 to A-Value
```

or

```
Move Function Factorial (4) to A-Value. returns 24 to A-Value
```

or

> Move Function Factorial (Function Factorial (3)) to A-Value. returns 720
> to A-Value

The Sum function returns a sum of numbers. Here is an example.

    01 A-Sum   Pic 9(05).

    ...

> Compute A-Sum = Function Sum (100, 200, 300) returns 600 to A-Sum

Sum may be used with the reserved word All. Here is an example of summing a table.

    01 A-Sum   Pic 9(05).
    01 A-Table.
       05 A-Table-Entry Occurs 10 times   Pic 9(02).

    ...

> Compute A-Sum = Function Sum (A-Table-Entry (All)))

DATE FUNCTIONS: CURRENT-DATE, DAY-OF-INTEGER, DATE-OF-INTEGER, INTEGER-OF-DATE, INTEGER-OF-DAY

The Current-Date function returns a 21-byte field that includes the century, year, month, day, hours, minutes, seconds, hundredths of seconds, and hours and minutes ahead or behind of Greenwich Mean Time. Here is the format.

    Pic X(21) ccyymmddhhmmsstt+-hhmmm (hhmmm is zero when not available)

Generally, most applications only need the first eight bytes and the function can be coded as follows:

    01 A-Current-Date   Pic X(08).

    ...

> Move Function Current-Date to A-Current-Date.

The **Day-Of-Integer** function returns a date in the form ccyyddd from an integer, where January 1, 1601 serves as the base integer and is equal to 1. Here is an example.

```
01 A-Date        Pic 9(08).
...
```
Move Function Day-Of-Integer (1) to A-Date. returns 1601001 to A-Date

The **Date-Of-Integer** function returns a date in the form ccyymmdd from an integer date. Here is an example.

```
01 A-Date        Pic 9(08).
...
```
Move Function Date-Of-Integer (1) to A-Date. returns 16010101 to A-Date

The **Integer-Of-Date** function returns an integer from a date in the form ccyymmdd. The following provides an example.

```
01 A-Date        Pic 9(08).
...
```
Move Function Integer-Of-Date (16010101) to A-Date. returns 1 to A-Date

The **Integer-Of-Day** function returns an integer from a date in the form ccyyddd. Here is an example of the code.

```
01 A-Date        Pic 9(08).
...
```
Move Function Integer-Of-Day (1601001) to A-Date. returns 1 to A-Date

MISCELLANEOUS

The **Continue** statement has been added to give COBOL a true null statement. For example:

```
Evaluate True
    When Input-Month = "Jan"
```

imperative statements
When other
Continue
End-Evaluate.

The reserved word **Filler** is optional.

```
01 A-Record.
    05 Input-Last-Name    Pic X(20).
    05                    Pic X(02).
    05 Input-First-Name   Pic X(20).
```

There is a **Justified** clause to right justify alphabetic or alphanumeric data that is declared with the **Picture**.

```
01 An-Input-Record    Pic X(80) Just Right.
```

Packed-Decimal and **Binary** may be specified in lieu of **Comp-3** and **Comp** as in the following example.

```
01 A-Value    Pic s9(04) Packed-Decimal Value 20.
```

```
01 A-Value    Pic s9(04) Binary Value 20.
```

The **Initialize** statement can be used to set one value or an entire table to a value. For example:

```
01 A-Value    Pic X(20).
    ..
Initialize A.                    moves spaces to A-Value
```

Here is an example of initializing all the entries in a table to spaces and zeros.

```
01 A-Table.
    05 Character-Entry    Occurs 100 Times Pic X(20).
    05 Numeric-Entry      Occurs 100 Times Pic 9(05).
```

Initialize A-Table.   moves spaces to Character-Entry, zeros to Numeric-Entry

For a complete list of features available in the COBOL 85/89 standard the reader is directed to the definitive ANSI references: X3.23 - 1985/X3.23a - 1989.

THE PROPOSED COBOL 97 LANGUAGE SYNTAX

The following composite language skeleton is from the October 1995 Working Draft 1.1 ISO/IEC/JTC1/WG4 document, Information Technology—Programming Languages, their environments and system software interfaces—Programming Language COBOL. In a nutshell, this is the COBOL standard as of October 1995.

Currently the standard is undergoing public review. A final version is expected to be published sometime in late 1997. There is the possibility the language will not be approved until 1998. This does not mean there is any time to waste, however. As you will see by looking through the draft, there is a wealth of new material in addition to the object-oriented extensions. The draft will change between now and final approval. The changes will, however, in all likelihood be minimal.

COBOL is an industry language and is not the property of any company or group of companies, or of any organization or group of organizations.

No warranty, expressed or implied, is made by any contributor or by the CODASYL COBOL Committee as to the accuracy and functioning of the programming system and language. Moreover, no responsibility is assumed by any contributor, or by the committee, in connection herein.

The authors and copyright holders of the copyrighted materials used herein

FLOW-MATIC (trademark of Sperry Rand Corporation), Programming for the UNIVAC ® I and II, Data Automation Systems copyrighted 1958, 1959, by Sperry Rand Corporation; IBM Commercial Translator Form No. F28-8013, copyrighted 1959 by IBM; FACT, DSI 27A5260-2760, copyrighted 1960 by Minneapolis-Honeywell

have specifically authorized the use of this material, in whole or in part, in the COBOL specifications. Such authorization extends to the reproduction and use of COBOL specifications in programming manuals or similar publications.

F.1 Program structure

F.1.1 COBOL compilation group

[{ source-unit } ...]

where source-unit is:

$$\left\{ \begin{array}{l} \text{program-definition} \\ \text{class-definition} \\ \text{interface-definition} \\ \text{method-definition} \end{array} \right\}$$

where program-definition is:

[<u>IDENTIFICATION</u> <u>DIVISION</u>.]

<u>PROGRAM-ID</u>. program-name-1 $\left[\ \text{IS} \left\{ \left\{ \begin{array}{l} \underline{\text{COMMON}} \\ \underline{\text{INITIAL}} \end{array} \right\} \right\} \text{PROGRAM} \right] \left[\ \text{WITH} \left\{ \begin{array}{l} \underline{\text{NATIVE}} \\ \underline{\text{STANDARD}} \end{array} \right\} \text{ARITHMETIC} \right]$.

[environment-division]

[data-division]

$\left[\begin{array}{l} \text{procedure-division} \\ [\ \{ \text{program-definition} \} ...] \end{array} \right]$

[<u>END</u> <u>PROGRAM</u>. program-name-1.]

where class-definition is:

[IDENTIFICATION DIVISION.]

CLASS-ID. class-name-1 [SIMPLE]

$$\left[\left\{ \begin{array}{l} \underline{\text{INHERITS}} \\ \underline{\text{REUSES}} \end{array} \right\} \{ \text{class-name-2} \} \, ... \right]$$

$$\left[\underline{\text{USING}} \left\{ \text{parameter-name-1} \left[\underline{\text{CONFORMING}} \text{ TO} \left\{ \begin{array}{l} \text{interface-name-1} \\ \text{class-name-3} \\ \underline{\text{UNIVERSAL}} \end{array} \right\} \right] \right\} \, ... \right].$$

[environment-division]

$$\left[\begin{array}{l} [\underline{\text{IDENTICATION DIVISION.}}] \\ \underline{\text{FACTORY.}} \\ [\text{ environment-division }] \\ [\text{ data-division }] \\ \left[\begin{array}{l} \underline{\text{PROCEDURE DIVISION.}} \\ [\{ \text{method-definition} \} \, ... \,] \end{array} \right] \\ \underline{\text{END FACTORY.}} \end{array} \right]$$

$$\left[\begin{array}{l} [\underline{\text{IDENTIFICATION DIVISION.}}] \\ \underline{\text{OBJECT.}} \\ [\text{ environment-division }] \\ [\text{ data-division }] \\ \left[\begin{array}{l} \underline{\text{PROCEDURE DIVISION.}} \\ [\{ \text{method-definition} \} \, ... \,] \end{array} \right] \\ \underline{\text{END OBJECT.}} \end{array} \right]$$

END CLASS class-name-1.

where method-definition is:

[IDENTIFICATION DIVISION.]

METHOD-ID. method-name-1

$$\text{IS [} \underline{\text{INVARIANT}} \text{] METHOD} \left[\begin{array}{l} \underline{\text{OVERRIDE}} \\ \underline{\text{PROTOTYPE}} \\ \text{OF [} \underline{\text{FACTORY}} \text{ OF] class-name-1} \end{array} \right].$$

[environment-division]

[data-division]

[procedure-division]

END METHOD method-name-1.

where interface-definition is:

[IDENTIFICATION DIVISION.]

INTERFACE-ID. interface-name-1

$$\left[\begin{Bmatrix} \underline{INHERITS} \\ \underline{REUSES} \end{Bmatrix} \begin{Bmatrix} class\text{-}name\text{-}1 \\ interface\text{-}name\text{-}2 \end{Bmatrix} \dots \right].$$

[environment-division]

[data-division]

$$\left[\begin{array}{l} \underline{PROCEDURE}\ \underline{DIVISION}. \\ [\ \{\ method\text{-}definition\ \}\ \dots\ ] \end{array} \right]$$

END INTERFACE interface-name-1.

F.1.2 End markers

$$\underline{END}\ \left\{ \begin{array}{l} \underline{PROGRAM}\ program\text{-}name\text{-}1 \\ \underline{CLASS}\ class\text{-}name\text{-}1 \\ \underline{FACTORY} \\ \underline{OBJECT} \\ \underline{METHOD}\ method\text{-}name\text{-}1 \\ \underline{INTERFACE}\ interface\text{-}name\text{-}1 \end{array} \right\}$$

F.2 Identification division

[IDENTIFICATION DIVISION.]

$$
\left\{
\begin{array}{l}
\text{program-id-paragraph} \\
\text{class-id-paragraph} \\
\text{factory-paragraph} \\
\text{object-paragraph} \\
\text{method-id-paragraph} \\
\text{interface-id-paragraph}
\end{array}
\right\}
$$

where program-id-paragraph is:

PROGRAM-ID. program-name $\left[\text{IS} \left\{ \left\{ \begin{array}{l} \text{COMMON} \\ \text{INITIAL} \end{array} \right\} \right\} \text{PROGRAM} \right] \left[\text{WITH} \left\{ \begin{array}{l} \text{NATIVE} \\ \text{STANDARD} \end{array} \right\} \text{ARITHMETIC} \right]$.

where class-id-paragraph is:

CLASS-ID. class-name-1 [SIMPLE]

$$
\left[\left\{ \begin{array}{l} \text{INHERITS} \\ \text{REUSES} \end{array} \right\} \{ \text{class-name-2} \} \dots \right]
$$

$$
\left[\text{USING} \left\{ \text{parameter-name-1} \left[\text{CONFORMING TO} \left\{ \begin{array}{l} \text{interface-name-1} \\ \text{class-name-3} \\ \text{UNIVERSAL} \end{array} \right\} \right] \right\} \dots \right] .
$$

where factory-paragraph is:

FACTORY.

where object-paragraph is:

OBJECT.

where method-id-paragraph is:

METHOD-ID. method-name-1

$$
\text{IS} [\text{INVARIANT}] \text{METHOD} \left[\begin{array}{l} \text{OVERRIDE} \\ \text{PROTOTYPE} \\ \text{OF} [\text{FACTORY OF}] \text{class-name-1} \end{array} \right] .
$$

where interface-id-paragraph is:

INTERFACE-ID. interface-name-1

$$
\left[\text{INHERITS} \left\{ \left[\frac{\text{FACTORY} \text{ OF}}{} \right] \text{class-name-1} \atop \text{interface-name-2} \right\} \dots \right]
$$

$$
\left[\text{USING} \left\{ \text{parameter-name-1} \left[\text{CONFORMING TO} \left\{ \text{interface-name-3} \atop \text{class-name-2} \atop \text{UNIVERSAL} \right\} \right] \right\} \dots \right].
$$

F.3 Environment division

ENVIRONMENT DIVISION.

[configuration-section]

[input-output-section]

F.3.1 Configuration section

CONFIGURATION SECTION.

[source-computer-paragraph]

[object-computer-paragraph]

[special-names-paragraph]

[repository-paragraph]

F.3.1.1 SOURCE-COMPUTER paragraph

SOURCE-COMPUTER. [computer-name [WITH DEBUGGING MODE] .]

F.3.1.2 OBJECT-COMPUTER paragraph

OBJECT-COMPUTER.

$$
\left[\text{computer-name} \left[\text{PROGRAM COLLATING SEQUENCE} \left\{ \begin{array}{l} \text{IS alphabet-name-1 [alphabet-name-2]} \\ \left\{ \begin{array}{l} \text{FOR } \underline{\text{ALPHANUMERIC}} \text{ IS alphabet-name-1} \\ \text{FOR } \underline{\text{NATIONAL}} \text{ IS alphabet-name-2} \end{array} \right\} \end{array} \right\} \right] \right] .
$$

F.3.1.3 SPECIAL-NAMES paragraph

SPECIAL-NAMES.

$$
\left[\begin{array}{l} \text{switch-name-1} \\ \left[\text{IS mnemonic-name-1} \left[\left\{ \begin{array}{l} \underline{\text{ON}} \text{ STATUS IS condition-name-1} \\ \underline{\text{OFF}} \text{ STATUS IS condition-name-2} \end{array} \right\} \right] \right] \\ \left\{ \begin{array}{l} \underline{\text{ON}} \text{ STATUS IS mnemonic-name-1} \\ \underline{\text{OFF}} \text{ STATUS IS mnemonic-name-2} \end{array} \right\} \\ \text{feature-name-1 IS mnemonic-name-2} \\ \text{device-name-1 IS mnemonic-name-3} \end{array} \right] \dots
$$

[alphabet-name-clause] ...

[symbolic-characters-clause] ...

$$
\left[\underline{\text{CLASS}} \text{ class-name-1} \left[\text{FOR} \left\{ \begin{array}{l} \underline{\text{ALPHANUMERIC}} \\ \underline{\text{NATIONAL}} \end{array} \right\} \right] \text{IS} \left\{ \text{literal-4} \left[\left\{ \begin{array}{l} \underline{\text{THROUGH}} \\ \underline{\text{THRU}} \end{array} \right\} \text{literal-5} \right] \right\} \dots \left[\underline{\text{IN}} \text{ alphabetic-name-4} \right] \right] \dots
$$

[CURRENCY SIGN IS literal-6]

[DECIMAL-POINT IS COMMA]

[CURSOR IS data-name-1]

[CRT STATUS IS data-name-2] .

where alphabet-name-clause is:

$$
\text{ALPHABET} \begin{cases} [\text{ FOR } \underline{\text{ALPHANUMERIC}} \text{] alphabet-name-1 IS} \begin{cases} \underline{\text{STANDARD-1}} \\ \underline{\text{STANDARD-2}} \\ \underline{\text{NATIVE}} \\ \text{code-name-1} \\ \{\text{ literal-phrase }\} \dots \end{cases} \\ \text{FOR } \underline{\text{NATIONAL}} \text{ alphabet-name-2 IS} \begin{cases} \underline{\text{NATIVE}} \\ \underline{\text{UCS}}\text{-2} \\ \text{code-name-2} \\ \{\text{ literal-phrase }\} \dots \end{cases} \end{cases}
$$

where literal-phrase is:

$$
\text{literal-1} \left[\begin{array}{l} \left\{ \begin{array}{l} \underline{\text{THROUGH}} \\ \underline{\text{THRU}} \end{array} \right\} \text{literal-2} \\ \{\ \underline{\text{ALSO}}\ \text{literal-3}\ \} \dots \end{array} \right]
$$

where symbolic-characters-clause is:

$\underline{\text{SYMBOLIC}}$ CHARACTERS

$$
\left[\text{FOR} \left\{ \begin{array}{l} \underline{\text{ALPHANUMERIC}} \\ \underline{\text{NATIONAL}} \end{array} \right\} \right]
$$

$$
\left\{ \{\text{ symbolic-character-1 }\} \dots \left\{ \begin{array}{l} \text{IS} \\ \text{ARE} \end{array} \right\} \{\text{ integer-1 }\} \dots \right\} \dots
$$

$$
[\ \underline{\text{IN}}\ \text{alphabet-name-3}\ ]
$$

F.3.1.4 REPOSITORY paragraph

$\underline{\text{REPOSITORY}}$.

$$
\left[\left\{ \begin{array}{l} \text{class-specifier} \\ \text{interface-specifier} \end{array} \right\} \dots\ . \right]
$$

where class-specifier is:

$$
\underline{\text{CLASS}} \text{ class-name-1} \left[\text{IS} \left\{ \begin{array}{l} \text{implementor-name-1} \\ \text{literal-1} \end{array} \right\} \right] \left[\underline{\text{OF}} \text{ class-name-2 } \underline{\text{USING}} \left\{ \begin{array}{l} \text{class-name-3} \\ \text{interface-name-1} \end{array} \right\} \dots \right]
$$

where interface-specifier is:

$$
\underline{\text{INTERFACE}} \text{ interface-name-2} \left[\text{IS} \left\{ \begin{array}{l} \text{implementor-name-2} \\ \text{literal-2} \end{array} \right\} \right] \left[\underline{\text{OF}} \text{ interface-name-3 } \underline{\text{USING}} \left\{ \begin{array}{l} \text{class-name-4} \\ \text{interface-name-4} \end{array} \right\} \right]
$$

F.3.2 Input-output section

INPUT-OUTPUT SECTION.

[file-control-paragraph]

[i-o-control-paragraph]

where file-control-paragraph is:

FILE-CONTROL. [file-control-entry] ...

where file-control-entry is:

SELECT [OPTIONAL] file-name-1

$$ASSIGN \begin{Bmatrix} TO \begin{Bmatrix} \text{device-name-1} \\ \text{literal-1} \end{Bmatrix} ... [\text{ USING data-name-1 }] \\ USING \text{ data-name-1} \end{Bmatrix}$$

$$\left[RESERVE \text{ integer-1} \begin{bmatrix} AREA \\ AREAS \end{bmatrix} \right]$$

$$\left[[ORGANIZATION \text{ IS }] \begin{Bmatrix} SEQUENTIAL \\ RELATIVE \\ INDEXED \end{Bmatrix} \right]$$

$$\left[PADDING \text{ CHARACTER IS } \begin{Bmatrix} \text{data-name-2} \\ \text{literal-2} \end{Bmatrix} \right]$$

$$\left[RECORD \text{ DELIMITER IS } \begin{Bmatrix} \text{STANDARD-1} \\ \text{feature-name-1} \end{Bmatrix} \right]$$

$$\left[ACCESS \text{ MODE IS } \begin{Bmatrix} SEQUENTIAL \\ RANDOM \\ DYNAMIC \end{Bmatrix} [RELATIVE \text{ KEY IS data-name-3}] \right]$$

$$\left[RECORD \text{ KEY IS } \begin{Bmatrix} \text{data-name-4} \\ \text{record-key-name-1 } SOURCE \text{ IS } \{ \text{ data-name-5 } \} ... \end{Bmatrix} \right]$$

$$\left[ALTERNATE \text{ RECORD KEY IS } \begin{Bmatrix} \text{data-name-6} \\ \text{record-key-name-2 } SOURCE \text{ IS } \{ \text{ data-name-7 } \} ... \end{Bmatrix} [\text{ WITH } DUPLICATES] \right] ...$$

[FILE STATUS IS data-name-8]

$$\left[COLLATING \text{ } SEQUENCE \begin{Bmatrix} \text{IS alphabet-name-3 [alphabet-name-4]} \\ \begin{Bmatrix} \text{FOR } ALPHANUMERIC \text{ IS alphabet-name-3} \\ \text{FOR } NATIONAL \text{ IS alphabet-name-4} \end{Bmatrix} \end{Bmatrix} \right] .$$

where i-o-control-paragraph is:

I-O-CONTROL. [[i-o-control-entry] .]

where i-o-control-entry is:

$$\left[\text{SAME} \begin{bmatrix} \underline{\text{RECORD}} \\ \underline{\text{SORT}} \\ \underline{\text{SORT-MERGE}} \end{bmatrix} \text{AREA FOR file-name-1} \; \{ \text{ file-name-2 } \} \; ... \right] \; ...$$

F.4 Data division

DATA DIVISION.

$$\left[\begin{array}{l} \text{FILE SECTION.} \\ \left[\begin{array}{l} \text{file-description-entry \{ record-description-entry \} ...} \\ \text{sort-merge-file-description-entry \{ record-description-entry \} ...} \end{array}\right] \text{...} \end{array}\right]$$

$$\left[\begin{array}{l} \text{WORKING-STORAGE SECTION.} \\ \left[\begin{array}{l} \text{77-level-description-entry} \\ \text{record-description-entry} \end{array}\right] \text{...} \end{array}\right]$$

$$\left[\begin{array}{l} \text{LINKAGE SECTION.} \\ \left[\begin{array}{l} \text{77-level-description-entry} \\ \text{record-description-entry} \end{array}\right] \text{...} \end{array}\right]$$

$$\left[\begin{array}{l} \text{COMMUNICATION SECTION.} \\ \text{[communication-description-entry [record-description-entry] ...] ...} \end{array}\right]$$

$$\left[\begin{array}{l} \text{REPORT SECTION.} \\ \text{[report-description-entry \{ report-group-description-entry \} ...] ...} \end{array}\right]$$

$$\left[\begin{array}{l} \text{SCREEN SECTION.} \\ \text{[screen-description-entry] ...} \end{array}\right]$$

F.4.1 File description entry

Format 1 (sequential):

FD file-name-1

   [IS EXTERNAL]

   [IS GLOBAL]

$$\left[\text{BLOCK CONTAINS [integer-1 TO] integer-2} \left\{\begin{array}{l}\text{RECORDS}\\\text{CHARACTERS}\end{array}\right\} \right]$$

$$\left[\text{RECORD} \left\{\begin{array}{l} \text{CONTAINS integer-3 CHARACTERS} \\ \text{IS VARYING IN SIZE [[FROM integer-4] [TO integer-5] CHARACTERS]} \\ \quad\text{[DEPENDING ON data-name-1]} \\ \text{CONTAINS integer-6 TO integer-7 CHARACTERS} \end{array}\right\} \right]$$

$$\left[\text{LINAGE IS} \left\{\begin{array}{l}\text{data-name-2}\\\text{integer-8}\end{array}\right\} \text{LINES} \left[\text{WITH FOOTING AT} \left\{\begin{array}{l}\text{data-name-3}\\\text{integer-9}\end{array}\right\} \right] \right.$$
$$\left. \left[\text{LINES AT TOP} \left\{\begin{array}{l}\text{data-name-4}\\\text{integer-10}\end{array}\right\} \right] \left[\text{LINES AT BOTTOM} \left\{\begin{array}{l}\text{data-name-5}\\\text{integer-11}\end{array}\right\} \right] \right]$$

   [CODE-SET IS alphabet-name-1] .

Format 2 (relative or indexed):

FD file-name-1

  [IS EXTERNAL]

  [IS GLOBAL]

$$\left[\underline{\text{BLOCK}} \text{ CONTAINS } [\text{ integer-1 } \underline{\text{TO}}] \text{ integer-2 } \left\{ \begin{array}{l} \underline{\text{RECORDS}} \\ \text{CHARACTERS} \end{array} \right\} \right]$$

$$\left[\underline{\text{RECORD}} \left\{ \begin{array}{l} \text{CONTAINS integer-3 CHARACTERS} \\ \text{IS } \underline{\text{VARYING}} \text{ IN SIZE } [\,[\underline{\text{FROM}} \text{ integer-4 }] [\underline{\text{TO}} \text{ integer-5 }] \text{ CHARACTERS }] \\ \quad [\underline{\text{DEPENDING}} \text{ ON data-name-1 }] \\ \text{CONTAINS integer-6 } \underline{\text{TO}} \text{ integer-7 CHARACTERS} \end{array} \right\} \right] .$$

Format 3 (report):

FD file-name-1

  [IS EXTERNAL]

  [IS GLOBAL]

$$\left[\underline{\text{BLOCK}} \text{ CONTAINS } [\text{ integer-1 } \underline{\text{TO}}] \text{ integer-2 } \left\{ \begin{array}{l} \underline{\text{RECORDS}} \\ \text{CHARACTERS} \end{array} \right\} \right]$$

$$\left[\underline{\text{RECORD}} \left\{ \begin{array}{l} \text{CONTAINS integer-3 CHARACTERS} \\ \text{IS } \underline{\text{VARYING}} \text{ IN SIZE } [\,[\underline{\text{FROM}} \text{ integer-4 }] [\underline{\text{TO}} \text{ integer-5 }] \text{ CHARACTERS }] \\ \quad [\underline{\text{DEPENDING}} \text{ ON data-name-1 }] \\ \text{CONTAINS integer-6 } \underline{\text{TO}} \text{ integer-7 CHARACTERS} \end{array} \right\} \right]$$

  [CODE-SET IS alphabet-name-1]

$$\left\{ \begin{array}{l} \underline{\text{REPORT}} \text{ IS} \\ \underline{\text{REPORTS}} \text{ ARE} \end{array} \right\} \{ \text{ report-name-1 } \} \ \dots \ .$$

F.4.2 Sort-merge file description entry

SD file-name-1

$$\left[\underline{\text{RECORD}} \left\{ \begin{array}{l} \text{CONTAINS integer-1 CHARACTERS} \\ \text{IS } \underline{\text{VARYING}} \text{ IN SIZE } [\,[\underline{\text{FROM}} \text{ integer-2 }] [\underline{\text{TO}} \text{ integer-3 }] \text{ CHARACTERS }] \\ \quad [\underline{\text{DEPENDING}} \text{ ON data-name-1 }] \\ \text{CONTAINS integer-4 } \underline{\text{TO}} \text{ integer-5 CHARACTERS} \end{array} \right\} \right] .$$

F.4.3 77-level description entry

{ 77 data-description-entry }

F.4.4 Record description entry

{ data-description-entry }

F.4.5 Data description entry

Format 1:

$$
\text{level-number} \left\{ \begin{array}{l} \text{data-name-1} \\ \underline{\text{FILLER}} \end{array} \right\}
$$

[<u>REDEFINES</u> data-name-2]

[IS <u>TYPEDEF</u> [<u>STRONG</u>]]

[IS <u>EXTERNAL</u>]

[IS <u>GLOBAL</u>]

$$
\left[\left\{ \begin{array}{l} \underline{\text{PICTURE}} \\ \underline{\text{PIC}} \end{array} \right\} \text{ IS character-string} \right]
$$

[usage-clause]

$$
\left[[\underline{\text{SIGN}} \text{ IS}] \left\{ \begin{array}{l} \underline{\text{LEADING}} \\ \underline{\text{TRAILING}} \end{array} \right\} [\underline{\text{SEPARATE}} \text{ CHARACTER}] \right]
$$

[occurs-clause]

$$
\left[\left\{ \begin{array}{l} \underline{\text{SYNCHRONIZED}} \\ \underline{\text{SYNC}} \end{array} \right\} \left[\begin{array}{l} \underline{\text{LEFT}} \\ \underline{\text{RIGHT}} \end{array} \right] \right]
$$

$$
\left[\left\{ \begin{array}{l} \underline{\text{JUSTIFIED}} \\ \underline{\text{JUST}} \end{array} \right\} \text{ RIGHT} \right]
$$

[<u>BLANK</u> WHEN <u>ZERO</u>]

$$
\left[\begin{array}{l} \underline{\text{VALUE}} \text{ IS literal-1} \\ \left\{ \left\{ \begin{array}{l} \underline{\text{VALUE}} \\ \underline{\text{VALUES}} \end{array} \right\} [\underline{\text{FROM}} (\{ \text{subscript-1} \} \dots)] \left[\begin{array}{l} \text{IS} \\ \text{ARE} \end{array} \right] \{ \text{literal-1} \} \dots \left[\underline{\text{REPEATED}} \left\{ \begin{array}{l} \text{integer-1 TIMES} \\ \text{TO } \underline{\text{END}} \end{array} \right\} \right] \right\} \dots \right]
$$

[<u>INVARIANT</u>]

$$
\left[\underline{\text{PROPERTY}} \left[\text{ WITH } \underline{\text{NO}} \left\{ \begin{array}{l} \underline{\text{GET}} \\ \underline{\text{SET}} \end{array} \right\} \right] \right]
$$

[<u>SAME</u> <u>AS</u> data-name-5]

[<u>TYPE</u> type-name-1]

[validation-clauses] .

where usage-clause is:

```
                 ⎛ BINARY                                              ⎞
                 ⎜ BIT [ ALIGN ]                                       ⎟
                 ⎜ COMPUTATIONAL                                       ⎟
                 ⎜ COMP                                                ⎟
                 ⎜ DISPLAY                                             ⎟
                 ⎜ INDEX                                               ⎟
[ USAGE IS ] ⎨   ⎜ NATIONAL                                           ⎬
                 ⎜                    ⎡ interface-name-1            ⎤ ⎟
                 ⎜                    ⎢ ⎡ ⎧ FACTORY ⎫    ⎤          ⎥ ⎟
                 ⎜ OBJECT [ REFERENCE ] ⎢ ⎨ CLASS   ⎬ OF ⎥ SELF     ⎥ ⎟
                 ⎜                    ⎢ ⎣ ⎩         ⎭    ⎦          ⎥ ⎟
                 ⎜                    ⎣ [ FACTORY OF ] class-name-1 [ ONLY ] ⎦ ⎟
                 ⎝ PACKED-DECIMAL                                     ⎠
```

where occurs-clause is:

```
⎡ OCCURS integer-3 TIMES                                                         ⎤
⎢                                                                               ⎥
⎢   ⎡ ⎧ ASCENDING  ⎫                   ⎤                                         ⎥
⎢   ⎢ ⎨ DESCENDING ⎬ KEY IS { data-name-3 } ... ⎥ ... [ INDEXED BY { index-name-1 } ... ]   ⎥
⎢   ⎣ ⎩            ⎭                   ⎦                                         ⎥
⎢ OCCURS integer-2 TO integer-3 TIMES DEPENDING ON data-name-4                   ⎥
⎢                                                                               ⎥
⎢   ⎡ ⎧ ASCENDING  ⎫                   ⎤                                         ⎥
⎢   ⎢ ⎨ DESCENDING ⎬ KEY IS { data-name-3 } ... ⎥ ... [ INDEXED BY { index-name-1 } ... ]   ⎥
⎢   ⎣ ⎩            ⎭                   ⎦                                         ⎥
⎢ OCCURS integer-2 TO integer-3 TIMES DEPENDING ON data-name-4                   ⎥
⎢                                                                               ⎥
⎢   EXTEND [ BY integer-4 ] [ UNTIL integer-5 ]                                  ⎥
⎢                                                                               ⎥
⎢   ...                                                                         ⎥
⎢                                                                               ⎥
⎢   [ INDEXED BY { index-name-1 } ... ]                                          ⎥
⎢ OCCURS [ integer-2 TO ] integer-3 TIMES [ DEPENDING ON data-name-4 ]           ⎥
⎢                                                                               ⎥
⎣   [ STEP integer-6 ]                                                          ⎦
```

where validation-clauses is:

[{ ALLOW [ONLY] literal-2 [OR literal-3] ... [WHEN condition-1] } ...]

$$\left[\text{CLASS IS} \left\{ \begin{array}{l} \text{NUMERIC} \\ \text{ALPHABETIC} \\ \text{ALPHABETIC-LOWER} \\ \text{ALPHABETIC-UPPER} \\ \text{class-name-2} \end{array} \right\} \right]$$

$$\left[\text{DEFAULT IS} \left\{ \begin{array}{l} \text{literal-4} \\ \text{identifier-1} \\ \text{NONE} \end{array} \right\} \right]$$

[DESTINATION IS { identifier-2 } ...]

$$\left[\left\{ \begin{array}{l} \text{ERROR STATUS IS} \left\{ \begin{array}{l} \text{literal-5} \\ \text{identifier-3} \end{array} \right\} \\ \text{NO ERROR STATUS IS} \left\{ \begin{array}{l} \text{literal-6} \\ \text{identifier-4} \end{array} \right\} \end{array} \right\} \quad ... \quad \left[\text{ON} \left\{ \begin{array}{l} \text{FORMAT} \\ \text{CONTENT} \\ \text{RELATION} \end{array} \right\} \text{FOR} \{ \text{identifier-5} \} ... \right] \right]$$

[{ INVALID [WHEN condition-2] } ...]

[PRESENT WHEN condition-3]

[VARYING { data-name-6 [FROM arithmetic-expression-1] [BY arithmetic-expression-2] } ...]

Format 2:

$$66 \text{ data-name-1 RENAMES data-name-2} \left[\left\{ \begin{array}{l} \text{THROUGH} \\ \text{THRU} \end{array} \right\} \text{data-name-3} \right].$$

Format 3:

$$88 \text{ condition-name-1} \left\{ \begin{array}{l} \text{VALUE} \\ \text{VALUES} \end{array} \right\} \left[\begin{array}{l} \text{IS} \\ \text{ARE} \end{array} \right] \left\{ \text{literal-1} \left[\left\{ \begin{array}{l} \text{THROUGH} \\ \text{THRU} \end{array} \right\} \text{literal-7} \right] \right\} ...$$

[WHEN SET TO FALSE IS literal-8].

Format 4 (validation):

$$88 \text{ [condition-name-2]} \left\{ \begin{array}{l} \text{INVALID} \\ \text{VALID} \end{array} \right\} \left\{ \begin{array}{l} \text{VALUE} \\ \text{VALUES} \end{array} \right\} \left[\begin{array}{l} \text{IS} \\ \text{ARE} \end{array} \right] \left\{ \text{literal-1} \left[\left\{ \begin{array}{l} \text{THROUGH} \\ \text{THRU} \end{array} \right\} \text{literal-7} \right] \right\} ...$$

[WHEN condition-4].

Format 5:

77 data-name

$$\left\{ \begin{array}{l} \left\{ \begin{array}{l} \underline{PICTURE} \\ \underline{PIC} \end{array} \right\} \text{ IS character-string} \\ [\ \underline{USAGE} \text{ IS}\ ]\ \underline{INDEX} \end{array} \right\}$$

   [other-data-description-entry-clauses]

F.4.6 Communication description entry (obsolete)

Format 1:

CD cd-name-1 FOR [INITIAL] INPUT

$$\left[\begin{array}{l} \left[\begin{array}{l} [\text{ SYMBOLIC } \underline{QUEUE} \text{ IS data-name-1 }] \\ [\text{ SYMBOLIC } \underline{SUB\text{-}QUEUE\text{-}1} \text{ IS data-name-2 }] \\ [\text{ SYMBOLIC } \underline{SUB\text{-}QUEUE\text{-}2} \text{ IS data-name-3 }] \\ [\text{ SYMBOLIC } \underline{SUB\text{-}QUEUE\text{-}3} \text{ IS data-name-4 }] \\ [\ \underline{MESSAGE} \ \underline{DATE} \text{ IS data-name-5 }] \\ [\ \underline{MESSAGE} \ \underline{TIME} \text{ IS data-name-6 }] \\ [\text{ SYMBOLIC } \underline{SOURCE} \text{ IS data-name-7 }] \\ [\ \underline{TEXT} \ \underline{LENGTH} \text{ IS data-name-8 }] \\ [\ \underline{END} \ \underline{KEY} \text{ IS data-name-9 }] \\ [\ \underline{STATUS} \ \underline{KEY} \text{ IS data-name-10 }] \\ [\ \underline{MESSAGE} \ \underline{COUNT} \text{ IS data-name-11 }] \end{array} \right] \\ \left[\begin{array}{l} \text{data-name-1 data-name-2 data-name-3} \\ \text{data-name-4 data-name-5 data-name-6} \\ \text{data-name-7 data-name-8 data-name-9} \\ \text{data-name-10 data-name-11} \end{array} \right] \end{array} \right]$$

Format 2:

CD cd-name-1 FOR OUTPUT

  [DESTINATION COUNT IS data-name-1]

  [TEXT LENGTH IS data-name-2]

  [STATUS KEY IS data-name-3]

  [DESTINATION TABLE OCCURS integer-1 TIMES [INDEXED BY { index-name-1 } ...]]

  [ERROR KEY IS data-name-4]

  [SYMBOLIC DESTINATION IS data-name-5] .

Format 3:

$$
\underline{CD}\ \text{cd-name-1 FOR } [\ \underline{INITIAL}\ ]\ \text{I-O}
\left\{
\begin{array}{l}
\left[
\begin{array}{l}
[\ \underline{MESSAGE}\ \underline{DATE}\ \text{IS data-name-1}\ ] \\[4pt]
[\ \underline{MESSAGE}\ \underline{TIME}\ \text{IS data-name-2}\ ] \\[4pt]
[\ \text{SYMBOLIC}\ \underline{TERMINAL}\ \text{IS data-name-3}\ ] \\[4pt]
[\ \underline{TEXT}\ \underline{LENGTH}\ \text{IS data-name-4}\ ] \\[4pt]
[\ \underline{END}\ \underline{KEY}\ \text{IS data-name-5}\ ] \\[4pt]
[\ \underline{STATUS}\ \underline{KEY}\ \text{IS data-name-6}\ ]
\end{array}
\right] \\[50pt]
\left[
\begin{array}{l}
\text{data-name-1 data-name-2 data-name-3} \\[4pt]
\quad\text{data-name-4 data-name-5 data-name-6}
\end{array}
\right]
\end{array}
\right\}
$$

F.4.7 Report description entry

$\underline{RD}$ report-name-1

$[\ \text{IS } \underline{GLOBAL}\ ]$

$$
\left[\ \underline{CODE}\ \text{IS}\ \left\{\begin{array}{l}\text{literal-1}\\ \text{identifier-1}\end{array}\right\}\ \right]
$$

$$
\left[\ \left\{\begin{array}{l}\underline{CONTROL}\ \text{IS}\\ \underline{CONTROLS}\ \text{ARE}\end{array}\right\}\ \left\{\begin{array}{l}\{\ \text{data-name-1}\ \}\ ...\\ \underline{FINAL}\ [\ \text{data-name-1}\ ]\ ...\end{array}\right\}\ \right]
$$

$$
\left[\ \underline{PAGE}\ \left[\begin{array}{l}\underline{LIMIT}\ \text{IS}\\ \underline{LIMITS}\ \text{ARE}\end{array}\right]\ \left[\begin{array}{l}\text{integer-1}\\ \text{integer-1}\ \left\{\begin{array}{l}\underline{LINE}\\ \underline{LINES}\end{array}\right\}\end{array}\right]\ \left[\ \text{interger-2}\ \left\{\begin{array}{l}\underline{COLS}\\ \underline{COLUMNS}\end{array}\right\}\right]\ \right]
$$

$$
\left[\ \underline{HEADING}\ \text{IS integer-3}\ \right]\ \left[\ \underline{FIRST}\ \left\{\begin{array}{l}\underline{DETAIL}\\ \underline{DE}\end{array}\right\}\ \text{IS integer-4}\ \right]
$$

$$
\left[\ \underline{LAST}\ \left\{\begin{array}{l}\underline{CONTROL\ HEADING}\\ \underline{CH}\end{array}\right\}\ \text{IS integer-5}\ \right]
$$

$$
\left[\ \underline{LAST}\ \left\{\begin{array}{l}\underline{DETAIL}\\ \underline{DE}\end{array}\right\}\ \text{IS integer-6}\ \right]\ \left[\ \underline{FOOTING}\ \text{IS integer-7}\ \right]
$$

F.4.8 Report group description entry

01 [data-name-1]

  [type-clause]

  [next-group-clause]

  [line-number-clause]

  [picture-clause]

$$\left[\ [\ \underline{USAGE}\ IS\ ]\ \left\{ \begin{array}{l} \underline{DISPLAY} \\ \underline{NATIONAL} \end{array} \right\} \right]$$

  [sign-clause]

  [justified-clause]

  [column-number-clause]

  [<u>BLANK</u> WHEN <u>ZERO</u>]

$$\left[\begin{array}{l} \text{source-clause} \\ \text{sum-clause} \\ \left\{ \begin{array}{l} \underline{VALUE} \\ \underline{VALUES} \end{array} \right\} \left[\begin{array}{l} IS \\ ARE \end{array} \right] \{\ \text{literal-1}\ \}\ ... \end{array} \right]$$

  [error-clause]

  [present-when-clause]

  [<u>GROUP</u> INDICATE]

  [<u>OCCURS</u> [integer-1 <u>TO</u>] integer-2 TIMES [<u>DEPENDING</u> ON identifier-1] [<u>STEP</u> integer-3]]

  [varying-clause] .

F.4.9 Screen description entry

Format 1 (group):

level-number $\left[\begin{array}{l} \text{screen-name-1} \\ \underline{\text{FILLER}} \end{array} \right]$

  [IS <u>GLOBAL</u>]

  $\left[\underline{\text{LINE}} \text{ NUMBER IS} \left[\begin{array}{l} \underline{\text{PLUS}} \\ \underline{\text{MINUS}} \end{array} \right] \left\{ \begin{array}{l} \text{identifier-1} \\ \text{integer-1} \end{array} \right\} \right]$

  $\left[\left\{ \begin{array}{l} \underline{\text{COLUMN}} \\ \underline{\text{COL}} \end{array} \right\} \text{NUMBER IS} \left[\begin{array}{l} \underline{\text{PLUS}} \\ \underline{\text{MINUS}} \end{array} \right] \left\{ \begin{array}{l} \text{identifier-2} \\ \text{integer-2} \end{array} \right\} \right]$

  [<u>BLANK</u> <u>SCREEN</u>]

  [<u>BELL</u>]

  [<u>BLINK</u>]

  $\left[\begin{array}{l} \underline{\text{HIGHLIGHT}} \\ \underline{\text{LOWLIGHT}} \end{array} \right]$

  [<u>REVERSE-VIDEO</u>]

  [<u>UNDERLINE</u>]

  $\left[\underline{\text{FOREGROUND-COLOR}} \text{ IS} \left\{ \begin{array}{l} \text{identifier-3} \\ \text{integer-3} \end{array} \right\} \right]$

  $\left[\underline{\text{BACKGROUND-COLOR}} \text{ IS} \left\{ \begin{array}{l} \text{identifier-4} \\ \text{integer-4} \end{array} \right\} \right]$

  $\left[\left[\underline{\text{SIGN}} \text{ IS } \right] \left\{ \begin{array}{l} \underline{\text{LEADING}} \\ \underline{\text{TRAILING}} \end{array} \right\} \right]$

  [<u>FULL</u>]

  [<u>AUTO</u>]

  [<u>SECURE</u>]

  [<u>REQUIRED</u>]

  [<u>OCCURS</u> integer-5 TIMES] .

Format 2 (elementary):

level-number $\left[\begin{array}{l}\text{screen-name-1}\\\underline{\text{FILLER}}\end{array}\right]$

[IS <u>GLOBAL</u>]

$\left[\underline{\text{LINE}}\text{ NUMBER IS }\left[\begin{array}{l}\underline{\text{PLUS}}\\\underline{\text{MINUS}}\end{array}\right]\left\{\begin{array}{l}\text{identifier-1}\\\text{integer-1}\end{array}\right\}\right]$

$\left[\left\{\begin{array}{l}\underline{\text{COLUMN}}\\\underline{\text{COL}}\end{array}\right\}\text{ NUMBER IS }\left[\begin{array}{l}\underline{\text{PLUS}}\\\underline{\text{MINUS}}\end{array}\right]\left\{\begin{array}{l}\text{identifier-2}\\\text{integer-2}\end{array}\right\}\right]$

$\left[\underline{\text{BLANK}}\left\{\begin{array}{l}\underline{\text{LINE}}\\\underline{\text{SCREEN}}\end{array}\right\}\right]$

$\left[\underline{\text{ERASE}}\left\{\begin{array}{l}\text{END OF }\underline{\text{LINE}}\\\text{END OF }\underline{\text{SCREEN}}\\\underline{\text{EOL}}\\\underline{\text{EOS}}\end{array}\right\}\right]$

[<u>BELL</u>]

[<u>BLINK</u>]

$\left[\begin{array}{l}\underline{\text{HIGHLIGHT}}\\\underline{\text{LOWLIGHT}}\end{array}\right]$

[<u>REVERSE-VIDEO</u>]

[<u>UNDERLINE</u>]

$\left[\underline{\text{FOREGROUND-COLOR}}\text{ IS }\left\{\begin{array}{l}\text{identifier-3}\\\text{integer-3}\end{array}\right\}\right]$

$\left[\underline{\text{BACKGROUND-COLOR}}\text{ IS }\left\{\begin{array}{l}\text{identifier-4}\\\text{integer-4}\end{array}\right\}\right]$

$\left[\left\{\begin{array}{l}\underline{\text{PICTURE}}\\\underline{\text{PIC}}\end{array}\right\}\text{ IS character-string}\right]$

$\left[\begin{array}{l}\left\{\left[\underline{\text{FROM}}\left\{\begin{array}{l}\text{identifier-5}\\\text{literal-1}\end{array}\right\}\right]\right\}\\\quad\left[\underline{\text{TO}}\text{ identifier-6}\right]\\\underline{\text{USING}}\text{ identifier-7}\\\underline{\text{VALUE}}\text{ literal-2}\end{array}\right]$

[<u>BLANK</u> WHEN <u>ZERO</u>]

$\left[\left\{\begin{array}{l}\underline{\text{JUSTIFIED}}\\\underline{\text{JUST}}\end{array}\right\}\text{ RIGHT}\right]$

$\left[\left[\text{ }\underline{\text{SIGN}}\text{ IS }\right]\left\{\begin{array}{l}\underline{\text{LEADING}}\\\underline{\text{TRAILING}}\end{array}\right\}\right]$

[<u>FULL</u>]

[<u>AUTO</u>]

[<u>SECURE</u>]

[<u>REQUIRED</u>]

[<u>OCCURS</u> integer-5 TIMES] .

F.5 Procedure division

Format 1 (with sections):

PROCEDURE DIVISION [USING { data-name-1 } ...] [RETURNING data-name-2] .

$$
\left[
\begin{array}{l}
\text{DECLARATIVES.} \\
\left\{
\begin{array}{l}
\text{section-name SECTION.} \\
\quad \text{use-statement.} \\
\text{[paragraph-name. [sentence] ...] ...}
\end{array}
\right\} \; ... \\
\text{END DECLARATIVES.}
\end{array}
\right]
$$

$$
\left\{
\begin{array}{l}
\text{section-name SECTION.} \\
\text{[paragraph-name. [sentence] ...] ...}
\end{array}
\right\} \; ...
$$

Format 2 (without sections):

PROCEDURE DIVISION [USING { data-name-1 } ...] [RETURNING data-name-2] .

{ paragraph-name . [sentence] ... } ...

Format 3 (factory object or interface):

PROCEDURE DIVISION.

$$
\left[
\begin{array}{l}
\text{DECLARATIVES.} \\
\left\{
\begin{array}{l}
\text{section-name SECTION.} \\
\quad \text{use-statement.} \\
\text{[paragraph-name. [sentence] ...] ...}
\end{array}
\right\} \; ... \\
\text{END DECLARATIVES.}
\end{array}
\right]
$$

[{ method-definition } ...]

F.5.1 ACCEPT statement

Format 1:

ACCEPT identifier-1 [FROM mnemonic-name-1] [END-ACCEPT]

Format 2:

$$
\text{ACCEPT identifier-2 FROM}
\left\{
\begin{array}{l}
\text{DATE} \\
\text{DAY} \\
\text{DAY-OF-WEEK} \\
\text{TIME}
\end{array}
\right\}
\text{[END-ACCEPT]}
$$

Format 3 (screen):

ACCEPT screen-name-1

$$\left[AT \left\{ \left\{ \begin{array}{l} \underline{\text{LINE}} \text{ NUMBER} \left\{ \begin{array}{l} \text{identifier-3} \\ \text{integer-1} \end{array} \right\} \\ \left\{ \begin{array}{l} \underline{\text{COLUMN}} \\ \underline{\text{COL}} \end{array} \right\} \text{ NUMBER} \left\{ \begin{array}{l} \text{identifier-4} \\ \text{integer-2} \end{array} \right\} \end{array} \right\} \right] \right.$$

[ON EXCEPTION imperative-statement-1]

[NOT ON EXCEPTION imperative-statement-2]

[END-ACCEPT]

Format 4 (Communication (obsolete)):

ACCEPT cd-name-1 MESSAGE COUNT

F.5.2 ADD statement

Format 1:

ADD $\left\{ \begin{array}{l} \text{identifier-1} \\ \text{literal-1} \end{array} \right\}$ ... TO { identifier-2 [ROUNDED] } ...

[ON SIZE ERROR imperative-statement-1]

[NOT ON SIZE ERROR imperative-statement-2]

[END-ADD]

Format 2:

ADD $\left\{ \begin{array}{l} \text{identifier-1} \\ \text{literal-1} \end{array} \right\}$ ... TO $\left\{ \begin{array}{l} \text{identifier-2} \\ \text{literal-2} \end{array} \right\}$

GIVING { identifier-3 [ROUNDED] } ...

[ON SIZE ERROR imperative-statement-1]

[NOT ON SIZE ERROR imperative-statement-2]

[END-ADD]

Format 3:

ADD $\left\{ \begin{array}{l} \underline{\text{CORRESPONDING}} \\ \underline{\text{CORR}} \end{array} \right\}$ identifier-1 TO identifier-2 [ROUNDED]

[ON SIZE ERROR imperative-statement-1]

[NOT ON SIZE ERROR imperative-statement-2]

[END-ADD]

F.5.3 CALL statement

Format 1 (archaic):

$$\underline{\text{CALL}} \left\{ \begin{array}{l} \text{identifier-1} \\ \text{literal-1} \end{array} \right\} \left[\underline{\text{USING}} \left\{ \begin{array}{l} [\text{ BY } \underline{\text{REFERENCE}}] \{ \text{identifier-2} \} \ldots \\ \text{BY } \underline{\text{CONTENT}} \{ \text{identifier-2} \} \ldots \end{array} \right\} \ldots \right]$$

[ON <u>OVERFLOW</u> imperative-statement-1]

[<u>END-CALL</u>]

Format 2:

$$\underline{\text{CALL}} \left\{ \begin{array}{l} \text{identifier-1} \\ \text{literal-1} \end{array} \right\} \left[\underline{\text{USING}} \left\{ \begin{array}{l} [\text{ BY } \underline{\text{REFERENCE}}] \{ \text{identifier-2} \} \ldots \\ \text{BY } \underline{\text{CONTENT}} \{ \text{identifier-2} \} \ldots \end{array} \right\} \ldots \right]$$

[ON <u>EXCEPTION</u> imperative-statement-1]

[<u>NOT</u> ON <u>EXCEPTION</u> imperative-statement-2]

[<u>END-CALL</u>]

F.5.4 CANCEL statement

$$\underline{\text{CANCEL}} \left\{ \begin{array}{l} \text{identifier-1} \\ \text{literal-1} \end{array} \right\} \ldots$$

F.5.5 CLOSE statement

$$\underline{\text{CLOSE}} \left\{ \text{file-name-1} \left[\begin{array}{l} \left\{ \begin{array}{l} \underline{\text{REEL}} \\ \underline{\text{UNIT}} \end{array} \right\} [\text{ FOR } \underline{\text{REMOVAL}}] \\ \text{WITH} \left\{ \begin{array}{l} \underline{\text{NO REWIND}} \\ \underline{\text{LOCK}} \end{array} \right\} \end{array} \right] \right\} \ldots$$

F.5.6 COMPUTE statement

Format 1 (arithmetic):

<u>COMPUTE</u> { identifier-1 [<u>ROUNDED</u>] } ... = arithmetic-expression-1

[ON <u>SIZE ERROR</u> imperative-statement-1]

[NOT ON <u>SIZE ERROR</u> imperative-statement-2]

[<u>END-COMPUTE</u>]

Format 2 (boolean):

<u>COMPUTE</u> { identifier-1 } ... = boolean-expression-1 [<u>END-COMPUTE</u>]

F.5.7 CONTINUE statement

<u>CONTINUE</u>

F.5.8 DELETE statement

DELETE file-name-1 RECORD

   [INVALID KEY imperative-statement-1]

   [NOT INVALID KEY imperative-statement-2]

   [END-DELETE]

F.5.9 DISABLE statement (obsolete)

DISABLE $\begin{Bmatrix} \text{INPUT [TERMINAL]} \\ \text{I-O} \\ \text{OUTPUT} \end{Bmatrix}$ cd-name-1

F.5.10 DISPLAY statement

Format 1 (low-volume-data):

DISPLAY $\begin{Bmatrix} \text{identifier-1} \\ \text{literal-1} \end{Bmatrix}$ ... [UPON mnemonic-name-1] [WITH NO ADVANCING] [END-DISPLAY]

Format 2 (screen):

DISPLAY screen-name-1

$$\left[\text{AT} \left[\left\{ \begin{array}{l} \text{LINE NUMBER} \begin{Bmatrix} \text{identifier-2} \\ \text{integer-1} \end{Bmatrix} \\ \begin{Bmatrix} \text{COLUMN} \\ \text{COL} \end{Bmatrix} \text{NUMBER} \begin{Bmatrix} \text{identifier-3} \\ \text{integer-2} \end{Bmatrix} \end{array} \right\} \right] \right]$$

   [ON EXCEPTION imperative-statement-1]

   [NOT ON EXCEPTION imperative-statement-2]

   [END-DISPLAY]

F.5.11 DIVIDE statement

Format 1:

DIVIDE $\begin{Bmatrix} \text{identifier-1} \\ \text{literal-1} \end{Bmatrix}$ INTO { identifier-2 [ROUNDED] } ...

   [ON SIZE ERROR imperative-statement-1]

   [NOT ON SIZE ERROR imperative-statement-2]

   [END-DIVIDE]

Format 2:

$$\underline{DIVIDE} \left\{ \begin{array}{l} \text{identifier-1} \\ \text{literal-1} \end{array} \right\} \underline{INTO} \left\{ \begin{array}{l} \text{identifier-2} \\ \text{literal-2} \end{array} \right\}$$

   $\underline{GIVING}$ { identifier-3 [$\underline{ROUNDED}$] } ...

   [ON $\underline{SIZE}$ $\underline{ERROR}$ imperative-statement-1]

   [$\underline{NOT}$ ON $\underline{SIZE}$ $\underline{ERROR}$ imperative-statement-2]

   [$\underline{END\text{-}DIVIDE}$]

Format 3:

$$\underline{DIVIDE} \left\{ \begin{array}{l} \text{identifier-2} \\ \text{literal-2} \end{array} \right\} \underline{BY} \left\{ \begin{array}{l} \text{identifier-1} \\ \text{literal-1} \end{array} \right\}$$

   $\underline{GIVING}$ { identifier-3 [$\underline{ROUNDED}$] } ...

   [ON $\underline{SIZE}$ $\underline{ERROR}$ imperative-statement-1]

   [$\underline{NOT}$ ON $\underline{SIZE}$ $\underline{ERROR}$ imperative-statement-2]

   [$\underline{END\text{-}DIVIDE}$]

Format 4:

$$\underline{DIVIDE} \left\{ \begin{array}{l} \text{identifier-1} \\ \text{literal-1} \end{array} \right\} \underline{INTO} \left\{ \begin{array}{l} \text{identifier-2} \\ \text{literal-2} \end{array} \right\}$$

   $\underline{GIVING}$ identifier-3 [$\underline{ROUNDED}$]

   $\underline{REMAINDER}$ identifier-4

   [ON $\underline{SIZE}$ $\underline{ERROR}$ imperative-statement-1]

   [$\underline{NOT}$ ON $\underline{SIZE}$ $\underline{ERROR}$ imperative-statement-2]

   [$\underline{END\text{-}DIVIDE}$]

Format 5:

$$\underline{DIVIDE} \left\{ \begin{array}{l} \text{identifier-2} \\ \text{literal-2} \end{array} \right\} \underline{BY} \left\{ \begin{array}{l} \text{identifier-1} \\ \text{literal-1} \end{array} \right\}$$

   $\underline{GIVING}$ identifier-3 [$\underline{ROUNDED}$]

   $\underline{REMAINDER}$ identifier-4

   [ON $\underline{SIZE}$ $\underline{ERROR}$ imperative-statement-1]

   [$\underline{NOT}$ ON $\underline{SIZE}$ $\underline{ERROR}$ imperative-statement-2]

   [$\underline{END\text{-}DIVIDE}$]

F.5.12 ENABLE statement (obsolete)

$$\text{ENABLE} \left\{ \begin{array}{l} \underline{\text{INPUT}} \; [\; \underline{\text{TERMINAL}} \;] \\ \underline{\text{I-O}} \; \underline{\text{TERMINAL}} \\ \underline{\text{OUTPUT}} \end{array} \right\} \text{cd-name-1}$$

F.5.13 EVALUATE statement

EVALUATE selection-subject-1 [ALSO selection-subject-2] ...

   { { WHEN selection-object-1 [ALSO selection-object-2] ... } ... imperative-statement-1 } ...

   [WHEN OTHER imperative-statement-2]

   [END-EVALUATE]

where selection-subject-n is:
$$\left\{ \begin{array}{l} \text{identifier-1} \\ \text{literal-1} \\ \text{arithmetic-expression-1} \\ \text{condition-1} \\ \underline{\text{TRUE}} \\ \underline{\text{FALSE}} \end{array} \right\}$$

selection-object-n is:
$$\left\{ \begin{array}{l} [\; \underline{\text{NOT}} \;] \text{ identifier-2} \\ [\; \underline{\text{NOT}} \;] \text{ literal-2} \\ [\; \underline{\text{NOT}} \;] \text{ arithmetic-expression-2} \\ [\; \underline{\text{NOT}} \;] \text{ range-expression-1} \\ \text{condition-2} \\ \text{partial-expression-1} \\ \underline{\text{TRUE}} \\ \underline{\text{FALSE}} \\ \underline{\text{ANY}} \\ \text{boolean-expression-1} \end{array} \right\}$$

range-expression is:
$$\left\{ \begin{array}{l} \text{identifier-3} \\ \text{literal-3} \\ \text{arithmetic-expression-3} \end{array} \right\} \left\{ \begin{array}{l} \underline{\text{THROUGH}} \\ \underline{\text{THRU}} \end{array} \right\} \left\{ \begin{array}{l} \text{identifier-4} \\ \text{literal-4} \\ \text{arithmetic-expression-4} \end{array} \right\}$$

F.5.14 EXIT statement

Format 1 (paragraph):

EXIT

Format 2 (program):

$$\text{EXIT PROGRAM} \left[\text{RAISING} \left\{ \begin{array}{l} \text{EXCEPTION exception-name-1} \\ \text{identifier-1} \\ \text{LAST EXCEPTION} \end{array} \right\} \right]$$

Format 3 (method):

$$\text{EXIT METHOD} \left[\text{RAISING} \left\{ \begin{array}{l} \text{EXCEPTION exception-name-1} \\ \text{identifier-1} \\ \text{LAST EXCEPTION} \end{array} \right\} \right]$$

F.5.15 GENERATE statement

$$\text{GENERATE} \left\{ \begin{array}{l} \text{data-name-1} \\ \text{report-name-1} \end{array} \right\}$$

F.5.16 GO TO statement

Format 1:

GO TO procedure-name-1

Format 2:

GO TO { procedure-name-1 } ... DEPENDING ON identifier-1

F.5.17 IF statement

$$\text{IF condition-1 THEN} \left\{ \begin{array}{l} \text{statement-1} \\ \text{NEXT SENTENCE} \end{array} \right\} \left\{ \begin{array}{l} \text{ELSE statement-2 [END-IF]} \\ \text{ELSE NEXT SENTENCE} \\ \text{END-IF} \end{array} \right\}$$

F.5.18 INITIALIZE statement

INITIALIZE { identifier-1 } ...

```
  ┌ ┌ ALL                         ┐       ┐
  │ │ ALPHABETIC                │       │
  │ │ ALPHANUMERIC              │       │
  │ │ ALPHANUMERIC-EDITED       │       │
  │ │ BOOLEAN                   │ TO VALUE │
  │ │ NATIONAL                  │       │
  │ │ NATIONAL-EDITED           │       │
  │ │ NUMERIC                   │       │
  └ └ NUMERIC-EDITED            ┘       ┘
```

```
  ┌                ┌ ALPHABETIC          ┐               ┐
  │                │ ALPHANUMERIC        │               │
  │                │ ALPHANUMERIC-EDITED │         ┌ identifier-2 ┐ │
  │ THEN REPLACING │ BOOLEAN             │ DATA BY │ literal-1    │ │
  │                │ NATIONAL            │         └              ┘ │
  │                │ NATIONAL-EDITED     │               │
  │                │ NUMERIC             │               │
  └                └ NUMERIC-EDITED      ┘               ┘
```

F.5.19 INITIATE statement

INITIATE { report-name-1 } ...

F.5.20 INSPECT statement

Format 1 (tallying):

INSPECT identifier-1 TALLYING tallying-phrase

Format 2 (replacing):

INSPECT identifier-1 REPLACING replacing-phrase

Format 3 (tallying and replacing):

INSPECT identifier-1 TALLYING tallying-phrase REPLACING replacing-phrase

Format 4 (converting):

INSPECT identifier-1 CONVERTING $\left\{ \begin{array}{c} \text{identifier-6} \\ \text{literal-4} \end{array} \right\}$ TO $\left\{ \begin{array}{c} \text{identifier-7} \\ \text{literal-5} \end{array} \right\}$ [after-before-phrase]

where tallying-phrase is:

$$\left\{ \text{identifier-2} \ \underline{\text{FOR}} \left\{ \begin{array}{l} \underline{\text{CHARACTERS}} \ [\ \text{after-before-phrase} \ ] \\[1ex] \underline{\text{ALL}} \ \left\{ \left\{ \begin{array}{l} \text{identifier-3} \\ \text{literal-1} \end{array} \right\} [\ \text{after-before-phrase} \ ] \right\} \cdots \\[2ex] \underline{\text{LEADING}} \ \left\{ \left\{ \begin{array}{l} \text{identifier-3} \\ \text{literal-1} \end{array} \right\} [\ \text{after-before-phrase} \ ] \right\} \cdots \end{array} \right\} \cdots \right\} \cdots$$

where after-before-phrase is:

$$\left\{ \left\| \begin{array}{l} \underline{\text{AFTER}} \ \text{INITIAL} \ \left\{ \begin{array}{l} \text{identifier-4} \\ \text{literal-2} \end{array} \right\} \\[2ex] \underline{\text{BEFORE}} \ \text{INITIAL} \ \left\{ \begin{array}{l} \text{identifier-4} \\ \text{literal-2} \end{array} \right\} \end{array} \right\| \right\}$$

where replacing-phrase is:

$$\left\{ \begin{array}{l} \underline{\text{CHARACTERS}} \ \underline{\text{BY}} \ \text{replacement-item} \ [\ \text{after-before-phrase} \ ] \\[2ex] \underline{\text{ALL}} \ \left\{ \left\{ \begin{array}{l} \text{identifier-3} \\ \text{literal-1} \end{array} \right\} \underline{\text{BY}} \ \text{replacement-item} \ [\ \text{after-before-phrase} \ ] \right\} \cdots \\[2ex] \underline{\text{LEADING}} \ \left\{ \left\{ \begin{array}{l} \text{identifier-3} \\ \text{literal-1} \end{array} \right\} \underline{\text{BY}} \ \text{replacement-item} \ [\ \text{after-before-phrase} \ ] \right\} \cdots \\[2ex] \underline{\text{FIRST}} \ \left\{ \left\{ \begin{array}{l} \text{identifier-3} \\ \text{literal-1} \end{array} \right\} \underline{\text{BY}} \ \text{replacement-item} \ [\ \text{after-before-phrase} \ ] \right\} \cdots \end{array} \right\} \cdots$$

where replacement-item is:

$$\left\{ \begin{array}{l} \text{identifier-5} \\ \text{literal-3} \end{array} \right\}$$

F.5.21 INVOKE statement

$$\underline{\text{INVOKE}} \ \text{identifier-1} \left\{ \begin{array}{l} \text{identifier-2} \\ \text{literal-1} \end{array} \right\} \left[\underline{\text{USING}} \left\{ \begin{array}{l} [\ \text{BY} \ \underline{\text{REFERENCE}} \ ] \ \{ \ [\ \underline{\text{INVARIANT}} \ ] \ \text{identifier-3} \ \} \cdots \\[1ex] \text{BY} \ \underline{\text{CONTENT}} \left\{ \begin{array}{l} \text{literal-2} \\ [\ \underline{\text{INVARIANT}} \ ] \ \text{identifier-3} \end{array} \right\} \cdots \end{array} \right\} \cdots \right]$$

[RETURNING identifier-4]

[ON EXCEPTION imperative-statement-1]

[NOT ON EXCEPTION imperative-statement-2]

[END-INVOKE]

F.5.22 MERGE statement

$$\underline{\text{MERGE}} \text{ file-name-1} \left\{ \text{ON} \left\{ \begin{array}{l} \underline{\text{ASCENDING}} \\ \underline{\text{DESCENDING}} \end{array} \right\} \text{KEY} \{ \text{data-name-1} \} \dots \right\} \dots$$

  [COLLATING SEQUENCE IS alphabet-name-1]

  USING file-name-2 { file-name-3 } ...

$$\left\{ \begin{array}{l} \underline{\text{OUTPUT}} \ \underline{\text{PROCEDURE}} \text{ IS procedure-name-1} \left[\left\{ \begin{array}{l} \underline{\text{THROUGH}} \\ \underline{\text{THRU}} \end{array} \right\} \text{procedure-name-2} \right] \\ \underline{\text{GIVING}} \{ \text{file-name-4} \} \dots \end{array} \right\}$$

F.5.23 MOVE statement

Format 1:

$$\underline{\text{MOVE}} \left\{ \begin{array}{l} \text{identifier-1} \\ \text{literal-1} \end{array} \right\} \underline{\text{TO}} \{ \text{identifier-2} \} \dots$$

Format 2:

$$\underline{\text{MOVE}} \left\{ \begin{array}{l} \underline{\text{CORRESPONDING}} \\ \underline{\text{CORR}} \end{array} \right\} \text{identifier-1} \underline{\text{TO}} \text{identifier-2}$$

F.5.24 MULTIPLY statement

Format 1:

$$\underline{\text{MULTIPLY}} \left\{ \begin{array}{l} \text{identifier-1} \\ \text{literal-1} \end{array} \right\} \underline{\text{BY}} \{ \text{identifier-2} [\underline{\text{ROUNDED}}] \} \dots$$

  [ON SIZE ERROR imperative-statement-1]

  [NOT ON SIZE ERROR imperative-statement-2]

  [END-MULTIPLY]

Format 2:

$$\underline{\text{MULTIPLY}} \left\{ \begin{array}{l} \text{identifier-1} \\ \text{literal-1} \end{array} \right\} \underline{\text{BY}} \left\{ \begin{array}{l} \text{identifier-2} \\ \text{literal-2} \end{array} \right\}$$

  GIVING { identifier-3 [ROUNDED] } ...

  [ON SIZE ERROR imperative-statement-1]

  [NOT ON SIZE ERROR imperative-statement-2]

  [END-MULTIPLY]

F.5.25 OPEN statement

$$
\underline{OPEN} \left\{ \begin{array}{l} \underline{INPUT} \; \{ \; \text{file-name-1} \; [\; \text{WITH} \; \underline{NO} \; \underline{REWIND} \;] \; \} \; ... \\[4pt] \underline{OUTPUT} \; \{ \; \text{file-name-2} \; [\; \text{WITH} \; \underline{NO} \; \underline{REWIN?} \;] \; \} \; ... \\[4pt] \underline{I\text{-}O} \; \{ \; \text{file-name-3} \; \} \; ... \\[4pt] \underline{EXTEND} \; \{ \; \text{file-name-4} \; \} \; ... \end{array} \right\} ...
$$

F.5.26 PERFORM statement

Format 1 (out-of-line):

$$
\underline{PERFORM} \; \text{procedure-name-1} \left[\left\{ \begin{array}{l} \underline{THROUGH} \\ \underline{THRU} \end{array} \right\} \text{procedure-name-2} \right] \left[\begin{array}{l} \text{times-phrase} \\ \text{until-phrase} \\ \text{varying-phrase} \end{array} \right]
$$

Format 2 (in-line):

$$
\underline{PERFORM} \left[\begin{array}{l} \text{times-phrase} \\ \text{until-phrase} \\ \text{varying-phrase} \end{array} \right] \text{imperative-statement-1} \; \underline{END\text{-}PERFORM}
$$

where times-phrase is:

$$
\left\{ \begin{array}{l} \text{identifier-1} \\ \text{integer-1} \end{array} \right\} \underline{TIMES}
$$

where until-phrase is:

$$
\left[\text{WITH} \; \underline{TEST} \left\{ \begin{array}{l} \underline{BEFORE} \\ \underline{AFTER} \end{array} \right\} \right] \underline{UNTIL} \; \text{condition-1}
$$

where varying-phrase is:

$$
\left[\text{WITH} \; \underline{TEST} \left\{ \begin{array}{l} \underline{BEFORE} \\ \underline{AFTER} \end{array} \right\} \right]
$$

$$
\underline{VARYING} \left\{ \begin{array}{l} \text{identifier-2} \\ \text{index-name-1} \end{array} \right\} \underline{FROM} \left\{ \begin{array}{l} \text{identifier-3} \\ \text{index-name-2} \\ \text{literal-1} \end{array} \right\}
$$

$$
\underline{BY} \left\{ \begin{array}{l} \text{identifier-4} \\ \text{literal-2} \end{array} \right\} \underline{UNTIL} \; \text{condition-1}
$$

$$
\left[\underline{AFTER} \left\{ \begin{array}{l} \text{identifier-5} \\ \text{index-name-3} \end{array} \right\} \underline{FROM} \left\{ \begin{array}{l} \text{identifier-6} \\ \text{index-name-4} \\ \text{literal-3} \end{array} \right\} \right.
$$

$$
\left. \underline{BY} \left\{ \begin{array}{l} \text{identifier-7} \\ \text{literal-4} \end{array} \right\} \underline{UNTIL} \; \text{condition-2} \right] ...
$$

F.5.27 PURGE statement (obsolete)

$\underline{PURGE}$ cd-name-1

F.5.28 RAISE statement

$$\underline{RAISE} \left\{ \begin{array}{l} \underline{EXCEPTION}\ exception\text{-}name\text{-}1 \\ identifier\text{-}1 \end{array} \right\}$$

F.5.29 READ statement

Format 1:

<u>READ</u> file-name-1 [<u>NEXT</u>] RECORD [<u>INTO</u> identifier-1]

   [AT <u>END</u> imperative-statement-1]

   [<u>NOT</u> AT <u>END</u> imperative-statement-2]

   [<u>END-READ</u>]

Format 2:

<u>READ</u> file-name-1 RECORD [<u>INTO</u> identifier-1]

$$\left[\underline{KEY}\ IS \left\{ \begin{array}{l} data\text{-}name\text{-}1 \\ record\text{-}key\text{-}name\text{-}1 \end{array} \right\} \right]$$

   [<u>INVALID</u> KEY imperative-statement-3]

   [<u>NOT</u> <u>INVALID</u> KEY imperative-statement-4]

   [<u>END-READ</u>]

F.5.30 RECEIVE statement (obsolete)

$$\underline{RECEIVE}\ cd\text{-}name\text{-}1 \left\{ \begin{array}{l} \underline{MESSAGE} \\ \underline{SEGMENT} \end{array} \right\} \underline{INTO}\ identifier\text{-}1$$

   [<u>NO</u> <u>DATA</u> imperative-statement-1]

   [WITH <u>DATA</u> imperative-statement-2]

   [<u>END-RECEIVE</u>]

F.5.31 RELEASE statement

<u>RELEASE</u> record-name-1 [<u>FROM</u> identifier-1]

F.5.32 RETURN statement

<u>RETURN</u> file-name-1 RECORD [<u>INTO</u> identifier-1]

   AT <u>END</u> imperative-statement-1

   [<u>NOT</u> AT <u>END</u> imperative-statement-2]

   [<u>END-RETURN</u>]

F.5.33 REWRITE statement

REWRITE record-name-1 RECORD [FROM identifier-1]

   [INVALID KEY imperative-statement-1]

   [NOT INVALID KEY imperative-statement-2]

   [END-REWRITE]

F.5.34 SEARCH statement

Format 1:

SEARCH identifier-1 $\left[\underline{VARYING} \left\{ \begin{array}{l} \text{identifier-2} \\ \text{index-name-1} \end{array} \right\} \right]$

   [AT END imperative-statement-1]

   $\left\{ \underline{WHEN} \text{ condition-1} \left\{ \begin{array}{l} \text{imperative-statement-2} \\ \underline{NEXT} \ \underline{SENTENCE} \end{array} \right\} \right\} \dots$

   [END-SEARCH]

Format 2:

SEARCH ALL identifier-1 [AT END imperative-statement-1]

   $\underline{WHEN} \left\{ \begin{array}{l} \text{data-name-1} \left\{ \begin{array}{l} \text{IS } \underline{EQUAL} \text{ TO} \\ \text{IS } = \end{array} \right\} \left\{ \begin{array}{l} \text{identifier-3} \\ \text{literal-1} \\ \text{arithmetic-expression-1} \end{array} \right\} \\ \text{condition-name-1} \end{array} \right\}$

   $\left[\underline{AND} \left\{ \begin{array}{l} \text{data-name-2} \left\{ \begin{array}{l} \text{IS } \underline{EQUAL} \text{ TO} \\ \text{IS } = \end{array} \right\} \left\{ \begin{array}{l} \text{identifier-4} \\ \text{literal-2} \\ \text{arithmetic-expression-2} \end{array} \right\} \\ \text{condition-name-2} \end{array} \right\} \right] \dots$

   $\left\{ \begin{array}{l} \text{imperative-statement-2} \\ \underline{NEXT} \ \underline{SENTENCE} \end{array} \right\}$

   [END-SEARCH]

F.5.35 SEND statement (obsolete)

Format 1:

SEND cd-name-1 FROM identifier-1

Format 2:

$$
\underline{SEND} \text{ cd-name-1 } [\underline{FROM} \text{ identifier-1 }] \left\{ \begin{array}{l} \text{WITH identifier-2} \\ \text{WITH } \underline{ESI} \\ \text{WITH } \underline{EMI} \\ \text{WITH } \underline{EGI} \end{array} \right\}
$$

$$
\left[\left\{ \begin{array}{l} \underline{BEFORE} \\ \underline{AFTER} \end{array} \right\} \text{ ADVANCING } \left\{ \begin{array}{l} \left\{ \begin{array}{l} \text{identifier-3} \\ \text{integer-1} \end{array} \right\} \left[\begin{array}{l} \text{LINE} \\ \text{LINES} \end{array} \right] \\ \text{mnemonic-name-1} \\ \underline{PAGE} \end{array} \right\} \right]
$$

[REPLACING LINE]

F.5.36 SET statement

Format 1 (index-assignment):

$$
\underline{SET} \left\{ \begin{array}{l} \text{index-name-1} \\ \text{identifier-1} \end{array} \right\} \dots \underline{TO} \left\{ \begin{array}{l} \text{index-name-2} \\ \text{identifier-2} \\ \text{integer-1} \end{array} \right\}
$$

Format 2 (index-arithmetic):

$$
\underline{SET} \; \{ \text{ index-name-3 } \} \dots \left\{ \begin{array}{l} \underline{UP} \; \underline{BY} \\ \underline{DOWN} \; \underline{BY} \end{array} \right\} \left\{ \begin{array}{l} \text{identifier-3} \\ \text{integer-2} \end{array} \right\}
$$

Format 3 (switch-setting):

$$
\underline{SET} \left\{ \{ \text{ mnemonic-name-1 } \} \dots \underline{TO} \left\{ \begin{array}{l} \underline{ON} \\ \underline{OFF} \end{array} \right\} \right\} \dots
$$

Format 4 (condition-setting):

$$
\underline{SET} \left\{ \{ \text{ condition-name-1 } \} \dots \underline{TO} \left\{ \begin{array}{l} \underline{TRUE} \\ \underline{FALSE} \end{array} \right\} \right\} \dots
$$

Format 5 (table-occurrences):

$$
\underline{SET} \; \underline{OCCURS} \text{ FOR identifier-4 } \underline{TO} \text{ arithmetic-expression-1}
$$

Format 6 (object-identifier-assignment):

$$
\underline{SET} \; \{ \text{ identifier-5 } \} \dots \underline{TO} \text{ identifier-6}
$$

Format 7 (attribute):

$$\underline{SET}\ screen\text{-}name\text{-}1\ \underline{ATTRIBUTE}\ \left\{ \left\{ \left\{ \begin{array}{l} \underline{BELL} \\ \underline{BLINK} \\ \underline{HIGHLIGHT} \\ \underline{LOWLIGHT} \\ \underline{REVERSE\text{-}VIDEO} \\ \underline{UNDERLINE} \end{array} \right\} \right\} \left\{ \begin{array}{l} \underline{OFF} \\ \underline{ON} \end{array} \right\} \right\} \dots$$

F.5.37 SORT statement

Format 1 (file):

$$\underline{SORT}\ file\text{-}name\text{-}1\ \left\{ ON \left\{ \begin{array}{l} \underline{ASCENDING} \\ \underline{DESCENDING} \end{array} \right\} KEY\ \{ data\text{-}name\text{-}1 \}\ \dots \right\} \dots$$

[WITH <u>DUPLICATES</u> IN ORDER]

[COLLATING <u>SEQUENCE</u> IS alphabet-name-1]

$$\left\{ \begin{array}{l} \underline{INPUT}\ \underline{PROCEDURE}\ IS\ procedure\text{-}name\text{-}1 \left[\left\{ \begin{array}{l} \underline{THROUGH} \\ \underline{THRU} \end{array} \right\} procedure\text{-}name\text{-}2 \right] \\[2mm] \underline{USING}\ \{ file\text{-}name\text{-}2\ \}\ \dots \end{array} \right\}$$

$$\left\{ \begin{array}{l} \underline{OUTPUT}\ \underline{PROCEDURE}\ IS\ procedure\text{-}name\text{-}3 \left[\left\{ \begin{array}{l} \underline{THROUGH} \\ \underline{THRU} \end{array} \right\} procedure\text{-}name\text{-}4 \right] \\[2mm] \underline{GIVING}\ \{ file\text{-}name\text{-}3\ \}\ \dots \end{array} \right\}$$

Format 2 (table):

$$\underline{SORT}\ data\text{-}name\text{-}2 \left[ON \left\{ \begin{array}{l} \underline{ASCENDING} \\ \underline{DESCENDING} \end{array} \right\} KEY\ [\ data\text{-}name\text{-}1\ ]\ \dots \right] \dots$$

[WITH <u>DUPLICATES</u> IN ORDER]

[COLLATING <u>SEQUENCE</u> IS alphabet-name]

F.5.38 START statement

$$\underline{START}\ file\text{-}name\text{-}1$$

$$\left[\underline{KEY} \left\{ \begin{array}{l} IS\ \underline{EQUAL}\ TO \\ IS\ = \\ IS\ \underline{GREATER}\ THAN \\ IS\ > \\ IS\ \underline{NOT}\ \underline{LESS}\ THAN \\ IS\ \underline{NOT}< \\ IS\ \underline{GREATER}\ THAN\ \underline{OR}\ \underline{EQUAL}\ TO \\ IS\ >= \end{array} \right\} \left\{ \begin{array}{l} data\text{-}name\text{-}1 \\ record\text{-}key\text{-}name\text{-}1 \end{array} \right\} [\ WITH\ \underline{LENGTH}\ arithmetic\text{-}expression\text{-}1\ ] \right]$$

[<u>INVALID</u> KEY imperative-statement-1]

[<u>NOT</u> <u>INVALID</u> KEY imperative-statement-2]

[<u>END-START</u>]

F.5.39 STOP statement

STOP RUN

F.5.40 STRING statement

STRING $\left\{ \left\{ \begin{array}{l} \text{identifier-1} \\ \text{literal-1} \end{array} \right\} \dots \left[\underline{\text{DELIMITED}} \text{ BY} \left\{ \begin{array}{l} \text{identifier-2} \\ \text{literal-2} \\ \underline{\text{SIZE}} \end{array} \right\} \right] \right\}$ ...

   INTO identifier-3

    [WITH POINTER identifier-4]

    [ON OVERFLOW imperative-statement-1]

    [NOT ON OVERFLOW imperative-statement-2]

    [END-STRING]

F.5.41 SUBTRACT statement

Format 1:

SUBTRACT $\left\{ \begin{array}{l} \text{identifier-1} \\ \text{literal-1} \end{array} \right\}$ ... FROM { identifier-2 [ROUNDED] } ...

    [ON SIZE ERROR imperative-statement-1]

    [NOT ON SIZE ERROR imperative-statement-2]

    [END-SUBTRACT]

Format 2:

SUBTRACT $\left\{ \begin{array}{l} \text{identifier-1} \\ \text{literal-1} \end{array} \right\}$ ... FROM $\left\{ \begin{array}{l} \text{identifier-2} \\ \text{literal-2} \end{array} \right\}$

   GIVING { identifier-3 [ROUNDED] } ...

    [ON SIZE ERROR imperative-statement-1]

    [NOT ON SIZE ERROR imperative-statement-2]

    [END-SUBTRACT]

Format 3:

SUBTRACT $\left\{ \begin{array}{l} \underline{\text{CORRESPONDING}} \\ \underline{\text{CORR}} \end{array} \right\}$ identifier-1 FROM identifier-2 [ROUNDED]

    [ON SIZE ERROR imperative-statement-1]

    [NOT ON SIZE ERROR imperative-statement-2]

    [END-SUBTRACT]

F.5.42 SUPPRESS statement

SUPPRESS PRINTING

F.5.43 TERMINATE statement

TERMINATE { report-name-1 } ...

F.5.44 UNSTRING statement

UNSTRING identifier-1

$$\left[\text{DELIMITED BY } [\text{ALL}] \left\{ \begin{array}{l} \text{identifier-2} \\ \text{literal-1} \end{array} \right\} \left[\text{ OR } [\text{ALL}] \left\{ \begin{array}{l} \text{identifier-3} \\ \text{literal-2} \end{array} \right\} \right] ... \right]$$

INTO { identifier-4 [DELIMITER IN identifier-5] [COUNT IN identifier-6] } ...

[WITH POINTER identifier-7]

[TALLYING IN identifier-8]

[ON OVERFLOW imperative-statement-1]

[NOT ON OVERFLOW imperative-statement-2]

[END-UNSTRING]

F.5.45 USE statement

Format 1 (file exception)

$$\text{USE } [\text{GLOBAL}] \text{ AFTER STANDARD } \left\{ \begin{array}{l} \text{EXCEPTION} \\ \text{ERROR} \end{array} \right\} \text{ PROCEDURE ON } \left\{ \begin{array}{l} \{ \text{file-name-1} \} ... \\ \text{INPUT} \\ \text{OUTPUT} \\ \text{I-O} \\ \text{EXTEND} \end{array} \right\}$$

Format 2 (reporting):

USE [GLOBAL] BEFORE REPORTING identifier-1

Format 3 (exception-name):

USE AFTER EXCEPTION { exception-name-1 } ...

Format 4 (exception-object):

$$\text{USE AFTER EXCEPTION } \left\{ \begin{array}{l} \text{class-name-1} \\ \text{interface-name-1} \end{array} \right\}$$

F.5.46 VALIDATE statement

VALIDATE { identifier-1 } ...

F.5.47 WRITE statement

Format 1:

WRITE record-name-1 [FROM identifier-1]

$$
\left[
\left\{ \begin{array}{l} \underline{BEFORE} \\ \underline{AFTER} \end{array} \right\}
\text{ADVANCING}
\left\{ \begin{array}{l} \left\{ \begin{array}{l} \text{identifier-2} \\ \text{integer-1} \end{array} \right\} \left[\begin{array}{l} \text{LINE} \\ \text{LINES} \end{array} \right] \\ \text{mnemonic-name-1} \\ \underline{PAGE} \end{array} \right\}
\right]
$$

$$
\left[\text{AT} \left\{ \begin{array}{l} \underline{END\text{-}OF\text{-}PAGE} \\ \underline{EOP} \end{array} \right\} \text{imperative-statement-1} \right]
$$

$$
\left[\underline{NOT} \text{ AT} \left\{ \begin{array}{l} \underline{END\text{-}OF\text{-}PAGE} \\ \underline{EOP} \end{array} \right\} \text{imperative-statement-2} \right]
$$

[END-WRITE]

Format 2:

WRITE record-name-1 [FROM identifier-1]

[INVALID KEY imperative-statement-1]

[NOT INVALID KEY imperative-statement-2]

[END-WRITE]

F.6 Intrinsic functions

FUNCTION ABS (argument-1)

FUNCTION ACOS (argument-1)

FUNCTION ALLOCATED-OCCURRENCES (argument-1)

FUNCTION ANNUITY (argument-1 argument-2)

FUNCTION ASIN (argument-1)

FUNCTION ATAN (argument-1)

FUNCTION CHAR (argument-1)

FUNCTION CHAR-NATIONAL (argument-1)

FUNCTION COS (argument-1)

FUNCTION CURRENT-DATE

FUNCTION DATE-OF-INTEGER (argument-1)

FUNCTION DAY-OF-INTEGER (argument-1)

FUNCTION DISPLAY-OF (argument-1 [argument-2])

FUNCTION E

FUNCTION EXCEPTION-FILE

FUNCTION EXCEPTION-LOCATION

FUNCTION EXCEPTION-STATEMENT

FUNCTION EXCEPTION-STATUS

FUNCTION EXP (argument-1)

FUNCTION EXP10 (argument-1)

FUNCTION FACTORIAL (argument-1)

FUNCTION FRACTION-PART (argument-1)

FUNCTION INTEGER (argument-1)

FUNCTION INTEGER-OF-DATE (argument-1)

FUNCTION INTEGER-OF-DAY (argument-1)

FUNCTION INTEGER-PART (argument-1)

FUNCTION LENGTH (argument-1)

FUNCTION LENGTH-AN (argument-1)

FUNCTION LOG (argument-1)

FUNCTION LOG10 (arugment-1)

FUNCTION LOWER-CASE (argument-1)

FUNCTION MAX ({ argument-1 } ...)

FUNCTION MEAN ({ argument-1 } ...)

FUNCTION MEDIAN ({ argument-1 } ...)

FUNCTION MIDRANGE ({ argument-1 } ...)

FUNCTION MIN ({ argument-1 } ...)

FUNCTION MOD (argument-1 argument-2)

FUNCTION NATIONAL-OF (argument-1 [argument-2])

FUNCTION NUMVAL (argument-1)

FUNCTION NUMVAL-C (argument-1 [argument-2])

FUNCTION ORD (argument-1)

FUNCTION ORD-MAX ({ argument-1 } ...)

FUNCTION ORD-MIN ({ argument-1 } ...)

FUNCTION PI

FUNCTION PRESENT-VALUE (argument-1 { argument-2 } ...)

FUNCTION RANDOM [(argument-1)]

FUNCTION RANGE ({ argument-1 } ...)

FUNCTION REM (argument-1 argument-2)

FUNCTION REVERSE (argument-1)

FUNCTION SIGN (argument-1)

FUNCTION SIN (argument-1)

FUNCTION SQRT (argument-1)

FUNCTION STANDARD-DEVIATION ({ argument-1 } ...)

FUNCTION SUM ({ argument-1 } ...)

FUNCTION TAN (argument-1)

FUNCTION UPPER-CASE (argument-1)

FUNCTION VARIANCE ({ argument-1 } ...)

FUNCTION WHEN-COMPILED

F.7 Compiler directing facility

F.7.1 Compiler directing statements

F.7.1.1 COPY statement

$$
\underline{\text{COPY}} \left\{ \begin{array}{l} \text{literal-1} \\ \text{text-name-1} \end{array} \right\} \left[\left\{ \begin{array}{l} \underline{\text{OF}} \\ \underline{\text{IN}} \end{array} \right\} \left\{ \begin{array}{l} \text{literal-2} \\ \text{library-name-1} \end{array} \right\} \right]
$$

$$
\left[\underline{\text{REPLACING}} \left\{ \begin{array}{l} \left\{ \begin{array}{l} ==\text{pseudo-text-1}== \\ \text{identifier-1} \\ \text{literal-3} \\ \text{word-1} \end{array} \right\} \underline{\text{BY}} \left\{ \begin{array}{l} ==\text{pseudo-text-2}== \\ \text{identifier-2} \\ \text{literal-4} \\ \text{word-2} \end{array} \right\} \\ \left\{ \left\{ \begin{array}{l} \underline{\text{LEADING}} \\ \underline{\text{TRAILING}} \end{array} \right\} == \text{partial-word-1} == \underline{\text{BY}} == \text{partial-word-2} == \right\} \end{array} \right\} \dots \right] .
$$

F.7.1.2 REPLACE statement

Format 1:

$$
\underline{\text{REPLACE}} \left[\underline{\text{ALSO}} \right] \left\{ \begin{array}{l} ==\text{pseudo-text-1}== \underline{\text{BY}} ==\text{pseudo-text-2}== \\ \left\{ \left\{ \begin{array}{l} \underline{\text{LEADING}} \\ \underline{\text{TRAILING}} \end{array} \right\} ==\text{partial-word-1}== \underline{\text{BY}} ==\text{partial-word-2}== \right\} \end{array} \right\} \dots .
$$

Format 2:

$$
\underline{\text{REPLACE}} \left[\underline{\text{LAST}} \right] \underline{\text{OFF}} .
$$

F.7.2 Compiler directives

Format 1 (extended-letters):

$$
>>\underline{\text{EXTENDED-LETTERS}} \left\{ \begin{array}{l} \text{cultural-repertoire-1} \\ \text{implementor-charset-1} \end{array} \right\}
$$

Format 2 (flag-85):

$$
>>\underline{\text{FLAG-85}} \left\{ \begin{array}{l} \text{ALL} \\ \left\{ \left\{ \begin{array}{l} \underline{\text{DIVIDE}} \\ \underline{\text{NOT}}\ \underline{\text{SIZE}} \\ \underline{\text{RECORD}}\ \text{AREA} \end{array} \right\} \right\} \end{array} \right\} \left\{ \begin{array}{l} \text{ON} \\ \underline{\text{OFF}} \end{array} \right\}
$$

Format 3 (list):

$$
>>\underline{\text{LISTING}} \left[\begin{array}{l} \text{ON} \\ \text{OFF} \end{array} \right]
$$

Format 4 (page):

>>PAGE [comment-text-1]

Format 5 (propagate):

>>PROPAGATE $\left\{ \begin{array}{l} \text{ON} \\ \underline{\text{OFF}} \end{array} \right\}$

Format 6 (source format):

>>SOURCE FORMAT IS $\left\{ \begin{array}{l} \underline{\text{FIXED}} \\ \underline{\text{FREE}} \end{array} \right\}$

Format 7 (turn):

>>TURN {exception-name-1} ... CHECKING $\left\{ \begin{array}{l} \text{ON} [\text{WITH} \underline{\text{LOCATION}}] \\ \underline{\text{OFF}} \end{array} \right\}$

F.8 Expressions

F.8.1 Concatenation expression

$$
\left\{
\begin{array}{l}
\text{literal-1} \\
\text{concatenation-expression-1}
\end{array}
\right\} \quad \& \quad \text{literal-2}
$$

F.8.2 Conditional expressions

F.8.2.1 Class condition

$$
\text{identifier-1 IS } [\ \underline{\text{NOT}}\ ]
\left\{
\begin{array}{l}
\underline{\text{NUMERIC}} \\
\underline{\text{ALPHABETIC}} \\
\underline{\text{ALPHABETIC-LOWER}} \\
\underline{\text{ALPHABETIC-UPPER}} \\
\underline{\text{BOOLEAN}} \\
\text{class-name-1}
\end{array}
\right\}
$$

F.8.3 Condition-name condition

condition-name-1

F.8.4 Relation condition (non-boolean)

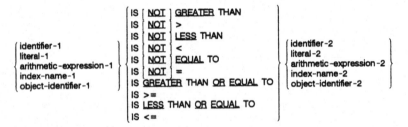

F.8.5 Relation condition (boolean)

$$
\text{boolean-expression-1}
\left\{
\begin{array}{l}
\text{IS } [\ \underline{\text{NOT}}\ ] \ \underline{\text{EQUAL}} \text{ TO} \\
\text{IS } [\ \underline{\text{NOT}}\ ] \ =
\end{array}
\right\}
\text{boolean-expression-2}
$$

F.8.6 Sign condition

$$
\text{arithmetic-expression-1 IS } [\ \underline{\text{NOT}}\ ]
\left\{
\begin{array}{l}
\underline{\text{POSITIVE}} \\
\underline{\text{NEGATIVE}} \\
\underline{\text{ZERO}}
\end{array}
\right\}
$$

F.8.7 Switch-status condition

condition-name-1

F.8.8 Negated condition

<u>NOT</u> condition-1

F.8.9 Combined conditions

condition-1 $\left\{ \left\{ \begin{array}{c} \underline{AND} \\ \underline{OR} \end{array} \right\} \text{condition-2} \right\}$ ...

F.8.10 Abbreviated combined relation condition

relation-condition-1 $\left\{ \left\{ \begin{array}{c} \underline{AND} \\ \underline{OR} \end{array} \right\} [\underline{NOT}] [\text{relational-operator-1}] \text{object} \right\}$ ...

F.9 Qualification

Format 1 (data-name and condition-name in FD or CD):

$$\left\{ \begin{matrix} \text{data-name-1} \\ \text{condition-name-1} \end{matrix} \right\} \left\{ \begin{matrix} \left\{ \left\{ \begin{matrix} \underline{\text{IN}} \\ \underline{\text{OF}} \end{matrix} \right\} \text{data-name-2} \right\} \cdots \left[\left\{ \begin{matrix} \underline{\text{IN}} \\ \underline{\text{OF}} \end{matrix} \right\} \left\{ \begin{matrix} \text{file-name-1} \\ \text{cd-name-1} \end{matrix} \right\} \right] \\ \left\{ \begin{matrix} \underline{\text{IN}} \\ \underline{\text{OF}} \end{matrix} \right\} \left\{ \begin{matrix} \text{file-name-1} \\ \text{cd-name-1} \end{matrix} \right\} \end{matrix} \right\}$$

Format 2 (paragraph-name):

$$\text{paragraph-name-1} \left\{ \begin{matrix} \underline{\text{IN}} \\ \underline{\text{OF}} \end{matrix} \right\} \text{section-name-1}$$

Format 3 (text-name):

$$\text{text-name-1} \left\{ \begin{matrix} \underline{\text{IN}} \\ \underline{\text{OF}} \end{matrix} \right\} \text{library-name-1}$$

Format 4 (linage-counter):

$$\underline{\text{LINAGE-COUNTER}} \left\{ \begin{matrix} \underline{\text{IN}} \\ \underline{\text{OF}} \end{matrix} \right\} \text{file-name-2}$$

Format 5 (page-counter and line-counter):

$$\left\{ \begin{matrix} \underline{\text{PAGE-COUNTER}} \\ \underline{\text{LINE-COUNTER}} \end{matrix} \right\} \left\{ \begin{matrix} \underline{\text{IN}} \\ \underline{\text{OF}} \end{matrix} \right\} \text{report-name-1}$$

Format 6 (data-name in RD):

$$\text{data-name-3} \left\{ \begin{matrix} \left\{ \begin{matrix} \underline{\text{IN}} \\ \underline{\text{OF}} \end{matrix} \right\} \text{data-name-4} \left[\left\{ \begin{matrix} \underline{\text{IN}} \\ \underline{\text{OF}} \end{matrix} \right\} \text{report-name-2} \right] \\ \left\{ \begin{matrix} \underline{\text{IN}} \\ \underline{\text{OF}} \end{matrix} \right\} \text{report-name-2} \end{matrix} \right\}$$

Format 7 (screen-name):

$$\text{screen-name-1} \left\{ \left\{ \begin{matrix} \underline{\text{IN}} \\ \underline{\text{OF}} \end{matrix} \right\} \text{screen-name-2} \right\} \cdots$$

Format 8 (record-key-name):

$$\text{record-key-name-1} \left[\left\{ \begin{matrix} \underline{\text{IN}} \\ \underline{\text{OF}} \end{matrix} \right\} \text{file-name-3} \right]$$

F.10 Miscellaneous formats

F.10.1 Identifier

F.10.1.1 Function-identifier

FUNCTION function-name-1 [({ argument-1 } ...)]

F.10.1.2 Qualified data-name

$$\text{data-name-1} \left[\begin{Bmatrix} \underline{\text{IN}} \\ \underline{\text{OF}} \end{Bmatrix} \text{data-name-2} \right] ... \left[\begin{Bmatrix} \underline{\text{IN}} \\ \underline{\text{OF}} \end{Bmatrix} \begin{Bmatrix} \text{cd-name-1} \\ \text{file-name-1} \\ \text{report-name-1} \end{Bmatrix} \right] [(\{ \text{subscript-1} \} ...)]$$

F.10.1.3 Reference modifier

identifier-1 (leftmost-character-position : [length])

F.10.1.4 Subscript

$$\begin{Bmatrix} \text{condition-name-1} \\ \text{data-name-1} \end{Bmatrix} (\begin{Bmatrix} \underline{\text{ALL}} \\ \text{arithmetic-expression-1} \\ \text{index-name-1} \left[\begin{Bmatrix} + \\ - \end{Bmatrix} \text{integer-1} \right] \end{Bmatrix} ...)$$

F.10.1.5 In-line invocation of methods

$$\text{identifier-1 !! literal-1} \left[(\begin{Bmatrix} \text{identifier-2} \\ \text{literal-2} \end{Bmatrix} ...) \right]$$

F.10.1.6 Object-modifier

$$\text{identifier-1 } \underline{\text{AS}} \begin{Bmatrix} [\underline{\text{FACTORY}} \text{ OF }] \text{ class-name-1 } [\underline{\text{ONLY}}] \\ \text{interface-name-1} \\ \underline{\text{UNIVERSAL}} \end{Bmatrix}$$

F.10.1.7 Exception-object

EXCEPTION-OBJECT

F.10.1.8 Object properties

property-1 OF identifier-1

F.10.1.9 Type-modifier

$$\text{identifier-1 } \underline{\text{AS}} \begin{Bmatrix} \text{type-name-1} \\ \underline{\text{ALPHANUMERIC}} \\ \underline{\text{BIT}} \\ \underline{\text{NATIONAL}} \end{Bmatrix}$$

F.10.2 Literals

F.10.2.1 Alphanumeric

"{character-1} ... "

F.10.2.2 Mixed-text alphanumeric

T"{character-1} ... "

F.10.2.3 Numeric

{character-1} ...

F.10.2.4 Boolean

B"{boolean-character-1} ... "

F.10.2.5 National

N"{character-1} ... "

PROGRAM INSTRUCTION FORMATS

Conventions for Instruction Formats

Notation	Example	Meaning
word is underlined	<u>Class-Id</u>	required key word in context given
word is not underlined	Class-Id	optional key word
Brackets [ ]	[Data Division]	optional
Braces { }	{identifier-1 identifier-2}	select one of the options
Angle Brackets < >	<Object Definition>	defined elsewhere
Ellipses	...	item may be repeated

GLOSSARY

abstract class
A class not meant to have object instances but to have subclasses. An abstract class specifies attributes or methods that its subclasses must have, thus guaranteeing consistency across a family of classes.

attribute
Characteristics of objects typically stored as an object's data. In terms of responsibility-driven design, what an object knows. Attributes can be simple data items, such as numbers or characters, or more complex recordlike structures. Attributes can also be references to other objects.

class
A template for creating individual object instances when a program is run. A class specification defines the attributes (data) and methods (code) that an object instance will have.

factory object
The unique object associated with every class definition in Object-Oriented COBOL. Factory objects handle the messages sent to classes for object creation and destruction.

information hiding
The term used to describe the fact that objects permit data to be "hidden" from program components external to the object. Information hiding has been a long-standing practice in software engineering, where program components intended for change are made inaccessible so that inadvertent coupling does not occur in the course of software maintenance and updates.

inheritance	The mechanism whereby one class can reuse the attributes and code of another class. As an example, the class battleship can inherit the properties of the class boat. This allows a programmer to define battleship by describing what it is over and above a boat. This makes for economy of expression.
instance	Another name for an object created based on a class definition.
instantiation	The process of creating an object based on a class definition.
message	A request for services sent to an object. Messages in Object-Oriented COBOL are sent via the reserved word Invoke and include an object reference, optional parameters, and return value.
method	The code that is executed as a result of an object receiving a message. There are both class methods and object-instance methods. Class methods are most commonly used for object creation and destruction. Object-instance methods are used to carry out application-specific tasks.
object	Packages of code and data that provide services with an object-oriented program. Objects are defined by their class definitions and are instantiated (come to life) during the running of a program. The code within an object is referred to as its methods and the data are called attributes. When doing analysis, we talk about finding the objects—the important entities within an application that we will later model with programmatic objects.
object-oriented programming	A modeling technique applied to software whose units of expression are objects that communicate by sending and receiving messages.
object-oriented programming (goal of)	An attempt to simulate reality by developing models of the real world in software.
polymorphism	A word with Greek origins literally meaning "many forms." Polymorphism refers to the fact that a message with the

same meaning with the same name may be sent to different object with different effects. For example, sending the message Compute-Fines to a Library-Book object, a Video object, and a Traffic-Ticket object may return very different values for each message. The advantage of polymorphism is that a programmer only has to remember one message name.

reuse   This occurs at different levels within object technology. Reuse occurs at the class level when classes serve as templates for the creation of object instances. Reuse also occurs when classes are extended through subclassing. Finally, reuse is possible when objects, defined by their interfaces, are available to other applications.

self   The reserved word that is used with a method to refer to the object that contains the method. It is used when one method of an object needs to invoke another method of the same object.

state   The value of an object's attributes at some point during program execution. Because an object can have both code and data, it can exhibit state-based behavior, meaning that it can respond differently at different times by checking its data. For example, if a file object is sent the message close twice consecutively, it may close the file the first time and change its state by setting an internal flag indicating file-closed. The second time it receives the same message it can check its state and respond with an error message.

subclass   A class that inherits the characteristics (data items and methods) of another class.

superclass   A class that is inherited from.

INDEX